Introducing East Asia

Introducing East Asia is an ideal textbook for those new to the study of one of the most exciting and important regions in the world. East Asia is a complex and culturally rich region, with the Chinese, Korean and Japanese civilizations among the oldest in the world. Over the past 50 years, Japan, South Korea, Taiwan and China have become economic powerhouses and leaders in the commercialization of science and technology. The countries are economically and culturally intertwined while at the same time burdened by a history of war and conflict. This textbook focuses on the historical and cultural roots of the contemporary political and economic ascendency of East Asia and explores the degree to which East Asian cultures, values and history set up the region for 21st century global leadership.

Features in this textbook include:

- Chapters on each of the countries and special economic zones that make up the region.
- Rich illustrations and timelines to guide the student visually.
- Focused textboxes on key figures and events, useful as research assignment and revision materials.

Providing undergraduate students with a solid introduction to East Asia, this textbook will be essential reading for students of East Asian studies, global studies and international studies.

Dr. Carin Holroyd is Professor in the Department of Political Studies, University of Saskatchewan. Her research focuses on the political economy of Japan, comparative East Asian political economy and national innovation systems. Her most recent book is *Green Japan: Environmental Technologies, Innovation Policy, and the Pursuit of Green Growth* (2018).

Introducing East Asia

History, Politics, Economy and Society

Carin Holroyd

LONDON AND NEW YORK

First published 2021
by Routledge
2 Park Square, Milton Park, Abingdon, Oxon OX14 4RN

and by Routledge
52 Vanderbilt Avenue, New York, NY 10017

Routledge is an imprint of the Taylor & Francis Group, an informa business

© 2021 Carin Holroyd

The right of Carin Holroyd to be identified as author of this work has been
asserted by him/her/them in accordance with sections 77 and 78 of the Copyright,
Designs and Patents Act 1988.

All rights reserved. No part of this book may be reprinted or reproduced or
utilised in any form or by any electronic, mechanical, or other means, now
known or hereafter invented, including photocopying and recording, or in any
information storage or retrieval system, without permission in writing from the
publishers.

Trademark notice: Product or corporate names may be trademarks or registered
trademarks, and are used only for identification and explanation without intent to
infringe.

British Library Cataloguing-in-Publication Data
A catalogue record for this book is available from the British Library

Library of Congress Cataloging-in-Publication Data
Names: Holroyd, Carin, author.
Title: Introducing East Asia / Carin Holroyd.
Description: 1 Edition. | New York : Routledge, 2020. |
Includes bibliographical references and index. |
Summary: "Introducing East Asia is an ideal textbook for those new to the
study of one of the most exciting and important regions in the world. East Asia
is a complex and culturally rich region with the Chinese, Korean and Japanese
civilizations among the oldest in the world. Over the past fifty years, Japan, South
Korea, Taiwan and China have become economic powerhouses and leaders in the
commercialization of science and technology. The countries are economically
and culturally intertwined while at the same time burdened by a history of war
and conflict. This textbook focuses on the historical and cultural roots of the
contemporary political and economic ascendency of East Asia and explores the
degree to which East Asian cultures, values and history set up the region for
21st century global leadership. Features in this textbook include: Chapters on
each of the countries and special economic zones that make up the region. Rich
illustrations and timelines to guide the student visually. Focused textboxes on
key figures and events, useful as research assignment and revision materials.
Providing undergraduate students with a solid introduction to East Asia, this
textbook will be essential reading for students of East Asian studies, global studies
and international studies. Dr. Carin Holroyd is a professor in the Department
of Political Studies, University of Saskatchewan. Her research focuses on the
political economy of Japan, comparative East Asian political economy, and
national innovation systems. Her most recent book is Green Japan: Environmental
Technologies, Innovation Policy, and the Pursuit of Green Growth (2018)"–
Provided by publisher.
Identifiers: LCCN 2020041186 | ISBN 9781138923973 (hardback) |
ISBN 9781138923980 (paperback) | ISBN 9781317409939 (adobe pdf) |
ISBN 9781317409922 (epub) | ISBN 9781317409915 (mobi)
Subjects: LCSH: East Asia–Economic conditions–21st century. |
East Asia–Economic integration–21st century. | East Asia–Foreign relations
21st century. | Information technology–East Asia.
Classification: LCC HC460.5 .H65 2020 | DDC 330.951–dc23
LC record available at https://lccn.loc.gov/2020041186

ISBN: [978-1-138-92397-3] (hbk)
ISBN: [978-1-138-92398-0] (pbk)
ISBN: [978-1-315-68469-7] (ebk)

Typeset in Times New Roman
by Deanta Global Publishing Services, Chennai, India

Contents

List of illustrations	vi
Acknowledgements	xi
Acronyms	xii

1	Introduction	1
2	China (People's Republic of China)	5
3	Japan	54
4	The Korean Peninsula: South Korea (Republic of Korea) and North Korea (Democratic People's Republic of Korea)	100
5	Taiwan (Republic of China)	142
6	Hong Kong, Special Administrative Region of the People's Republic of China	161
7	Macau, Special Administrative Region of the People's Republic of China	179
8	Connections and commonalities in East Asia	188
9	Security and regional tensions in East Asia	199
10	21st-century political economy in East Asia: National science, technology and innovation strategies	212
11	East Asia in the 21st century	224
	Index	231

Illustrations

Figures

2.1 Administrative map of China. *Source*: China Administrative, Central Intelligence Agency. [Public Domain]   6

2.2 Modern course of the Grand Canal of China. *Source*: Depiction of the modern course of the Grand Canal of China. Selected rivers and lakes shown includes Yellow, Yangtze, Yongding, Hai, Jiya, Wei, Huai, Qiantang, Luoma, Weishan, Hongze, Shaobo, Gaoyou, and Tai. Ian Kiu, 2008. [Permission is granted to copy, distribute and/or modify this document under the terms of the GNU Free Documentation License and Wikimedia Commons.]   9

2.3 The Great Wall of China. *Source:* The Great Wall of China at Mutianyu, near Beijing, in July 2006. Nicolas Perrault III, 2006. [Permission is granted to copy, distribute and/or modify this document under the terms of the Creative Commons CC0 1.0 Public Domain licence.]   12

2.4 Map of the Long March. *Source:* The Long March in China, *1934–1935*. Rowanwindwhistler, 2015. [Permission is granted to copy, distribute and/or modify this document under the terms of the Creative Commons CC0 1.0 Universal Public Domain Dedication.]   18

2.5 Paramount Leader of China Deng Xiaoping, Billboard in Shenzhen, 1978–1992. *Source:* Roadside billboard of Deng Xiaoping at the entrance of the Lychee Park in Shenzhen. Brücke-Osteuropa, 2007. [Public Domain]   25

2.6 The Belt and Road Initiative. *Source:* China in Red, the members of the Asian Infrastructure Investment Bank in orange. The 6 proposed corridors in black. Anonymous, 2017. [Permission is granted to copy, distribute and/or modify this document under the terms of the Creative Commons Attribution-Share Alike 4.0 International license.]   30

2.7 Parallel Organization of the Chinese Government and the Communist Party. *Source*: Adapted from Patrick H. O'Neil, Karl Fields and Don Share, Cases in Comparative Politics, W.W. Norton & Company, 6th Edition 2017.   34

3.1 Map of Japan. Map of the regions and prefectures of Japan with Titles. *Source*: Tokyoship, 2011. [Public Domain]   55

Illustrations vii

3.2 Portrait of Minamoto, Yoritomo, the first Shogun. *Source:* Minamoto no Yoritomo. Hanging scroll; color on silk. Fujiwara Takanobu, 1179. [Public Domain] 59

3.3 Atomic bombings of Hiroshima and Nagasaki. *Source*: Mushroom cloud over Hiroshima and Atomic Cloud Rises Over Nagasaki, 1945, taken by Charles Levy. United States Department of Energy. [Public Domain] 71

3.4 Signing the Japanese Instrument of Surrender on the USS Missouri—September 2, 1945. *Source*: Japanese Foreign Minister Mamoru Shigemitsu signs the Instrument of Surrender on behalf of the Japanese Government, on board USS Missouri (BB-63), 2 September 1945. Lieutenant General Richard K. Sutherland, U.S. Army, watches from the opposite side of the table. Foreign Ministry representative Toshikazu Kase is assisting Mr. Shigemitsu. Army Signal Corps photographer LT. Stephen E. Korpanty, 1945. [Public Domain] 72

3.5 Japanese war crime trials—International Military Tribal for the Far East. *Source*: Maj Ben Bruce Blakenle (defense counsel) addresses the court at the International War Crimes Tribunal for the Far East, 1946. Photo by the Occupation administration, U.S. Federal Government. [Public Domain] 74

3.6 Shinto Shrine. *Source*: Photo by author, Kumano Hayatama Taisha Shrine, March 4, 2019 91

3.7 U.S. military bases in Okinawa. *Source*: US military bases in Okinawa Prefecture, Japan. Created by Wikmedia Commons user Misakubo, 2010. [Permitted under the GNU Free Documentation License.] 95

4.1 Statue of King Sejong. *Source*: A statue of a seated King Sejong at Gwanghwamun Plaza. King Sejong was the fourth king of the Joseon Kingdom (1392-1910) who created Hangeul with his scholars. Republic of Korea, 2009. [Permission is granted to copy, distribute and/or modify this document under the terms of the Creative Commons Attribution-Share Alike 2.0 Generic license.] 103

4.2 Korean provinces and main cities. *Source*: South Korean Administrative Map, Central Intelligence Agency. [Public Domain] 108

4.3 Reception Center at Cheongwadae or "Blue House", the South Korean presidential residence in Seoul South Korea. *Source*: Reception Center at Cheongwadae or "Blue House", the South Korean presidential residence in Seoul South Korea. Photo by Wikmedia Commons user Steve46814, 2010. [Permitted under the Creative Commons Attribution-Share Alike 3.0 Unported license.] 117

4.4 Jogyesa Buddhist temple, Seoul. *Source*: Jogyesa Temple. Francisco Anzola, 2007. [Permitted under a Creative Commons Attribution 2.0 Generic license.] 122

4.5 Official North Korean portrait of Kim Il-sung (posthumous). *Source*: North Korean posthumous portrait of Kim Il-sung. Unknown author, 2019. [Permitted under the Creative Commons CC0 1.0 Universal Public Domain Dedication.] 127

viii *Illustrations*

4.6   Official North Korean portrait of Kim Jong-il (posthumous). *Source*:
      North Korean posthumous portrait of Kim Jong-il. Unknown author, 2019.
      [Permitted under the Creative Commons CC0 1.0 Universal Public Domain
      Dedication.]   128
4.7   North Korean ballistic missile. *Source*: North Korea's ballistic missile -
      North Korea Victory Day-2013. Stefan Krasowski, 2013. [Permitted under
      the Creative Commons Attribution 2.0 Generic license.]   133
4.8   Kim-Trump summit in Hanoi, February 2019. *Source*: President Donald
      J. Trump and Kim Jong Un, Chairman of the State Affairs Commission
      of the Democratic People's Republic of Korea meet for a social dinner
      Wednesday, Feb. 27, 2019, at the Sofitel Legend Metropole hotel in Hanoi,
      for their second summit meeting. (Official White House Photo by Shealah
      Craighead). The White House from Washington, DC, 2019. [Public Domain]   138
5.1   Map of Taiwan. *Source*: A political division map of Taiwan, ROC. Created
      by Wikimedia Comons user Luuva, 2008, modified by user Ran, 2009.
      [Permitted under the Creative Commons Attribution-Share Alike 3.0
      Unported license.]   143
5.2   Taiwan's COVID-19 response. *Source*: Courtesy of the Macdonald-Laurier
      Institute. Used with permission.   147
5.3   Canadian trade office in Taipei. *Source*: Courtesy of the Canadian Trade
      Office in Taipei. Used with permission.   148
5.4   Ma Ying-jeou and Xi Jinping meeting on November 7, 2015. *Source*: Presi-
      dent Ma Ying-jeou and General Secretary Xi Jinping, leaders of Taiwan
      and the mainland. Office of the President of the Republic of China, 2016.
      [Public Domain]   153
6.1   Map of Hong Kong. *Source*: Hong Kong Base Map, 2008. Created by
      Wikimedia Comnmons users Sambeoat and Raphaelmak. [Public Domain]   162
6.2   Umbrella Movement protests 2014. *Source:* 31th Day Hong Kong
      Umbrella Revolution. Courtesy of Studio Incendio, 2014. [Permitted under
      the terms of the CC BY 2.0 License]   168
6.3   2019 Hong Kong anti-extradition bill protest. *Source*: *2019* Hong Kong
      anti-extradition bill protest. Courtesy of Studio Incendio, 2019. [Permitted
      under the terms of the CC BY 2.0 License]   170
6.4   Hong Kong Central and Victoria Harbour. *Source*: Panorama of the Hong
      Kong night skyline, taken from Lugard Road at Victoria Peak. Picture by
      Base64 and CarolSpears Finalist, Picture of the Year 2008. Jim Trodel.
      [Licensed under the Creative Commons Attribution-Share Alike 2.0
      Generic license.]   177
7.1   The Pearl River Estuary. Eastern portion, in Guangdong Province. *Source:*
      Croquant, 2007. [This file is licensed under the Creative Commons Attribu-
      tion 3.0 Unported license]   180
7.2   Map of Macau. *Source:* Macau Physiography, Central Intelligence Agency
      [Public Domain]   181

Illustrations ix

7.3 Saint Dominic's Church. St. Dominic's, Macau. *Source:* Created by Wikimedia Commons user Whhalbert, 2008. [Permission is granted to copy,
distribute and/or modify this document under the terms of the GNU Free
Documentation License.]   182

7.4 Casino lights in Macau, 2009. Author unknown. [Public Domain]   185

8.1 Ink wash painting—English: "Pine Trees" by Hasegawa Tōhaku (Japanese,
1539–1610). The painting has been designated as National Treasure in the
paintings category. 16th century [Public Domain]   189

8.2 Japanese pop group AKB48—COOL JAPAN FEST 2018 in
台北圓山大飯店』 *Source:* AKB48 Team TP. Photo by AKB48-Taiwan
Clubs 李承儒, 2018. [Licensed under the Creative Commons
Attribution-Share Alike 2.0 Generic license.]   194

9.1 Japan, its neighbours and territorial disputes. *Source*: Courtesy of European
Parliamentary Research Service. Used with permission.   200

9.2 Korean tourists visiting Dokdo/Takeshima Islands, 2009. *Source*:
Wikimedia Commons user Ulleungdo [Public Domain]   202

10.1 Honda's Humanoid Robot Asimo—Asimo Robot, California Disneyland,
2012. Photo by World Wide Gifts. [Permitted under the Creative Commons
Attribution-Share Alike 2.0 Generic license.]   213

10.2 Digital Media City—a sign of Digital Media City Station on Seoul Subway
Line 6, 2019. Created by Wikimedia Commons user LERK. [Permitted
under the Creative Commons Attribution-ShareAlike 4.0 licence.]   219

10.3 Cool Japan Fest, 2018. Photo by Flickr Commons user AKB48-Taiwan
Clubs 李承儒. [Permitted under the Creative Commons Attribution-Share
Alike 2.0 Generic license.]   220

10.4 Seoul Animation Centre, 2015. Photo by Wikimedia Commons user
Bonnielou2013. [Permitted under the Creative Commons Attribution-Share
Alike 4.0 International license.]   222

11.1 Army disinfecting city streets, Taiwan 2020—
中文（台灣）：蔡總統視導33化學兵群/ English: Disinfectant being
sprayed in Taiwan. 軍聞社記者周力行攝 / Military News Agency Zhou
Lihang. February 7, 2020. Army disinfecting city streets, Taiwan, 2020.
Source: Military News Agency Zhou Lihang, February 2020. [The copyright holder of this file allows anyone to use it for any purposes, provided
that the copyright holder is properly attributed. Attribution: 軍事新聞通訊社)]   228

Tables

3.1 Japanese population over age 65 compared with the equivalent population
in other countries (%). *Source*: Patrick H. O'Neil, Karl Fields and Don
Share, Cases and Concepts in Comparative Politics, W.W. Norton &
Company, pp. 332–353; World Bank. https://data.worldbank.org/indicator/
SP.POP.65UP.TO.ZS; https://knoema.com/atlas/China/Population-aged-
65-years-and-above   92

x   *Illustrations*

3.2   Urban-rural population in Japan by percentage, 1950–2050. *Source*: World
Urbanization Prospects, 2018, United Nations, Department of Economic
and Social Affairs. https://population.un.org/wup/Country-Profiles/   97

6.1   Hong Kong identity survey. *Source*: Centre for Communication and Public
Opinion Survey, Chinese University of Hong Kong. http://www.com.cuhk.
edu.hk/ccpos/en/tracking3.html   175

8.1   Programme for international student assessment (PISA) 2018—average
score of mathematics, science and reading. *Source*: FactMaps: PISA 2018
Average Score of Mathematics, Science and Reading. http://factsmaps.
com/pisa-2018-worldwide-ranking-average-score-of-mathematics-science-
reading/   193

Acknowledgements

I would like to express my sincere appreciation to the University of Saskatchewan for the sabbatical that allowed me to complete this book. Many thanks to the Taylor & Francis production team, especially Stephanie Rogers and Emily Pickthall. I greatly appreciate the comments and feedback from the anonymous reviewers.

I am very grateful to my academic friends who took time out of their busy schedules to review various chapters for me. Their excellent and thoughtful comments and questions were of great assistance. Thank you to Leila Tang, David Welch, Bill Sewell, Kimie Hara, Owen Griffiths, Stephen Nagy, Simon Sung and Young G. Kim. Thank you to Heather McWhinney for her fantastic editorial work.

As always, my deepest thanks and appreciation are for my husband, Ken Coates.

Acronyms

ADIZ	Air Defense Identification Zone
AWF	Asian Women's Fund
CCP	Chinese Communist Party
DMZ	Demilitarized Zone (the 4 km wide strip of land between North and South Korea)
DPRK	Democratic People's Republic of Korea or North Korea
EEZ	Exclusive Economic Zone
GDP	Gross Domestic Product (the value of goods and services produced in a country in a year)
KMT	Kuomintang or Nationalist Party (in China between 1912 and 1949 and in Taiwan from 1949)
MITI/METI	Japan's Ministry of International Trade and Industry, which became the Ministry of Economy, Trade and Industry
OECD	Organisation for Economic Development and Cooperation
PCA	Permanent Court of Arbitration
PLA	People's Liberation Army (the armed forces of the People's Republic of China)
PPP	Purchasing Power Parity
PRC	People's Republic of China
MRT	Mass Transport Railway (Hong Kong's transit system)
ROC	Republic of China (Taiwan)
ROK	Republic of Korea or South Korea
SAR	Special Administrative Region of China—Hong Kong and Macau
SCAP	Supreme Command of Allied Powers
SEZ	Special Economic Zone
SME	Small- and Medium-Sized Enterprises
SOE	State-Owned Enterprises
STDM	Sociedade de Turismo e Diversões de Macau or Macau Travel and Amusement Company
TEAM	Traditional East Asian Medicine
TRA	Taiwan Relations Act
THAAD	Terminal High-Altitude Area Defense system
UN	United Nations
UNCLOS	United Nations Convention on the Law of the Sea
UNSCR	United Nations Security Council Resolution
WHO	World Health Organization

1 Introduction

Introducing East Asia: History, Politics, Economy and Society seeks to introduce readers to one of the most exciting and important regions in the world. The Chinese, Korean and Japanese cultures are among the oldest in the world, dating back over 3,000 years. For centuries, China was the world's most innovative country, responsible for one-quarter of estimated global GDP in the decades before the arrival of Europeans in the region. The Chinese introduced the world to gun powder, the rudder, moveable type, the compass and paper making, to name just a few Chinese inventions. Korean early contributions include the *ondol*, a famous underground heating system created 2,500 years ago and still in use today, green celadon pottery, moveable metal-type printing and one of the world's first astronomical observatories. A Japanese noblewoman wrote the world's first novel (*The Tale of Genji* by Murasaki Shikibu in around A.D. 1000). Japanese martial arts, including karate, judo, jujitsu, kendo and aikido, all began during Japanese medieval times when the samurai had to be prepared to fight.

East Asia is home to several of the world's dominant religions. Buddhism began in India but later took root in all the countries of East Asia. Confucianism, based on the writings of Confucius, a Chinese philosopher from 6th century B.C., is an ethical philosophy that remains dominant across the entire East Asian region. Daoism, founded by the Chinese philosopher Laozi, who was a contemporary of Confucius, has 20 million followers across China, Taiwan, Hong Kong and Macau. Socially and culturally, East Asia is diverse and rich. Understanding the interaction of many influences and forces, perceiving the historical and cultural roots of contemporary East Asia and recognizing the complex interactions between the peoples and the nations are, as the book shows, fundamental to making sense of 21st-century East Asia.

China, Japan and South Korea have complicated and interwoven histories. Their societies have intersected over the centuries in peace and in war, resulting in both cultural closeness and outrage and anger. The ascendency of Japanese imperialism in the late 19th century damaged established relationships, and World War II effectively ended them. Japan's dreams of the Greater East Asia Co-Prosperity Sphere (an imperialist Japanese concept promoting a self-sufficient group of Asian countries led by Japan) died at the end of World War II, when East Asia was in ruins. Japan, the regional military and industrial superpower, had been ravaged by a disastrous and losing war. Citizens struggled to survive on the streets of cities destroyed by Allied bombs, including the only nuclear weapons ever exploded in wartime. China collapsed into political chaos and civil war. The Chinese Communist Party drove the Nationalist forces to a final fortress on the island of Taiwan while in 1949 establishing the People's Republic of China on the mainland. Korea, finally freed from Japanese control, soon stood occupied by American and Allied troops in the South and by the Soviet soldiers in the North. The Korean peninsula became the front line of the most frightening and dangerous

2 *Introduction*

conflict on the planet: the nuclear-based Cold War standoff between the United States and the Soviet Union.

Hong Kong, the United Kingdom's commercial jewel in the Far East and Europe's primary entrance point to China, had been overrun by Japanese forces in 1941–1942. Liberated, it raced to rebuild during the political and economic uncertainties of the post-war period. The Japanese threat had been beaten back, and in most of the world, East Asia faded into the background. Based on fanciful notions of Asian exoticism and pre-modern cultures, the uniqueness of the Far East intrigued Westerners, but these images created false impressions about the reality of economic, social and cultural development in the region.

Skip forward to the early decades of the 21st century. With two of the world's three largest economies, East Asia is now the globe's most economically powerful region, producing much of the hardware and software that sustains the global digital economy. China's industrial machinery has a huge demand for natural resources; its manufacturers fill stores, homes and industrial plants around the world. Taiwan, a struggling agrarian state only 40 years ago, is an electronics powerhouse with an increasingly prosperous population, while Japan, having flirted in the 1980s with the possibility of becoming the world's largest economy, remains one of the most technologically innovative places on the planet. Japan is also leading the industrial nations through the uncertain transition to the realities of the post-industrial, environmentally aware and rapidly ageing world. China now has the world's second largest economy to go with the world's largest population (although India's population is growing fast and due to overtake China's by 2030). With its growing middle class now offsetting the persistent poverty of the country's declining rural population, China's economic and political presence is expanding across Asia and Africa as the country competes with the United States to be the world's most dominant economic power. Like China, South Korea is enjoying the prosperity of a creative and globally competitive economy.

Post–World War II transformations propelled East Asia into global prominence, but the transformation has been far from flawless and remains incomplete. After prospering for two decades from the economic resurgence of China, the city-state of Hong Kong is struggling to maintain a modicum of autonomy in the face of Chinese control; the streets of the city have become the front lines of the global pro-democracy movement. The Korean peninsula remains locked in the painful legacy of the Cold War, with North Korea a rogue pariah state in the grasp of a brutal dictatorship. Although intensive economic integration is slowly offsetting decades of ill-will and animosity in the region, historical memories run deep and strong, and East Asia has wrestled with the challenge of setting aside the tensions of the immediate post–World War II era. Tensions between South Korea and China with Japan continue to flare up regularly.

In spite of these challenges, the world has slowly started to appreciate the region's massive investments that now drive numerous resource and industrial economies, influence international public affairs, share popular culture through exports of food, animation, video games and clothing styles and exert powerful influences over the lives of people around the planet.

Today, East Asia is no longer hidden behind a wall of mystery and intrigue. While some areas are inaccessible—breaching the intricacies of China's political system and the nature of internal opposition forces remains a formidable challenge—Japan, North Korea, South Korea, China (including Hong Kong and Macau) and Taiwan have attracted increasing academic, business and government interest. Western popular culture flows into the region, and East Asian influence filters out internationally.

Despite the West's growing appreciation and increasing interest in East Asia, global understanding of the region remains woefully weak. The international appetite for Chinese food, sushi and, now, Korean food has created a culinary fascination with the region that, sadly, does not penetrate deeply into the global consciousness. The region remains off the beaten track for Western tourists and student travellers. Although interest is growing, only a small number of outsiders have visited the area. Few people of non-East Asian ancestry can speak Mandarin, Cantonese, Japanese or Korean—even as over half a billion regional residents are actively learning English. Conversely, the vast Asian diaspora, particularly from China, has an outsized economic impact on countries around the world. Indeed, if the Chinese population outside mainland China was a single national economy, it would be the third largest and one of the most dynamic in the world.

Westerners know little about the nuances of East Asian national politics, business and society. Even a long-standing leader, such as former Prime Minister Abe of Japan, is not well known internationally. The strong man of China, Xi Jinping, General Secretary of the Chinese Communist Party (CCP) and the President of the People's Republic of China (PRC), is better known, and increasingly feared, but he remains a global enigma. Commercially, core East Asian brands are now ubiquitous (e.g. Huawei, Toyota, Alibaba, Samsung, Toshiba, Hyundai, Taiwan Semiconductor, LG Electronics, Alibaba, Tencent and Sony). Yet the complex interactions between East Nations countries and the ebbs and flows of East Asian business and technological innovation are typically understood only superficially. Other dimensions of East Asian society are also little understood outside the region: striking demographic transitions like the dramatic ageing of Japan and China, the rise of East Asia's world-class cities, rapid cultural evolution and the area's swiftly changing role in global affairs. East Asia is a major international force. Developing an understanding of the foundations of East Asia—the area's history, cultures, politics, economics and social trends—helps to make sense of a region that is leading the world's transformation and that will shape global affairs in the coming decades.

East Asia is a region in more than geographic or economic terms. It may be divided by political regimes and historical encounters—China's Communist Party and Japan's Liberal Democratic Party (LDP) share precious little in common. Yet there is a common foundation to East Asian society rooted in the ethical and moral philosophy of Confucianism. Confucius (551–479 B.C.) established the conceptual and cultural underpinnings of the region. His system of ethics valued order and stability and offered moral codes for government and society at large. Confucianism emphasized loyalty to the nation, a commitment to social conventions, a deep belief in the efficacy of education and a hierarchical structure that established the feudal system. Social hierarchy, in turn, reflected the belief that "right form leads to proper inner behaviour." (Right form means the appropriate way of doing things.) This approach, in turn, emphasized paternalism among the leaders and a society-wide emphasis on respect and obedience.

East Asian society is, with variations, spiritual and respectful. The cultures highlight "inside-outside" concepts (differences in how one should behave with one's family, company or in-group of some sort and those outside), a powerful sense of obligation to family and country and hierarchical senior–junior relationships. All societies in the region place a great deal of emphasis on "face"—and what the Japanese call *tatemae* and *honne*, or the difference between what a person shows in public and their real feelings. More than anything, and in sharp contrast to Western democracies, East Asian societies highlight the importance of the group and the priority attached to the common good over the individualism personified by the United States. These values and assumptions have coalesced into a deeply held concern for long-term outcomes over short-term benefits, a focus that rebounds through East Asian societies. East Asian politics, government, culture and business reflect, in many diverse ways, Confucian values made real and given human and societal form.

4 *Introduction*

Introducing East Asia: History, Politics, Economy and Society explores three core and interrelated elements: the evolution and character of the individual nations and regions of East Asia (China, Japan, South Korea, North Korea, Taiwan, Hong Kong and Macau), the connections and conflicts within the East Asian region and the emergence of the region as a global powerhouse. The interplay of culture, nation, region and global force is crucial to the understanding of the region and, more broadly, to the global dynamics of the 21st century.

Exploring East Asia is fascinating and important on its own merits. This is a dynamic and culturally rich region with complex national histories, but it is also a region of immense and growing global significance, certain to be at the centre of major political, diplomatic, economic and social developments for the next 50 years and beyond. It is important, finally, to approach East Asia on its own terms, not as a region defined, experienced and shaped by Western influences but as a network of cultures, nations and histories that only rather late in its evolution intersected with European and North American empires. This volume seeks to explain the region from the inside out, understanding culture and histories that shaped the peoples of the area and the interplay of nations that created the diversity, intensity and creativity of contemporary East Asia.

Learning about and from East Asia begins with human settlement and with the establishment of regions with unique cultures that, long before outsiders arrived, developed, fought, conquered and shaped each other. Studying East Asia requires, intellectually, a mental shift of the globe, moving Europe and North America from the centre of the map and restoring East Asia to its long prominent role as the most dynamic and creative force in the world. This shift does not diminish the importance or impact of Europe's colonial powers or American economic and military expansion. Rather it allows this region to be seen as part of a complex process of social, political and economic change. East Asia has evolved a great deal over the past centuries, and it is changing still. As the world moves into a century of technological, demographic, economic and social uncertainty, it is abundantly clear that East Asia will feature prominently in the transitions and transformations that lie ahead.

2 China (People's Republic of China)

Introduction

Over the past 40 years, China has transformed itself from a developing country to one of the world's greatest economies. The shift towards state-managed capitalism brought about a dramatic increase in the size of the Chinese middle class, a rise in per capita incomes and an improvement in people's quality of life, particularly in Beijing, Shanghai, Guangzhou and the coastal cities. The country raised 400 million people out of abject poverty, one of the fastest such transformations in world history. China's economic rise sparked a global economic boom, as the country produced manufactured goods for international consumers and purchased minerals, lumber, foodstuffs, oil and gas and other supplies from around the world. The re-integration of China into the global economy has had transformative effects both inside the country and internationally, upsetting the global order. This profound change in China represented not the standard transition from a developing to a developed country but the re-emergence of the country as a global superpower. As this chapter demonstrates, for most of its long history, China was, in fact, the world's largest economy and one of the most advanced and sophisticated civilizations. China brought the world major developments in science and technology, art, architecture, literature, writing systems, government systems, philosophy and religion.

China, officially the People's Republic of China (PRC), has a land area of 9.6 million km², making it slightly bigger than the United States and the third largest country in the world after Russia and Canada. With about 7 percent of the world's land area, China is home to 20 percent of the world's population. Its population of almost 1.4 billion people is the largest in the world but will soon slide into second place behind India. The vast majority of that population lives in the eastern plains and along China's coastline. The country is geographically diverse and mountainous, particularly in the west, with high plateaus and desert areas. China's rivers, including the Yellow and Yangzi rivers, flow eastward from the high mountains into the plains and on to the China Sea. China shares a land border with 14 different countries: Mongolia to the north; North Korea to the east; Russia to the northeast; Kazakhstan, Kyrgyzstan and Tajikistan to the northwest; Afghanistan, Pakistan, India, Nepal and Bhutan to the west and southwest; and Vietnam, Laos and Myanmar to the south. China has 23 provinces, which are shown in Figure 2.1.

Figure 2.1 Administrative map of China.

Early Chinese history: 1600 B.C.–A.D. 1368

Chinese history reaches back to the Neolithic period, over 5,000 years ago. See Textbox 2.1 for a list of dynasties that ruled China from 1600 B.C. to 1911. The first dynasty for which there is archaeological and documentary evidence was the Shang dynasty, which ruled from approximately 1600 to 1046 B.C. Long before anywhere else in the world, the Shang fashioned weapons and containers from bronze and used a formal writing system. In the intellectual ferment of the Zhou dynasty (1047–221 B.C.) that followed the Shang, two major thinkers emerged: Laozi, a philosopher and founder of Daoisim, and Confucius

China (People's Republic of China) 7

(see Chapter 8), a philosopher whose system of ethics for government and moral code for society still influence thought and behaviour across East Asia.

Textbox 2.1 Different periods in Chinese history

- Shang dynasty (1600–1046 B.C.)
- Zhou dynasty (1047–221 B.C.)
- Qin dynasty (221–206 B.C.)
- Han dynasty (206 B.C.–A.D. 220)
- Jin dynasty (265–420)
  - Sixteen Kingdoms or dynasties (304–409)
- Southern and Northern Dynasties (420–589)
- Sui dynasty (581–618)
- Tang dynasty (618–907)
- Five dynasties and 10 kingdoms (907–960)
- Song dynasty (960–1279)
  - Jin dynasty in the north (1115–1234)
- Yuan dynasty (1279–1368) (Mongol)
- Ming dynasty (1368–1644)
- Qing dynasty (1644–1911) (Manchu)

The kings of the Zhou dynasty were the first to use the political and religious doctrine of the Mandate of Heaven, the belief that a just ruler is given a blessing to rule directly from heaven. If a ruler is overthrown, he loses that mandate; if natural disasters occur, heaven must be displeased with the ruler. This belief in the Mandate of Heaven explains why public revolts occurred after natural disasters. People believed that the ruler had lost his mandate, an approach that continued for the next two millennia over various dynasties.

The short-lived Qin dynasty (221–206 B.C.) marked the beginning of China's imperial (relating to an empire or emperor) system, which, remarkably, lasted until 1912. Under Qin Shi Huangdi, the first emperor, China was united and authority centralized. The newly created central government developed infrastructure such as roads, canals and the beginnings of what would become the Great Wall of China. The Qin also introduced a standard currency and standardized weights and measures. The equally significant and longer lasting Han dynasty (206 B.C.–A.D. 220) followed. These four centuries witnessed enhanced economic growth and prosperity. Education, literature and philosophy flourished. Major progress was made in science and technology in fields as diverse as papermaking, the development of the rudder to steer ships and the creation of a basic seismometer to measure earthquakes. Exploration and trade also expanded. The Han built trade networks throughout what is now Central Asia, India and Pakistan, all the way to Europe. These routes came to be known as the Silk Road.

At this time, China's borders were the edges of its cultural influence, meaning that people who accepted the Chinese ruler as the "Son of Heaven" were part of China and those who did not were outside China and referred to as barbarians. (There were, though, some places that did not accept Imperial rule in which Han influence could be seen.) China's borders shrank and expanded accordingly. Between the end of the Han dynasty and the beginning of the Jin dynasty that followed, China was divided into three states: Wei, Shu and Wu. This era of the

8 China (People's Republic of China)

Three Kingdoms was extremely violent, with each kingdom's emperor claiming control over the rest of China and willing to fight battles to maintain or extend that control.

China was eventually briefly reunified under the Jin dynasty (266–420), China's second imperial dynasty, but the reunification did not last long. A series of rebellions led by ethnic tribal groups, referred to as the Uprising of the Five Barbarians, overthrew the Jin dynasty and established their own kingdoms in the north. Leaders of four of these ethnic groups would divide northern China into a number of independent kingdoms, named the Sixteen Kingdoms. Despite losing much of its northern territory, the Jin maintained control of southern China, with their capital near modern day Nanjing, for another century.

After the end of the Jin dynasty in A.D. 420, China was divided in an era known as the Southern and Northern Dynasties period (420–589). The south was ruled by four brief dynasties (Song, Zi, Liang and Chen), while the north's 16 small kingdoms were separately unified by the Tuoba, a northern ethnic group, under the North Wei dynasty, which lasted until 534. Although this was a time of great turmoil, war and chaos, it was also one of technological and scientific advancement in medicine, mathematics, cartography and astronomy. The stirrup, invented in the Jin dynasty, made the use of cavalry in war possible. Buddhism and Daoism spread throughout the north and south.

In 589, Emperor Wen of the Sui dynasty united China again. Other than a short time under the Jin, this was the first time China had been unified after centuries of internal warfare. Although the Sui dynasty lasted less than 40 years, it was of considerable importance. The Sui put ethnic Chinese back in control of the whole of China and *sinicized* (made Chinese), the ethnic minorities in the north. Under Sui rule, numerous initiatives were made to reduce economic inequality by improving agriculture and developing infrastructure, resulting in increased population growth. The Sui undertook mega projects such as building the city of Luoyang as an eastern capital, extending the Great Wall and constructing the Grand Canal, the oldest artificial river in the world. Built to move grain from agricultural areas to Beijing and to facilitate military movements, the Grand Canal transported goods and people for hundreds of years. Now a UNESCO world heritage site, the Grand Canal stretches 1,776 km from Beijing through Tianjin and four provinces to Hangzhou (see Figure 2.2). Although impressive, the reforms and construction projects, along with ongoing military campaigns to consolidate the country, eventually exceeded what the country could support. Reeling from revolts against heavy taxes and labour conscription and defeated after invading the Goguryeo, one of the Three Kingdoms of Korea, the dynasty finally fell.

As the Sui empire collapsed, the Li family seized power, founding the Tang dynasty (618–907), which was to become an important Chinese dynasty. (Interestingly, the rule was interrupted by a brief inter-regnum between 690 and 705, when Empress Wu Zetian took the throne, becoming the only female monarch.) The first half of the Tang dynasty was generally a time of peace and prosperity. Scholar-officials were recruited through civil service exams, creating a stable civil service, a new legal code was implemented, attempts were made at obtaining an accurate census and a new tax system was put in place. Buddhism, which had grown in popularity under the Sui dynasty, became a significant force in Chinese culture until it was banned by Emperor Wuzong in the 840s. Art, literature and poetry flourished, and many famous Chinese poets and painters lived during the Tang dynasty. Wood block printing was also developed at this time. Sometimes referred to as a golden age of Chinese culture, the Tang dynasty had influence beyond that of previous Chinese dynasties, extending further west and expanding to Japan, Korea and India. Using the Silk trade routes, China traded silk, spices and jade for ivory, gold and other treasures from the Middle East, India, Persia and Central Asia. In the second half of the Tang dynasty, centralized authority declined,

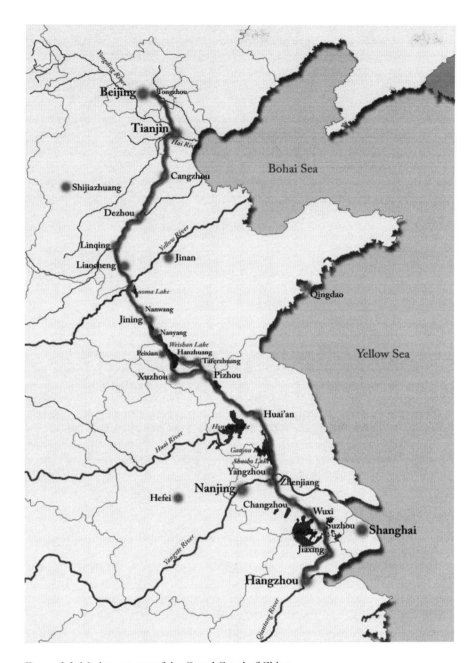

Figure 2.2 Modern course of the Grand Canal of China.

10   *China (People's Republic of China)*

precipitated by the An Lushan Rebellion, beginning in December 755 when General An Lushan proclaimed himself emperor and tried to establish a rival dynasty. The rebellion lasted until 763 and caused many millions of deaths and enormous destruction, greatly weakening the Tang empire, opening the door to other rebellions and unrest and leading to the downfall of the dynasty.

After the collapse of the Tang dynasty, China fell into a time of turmoil. The next 50 years were filled with power struggles, fighting and political division. In the north, around the Yellow River, five dynasties quickly followed one after another. As the leaders of various kingdoms fought for dominance, there was constant warfare. In the south, ten kingdoms governed their own territories concurrently. Aptly named the Five Dynasties and Ten Kingdoms (907–960), this time in Chinese history witnessed military developments, such as the country's first use of gunpowder, and social change, such as the forced binding of women's feet (signifying that the family was well off as the women were not needed to do physical work). Literary developments also occurred: the printing of books, which had begun during the Tang dynasty, expanded and the Five Classics (Confucian texts) were printed for the first time in 953.

The Song dynasty began in 960 but is divided into two periods: the Northern Song (A.D. 960–1125) and the Southern Song (A.D. 1125–1279). The Northern Song had its capital in the northern city of Kaifeng and ruled a relatively unified China. However, by the late 11th century, the regime began to crumble. In the early 12th century, the Jurchen (a tribal group from Siberia and Northeast Asia) invaded and conquered the Northern Song. The Jurchen established the Jin dynasty (1115–1234) and controlled much of northern China until the Mongol conquest in 1234. With the establishment of the Jin state in the north, the Song moved their capital further south to Hangzhou. The Song had an advanced system of government with a strong civil service. Under its rule, the population increased, cities grew, the economy rapidly expanded, the world's first bank notes were issued and the first permanent Chinese navy was created. Great progress continued in technology (including in weapons, moveable type, engineering and navigation) and agriculture. Fine arts, especially calligraphy and painting, and literature flourished, and Song Ci, a new type of lyric poetry with fixed rhythmic and tonal patterns, was created. Despite its economic progress and wealth, Song China was unable to militarily beat back the Mongol invaders. The Mongols conquered the Jin dynasty in the north in an alliance with the Song. When the alliance broke down, they invaded and conquered the Song.

It was Kublai Khan, the grandson of Genghis Khan, who defeated the Song in 1279. Kublai subsequently founded the Yuan dynasty and became its first emperor. The Mongols ruled China until 1368, the first foreign-led government in China. Although the Yuan was a foreign dynasty, the Mongols invoked the Mandate of Heaven to legitimize their rule. They continued with the Chinese style of bureaucracy, including imperial exams, although the Chinese elite were not given much power or respect. During the Yuan dynasty, Beijing became the capital of China, infrastructure like the Grand Canal, roads and the postal system were improved, foreign trade and diplomacy were greatly expanded and Chinese inventions and products were increasingly sold in Europe and Asia.

In 1274 and 128, Kublai Khan launched two unsuccessful invasions of Japan, both of which were affected by enormously strong winds, which the Japanese called *kamikaze* or divine winds. Other expensive and unsuccessful wars in Southeast Asia drained the Yuan treasury. These expenditures, combined with fighting among the Mongol leaders and a number of natural disasters, including famines and plagues, led to peasant rebellions and the decline and eventual end of the Mongol empire. Between 1353 and 1368, the Yuan dynasty

China (People's Republic of China) 11

was plagued by a series of uprisings perpetrated by the Red Turban movement (named after the fighters' red turbans and red banners). One of the most important Red Turban leaders was Zhu Yuan Zhang. After winning a series of military campaigns, Zhu proclaimed himself emperor in 1368.

Ming dynasty (1368–1644)

The Ming dynasty is an important dynasty in Chinese history. Over the 276 years of the Ming dynasty, 17 emperors ruled and China's population doubled. Zhu Yuan Zhang was the first Ming emperor; he was known as the Hongwu Emperor. One of the only Chinese emperors to have been born to a peasant family, Zhu was orphaned at a young age. Over his 30-year rule, he rebuilt a country devastated by war. After making Nanjing the first Ming capital city, he set up a new system of government, promoted agriculture, reduced corruption, protected peasants' land and outlawed private slavery.

Following Zhu's rule, the Yongle Emperor (1402–1424) moved the capital to Beijing in the early 1400s. Construction of the imperial palace, what is now the Forbidden City, began in 1406 lasted 14 years and involved a million labourers. Concerned about potential enemies, the Yongle Emperor created a spy network to monitor potential opposition and ordered the execution of those he believed were disloyal and their family members. Intent on demonstrating Chinese power not only within China but also to the world, the Yongle Emperor commissioned the construction of 3,500 enormous ships. (To give a sense of size, one of the larger Ming ships was 400 feet long compared to the Santa Maria, Christopher Columbus' largest ship, which was launched in 1492 and was 160 feet long.) Between 1405 and 1433, Admiral Zheng He commanded seven "Ming treasure voyages," ocean expeditions to the South China Sea, the Indian Ocean, the Arabian Peninsula and even East Africa. Along with the main nine-mast treasure ships, on each voyage would be over 100 ships of various sizes, carrying treasure, horses, food, tens of thousands of military troops and other personnel. These expeditions are astonishing to contemplate for their size and expeditionary reach.

After these expeditions, however, little geographic exploration happened during the Ming dynasty. Subsequent Ming emperors closed the country to foreigners and foreign ideas, strengthening and expanding the Great Wall to keep out foreign invaders. It is estimated that by the end of the Ming dynasty, the Great Wall was 5,500 miles long (see Figure 2.3).

The Ming believed in Chinese superiority—and at the beginning of the dynasty, China was ahead of the rest of the world in a wide range of fields, including weaponry and navigation—and decided to isolate China from outside influences. [China was not entirely isolated. Merchants (primarily from Fujian) established Chinese trade across Southeast Asia, and the Ming were also engaged in diplomacy with neighbours, even invading Vietnam at one point.] On the scientific front, over the years China's progress slowed and fewer discoveries were made. The country's isolationism meant it did not keep abreast of discoveries happening elsewhere in the world. Thus, China began to lose some of its scientific and technological lead. However, trade continued between Ming China and Europe and Japan, with China selling silk and porcelain in return for silver as there was not much the country wanted from Europe.

The Ming dynasty is known and remembered for the arts, including drama, literature, architecture, textiles, lacquers and, especially, porcelain. Ming porcelain, particularly the blue and white, was in high demand in the 15th century and is still highly prized by collectors today. Ming porcelain's fame was such that over time all fine white porcelain dishes came to be called china.

Figure 2.3 The Great Wall of China.

A variety of factors contributed to the end of the Ming dynasty. These included a series of weak emperors, a financial crisis partly due to the costs of repelling the Mongols and fighting with Japan, an agricultural disaster because of unusually cold temperatures, a major earthquake in 1626 (a sign that the Heavens were angry) and a peasant rebellion. Most significantly, the Ming had been in conflict with the Manchu clan for years. In 1636, the Manchus expelled the Ming from the Liaodong Peninsula in northeast China and established the Qing dynasty. The last Ming emperor committed suicide in 1644. That same year, the Manchus drove out a rebel leader who had captured Beijing and established the Qing dynasty.

Qing dynasty (1644–1911)

The last Chinese dynasty was the Qing dynasty under the Manchus, who came from the north and were one of the "barbarian" groups the Great Wall was designed to keep out. Although the Qing dynasty was established in 1644, it took almost 40 years before the Qing had control of the whole country. Initially, the Qing differed substantially from the Han Chinese. They imposed a few of their ways on the Han, including forcing the men to wear their hair in a queue (the front of the head is shaved while the rest of the hair is grown long and put into a braid), but otherwise the Chinese were allowed to continue as they had been, as long as they accepted Qing rule.

The most famous and celebrated of the Qing rulers is the Kangxi Emperor, the fourth emperor of the Qing dynasty but the second to rule over a united China. Ascending to the throne at the age of seven in 1661, he ruled until 1722, his 61-year reign making him the longest reigning emperor in Chinese history.[1] The Kangxi Emperor had several significant military victories. He defeated a major Ming loyalist rebellion in southern China (the Revolt of the Three Feudatories), which lasted from 1673 to 1681. In 1683, he annexed Taiwan and expanded the Chinese empire to the north and northwest as his armies defeated numerous Mongol tribes and brought them under Qing rule. He also signed a border and trade treaty with Russia, the Treaty of Nerchinsk (1689), which confirmed China's northern border.

The reign of the Kangxi Emperor and the next few emperors who followed him brought stability and prosperity to China after decades of war. This was also a time of cultural revival. The Kangxi Emperor ordered the completion of a standard Chinese dictionary (now referred to as the Kangxi dictionary) and also funded surveys to create maps of China. Later, the Qianlong Emperor focussed on preserving the Manchu culture and on writing poetry. However, as Qing society became more conservative over the years, the dynasty declined. By 1850, China's population topped 430 million, outgrowing the ability of its agricultural system to support the people. Many peasants who made up the majority of the population were exploited by their landlords and by greedy local government officials. Conflicts and rebellions with the Qing leadership grew. Although it was becoming increasingly corrupt and incompetent, the imperial bureaucracy did promote practical reforms in areas like agriculture. Civil servants, however, were still selected based on exams on ancient Confucian texts and not on their knowledge of science, technology or agriculture. China's isolationist tendencies meant that the Chinese were not aware of the impact of the Industrial Revolution underway in Great Britain. As the Western powers were growing stronger, China was weakening. The country was becoming increasingly unable to ignore the rest of the world but when engagement came the consequences of having fallen behind were made abundantly clear.

In the early part of the 19th century, the Qing rulers fought to curtail foreign influence, including trade. As a result, British trade with China was primarily one-way. The British loved Chinese tea, silk and porcelain, but because there was little Chinese demand for goods from Britain, China insisted that it be paid in gold and silver. The British were frustrated with China as they wanted the country to open up its ports and markets to trade. They also wanted the British Empire to be recognized as equal to China and to establish formal diplomatic ties between the two countries. But the Qing Court showed little interest.

Britain eventually found one thing the Chinese would buy: opium, a strong narcotic that the British imported from their colony in India. Although the emperor made the trade in opium illegal, the British smuggled in enough opium that it soon reversed the trade balance in Britain's favour. The level of opium addiction in China skyrocketed, affecting all classes of society, including the elite and the military, and causing serious social and economic problems. The Chinese tried hard but unsuccessfully to stop the opium trade, including by writing a letter of appeal to Queen Victoria (which was not delivered) and offering the foreign companies tea in exchange for their opium. In 1839, the Chinese government confiscated and burned over 20,000 chests of opium (about 1,300 tons) in warehouses in Canton. They then blockaded foreign ships to force them to give up their opium.

14　*China (People's Republic of China)*

Britain retaliated by sending in its Royal Navy and decisively defeating China in the first Opim War (1839–42). In 1842, China was forced to sign the Treaty of Nanjing (the first of what would be called the unequal treaties), which required China to pay compensation, open up five Chinese ports to the British and cede the island of Hong Kong to Britain in perpetuity. The next year an additional treaty granted Britain extraterritoriality (any of its citizens accused of a crime could be tried in British courts) and the right to any concessions China might grant to any other country in the future.

Fifteen years later, tensions reignited over trade and diplomatic relations between the British and the Chinese. In 1856, Chinese officials boarded a British ship, the *Arrow*, when it was docked in Canton and arrested some of the Chinese crew. In response, the British attacked Canton. The Chinese then burned down foreign trading warehouses. The French joined the British in fighting the Chinese in a war that lasted until 1860. This Second Opium War (also called the *Arrow* War) resulted in the 1860 Convention of Beijing, which comprised three separate treaties with the United Kingdom, the French Empire and the Russian Empire (even though Russia was not involved in the conflict, it used the opportunity to press for demands). The treaties obliged China to pay silver to Britain and France and to open up ten additional ports and the interior of China to foreigners. Britain, France and Russia were given the right to establish legations (small embassies) in Beijing. The Russian-Chinese border was also revised, and, most significantly, the Kowloon Peninsula (across from Hong Kong) was ceded to the United Kingdom.

China paid a heavy price for its isolation. The Western countries had made technological advances that gave them power over China. At the same time, China was being badly beaten by the Western powers and forced to make difficult concessions, the country was fighting internal protests and unrest. The Taiping Rebellion against the Qing dynasty occurred between 1850 and 1864, overlapping with the Second Opium War. The Taiping were followers of the God Worshipping Society led by a self-proclaimed prophet Hong Xiuquan (who eventually amassed 2 million followers). Hong and his followers took control of Nanjing and held it for 11 years. The Taiping Rebellion eventually collapsed, but as many as 20 million people died in the conflict, approximately the same number as all the fatalities associated with World War I.

In 1894–1895, China and Japan went to war over influence in the Korean peninsula. The Sino-Japanese War demonstrated the failure of the Qing government to improve its military in comparison with the modernization undertaken by Meiji Japan. China lost the war and ceded the Liaodong Peninsula (although Russia, France and Germany forced Japan to give it back within a week), Taiwan and the Penghu Islands to Japan in perpetuity, cementing Japan's dominance in the Korean peninsula and undermining Chinese ambitions for that region. Japan's victory in the Russo-Japanese War (1904–1905) kept the Russians out of the Korean peninsula and brought the Japanese into southern Manchuria.

China had now been defeated in several wars with foreign powers. As a result of these defeats, the country had been forced to make payments, give up territory and open up to foreign companies and missionaries. (After the Beijing Convention of 1860, foreign missionaries had been free to travel throughout China and to construct churches, which they had done in substantial numbers.) These foreigners were also accorded extraterritorial rights and were not subject to Chinese law. Not surprisingly, many Chinese resented the havoc foreigners were wreaking on their country.

China (People's Republic of China)   15

Between 1889 and 1901, a Chinese organization called the Society of the Righteous and Harmonious Fists, referred to by Westerners as the Boxers, led an uprising in northern China. While rebelling against the Qing leaders and frustrated with an ongoing drought, the Boxers also fought against the spread of foreign influence in China. In 1900, the Boxers reached Beijing, where they started killing foreigners and Chinese Christians and laid siege to the foreign legation district of Beijing. Power at the time rested with the Empress Dowager (widow of the former emperor) Cixi, who supported the Boxers and declared war on foreign countries with ties in China. The siege continued for weeks, causing suffering to the diplomats and their families and staff. Thousands of Chinese Christians were killed during this time as were a few hundred foreigners, primarily missionaries. After the siege had continued for almost two months, an international military coalition of troops from eight countries took control of Beijing and rescued the Christians and the foreigners. The signing of the Boxer Protocol in 1901 marked the official end of the Rebellion. Under the protocol, along with punishment for the Boxer leaders and any Chinese officials involved in the Rebellion, China was obliged to pay millions of dollars in reparations to the countries involved. Foreign legations were henceforth permitted to have military forces in Beijing for protection.

The Boxer Rebellion further weakened the Qing dynasty, which ultimately fell in 1911. Elements within the population were becoming increasingly frustrated and angry at their Manchu rulers and at the foreigners who had taken so much from China. Revolutions and riots rocked the country. Although the Xinhai Revolution, which ultimately toppled the Qing dynasty, occurred in 1911, it had been building for years. Various groups of Chinese people, both in China and overseas, spent years talking about how to strengthen China and whether to overthrow the emperor and even the imperial system. A number of small but unsuccessful rebellions took place.

In 1911, in the wake of a government announcement of plans to nationalize a group of private railways in central China, protests turned into riots. Eventually, a larger rebellion against the Qing erupted. The Revolutionary Alliance, a secret underground resistance group formed by physician and revolutionary leader Sun Yat-sen and others in 1905 from the merger of many smaller revolutionary groups, saw an opportunity to end the imperial system after leading seven unsuccessful revolts against the Qing in the previous six years. The Qing government agreed to the demands to create a constitutional monarchy, and Yuan Shikai, a top general, was appointed as China's first prime minister. However, it proved to be too late as, one by one, provinces began declaring their opposition to Qing rule. Former Qing military commanders from Zhejiang and Jiangsu provinces (which had declared independence) led the war against the Qing in Nanjing and captured the city. Soon after, provincial representatives arrived in Nanjing for the first national assembly. On December 29, 1911, the assembly elected Dr. Sun Yat-sen as the provisional president of the new Republic of China (ROC), although many analysts questioned the legality of this election, seeing it as part of a power struggle between Sun Yat-sen and Yuan Shikai. Meanwhile, Yuan Shikai and his followers negotiated with the Qing for a peaceful abdication of the child emperor Puyi (see Textboxes 2.2 and 2.3). Yuan Shikai and the Qing agreed that if the emperor and the royal family abdicated, then Yuan Shikai would be the president. In February 1912, the emperor and the royal family abdicated. Yuan Shikai was sworn in as the provisional president, and Beijing was made the capital.

Textbox 2.2 Puyi, the last emperor of China

When the Guangxu Emperor died in 1908, Puyi ascended to the Manchu throne at the age of 2 years and 10 months. He became the Xuantong Emperor and ruled under a regency (a regent was appointed to rule for him as he was a child) until he was forced to abdicate on February 12, 1912. This ended the 267 years of the Qing dynasty (1644–1911) and the 2,000 year old imperial system. Puyi continued to live in the Forbidden City (the palace complex in central Beijing). He was placed back on the throne as emperor from July 1 to 12, 1917, when an army general led a coup to restore the monarchy. Sir Reginald Johnston was Puyi's tutor between 1919 and 1924, an experience which Johnston describes in his book *Twilight in the Forbidden City*.

In 1932, Puyi accepted the offer to be the Chief Executive of the Japanese puppet state of Manchukuo or Manchuria in China's northeast. In 1934, he was installed as the emperor of Manchukuo; his reign continued until the end of World War II in August 1945 at which time he was taken prisoner by the Russians. The Russians returned him to China in 1950 and he was tried and convicted as a war criminal. He was released in 1959. The Oscar winning film *The Last Emperor* was based on Puyi's autobiography and portions were filmed inside the Forbidden City.

Textbox 2.3 China's rise, fall and return

From several years B.C. until the early 19th century, China was the world's largest economy, responsible for 25–35 percent of global estimated GDP from 1600 until the early to mid-1800s (see Figure 2.4). China was responsible for the creation of philosophies, religions, writing systems, art and architecture that reached far beyond its borders. Much of what was created in China endures to this day. The opening ceremonies of the 2008 Beijing Summer Olympics showcased four of China's greatest ancient inventions: the compass, printing, paper making and gun powder. Joseph Needham, Cambridge historian of China's science and technology, remarked that from early times until well into the Middle Ages, China was far ahead of the rest of the world in almost every discipline of science and technology (Needham, 2013). It is little wonder that China saw itself as the centre of the universe, the self-described celestial kingdom.

However, internal and external challenges set in. Over a hundred years, China went from being one of the world's great empires to one of the poorest countries in the world. In the 4,000 years of Chinese history, the 120 years in which China lost its place at the top of the world is only a blip. Today, when academics and politicians talk about the rise of China, China talks about its return to pre-eminence.

Republican China

The establishment of the new government of the Republic of China did not solve China's problems. The new government now had to unify the country—no easy task. The loss of the Qing left a power vacuum quickly filled by local warlords, who ruled their own territories with little attention to the national government. While Sun Yat-sen advocated a Western style approach to government, others were not as enthusiastic and searched for other ideas on how to run the country. In 1917, an army general led a coup to restore the monarchy. The last emperor, Emperor Puyi, briefly ascended to the throne (see Textbox 2.2). Over the next decade, two main political organizations emerged. Both parties were influenced by the New Culture Movement (circa 1915–1925), which grew out frustration with the inability of the new Chinese republic to deal with China's difficulties. Scholars and others associated with the New Culture Movement rejected Confucianism and promoted democratic and egalitarian values, a renewal of China's place in the world and a focus on the future. In 1919, the May Fourth Movement grew out of student protests in Beijing. The protests were focussed on the Treaty of Versailles (1919), which allowed Japan to keep the concession (a grant of land) on the Shandong peninsula.[2] The May Fourth Movement resulted in a surge of nationalism and a move away from intellectual elites and traditions towards mass political mobilization.

The Nationalist Party or Guomindang (GMD)/Koumintang (KMT) emerged out of the Revolutionary Alliance. The KMT became a political party in 1912, dissolved in 1913 and reformed in 1919, with Sun Yat-sen as its leader. At that time, the party intended to promote Chinese identity, modernize and break from traditional Chinese values. The Communist Party of China (CPC) was founded in Shanghai in 1921. (The English translation and abbreviation most commonly used now is the Chinese Communist Party or CCP so that will be used in this book.) Marxist ideas had been discussed during the May Fourth Movement and now began to spread. The CCP encouraged the Chinese working class to overcome both domestic and foreign exploitation. The Moscow-based Comintern (Communist International) initially supported both the KMT and the CCP and advised the CCP to join the KMT until it was stronger, whereas the Soviets saw the larger KMT as more likely to gain power and hoped to bring it under their influence.

The KMT and CPC did in fact unite to fight the warlords and reunify China under a central government. The KMT-CCP Alliance or the First United Front was formed in 1924. Sun Yat-sen died in 1925, and Chiang Kai-shek became the new leader of the KMT. After forming a National Revolutionary Army, the First United Front set out in 1926 on the Northern Expedition, a military operation against the warlords. However, while the KMT wanted to use the Front to control the Communists, the CCP members wanted to spread communism. In 1927, halfway through the Northern Expedition, Chiang Kai-shek purged the Communists from the First United Front. His actions exacerbated the civil war raging among various warlords but, by 1928, the KMT under Chiang had subdued the warlords and suppressed the CCP. The KMT was now in power, albeit in a somewhat limited way. Although Moscow intended for the CCP to concentrate on building a base of urban workers, the KMT and their military forces controlled the cities. The CCP's urban-focussed strategy attracted resistance, prompting some Communist leaders to begin to organize the countryside. The Communist Party established bases for its newly established Soviet Republic of China in Jiangxi and Fujian provinces.

The Long March (1934–1936)

As Chiang Kai-shek's Nationalists encircled the bases of the Soviet Republic of China, the Communist Party and its Red Army members attempted to break out of the encirclement and evade the KMT forces, in what came to be known as the Long March. There were actually a series of marches, but the most well-known march began in October 1934 in the Communist enclave in Jiangxi province, from where the Communists escaped to the north and the west. Over the next year, the 85,000 troops plus additional personnel travelled 9,000 kilometres, retreated west and then north through 11 provinces and across difficult terrain, including 4,000 metre mountains, with KMT forces in pursuit (see Figure 2.4). Although the group

18 China (People's Republic of China)

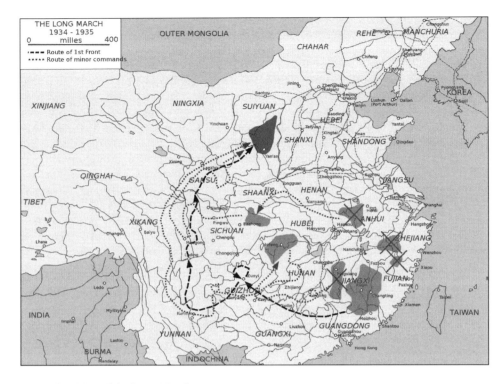

Figure 2.4 Map of the Long March.

finally reached their destination of Yan'an in north central China, many members had died of illness, exhaustion and hunger. Historians estimate that only 7,000 of the original 100,000 people who set off on the march survived.

During the Long March, the Communists developed strong relationships with the peasantry in the countryside. Emerging from the March as a hero and leader of the Communists was Mao Zedong. Inspired by the dedication and determination of the participants in the Long March and the reforms Mao organized in the countryside, many young people enlisted in Mao's army. Mao believed the peasantry, 85 percent of China's population at the time, would be the base of the Communist Party. Downtrodden and exploited, the peasants looked to the Communist Party to improve their futures.

In 1931, the Japanese military staged an explosion on the Japanese-owned South Manchuria Railway near Mukden (now Shenyang) and blamed it on Chinese dissidents. The Mukden Incident became the pretext for Japan's subsequent invasion of northeast China (Manchuria.) Japan quickly established a puppet state in the area called Manchukuo. Soon after, some elements of the Japanese army began casting expansionist eyes on other parts of a China badly weakened by the prolonged and vicious civil war. To resist a Japanese invasion, the Kuomintang (Nationalists) and the Communist Party formed an alliance known as the Second United Front. Although tensions and strife between the two sides remained, the combatants suspended the Chinese Civil War between 1937 and the end of World War II in 1945. Sparked by a clash between Chinese and Japanese troops at the Marco Polo Bridge near Beijing, the Second Sino-Japanese War began in 1937.

China (People's Republic of China)   19

The ensuing struggle for China, waged largely outside the view of the world, involved millions of soldiers, mass death and civilian dislocation and hardship. The conflict unleashed one of the greatest refugee movements in world history, with estimates suggesting that 90 million Chinese citizens were forced off their lands and out of their homes. The Japan-China struggle was as bitter and hate-filled as the later Japanese-American conflict would be, taking on a "fight to the death" character that would deeply poison relations in the region for decades to come. Brutality reigned, marked by the Japanese murderous "rape of Nanjing" (see Chapter 3) and the equally destructive China-led flooding of the Yellow River (an attempt to stop Japanese troops), which killed hundreds of thousands of people and caused an internal refugee crisis. Bitter battles raged for years between the Japanese occupiers and the Chinese and between Chinese rivals. Efforts to understand the deep distrust that exists between China and Japan begin with understanding the intense legacy of the wartime conquest and subsequent struggles. In the mid-1930s, many in East Asia saw Japan as a bulwark against American and Western intrusions; those witnessing Japan's brutal and violent occupation of China understood that the Japanese "cure" was as bad or worse as the purported Western threat.

The Chinese-Japan conflict, long seen as a sideshow to World War II, proved to be pivotal to the future of East Asia. It drove deep divisions between China and Japan that linger in the public memories of both countries, and the fracturing of Chinese politics created an opening for Mao Zedong (see Textbox 2.4) and the Communists. Battered and damaged by the wartime conflicts and undermined by Japan's militaristic colonialism, China had no option but to reinvent itself after World War II, a struggle for identity that led directly to the dominance of the Communist Party.

Textbox 2.4 Mao Zedong (1893–1976)

The most dominant individual in modern Chinese history, Mao Zedong, was born in a village in Hunan province, the son of a prosperous peasant farmer. As a young man, he was influenced by the Xinhai Revolution of 1911 and the 1919 May Fourth Movement (the intellectual revolution that promoted national independence and a major reform of Chinese society). Mao became a Marxist-Leninist and a founding member of the Communist Party of China. Mao emerged as the leader of the Party during the first Chinese Civil War between the CCP and the KMT during 1927–1937, and especially the Long March— the military retreat undertaken by the Red Army of the CCP during 1934–1936. During World War II, against the Japanese, the CCP and its Red Army strengthened significantly. After World War II, with the USSR's military and financial support, the CCP and its Red Army under Mao's leadership won the second part of the civil war against the KMT. In 1949, Mao proclaimed the founding of the People's Republic of China.

Mao's variety of Marxism-Leninism focussed on creating a socialist revolution in a primarily agricultural and rural China. Under Mao's leadership, the economic, political and academic systems were established in China by copying those of the USSR. Mao's Great Leap Forward movement (see below) led to the Great Famine during 1959–1961, which caused tens of millions of deaths. Mao initiated numerous political movements after he became the leader of the CCP to reinforce his paramount leadership and authority. This included the Cultural Revolution (see below) during which many people were killed, tortured, exiled and imprisoned. Under Mao, the country disconnected from its religions and traditions, especially Confucianism, and substituted Communism and the Cult of Personality of Mao as the nation's sole ideologies.

Mao brought China into the Korean War to back North Korea and into the Vietnam War to support the Communist forces in Vietnam. During the Cold War, with the deterioration of the relationship between the CCP and the Communist Party of the Soviet Union after Joseph Stalin's death, Mao accepted the engagement initiated by U.S. President Richard Nixon, which led to the opening of China to the West in the late 1970s. Thus, Mao both created China as an outcast state and navigated its re-entry into global affairs. His collective writings on his ideas, policies and strategies about this socialist revolution are referred to as Maoism.

According to current CCP ideology, Mao is now regarded as the great founding father of the CCP and the PRC who made minor mistakes during his leadership. Within China, an honest exploration and reflection on Mao's actions and Maoism has been prohibited. Hence, Mao is both revered and despised, beloved and hated by Chinese people depending on their ability to access accurate information and their personal memories of the last 60 years.

The resumption of China's Civil War: 1945–1949

In the aftermath of World War II, the global order was hastily reconstructed. An iron curtain descended between Western and Eastern Europe. The Union of Soviet Socialist Republics, recovering from millions of civilian and military deaths, pushed its Communist alliances internationally. Awoken by war from self-imposed isolation, the United States extended its economic leadership around the world. Peoples freed from Germany or Japan pressed for independence or autonomy but also struggled to break away from the Capitalist-Communist stand-off that defined the post-war era. The Axis powers of Germany, Japan and Italy, recovering from the devastation of wartime battles and occupation, quickly began to rebuild, largely through American aid.

In 1945, China began to attempt to recover from almost a decade of brutal Japanese occupation. The Kuomintang (KMT or Nationalists) and the Communists had united in a shared hatred of Japan, but with the enemy defeated, they vied for control of post-war China. The conflict was complicated by the presence of the Soviet Union, which had muscled its way into the war near the end, primarily so that it could have a role in the post-war settlement. Within a year of the end of World War II, the conflict between the CCP and the KMT had erupted into a full-scale war. The civil conflict saw the Communist Party under Mao Zedong metaphorically push the Kuomintang led by Chiang Kai-shek into the sea. Both groups claimed to represent all of China, and both parties believed that the ascendency of the other would be disastrous for the country. Chiang Kai-shek had well over a million troops in the field and a stronger military organization, but the Nationalists lacked the ideological passion and reserve army that the Communists would soon call on.

Armed with captured Japanese weapons controlled by the Soviet Union and supported by the rapid growth of their army, the increasingly hard-line CCP rapidly gained the upper hand. Peasants rallied to the cause in ever-growing numbers that quickly exceeded 5 million soldiers, many drawn by the Communists' promise to break up large landholdings and redistribute the land to the poor. Although the KMT army was technologically superior and better trained, the Communists eventually gained the support of more of the Chinese people, at least partly because of their time in the countryside with the peasantry during the Long March.

Seen as defenders of the pre-World War II economic order, the Nationalists became increasingly dependent on conscripts. Their cause was not helped by their decision to return to the areas occupied by the Japanese as conquerors and to accuse the Chinese there of being collaborators. In the chaos of post-war China, with economic despair across the land and with the Americans stepping in to prop up non-Communist regimes and political parties around the world, China's Civil War took on global implications. The Communist-National conflict became one of the first battlegrounds in the Cold War.

The struggle began in earnest in the northeast quadrant of the country, rapidly spreading to the south and towards the coast before moving further south. With a much larger army and better supplies, the Communist Party soon had the upper hand, but the United States continued to supply aid, largely in the form of surplus military materials, to Chiang Kai-shek's Nationalist forces, which were clearly on the defensive. The Communist Party's war of attrition worked, slowly draining the life out of the Nationalist armed forces and leaving the Communists in control of most of the country. What the CCP took to calling the "War of Liberation" moved steadily in its favour. Casualties mounted on both sides, with the CCP better able to withstand the staggering losses. Tens of thousands of non-combatants died from war-induced starvation. In 1948, for example, the Communists prevented people from leaving the city of Changchun, exhausting the KMT food supplies and resulting in the eventual death by starvation of 150,000 civilians. The Communists pushed every advantage, rejecting suggestions for a cease fire or a portioned country and pursuing Chiang Kai-shek's retreating armies.

The Chinese Civil War resulted in the death of many millions of civilians and Nationalist and Communist soldiers. By 1949, it was evident that Chiang Kai-shek and his KMT Nationalist forces faced defeat. Chiang and 1.2 million of his military, political and commercial elite fled to Taiwan, bringing with them many treasures of imperial China. Once there, under the name of the Republic of China, the KMT insisted for decades that it had the right to rule China. Pockets of Nationalist supporters remained on mainland China, but the resistance faded.

The early years of the People's Republic of China

In Beijing on October 1, 1949, Mao declared the founding of the People's Republic of China. With the exception of the island of Taiwan, Tibet, Yunnan, Guangxi and Hainan Island, almost all of China was now under Communist control. Victory had come sooner than the Communists had predicted, and the new government was suddenly faced with figuring out how to unify, rebuild and modernize a country of over 600 million people. Most of the Communist leadership was from the peasantry. They knew how to fight but not how to govern.

China began its process of aggressive industrial expansion by focusing on central planning, nationalizing most private industry and collectivizing agriculture. Land reform was one of the first changes Mao implemented, shifting the land management system from one in which landlords owned the farmland and tenant peasants worked their land to one in which peasants owned and worked the land themselves. In 1950, land was redistributed to 300 million formerly landless peasants to own individually, and, by 1952, peasants were required to form agricultural cooperatives. During this campaign, however, hundreds of thousands of landlords were murdered, China's rural gentry who for thousands of years had been the backbone of the countryside. The Communist Party destroyed the landlord class completely

22 *China (People's Republic of China)*

and put in place tight administrative control over villages and rural families. Land reform therefore had significant economic, political and cultural impacts on Chinese society.

Communist China could not turn to the West for help, but it could and did call on the Soviet Union. The CCP received a great deal of assistance in the beginning. China relied on Soviet experts and modelled its economic development plan after those of the Soviet Union. However, the Soviet model was based on capital-intensive industrialization, and China was poor. Although China borrowed from the Soviets, this money had to be repaid. Gradually, elements within the CCP led by Mao doubted the applicability of the Soviet model for China. Mao proposed a different Chinese model of economic development that took into account China's poverty and huge population. This Maoist model substituted human power for capital equipment.

The Great Leap Forward

Mao launched his model of economic development in 1958 under a five-year plan he called the Great Leap Forward. The goal of the Great Leap Forward was for China to catch up to the industrialized Western nations by developing the country's industrial and agriculture sectors simultaneously. Industry could only succeed if its workforce was well fed, and agriculture needed industry to make the tools required to grow food. Mao organized the population into communes for which people worked. Everything from tools to animals was owned collectively, while education and health care were provided by the commune. The communes were divided into work teams with numerous families in one work team. By the end of 1958, the country's 700 million people had been divided into over 26,000 communes.

The communes were responsible for both agriculture and industrialization, which took place through a program of "backyard" furnaces to smelt iron. Believing that the quantity of steel produced was the most important indicator of successful industrialization, Mao and the CCP initiated the "Everybody Produces Steel" campaign. Whether in cities or in rural communities, everybody was encouraged to help produce steel, and propaganda exhorted the population to meet and beat production targets. People made simplified or "backyard" furnaces to melt their pots or spoons, which were believed to have iron inside. The Maoist model taught that as long as people had the "proper revolutionary consciousness," meaning a commitment to Communism, they could accomplish anything; revolutionary consciousness was more important than expertise. As a result, criticism was unwelcome and could even result in imprisonment.

But the Everybody Produces Steel campaign went badly wrong. The steel produced by the backyard furnaces was of poor quality, items built with it fell apart, and inexperienced and exhausted workers had accidents and were injured or died. Although the weather in 1958 was excellent for agriculture, there were not enough workers to harvest the crop as many people were busy with the steel furnaces. In the following two years, China was affected by droughts and flooding, and an exceptionally poor harvest resulted in food shortages in many parts of the country. A disastrous failure, the Great Leap Forward was responsible for the decline of industrial and agricultural production and death by starvation of an estimated 20–30 million people. Most of these deaths occurred between 1959 and 1962, a period that came to be known as the Great Famine.

Mao took responsibility for the failure of the Great Leap Forward by resigning as the head of state and passing responsibility for economic decision making to Liu Shaoqi. Although he was still the Chairman of the Central Committee of the CCP, for the next few years Mao remained in the background. Unsurprisingly, Mao did not stay silent long as he did not agree with the more practical economic policies implemented by Liu Shaoqi. In 1966, Mao launched the Great Proletarian Cultural Revolution. Putting himself back at the centre of power, he declared that the Party needed to be even more radical. He would restore a revolutionary spirit to the Chinese people and ensure that they did not abandon socialism.

The Cultural Revolution

From the progress China had made since 1949, Mao saw a privileged class (e.g. engineers, scientists, managers and teachers) gaining too much power (perhaps at his expense) with little understanding of what life was like for regular people in China. Since the founding of the People's Republic of China, Mao had advocated for the creation of a country in which everyone was equal and working for China. He and his supporters aimed to purge capitalism and tradition from Chinese society and to make Maoism (known in China as Mao Zedong Thought) the central ideology. Mao's real aim, though, was to strengthen the power of the Communist Party and his authority within the party and the country.

To assert that authority, Mao capitalized on growing class tensions within China and accelerated social and economic class divisions within Chinese society, promoting hatred, abuse and discrimination between social classes. Landlords, intellectuals, Party officials who had different ideas from Mao, business/factory owners, various type of professionals, army leaders who didn't absolutely agree with Mao's preferences and so on—all were targeted in numerous massive political campaigns from 1949 through the Cultural Revolution. Mao could easily label one group (depending on the situation and Mao's enemy of the moment) and instruct others to hate, torture and kill this targeted group and their families, all the while claiming that by doing this a socialist society equal for everyone would be built and all privilege would be eliminated. It is difficult to know whether Mao genuinely believed in an equal society for everybody, changed his policies in response to circumstances or stayed true to his real goal—to hold absolute power and destroy anyone who could present any challenge/question to his rule. As happened with other revolutionaries in power, Mao had created a political system that prevented critical feedback or criticism. A full accounting of the human cost of the Cultural Revolution will never be possible. Tens of millions of people were persecuted, tortured and abused. Historians debate the number of deaths with estimates ranging from half a million to 2 million people, some of whom were driven to suicide (Yang, 2011; Yongyi 2011, 315–327; Walder, 2014, 513–539).

After the Great Leap Forward, Mao had lost a good deal of his power, while Liu Shaoqui and his faction had gained trust and influence by implementing more practical economic policies. To re-establish his absolute authority within the Party and the government, Mao initiated the Cultural Revolution to use the masses, especially the youth, to purge and reshape the government. Mao directed massive political campaigns targeting Liu's faction within the Communist Party, accusing it of having "taken the capitalist road." To maximize his influence and authority with the general public, Mao and his followers ignited a cult of personality around him. The publication *Quotations from Chairman Mao Zedong*, which contained quotations from Mao's speeches and statements, was read by everyone. Nicknamed the "little red book," the book's image was on posters and pictures everywhere in late 1960s China.

Red Guards, groups of militant young people who formed into units, implemented Mao's directions. By promoting the idea that a privileged class was developing and oppressing the masses, Mao encouraged the Red Guards to attack anyone in a position of any authority or prestige in the government or society generally—bureaucrats, teachers, professors, managers, writers, musicians, scientists, Party and state leaders and intellectuals or anyone

24 China (People's Republic of China)

the Red Guards determined was acting in a superior way. In many cases, those targeted and others who showed mercy or compassion to them were publicly humiliated, beaten, tortured, jailed, murdered or exiled to the countryside. People protected themselves by attacking others. Children turned on parents, and friends turned on each other. People were tortured until they "admitted" or "confessed" to their "bourgeois" or "rightist" ways. The government was paralyzed, and Mao was once again the most powerful person in China.

Society descended into chaos and violence. Schools and universities were closed. Many historic buildings, religious facilities, works of art and literature, musical instruments and even furniture or home decorations with Western or traditional Chinese features were destroyed as they were seen to represent the bourgeoisie or traditional China. Books, music, paintings, sculptures, movies and theatre shows were allowed only if they championed Maoist ideas. Many of China's brightest individuals were sent to toil in the countryside, and a generation of young people missed all or part of their education. Approximately 80 million people, about 10 percent of China's population at the time, were targets of the Cultural Revolution. The estimated number of people who died ranges from hundreds of thousands to many millions. The economy was devastated.

During the 10 years of the Cultural Revolution (1966–1976), policies and the faction in power changed frequently while still under Mao's control. After 1969, the massive political movements and violence began calming down, but the power struggles and unrest continued until Mao's death in 1976. Although Mao began the Cultural Revolution and bears most of the responsibility for it, his successors in the Communist Party put much of the blame on four Chinese Communist Party officials (one of whom was Mao's wife Jiang Qing), nicknamed the "Gang of Four." Shortly after Mao died, the Gang of Four were arrested, tried and convicted for their actions during the Cultural Revolution.

Textbox 2.5 Deng Xiaoping (1904–1997)

Deng Xiaoping, a Chinese politician who rose to power after Mao Zedong's death in 1976, led the economic resurgence of China. Deng served as China's Paramount Leader from 1978 until 1992. Deng joined the Communist Party of China in 1923 and participated in the Long March. After the founding of the People's Republic of China, Deng became the Party's Secretary General in the 1950s, joining the Political Bureau in 1955. Deng's economic approach was pragmatic and focussed on the use of incentives and individual self-interest to spark economic development. He believed that China needed to build an elite group of highly trained individuals with strong technical and managerial skills, supported the unprecedented expansion of the country's university system and encouraged leading students to study internationally. This thinking put him in opposition to Mao. Deng was purged twice during the Cultural Revolution. He and his family were targeted; his son, Deng Pufang, was tortured and fell, or was pushed, from an upper-story window.

After Mao's death, Deng was rehabilitated by the Party. He soon was in a senior position and turned his attentions to putting China on a path of economic development. Deng Xiaoping became Paramount Leader, an informal term used to describe the most important person in the PRC leadership. In 1978. Deng instituted a broad range of economic reforms, beginning in the countryside and expanding into the urban areas (see p. 27). Deng was also responsible for implementing China's One Child Policy in an attempt to control the country's booming population.

Figure 2.5 Paramount Leader of China Deng Xiaoping, Billboard in Shenzhen, 1978–1992.

Although not a charismatic presence on the world stage, Deng restored stability to China after the chaos of the Cultural Revolution. He jump-started China's economy, bringing a burst of growth that thrust the country into global prominence. During his time as leader, China's economy grew rapidly, standards of living improved and China's ties to the world economy were strengthened. Deng was a proponent of collective leadership within the Chinese Communist Party. He did not want a repeat of the one person dictatorship and the cult of personality that had been seen with Mao. Deng was, however, still a very strong protector of the CCP's absolute control over the country. He ordered the crackdown on the Tiananmen Square protestors in 1989, a stunning act of repression, which dashed international hopes that China was on a path to liberalization.

Deng's tour of Southern China in 1992, designed to highlight, both domestically and internationally, the success of the country's economic reforms served as the country's industrial "coming out party." Deng died in 1997, having been an integral part of the modern history of the People's Republic of China, from its descent into isolationism and internal repression to its re-emergence as an economic powerhouse in the late 20th century (see Figure 2.5).

Reform and Opening

With Mao's death and the subsequent arrest of the Gang of Four, the Cultural Revolution drew to a close, marking the end of radical policies and continuous revolution. New men stepped forward to lead the Communist Party, some of whom had themselves been victims of the Cultural Revolution. Deng Xiaoping, a top Communist Party official who had been

26 *China (People's Republic of China)*

purged twice, consolidated power and became the most prominent political leader in the PRC (see Textbox 2.5). Deng opened China to the outside world and implemented pragmatic reforms that liberalized the country economically and, to a more limited extent, politically. Deng pursued his "reform and opening" policies whether or not they meshed with Communist ideology, stating "Whether a cat is black or white makes no difference. As long as it catches mice, it is a good cat." By this he meant that if capitalist methods helped China modernize and improve its economy, then he would use them. Agriculture and then business were allowed to be privatized, and foreign trade and investment were promoted. Over the next decade, the economy saw an annual average growth rate of about 10 percent.

On the political side, the CCP still maintained control. Not all of the CCP leadership was happy about the economic liberalization, and there were campaigns against "spiritual pollution" (the erosion of Communist values), corruption and crime. At the same time, some of the Chinese population, particularly students, began to push for further freedoms. In the spring of 1989, students and other activists began demonstrating in Beijing's Tiananmen Square, pushing back against the authoritarianism of the government and calling for democratic reform. The protests started out small but gradually grew and spread to other cities throughout China. A group of Beijing students went on a hunger strike in the Square at a time that happened to coincide with the state visit of Soviet leader Mikhail Gorbachev. The demonstrations had now become a public embarrassment to the CCP.

While the central government wrestled with how to respond, martial law was declared in Beijing. The hardliners won, and on June 4th, the government sent in the military and one of the most violent modern political crackdowns ensued. Chinese soldiers fired directly into the crowds of people in the Square, killing or injuring many people. The estimated death toll ranged from 200–300 (PRC government figures) to 2,000–10,000. Thousands of people connected to the process were arrested. A photograph of an unidentified man standing in front of a tank became the most iconic image of the Tiananmen Square Massacre, referred to in Chinese as the June Fourth Incident. Knowledge of the June Fourth Incident in China today is limited. China has repressed all discussion of what occurred and young people are not taught about it in school.

Economic system

For the first 30 years of the People's Republic of China, from its founding in 1949 until 1979, China's economy was centrally planned and controlled. China copied this model of centralized planning from the Soviet Union. Part of the appeal of this model was the need to unify and control the country after decades of instability, internal strife and economic difficulties. In a centralized planned economy, the leadership sets out the nation's economic policies. Mao and the CCP leadership decided the country's political goals and ideology and set targets for agriculture and industry. The state had ownership of all the country's resources—labour, raw materials, money and land—and government planning committees allocated resources and set targets and quotas. Farmers planted the crops they were told to plant, and factories produced the goods they were told to produce. In return, the population was promised an "iron rice bowl" (a job for life). This system is clearly a very different system from a capitalist laissez-faire economy in which the market is relatively free from government intervention and the creation and distribution of goods depends on the forces of supply and demand. Gradually, it became clear that China's highly centralized system, which paid little attention to profitability or consumer demand, was inefficient and inflexible.

China's industrial sector was dominated by State-Owned Enterprises (SOEs), whose primary objectives were to maximize employment and output with little concern for whether there was a market for what the company produced. The government would set production goals for a factory without knowing if there were any customers for the product. Since the factory management was not responsible for marketing, it was not concerned. The government would keep poorly performing factories open because it was reluctant to lay off workers. See the following textbox for more on state-owned enterprises.

State-owned enterprises (SOEs)

State-owned enterprises were notoriously inefficient. Factories had to get permission from the government's planning unit to buy supplies, purchase machinery, decide what to produce or when to hire workers. The system was highly inefficient, and productivity was very low as the "iron rice bowl" meant that employees were paid the same no matter what they did or how hard they worked. Promotions were primarily based on seniority and loyalty to one's boss and to the party. Because in theory everyone (e.g. all citizens) owned each SOE, in practice no one took responsibility for the factory or the company. Production statistics were falsified to put companies in a favourable light, and managers and employees tried to benefit from the SOE as much as possible.

SOEs controlled all aspects of their employees' lives—not only their work but also their personal lives. An employee would have to receive permission to travel, get married or have children, and workers were bound for life to their work unit or *danwei*, which supplied housing, child care and education. Through the danwei system, party policy was easily communicated and implemented. Later, the danwei system would facilitate the One Child Policy, for example, as workers could be both easily monitored and easily punished (e.g. through pay cuts or downgraded accommodation) if they did not comply. Eventually, the work unit's power faded. In 2003, employees no longer needed permission from their work unit to marry.

Under Deng Xiaoping's leadership, the economy gradually improved, beginning in the rural areas around 1978. The agricultural communes were disbanded, and a new system put in place that required farmers to sell a percentage of their produce to the state at a price set by the government but gave them the freedom to sell the rest privately. Over the years, the government monopoly on the buying and selling of agricultural products was relaxed. Government-determined prices were loosened and farmers were permitted to engage in other forms of business. As a result, agricultural outputs soared, doubling in the 1980s and continuing to grow from then. Today, China is one of the world's top producers of a range of agricultural products including rice, wheat, barley, sorghum, potatoes, tomatoes, tea and soybeans.

In 1984, economic restructuring spread to the industrial sector, which was gradually opening to private companies, although they were heavily regulated at the beginning. Opportunities for individuals to establish their own companies and to generate revenue emerged, and the government began to set national economic goals and targets, such as increasing GDP to a certain level by a set year. At the same time, much economic decision making was devolved to the provincial and local levels. To attract foreign direct investment, China created four

28   *China (People's Republic of China)*

Special Economic Zones (SEZs) in Guangdong province (Shantou, Shenzhen and Zhuhai) and in Fujian province (Xiamen). In an effort to make them attractive to visitors, laws and regulations within the SEZs were much less onerous than in the rest of China. Companies that set up in the SEZs could even follow Western human resources practices like dismissing an unsatisfactory employee.

As China's economy liberalized, SOEs found themselves increasingly in competition with private companies and with foreign multinationals. Many SOEs struggled in the face of this increased competition. In the late 1990s, Beijing implemented an SOE Reform Program, which allowed for the privatization of many of the SOEs, causing both unemployment and corruption as officials benefitted from the privatization of collective resources. With time, SOEs became a smaller part of China's economy. Nonetheless, in 2019, state-owned enterprises contributed approximately 25 percent of China's GDP and were responsible for about 10 percent of employment. The remaining SOEs are arguably China's largest and most important companies in strategic sectors like energy, transportation and telecommunications that were not allowed to be privatized. Of the 119 Chinese companies on the 2019 Fortune 500 list, 82 were state owned, 37 privately owned and 10 were from Taiwan). SOEs are supported by the government through preferential access to financing, access to markets and other privileges.

Deng's economic restructuring bore fruit: China's economy grew rapidly averaging about 10 percent annually for three decades. However, the economic reforms and growth did not come without their challenges and implications. Firstly, goods that had been owned collectively (tractors, boats, equipment, fields) had to be divided up. Secondly, the transition to a market economy meant that companies were now focussed on profit, making employment suddenly precarious for many. Workers used to the guarantee of an iron rice bowl were suddenly faced with job uncertainty and even the prospect of unemployment. Thirdly, tens of millions of peasants in the countryside left the land hoping to find more lucrative employment in the cities, but those who moved could not always find work, resulting in social instability and crime. As the cities grew wealthier, the gap between life in the city and that of the 40 percent of the population that lived in the countryside became more apparent. Because the CCP and its government had the absolute power over all the resources and the market, rent seeking (gaining wealth without any productivity contribution) was very common through tax avoidance, bribery, embezzlement and other forms of corruption. The Chinese government eventually implemented a series of anti-corruption campaigns.

China has definitely become a capitalist economy, with the caveats that private property is not always protected and the market is not totally open as key sectors are protected. China is an integral part of the global economy. In 2001, it joined the World Trade Organization (WTO), which dramatically boosted its economy. In just 32 years, from 1978 to 2010, China transformed itself from a closed economy with no imports and exports to the second largest economy in the world after the United States. By 2014, China's GDP adjusted for purchasing power parity (PPP) had surpassed that of the United States. In 1978, China's international trade was worth $20.6 billion (1 percent of world trade); by 2017, it was 200 times more at $3.7 trillion (Amighini, 2018). Foreign direct investment into and out of China also grew exponentially: in 1990, China attracted $19 billion in foreign direct investment; by 2018, that figure had grown to $1.62 trillion (Graham and Wada, 2001; Texter, 2020).

China is unusual in that it dominates in both low- and high-technology sectors. The country's low labour costs allow it to dominate sectors that other industrialized countries have generally left behind, including toys, textiles, shoes, electrical household appliances, coal

China (People's Republic of China)   29

and mining. At the same time, China is a world leader in a whole range of high-technology sectors, including artificial intelligence, alternative energy, e-commerce and telecommunications. In 2017, the record for the world's fastest long-distance bullet train (at 350 km/h) was set in China. To support high-technology industries, the Chinese government has put in place new industrial policies for a range of advanced sectors, including aerospace, robotics, medical devices and new materials.

Despite this support for its industries, China's economy has been slowing. Into the mid-2000s, the country was still experiencing double-digit growth, but since 2012, GDP growth has been between 6 and 7 percent. While not an insignificant rate of growth (it would be the envy of all developed countries), it is a substantial slowdown. As countries become more developed, their economic growth rates typically slow, so while concerning, it is in some ways not surprising that China's economy is slowing after 30 years of breakneck growth. Nevertheless, it is important to note that while China is the largest economy in the world, in GDP per capita (an approximation for per capita income), China ranked 73rd in the world in 2018; 30 million Chinese still live in poverty, primarily in the rural parts of the country. To continue lifting people out of poverty and to improve the living standards of many others, China needs the economy to continue to grow.

A Chinese economy growing at a slower rate has an impact not only on China but also on the rest of the world. Because China is a key engine for global economic growth, a slower Chinese economy means less demand for everything from agricultural products to machinery. It is estimated that every 1 percent drop in China's growth causes a 0.2 percent drop in global growth (Nicocali da Costa, 2019). Although some of China's economic slowdown is inevitable, analysts point to domestic and international issues that have likely contributed to slowing Chinese growth. These include an ageing population, rising wages, outbreaks of the swine flu, which severely affected pork producers, and the trade war with the United States. The coronavirus, which appeared in December 2019, curtailed the major Lunar New Year holiday (the source of much spending) and caused 780 million people to be under quarantine or travel restrictions for many weeks, and it will have severe effects on China's economy in 2020 (Textbox 2.6).

Textbox 2.6 Belt and Road Initiative

The Belt and Road Initiative (formerly One Belt, One Road) is the Chinese government's $5 trillion infrastructure development plan to connect Asia, Africa and Europe through an enormous network of transportation and infrastructure links, requiring the construction of roads, railroads, pipelines, ports and airports. Made public in 2013 by President Xi, the goal of the initiative is to better connect China to Asia and the rest of the world, to build commercial opportunities for China's multinational companies and to showcase China's leadership on the world stage. Along with the Asian Infrastructure Investment Bank (AIIB), a new China-led multilateral investment development bank, the Belt and Road is the mark of a more assertive China, with the Chinese government willing to fund the endeavours it claims to support. Already it is estimated that China has spent $200 billion on the Belt and Road.

The Belt refers to road and rail routes, while, confusingly, the Road or Maritime Silk Road refers to sea routes. Six main corridors are planned (see Figure 2.6), which are in different stages of development: (1) the China–Pakistan Economic Corridor linking

30 *China (People's Republic of China)*

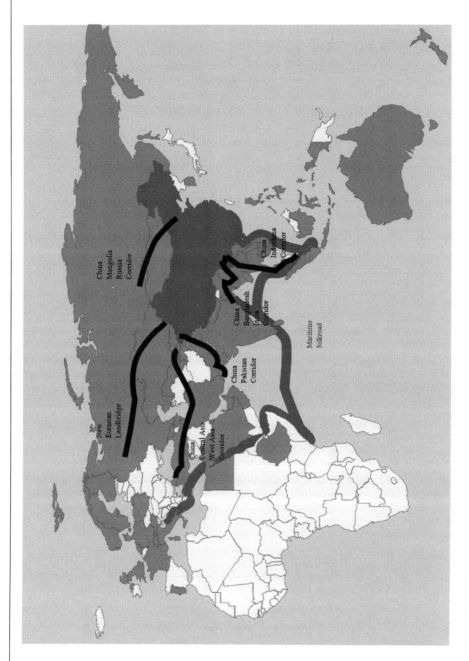

Figure 2.6 The Belt and Road Initiative.

Xinjiang in western China to the Pakistani deep-water port of Gwadar on the Arabian Sea; (2) the New Eurasian Land Bridge connecting China by rail to Europe via Russia and Central Asia; (3) a corridor connecting northeastern China to Mongolia; (4) the China–Central Asia–West Asia Economic Corridor connecting rail networks through Central and West Asia to the Mediterranean; (5) a corridor between China and Southeast Asia through the construction of railways and ports; and (6) a route connecting China, India, Bangladesh and Myanmar (China and India are still in initial negotiations).

Potential Maritime Silk Road routes go from India to Africa and from Africa through the Red Sea and the Suez Canal to Europe. China plans to invest in port development along these routes.

The Belt and Road Initiative is an audacious project. There is a great need for improved infrastructure across these regions, so China's initiative has been met with enthusiasm by many. Over 70 countries and international organizations have become involved. However, the initiative has also sparked concern as the United States, India, Japan, France and other countries worry about the nature of China's overall ambitions.

Despite the enthusiasm, there are criticisms of the Belt and Road Initiative, the biggest concern being the large debt countries must take on to fund these infrastructure projects. Some call it a "debt trap" to give huge loans to countries already deeply in debt, while other analysts say the situation is more complicated than that. The example most often cited to support this criticism is the case of Sri Lanka, which was unable to make its debt payments and was therefore forced to relinquish to China its Hambantota port and the land around it on a 99-year lease (Shepard, 2020; Sautman and Hairong, 2019). Other criticisms centre around the hiring of Chinese firms and labour for the project, leaving locals without employment opportunities. The Chinese government argues that these initiatives help developing nations in need of infrastructure funds, which no other country or organization is providing. It disputes the debt narrative, claiming that both China and the country involved carefully evaluate the feasibility of a Belt and Road Initiative project.

Political system

The CPC is the centre of power and policy in China. As of 2018, the CPC had 90.6 million members, representing 6.5 percent of the country's population. Being selected to be a member of the party involves a year-long rigorous vetting process, which includes completing a detailed application, taking courses, testing, screening and providing references. Candidates who succeed this far then have a year-long probationary period. Once admitted, the new member takes an oath in front of the Communist Party flag. Less than 10 percent of applicants are successful. In 2014, for example, 2 million people were accepted out of the 22 million who applied.

People join the Party for a variety of reasons. Certainly, for those who are ambitious, Party membership is vital. It is the main path to political advancement and opens doors to economic opportunities. Communist Party members dominate the senior positions in government, business, academia, the legal system, the army and public services, such as hospitals and elementary schools. For those who are not members, there are limits as to how high they can rise in society.

The Party seeks to attract the best people it can find. In the 1980s, Deng Xiaoping began to discuss the importance of expertise in addition to ideological conformity, welcoming

32 China (People's Republic of China)

professionals and academics into the party. In 2001, the then president Jiang Zemin launched his "Three Represents," which described what the Party stands for or represents. One of these Represents was for the Party to represent the interests of the overwhelming majority of the Chinese people. This goal was taken to mean that the Party should expand its membership to include not only workers and peasants but also intellectuals and businesspeople. Although three-quarters of the membership is male, the Party now includes people from a range of backgrounds and occupations. Forty percent of new recruits are university students, suggesting that the Party is taking steps to attract educated people. Most of China's wealthiest individuals are CCP members (see Textbox 2.7).

Textbox 2.7 China's Paramount Leaders

- Mao Zedong 1935–1976
- Deng Xiaoping 1979–1992
- Jiang Zemin 1992–2002
- Hu Jintao 2002–2012
- Xi Jinping 2013–

Constitution

China's current Constitution was adopted by the Fifth National People's Congress in 1982. It outlines the rights and duties of citizens, the structure of the state and the national flag, anthem and emblem. The Constitution states that there is respect for equality, freedom of speech, assembly and religion. The Constitution has been amended several times since 1982, most significantly in 2018. The 2018 amendments, the first in 14 years, overturned numerous constitutional reforms that had been made under Deng Xiaoping. In previous versions of the Constitution, except for in the preamble, the role of the all-powerful Communist Party had been largely absent. The 2018 revisions added the following to Article 1: "The defining feature of socialism with Chinese characteristics is the leadership of the Communist Party of China." This makes the Communist Party front and centre in the Constitution.

Another 2018 amendment added "Xi Jinping Thought on Socialism with Chinese Characteristics for a New Era" to the section in the preamble that outlines China's guiding ideologies (Marxism-Leninism, Mao Zedong Thought, Deng Xiaoping Theory and the Three Represents). This marks the first time a Chinese leader's thoughts have been enshrined in the Constitution while he is still alive. The new "Xi Jinping Constitution" also eliminated the clause stating that the president and vice president serve no more than two terms. In 1982, when the original Constitution was adopted, the two-term limit had been an intentional insertion, aimed at preventing a leader from gaining too much power and preventing the reoccurrence of an event like the Cultural Revolution, which emerged from the personality cult surrounding Mao Zedong. The final 2018 revision was the addition of articles establishing a central State Supervisory Commission to oversee corruption under the Structure of the State section of the Constitution.

Head of state

China's president is Head of State. The president is elected by the National People's Congress (NPC) as per the Constitution. Since President Jiang Zemin (1992–2002), the president has also held the powerful positions of General Secretary of the Communist Party and Chairman of the Central Military Commission, which makes him commander in chief of China's armed forces. He is thus often referred to as the Paramount Leader.

Until under President Xi Jinping, term limits were removed, presidents were limited to two successive terms. Xi Jinping became General Secretary of the Communist Party in the fall of 2012 and President of China in the spring of 2013. He started his second five-year term in October 2017. See Textbox 2.8 for more about Xi Jinping.

Textbox 2.8 Xi Jinping (1953–)

Xi is the son of an important Communist revolutionary Xi Zhongxun who fought beside Mao Zedong during the Chinese Civil War. His father was purged during the Cultural Revolution, and along with millions of other urban young people, Xi was sent to the countryside to be "re-educated" by farmers. He was sent to Yan'an in Shaanxi province, where for six years he lived in a cave and did manual work on an agricultural commune. When he returned to the city, he applied to the Communist Party multiple times before it accepted him. He studied chemical engineering at Tsinghua University. In his early political career, he took on increasingly larger and more senior roles from vice mayor of the city of Xiamen (population 3.5 million) to governor of Fujian province (population 38 million). In 2007, he became a member of the Politburo Standing Committee. He is married to Peng Liyuan, a famous singer.

Since he became Paramount Leader, President Xi has progressively strengthened his power over the elite. He reduced the size of the Politburo Standing Committee from nine members to seven, moved away from the collective leadership approach of his predecessors and established new working groups with himself in charge. He has tightened controls on social media and reacted quickly to stem any forms of dissent.

Head of government

The leader of China's State Council and the head of government, the premier is formally nominated by the president and then approved by the National People's Congress. However, in practice, it is usually the Standing Committee of the Politburo that selects the premier. The premier nominates a government cabinet and oversees the cabinet ministries. The current premier is Li Keqiang.

Political institutions: Parallel government and Communist Party institutions

The Communist Party of China controls the state, society and economy of the country. While in theory the Party and the state are distinct from one another, in reality they overlap. In a

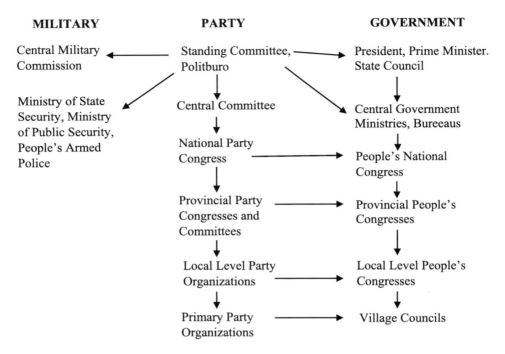

Figure 2.7 Parallel Organization of the Chinese Government and the Communist Party.

system of "organizational parallelism," all the levels of state government are matched by a corresponding Party organization (see Figure 2.7). Most importantly, ultimate power rests with the Chinese Communist Party. The Party supervises the work of the government to ensure that the party's intentions are carried out. This same organizational control is also maintained at provincial, regional and local levels of government.

- National People's Congress/National Party Congress—approximately 3,000 members
- NPC Standing Committee/Central Committee—approximately 150–300 members
- State Council/Politburo—25–35 members, State Council led by the premier; Politburo by the Secretary General
- Executive meetings of the State Council/Politburo Standing Committee—seven to nine members

Branches of government

The National People's Congress is the national unicameral legislature for the People's Republic of China. Approximately 3,000 delegates representing geographic and functional (e.g. industry, military, provinces) constituencies are elected for five-year terms. About one-quarter of the delegates are women. Delegates attend the annual two-week session of the National People's Congress and vote on legislation. In theory, the NPC has the power to make laws and legislation, but, in reality, the Party drafts the legislation, which is passed on to the NPC for its consideration and approval. Although the NPC has asserted some independence at times, it is not intended to be like a Western parliament. Many critics describe it as simply a rubber-stamping body.

The National People's Congress also elects the president and vice president and a variety of other senior positions from the nominations it receives.

National People's Congress Standing Committee

The NPC Standing Committee comprises about 150 members selected from the NPC. It meets every two months as a legislative assembly. The top leader must also be a member of the National Party Congress Standing Committee (the Communist Party's parallel organization—see Figure 2.7—which ensures that the Party is closely involved and aware of legislative affairs).

State Council

The State Council is China's executive branch, led by the premier. The council of about 35 members meets every six months to oversee the work of China's ministries and commissions and implement laws and regulations.

Executive Meetings of the State Council

The Executive Meeting of the State Council has ten members, including the premier and numerous vice premiers and state councillors. The executive meets weekly and more closely supervises the work of the Chinese government.

Communist Party institutions

The Party likes to point out that to reach the top levels of the Communist Party, individuals must emerge from a system that rewards merit and experience. In democracies, according to the CCP, leaders can attain powerful positions simply by virtue of having money or the ability to raise it and a speaking style that appeals. In contrast, the Chinese system requires bureaucrats to pass exams and gain experience in various levels of government and in the party. For example, Xi Jinping had served in various senior capacities in four provinces and in the bureaucracy of the party before he became the president and General Secretary.

The Communist Party is structured as a hierarchy of party congresses and committees that stretch from the grassroots to various higher levels of authority. Throughout the system, lower organizations are subordinate to those above them. There is considerable discipline throughout the party. Although there are opportunities for discussion and contrary views can be expressed under the proper circumstances, decisions from the top are binding, and no dissent is tolerated once these decisions have been made. The highest-level decision-making bodies are the National Party Congress, the Central Committee, the Politburo, and the Standing Committee of the Politburo.

National Party Congress

The National Party Congress is the highest-level organization within the Communist Party. Every five years, approximately 2,200 party members meet for a week at the Great Hall of the People in Beijing. These delegates are selected by provincial level party congresses to represent all the members of the Communist Party of China. The National Party Congress is the venue at which the Communist Party makes leadership changes, reviews the Constitution, endorses the party's ideology and vision and selects its Central Committee.

The 19th National Party Congress, the most recent, took place in October 2017 and was attended by 2,280 delegates from across the country. Part of the delegates' responsibility is to select/confirm the 376 members of the Central Committee, 25 members of the Politburo and 7 of the Politburo Standing Committee. The announcement of the Politburo Standing Committee is the most closely watched. Negotiations happen in secret. At the 18th National Party Congress, analysts pointed to a power struggle between two factions in the party, one faction connected to former president Jiang Zemin and the other to outgoing president Hu Jintao. Those connected to Jiang Zemin have been referred to as princelings (sons of Chinese Communist revolutionaries), who tend to favour greater state control over the economy, no substantive political reforms and a more assertive China on the world stage. The Hu Jintao faction members tend to come from more humble beginnings and have a shared history in the Communist Youth League. The Hu faction is more populist and open to greater freedoms, committed to decreasing inequality and concerned about issues of social justice. Hu Jintao's candidate to be his successor was Li Keqiang. After the selections were made by the delegates, four of the seven members of the Standing Committee were found to be princelings, including Xi Jinping who, although a princeling himself, was a compromise candidate between the two factions. Li Keqiang was named deputy leader and, ultimately, as expected, became the premier. There had been indications and wide speculation in advance of the National Party Congress that Xi and Li would become the leader and deputy leader, so these announcements were not a surprise.

At the 19th National Party Congress in October 2017, the new Politburo Standing Committee was unveiled. Xi Jinping and Li Keqiang remained, but the other five members were new, and senior officials who had been anticipated to succeed Xi in 2022 were not included.

Central Committee

The Party members selected to be on the Central Committee are China's political elite, the most important national or provincial leaders, from among whom China's top leaders emerge. The committee has about 200 members and approximately another 170 alternate members who can participate in discussions but do not have voting rights. The committee meets at an annual conference to discuss policy issues and the work of the party.

Politburo

The Politburo is composed of 25 members, who meet monthly to oversee the Communist Party as a whole. Although the Selection Committee nominally selects the Politburo (short for Political Bureau), those who analyse Chinese politics believe that former and current members of the Politburo play a major role in the selection (Li, 2016).

Politburo Standing Committee

Usually, between seven and nine members of the Politburo make up the Politburo Standing Committee, China's most powerful body. One of the members is the Secretary General of the Communist Party of China (who has in recent history also been the president). The Standing Committee comprises the very top political leadership of China. It makes policy decisions and supervises all levels of the Party and the government.

Political succession

Political succession is a challenge for the Party, as is revealed at the National Party Congress every five years. Because there is no identified vice leader, years of negotiations and jockeying for power takes place in advance of the Congress. Often the next leader has been identified at the Congress prior to the one at which he would assume the role, in other words, five years earlier. Since there was a great deal of infighting when Mao died, Deng tried to put in place a system of succession that would prevent this instability from occurring. Deng selected not only his replacement, Jiang Zemin, but also the leader who succeeded Jiang—Hu Jintao. The recent removal of presidential term limits will clearly impact any succession planning.

Provincial and local government

Over the centuries, Chinese authorities have believed in the importance of strong centralized leadership to keep the country united and stable. However, given the size of the country and its large population, of necessity China has been divided administratively since ancient times. Currently, underneath the national government, there are five main levels of governance. The highest level is the provincial one, which includes 22 provinces (China includes Taiwan as a 23rd), 5 autonomous regions, 4 mega municipalities and 2 special administrative regions. The next level of governance is the prefecture-level divisions made up of 7 prefectures, 293 prefecture-level cities, 30 autonomous prefectures (home to large ethnic minority populations) and 3 leagues (the prefectures of Inner Mongolia.) These are followed, in descending order of size, by counties, townships and villages. Each level of governance is modelled on the central government.

Since provincial and local governments have no powers of taxation (they are transferred a portion of personal and corporate income taxes), they rely on the funds transferred to them, as well as any fees or penalties they are able to charge their citizens and the sale of land and land-use rights.

People's Liberation Army

The People's Liberation Army (PLA) is the largest military force in the world with approximately 2.2 million members among its land, sea and air forces. After the United States, China's military spending is the highest in the world. The PLA falls under the Central Military Commission, which reports directly to the Politburo, and the Commander in Chief of the PLA is the General Secretary of the Communist Party. In many ways, the People's Liberation Army can be considered the armed forces of the Communist Party of China rather than the country's or government's army. In 2016, President Xi implemented a series of reforms to improve the PLA as a fighting force, to rid the PLA of corruption and to strengthen the party's hold on it. The PLA organizations responsible for troop recruitment, weapons procurement, logistics and supervision are now all subsumed under the Central Military Commission.

Society

"Chinese society was shaped for a long time by Confucianism and then by Communism and now by making money" (Hays, 2015).

38 China (People's Republic of China)

China is such a large, heavily populated and very diverse country that it is hard to make generalizations about Chinese society. Nonetheless, despite all the regional, linguistic and cultural differences, people feel bound together as part of the same Chinese society. That Chinese society has been through enormous economic and social changes over the past 70 years. Traces of Confucianism with its emphasis on knowing one's role in society, respect for family and elders and emphasis on education remain an element of Chinese life. The Communist Party with its centralized control has a major impact on daily Chinese life and society. The lessons and complex repercussions of the Great Leap Forward, the Cultural Revolution, the reform and opening up and the huge jump in standard of living for hundreds of millions of Chinese over a 30-year period, all changed Chinese society.

Although China has 55 official ethnic groups, over 90 percent of the population is Han Chinese. The Han have shared a written language for the past 2,000 years, but there are eight main Han-speaking language groups, and many dialects within these. The written characters are pronounced differently depending on the language. After the CCP came to power, it decided that to unify the country, a common language was needed. The northern language of Mandarin was made the official language of government, and all schools were required to teach it. Other languages and dialects, though, are alive and spoken in people's home regions.

Religion

The Chinese Communist Party is officially atheist. Members are not allowed to belong to religious organizations, but the Chinese Constitution officially allows freedom of religious belief. There are five religions approved to operate, under the supervision of the State Administration for Religious Affairs: Buddhism, Catholicism, Daoism, Islam and Protestantism. Other faiths are prohibited, although Chinese folk religions are usually tolerated. Chinese folk religions include animistic beliefs (that non-living things have spirits that should be worshipped), ancestor worship beliefs (that the dead and living can communicate and that sacrifices ritually made to the dead can improve life for the living) and a mixture of Buddhist and Daoist practises and beliefs. Although the number of people who follow traditional religious folk practices is difficult to measure, it is estimated at about 20 percent of the population.

Always concerned about keeping control, the CCP is nervous about any grassroots organizations, especially religious organizations that could undermine or compete with it in any way. In a major speech in 2016, Xi Jinping encouraged the "sinicization of religion," meaning that religious leaders should merge their teachings with Chinese socialist thought, and that the religion should be operated under CCP control.

Since Xi came to power, Beijing has been strengthening control of religion. Believers across faiths have been facing heightened controls, increasing repression and even persecution, particularly of those who practise Islam on which there has been a major crackdown (see the section titled Xinjiang on p. x). Two hundred and sixty million people, about 19 percent of China's population, are Buddhist. Seen as a more traditional Chinese religion than some of the others, Buddhism has an extremely long history in China. As a result, since the 1980s, the CCP has been more tolerant of Buddhism than of other religions. Many influential monks who manage some of China's larger Buddhist temples are well connected to the party. This tolerance does not extend to Tibetan Buddhism, however, whose adherents have faced serious religious persecution.

Christian organizations are also facing increased state repression. The number of Christian organizations in China has increased since the 1980s. The estimated number in 2019 ranges from 30 million to 100 million. In recent years, there have been campaigns against both house churches and party-approved churches and organizations. Churches have been forced to close or remove crosses from their rooftops, and hundreds of pastors and priests have been detained or imprisoned. Churches allowed to remain open have often been required to install facial recognition cameras, add state messages to their sermons or close off services to those under 18.

Although the Vatican has not had diplomatic ties with China since 1951, the country remains home to over 10 million Catholics. A major point of tension between the Catholic Church and the Chinese authorities has been the approval of bishop appointments. During the 1950s, a CCP-controlled organization, the Chinese Catholic Patriotic Association (CCPA), began appointing bishops. At the same time, the Vatican continued to appoint its own bishops, often secretly to protect them from harassment. These Vatican-appointed bishops ran their own "underground" secret churches, which a large number of Chinese Catholics attended.

In 2018, China and the Vatican signed an agreement in which the Pope officially recognized seven living and one deceased Chinese-state-appointed bishops who had previously been excommunicated as they were not approved by the Church. The agreement also stated that Chinese Catholics would register with the CCPA. From the Church's perspective, the goal is to bring the Chinese Catholic community together and for this to be the first step towards a broader agreement. However, the main remaining problem is the split between the CCPA and the underground churches. For example, a number of Vatican-appointed bishops have not been recognized by the CCPA. Many underground priests and parishioners who suffered greatly by remaining loyal to the Pope have no intention of supporting a state-backed Catholic Church. Additionally, the Vatican is one of only 15 states that have full diplomatic relations with Taiwan, and severing those ties is likely to be one of China's conditions of a future broader agreement.

Sensitive "core" issues

For the Chinese Communist Party, certain issues are particularly sensitive. These are issues that the Party believes would threaten its control over China or would undermine the country's territorial integrity. Discussions of these topics are generally censored within the country and foreign companies doing business in China generally engage in self-censorship to avoid angering the government and their customers. Below is a brief introduction to a number of particularly sensitive issues.

Falun Gong

Falun Gong or Falun Dafa is a Chinese religious practise centred on meditation and qigong, an ancient practice of deep breathing and movement. Falun Gong draws on Buddhist and Daoist teachings and the moral tenets of truth, compassion and forbearance. Followers wish to rid themselves of attachments and reach spiritual enlightenment. The religion was founded in 1992 by Li Hongzhi in northeast China at a time when qigong was proliferating. Falun Gong's popularity grew very quickly: by 1999, it had 70 million practitioners. This rapid rise in popularity upset the Chinese government, which now saw Falun Gong as a threat. In July 1999, the Communist Party launched a crackdown against the Falun Gong and set out to eliminate it. Hundreds of thousands of Falun Gong followers have been subject to torture, imprisonment and other forms of abuse. Falun Gong is still practised secretly in China and has many followers outside of China. Those outside the country try hard to bring attention to the persecution faced by Falun Gong practitioners in China.

China (People's Republic of China)

Xinjiang

Xinjiang is an autonomous region in northwest China, whose indigenous population is primarily Uyghurs (also spelt Uighurs), a Turkic-speaking Muslim ethnic minority. The Chinese leadership has been concerned about Xinjiang for decades because of separatist movements and growing Islamization. Some Uyghurs are separatists who claim that East Turkestan, as they call the region, is not a part of China. They point to the establishment of the Second East Turkestan Republic that existed, with Soviet support, between 1944 and 1949 in three of Xinjiang's northern districts. The separatists contend that in 1949, the People's Liberation Army annexed the Republic. Since the 1980s, when China began to allow the revitalization of local cultures, Uyghur participation in Islamic culture and practices has increased. When the Soviet Union broke up in 1991, ties between Xinjiang and China's Islamic border states (Kazakhstan, Kyrgyzstan and Tajikistan) and with Afghanistan and Pakistan grew.

Beginning in 1955, the Communist Party began encouraging the migration of Han Chinese into Xinjiang to exploit the region's mineral, oil and agricultural wealth. The encouragement worked: in 1949, the population of Han Chinese in the region was 6.7 percent; the 2010 census showed that 40.5 percent of the population was Han and 46 percent Uyghur. To improve the local economy, the Chinese government has made major investments in Xinjiang, but many Uyghurs believe that these investments disproportionately benefitted the Han. When tensions intensified between the Han and the Uyghurs, Beijing became increasingly concerned. Between 1997 and 2014, numerous incidents of violence and unrest occurred, including bus bombings and riots in Urumqi (the capital of the region), communal violence in Southwestern Xinjiang related to the police custody death of a Uyghur businessman and knife attacks in Kashgar, Hotan and Kunming. A knife attack and bombing in Urumqi in April 2014 when President Xi Jinping was visiting is said to have persuaded Xi to instigate a major crackdown against the Uyghurs.

The crackdown began with mass surveillance through social media and face and voice recognition. Then, a law prohibiting long beards and the wearing of veils was passed, and, in 2017, large numbers of Uyghurs began to be detained. Over a million Muslims (most of them Uyghurs but some ethnic Kazakhs, Uzbeks and even Hui who are often called Chinese Muslims) are estimated to be detained in "re-education camps" (Kuo, 2018). If both parents are detained, their children are put into state care. Most of these detainees have not done anything wrong or been charged with anything; simply practising their religion has made them a target. Initially, the Chinese authorities denied the existence of the camps and then described them as boarding schools and vocational training centres. Now Chinese officials say the Uyghurs are participating in vocational training designed to fight religious extremism and terrorism. Although the camps are closely guarded and investigators have not been permitted to enter, in late 2019, leaked Chinese government documents confirmed many details about the detention camps, including that the Uyghurs are locked up and prevented from leaving.

Conditions in the camps are said to be harsh, with reports of torture, sexual abuse, constant surveillance and crowded cells. Detainees undergo political indoctrination and must renounce Islam and pledge allegiance to the Chinese Communist Party. To strengthen their identity as Chinese citizens, they are taught Mandarin and theories about Communism. The governments of many countries and human rights groups have condemned the mass detention of Uyghurs and strongly encouraged the Chinese government to change its policies and close the camps. Notably absent among the countries speaking out are many of the

Muslim-majority countries, with the exception of Turkey. In 2020, reports emerged that tens of thousands of Uyghurs from the camps were being sent to work as forced labour in factories in Xinjiang and other parts of China.

Tibet

The Tibetan Autonomous Region is located in southwest China. Known as "the roof of the world," Tibet is the highest region in the world and includes vast plateaus and mountains, of which Mount Everest is the highest. Tibet is another contentious topic for the Chinese Communist Party and government. Elliot Sperling of the East-West Centre summed up the background nicely when he wrote, "China maintains that Tibet is an inalienable part of China. Tibetans maintain that Tibet has historically been an independent country. In reality, the conflict over Tibet's status has been a conflict over history" (Sperling, 2004). The PRC's view is that Tibet has been legally recognized as part of China since the Yuan dynasty in the 13th century. Subsequent Chinese governments that succeeded the Yuan government, therefore, continued to have sovereignty over Tibet through to the Republic of China's (KMT) rule and then the People's Republic of China. Although the Republic of China did not actually control Tibet between 1912 and 1951, the PRC argues that this does not mean that Tibet was independent during these years; no more than it would mean that when the country was torn apart by warlordism that those regions were independent. The Republic of China's provisional Constitution of 1912 stated that Tibet was a province of the ROC.

The position of the Tibetan Government in Exile is that for centuries Tibet has had its own culture, language, religion and political system. While never a nation-state in the sense in which this term is currently defined, and influenced by numerous foreign powers, including China, Tibet has not been a part of China for 800 years. (Pointing to Mongol and Machu rule, the Tibetan Government in Exile also argues that even China was not always under Chinese rule.) At times, the relationship between Tibet and China was one of "patron and priest" but never one of subordination. Furthermore, in 1913, the 13th Dalai Lama, the spiritual leader of the Tibetan people, proclaimed Tibetan independence as the Qing dynasty collapsed and Qing troops were chased out of Tibet. Soon after the proclamation, Tibet established an army and issued its own flag, currency, postage stamps and passports. Tibet ruled itself until the PRC invaded and incorporated Tibet into China in 1949–1950.

In 1950, the Communist government of the new People's Republic of China and 40,000 PLA troops invaded Tibet. Tibet's natural resources and strategic location made it of great value to China. Militarily outstripped, the following year, the Tibetan government signed a 17-point agreement with Beijing that granted China sovereignty over Tibet in exchange for a commitment not to change Tibet's political system and to protect the Dalai Lama and Tibetan Buddhism. Unfortunately, relations unravelled quickly. In 1959, Tibetan resistance, which had been building over the past number of years, peaked. Hundreds of thousands of Tibetans surrounded the Potala Palace in Lhasa, fearing that the Dalai Lama might be kidnapped or killed, and tried to offer him protection. As Chinese troops began to surround the city of Lhasa and artillery was aimed at the palace, the Dalai Lama fled into exile in India. Approximately 100,000 Tibetans followed the Dalai Lama to India. Shortly after the Dalai Lama's escape, the People's Liberation Army easily suppressed the Tibetan rebels and ended the uprising over three violent days. China wasted no time closing down the Tibetan government, destroying monasteries and their inhabitants and bombing the Potala Palace.

42   *China (People's Republic of China)*

Since 1959, the Dalai Lama has been in permanent exile in Dharamsala in northern India. There he established the Central Tibetan Administration, often referred to as the Tibetan Government in Exile. Not intended to take over the government in Tibet from the Chinese, the Tibetan Government in Exile advocates for Tibet and supports Tibetans in India. The Dalai Lama has led the Tibetan Government in Exile for many years, but his political authority has now been transferred to a democratic administrative system. Highly respected as a moral and spiritual leader and an advocate for Tibet, the Dalai Lama insists he is not pushing for independence from China but for more autonomy for Tibetans. Despite the respect and reverence felt for the Dalai Lama, not all Tibetans support his approach; some aspire towards full independence and are militant about reaching this goal. For his nonviolent campaign to end the Chinese domination of Tibet, the Dalai Lama was awarded the 1989 Nobel Peace Prize. This greatly angered the government of China. To members of the CCP, the Dalai Lama is a threat— subversive and "splittist." They do not believe him when he claims not to be seeking independence for Tibet. The Chinese government and the Communist Party express disdain for foreign leaders when they meet with the Dalai Lama, believing that these meetings give credibility to his claims about Tibet and challenge China's sovereignty.

As the current 14th Dalai Lama is 84 years old, the issue of his successor is of paramount importance. In Tibetan Buddhism, the Dalai Lama is the reincarnation of his predecessor. The next Dalai Lama is usually found by senior monks based on spiritual signs. China, however, has stated that the selection process must comply with Chinese laws and that the next Dalai Lama must have China's approval. In the future, it is likely there could be two Dalai Lamas: one selected by China and one selected by Tibetan monks.

The legacy of China's rule in Tibet from 1949 to 1979 is sobering: 1.2 million Tibetans dead, tens of thousands of people imprisoned or in labour camps, over 6,000 monasteries destroyed, Tibetan literature burned, forests cleared and sections of what was Tibet added to bordering provinces with only a portion left as the Tibet Autonomous Region (Avedon, 1987). The government sponsored the migration of large numbers of Han Chinese into Tibet as part of its efforts to make Tibet an integral part of China. In the 1980s, China pursued a liberalization and economic development program in Tibet. The region has received government funding and investment, and tourism has boomed. Unfortunately, most of the benefit of this economic growth appears to have gone to the Han population living in Tibet rather than to the Tibetans. Tibet remains poor, and China's moratorium on the Tibetan language, culture and religion remains tight. To protest Chinese rule, many Tibetans have self-immolated (setting oneself on fire). Between 2009 and 2019, 156 self-immolations took place across Tibet.

The future for democracy

What does the future look like for democracy and human rights in China? At the outset, it is important to note that China's political system reflects a history, political culture and even set of values different from those in the West. For a millennium, the focus of Chinese philosophy and political theory has not been on individual rights, privacy and the appropriate limits on state power. The Chinese political tradition is based much more on authoritarian values like obedience and respect for authority. Confucian teachings described all relationships as being like those between the ruler and the ruled, in which the person in the senior position looks after and takes care of the junior person and in return is granted respect and compliance. Rulers or those in more senior positions are there because they have earned these positions through experience, expertise and wisdom.

China's leaders have always been more focussed on establishing authority and uniting the country than on protecting individual rights. For many Chinese, and especially the Chinese political leadership, their greatest fear is losing authority. They look at the liberal democratic model of governance and see the potential for, and often the reality of, chaos. How, they wonder, can this possibly be a better system for 1.4 billion people spread across the third largest country in the world?

Is democracy likely to come to China? Joseph Wong, Canada Research Chair at the Munk School of Global Affairs at the University of Toronto, has considered this question:

> Scholars tell us that there is the potential for democratic reform in China. Some imagine a more peaceful transformation, while others envisage a more violent process of political change. Either way, democracy is possible in China. In fact, folks in China tell me that real democratic reform is inevitable. It is just that China is not ready, they argue. China is, at this moment, ill-suited for "liberal" democracy. As such, China chooses not to democratize, citing deep structural reasons for its reticence.
>
> (Wong, n.d.)

Wong argues that China is ready. If democracy is actually inevitable, then the Chinese Communist Party can engineer a transition that it knows it can win:

> China is ready. And more importantly, the ruling party—the main "agent" which can initiate a peaceful democratic transformation—is in a strategically advantageous position. By having readying (sic) China over the past three decades, the CCP has earned its legitimacy, its popularity, its centrality in people's daily lives and their future aspirations. For these reasons, the party ought to be more confident that it will not, or maybe even cannot, lose. Democratic transition is about calculated risks and probabilities, and they weigh heavily in the CCP's favor.
>
> (Wong, n.d.)

Wong made this argument 12 years ago in 2008, but from the vantage point of the early 2020s, it does not appear likely that either democracy or improved human rights are coming to China any time soon. Since he became Paramount Leader in 2012–2013, President Xi has become more dominant, consolidating his power within the party and clamping down on any political dissent outside it. This consolidation of power is evidenced by the enshrinement of Xi Jinping Thought on Socialism with Chinese Characteristics for a New Era in the Constitution, the abolishment of a two-term limit on the presidency and the lack of any potential successor to replace Mr. Xi as General Secretary of the Communist Party.

Human rights

China's record on human rights has long been a cause of international dissatisfaction. Criticism focuses firstly on the legal system, which is not independent but run under the Chinese Communist Party. Arbitrary arrests, rapid judgements, lengthy sentences for political dissidents and corruption within the police and the judiciary are all common concerns. China makes extensive use of capital punishment. Although the exact number of executions annually is not released publicly, Amnesty International estimates that China executes more people than the rest of the world combined. The second set of criticisms relates to the lack of freedom of

44 China (People's Republic of China)

speech, of religion and of minority rights. There was no space for civil society under Mao. In the opening and reform period that followed, the party created government-operated non-governmental organizations (e.g. the Women's Federation, the all-China Federation of Trade Unions) to mobilize society to work under party officials towards national goals. In the 1990s, China signed and ratified the International Covenant on Economic, Social and Cultural Rights (ICESCR), one of the two UN covenants on human rights. However, rather than using the official Chinese language version of the covenant, the Chinese government often uses its own translation which omits some statements and waters down others.

In the first decade of the 2000s, the Communist Party became slightly more permissive, and except for the core sensitive issues (criticism of the Party or the government, human rights, Tibet, Xinjiang and the Falun Gong), there was freedom to discuss almost everything else. Along with bringing more businesspeople into the party, non-governmental organizations were now permitted to play a role in non-political areas such as social welfare program delivery. But as David Shambaugh, China expert from George Washington University, expressed in his 2016 book *China's Future*, the country is now on a "hard authoritarianism" path (Shambaugh, 2016). Since 2012, the space for civil society and political activism in China has become very small. Surveillance, censorship and arbitrary arrests are increasingly common. Activists are harassed and threatened; the less fortunate are detained, tortured or disappeared:

> Running a nonprofit advocacy organization, working as an investigative journalist, practicing one's faith, or simply sharing a political joke with friends on social media is more difficult and risky in today's China than it was even three years ago. Some long-standing civil society groups are closing their doors, prominent journalists are changing careers, and ordinary Chinese are more careful about their online communications.
>
> (Cook, 2019)

China has been using various digital technologies, including big data collection, to closely monitor its citizens. There are 200 million CCTV cameras equipped with facial recognition software around the country. Over the past few years, the Chinese government has launched a social credit system that analyses the behaviour of all citizens by using government data, social media, facial recognition and other technologies. All of these data are analysed, and individuals are given a social credit score that rates their trustworthiness. Actions that lower your score include everything from bad driving to frivolous spending to posting fake news online. Good scores are rewarded and bad scores punished. Punishments include being unable to buy domestic airline or train tickets, throttled Internet speed, being unable to secure a job in a state-owned enterprise or being unable to enrol your child into one of the better schools. Depending on one's behaviour, one's score can go up and down. Westerners hearing about the social credit system are horrified, and, indeed, focussing on the implications for human rights and privacy, it is easy to see the system as part of some dystopian nightmare. Many Chinese, however, welcome or at least are unbothered by the social credit system. There is a crisis of trust in China, these Chinese say, pointing to fraud cases and food safety scandals, and they are willing to give up some privacy for more security.

Recently, China has also been more closely monitoring Chinese citizens overseas, both PRC nationals working or studying in foreign countries and the Chinese diaspora more broadly. Beijing keeps a close eye on Chinese students studying overseas, often working with local branches of the Chinese Students and Scholars Association (CSSA). The CSSA helps China promote a pro-China agenda and curb any activities or speakers deemed to be critical of the country. When students and other Chinese citizens return to China, they can be arrested if they were critical of the government or country while they were away, as recently happened to a 20-year-old University of Minnesota student, who was sentenced to six months of imprisonment for his social media posts (Bloomberg, 2020). Although some Chinese immigrants overseas are upset by human rights abuses in China, they fear if they express their criticism openly, their ability to return to China could be affected, and their family members could be in danger.

Challenges

Environmental problems

China's years of rapid economic growth have had a devastating impact on the environment. While far from the first industrializing country to have environmental problems, China's huge population and rapid industrialization with a growth at all cost mentality have exacerbated its problems. Toxic levels of air pollution have made visibility poor and breathing dangerous, with half a billion Chinese breathing air that is hazardous to their health. In 2015, for example, based on American standards, Beijing's air quality was considered unsafe, and often extremely unsafe, 62 percent of the time. Estimates are that between half a million and one and a half million Chinese die premature deaths caused by air pollution every year. Emissions from coal combustion are the biggest cause of China's air pollution, as 65 percent of China's energy comes from coal. Another environmental problem is water pollution, which is so serious that the World Bank has stated that there could be "catastrophic consequences for future generations" (Gibson, 2018). The dumping of human, agricultural and industrial waste has contaminated China's lakes, rivers, streams and groundwater. Because much of rural China lacks wastewater treatment, the population must rely on contaminated water. At the same time, much of China, and particularly the north, has been facing severe water shortages. China's rivers are drying up, and its forests are being cut down. The country is the world's largest emitter of greenhouse gases, responsible for about 27 percent of emissions. Rising sea levels caused by climate change have already eroded part of the coast in China's southern Guangdong province. The World Bank has warned that the city of Guangzhou, the capital of Guangdong province, will likely face more serious economic losses from sea level rise than any other major city.

In the face of so much environmental degradation, China is now taking climate change seriously. The Chinese played a leadership role at the Paris climate talks in 2015 and have continued to do so since then. The government feels pressure from the country's urban middle class, which has become more concerned about the environment and about their quality of life. As a result of this pressure, the government has improved China's environmental situation, making substantial investments in solar, wind and clean coal technologies. In fact, China is now the world's largest manufacturer and consumer of both wind and solar energy. More environmental regulations are being put in place along with stricter enforcement measures. At the same time, China is faced with the challenge of a growing middle class with the same aspirations and desires for goods and services as others in the developed and developing world. If China were to have the same number of cars per capita as the United States, the country would have over a billion cars. (Currently there are 340 million cars on the roads in China and 1.4 billion cars in the world.) Balancing the desires of the population for a better life with the need to reduce environmental destruction is a huge challenge for the government and for the Chinese population.

Growing inequality

China's three decades of double-digit economic growth improved the lives of many millions of Chinese, lifting people out of poverty and raising incomes. However, while the vast majority of the Chinese population benefitted from this growth, the benefits were not spread equally. Some increase in inequality is to be expected as a country develops, but China's has been quite dramatic. In the 1970s, the level of inequality in China was low; by 1990, China was moderately unequal, and by 2018, it had reached levels of inequality close to those of the United States and Mexico. China's GINI coefficient, a measure of income inequality where zero is perfectly equal and 1 is completely unequal, was 0.47 in 2018, a big jump from 0.35 in 1990. In China today, the bottom earning half of the population earns 15 percent of total national income, and the top 1 percent earns 14 percent. Another way of looking at the inequality is that the bottom 25 percent of the population controls 1 percent of the wealth, while the richest 1 percent controls one-third.

The biggest differences in income and wealth are between people in the rural areas and those in the cities. In the countryside, public services and social security supports are much weaker and educational attainment, an important inequality driver, is much lower. To address rising inequality, China has implemented policies such as raising the minimum wage and setting a minimum income threshold for paying income tax. The government has also begun to improve public services in rural China. It appears these policies are having some effect, as the GINI coefficient has been slowly declining, in other words improving, having peaked in 2008 at 0.49.

Although educational attainment has helped reduce inequality in China, lack of professional opportunities is impeding the progress of many. After working extremely hard to pass their dreaded college entrance exams and receive their degrees, many students find themselves unemployed or underemployed. This problem is not unique to China, but it is particularly severe there. Matching an ever-increasing number of university graduates with dignified and rewarding employment has been a challenge for over two decades. In the 1990s, the government invested heavily in higher education, and, as a result, the number of undergraduates in China skyrocketed. While this investment in higher education has brought many benefits, the escalating number of graduates (8.3 million in 2019) may be outstripping the ability of the labour market to absorb them. MyCos, a Beijing education consultancy, estimates that in 2018 only about 74 percent of graduates found work within six months of their graduation ("Idle Hands," 2019). Other studies show college graduate unemployment after six months to be only 8 percent but highlight falling wages and chronic underemployment (Minter, 2019).

Rural unrest and migrant workers

There are two major sources of rural unrest in China. The first is the seizure of village land by the government, often in partnership with private developers, who then resell the land at prices many multiples of the compensation that is given to the villagers. Over 100,000 protests happen annually in rural China, and approximately 65 percent of those relate to loss of land. Every year, local governments expropriate the land of about 4 million rural Chinese citizens. The second source of rural unhappiness is the growing gap between the quality of life in rural and urban settings. China's prosperity has not been shared evenly; indeed, the rural areas are being left behind. To improve their lives, millions of rural Chinese migrate to the cities to seek work. To discourage people from settling in the cities, China's household registration system, known as *hukou*, intentionally limits where people may legally work. The migrants are therefore unable to access social services or education for their children. Tens of millions of children remain with their grandparents or other relatives in the country-side, while their parents work sometimes thousands of miles away. Children grow up without parents, while their parents work 10–12 hours per day, six or seven days a week all year to send money home for their support. Often the only time the entire family is together is during the Lunar New Year holiday when everyone travels home.[3] Nonetheless, this migration from the rice paddies to the factories has made both individuals and the country as a whole much wealthier. In 2015, over 158 million migrant workers worked outside their home province, and another 94 million worked within their home province.

China has recently begun relaxing *hukou* residency rules in its smaller cities as part of its urbanization plan. However, although rural migrant workers are essential to China's economy, they often feel the disdain of their city neighbours and are frequently targeted by the police and other authorities. Many city people believe that those from the countryside are inferior and would prefer that these "country bumpkins" not go to school with their children. Annually there are numerous migrant protests over poor pay and working conditions. Clashes, which sometimes turn into riots, between migrants and locals and migrants and police have occurred throughout China over the past decades.

Corruption

Corruption has been a serious problem in China for decades. The 1989 Tiananmen Square protests were actually motivated more by anger at massive corruption by Party/government officials and their cronies than by a call for democracy. Economic reform and a wealthier economy have created opportunities for officials to use their power and control over bureaucratic approvals and resources for private gain, all the more so as authority has devolved to local level governments. Party and state authorities have positions that present many opportunities to make a profitable arrangement. Officials trade approvals or "looking the other way" for everything from starting up a business, initiating a project, accessing good schools for their children or better housing to, particularly in the past, goods in short supply. Bribery, kickbacks and nepotism are all too common.

Along with the economic costs, corrupt practices undermine the legitimacy of the government, increase inequality and build up frustration within society. In an effort to stop corruption, the party has launched various campaigns, the most recent and serious of which began soon after President Xi assumed the leadership in 2012. Popular with the general public, fighting corruption has continued to be one of the main planks in Xi's presidency, targeting both "tigers" and "flies"—the elite and the ordinary—and arresting and charging over 1 million officials. Close observers of Chinese politics point out that the anti-corruption campaign has also been an ideal opportunity for Xi to eliminate his enemies and strengthen his own power (Lorentzen and Lu, 2018, Hui 2020). High-level leaders, including two military generals and a Politburo Standing Committee member, are now in prison. Strikingly, Xi's family has somehow managed to amass over $1 billion in wealth.

Chinese analysts suggest that the challenge of corruption in China is complex since corruption is built into the country's institutional structure. The most serious corruption involves people in senior positions plundering national resources. These administrators are presented with tempting opportunities for personal gain because there is little oversight in the awarding of government contracts and the transferring of public assets into private hands. Matters are

48 China (People's Republic of China)

compounded by a weak rule of law and unclear relations between private and state-owned companies. Rooting out this kind of corruption would require deep institutional reforms like strengthening the rule of law, establishing more transparent property rights, allowing oversight by the media and civil society and granting greater judicial independence. But Xi has not pursued these kinds of reforms and the plundering of state assets continues (Hui, 2020).

Demographics

China faces two major demographic challenges. The first is that its population will soon rapidly decline. Over the past 70 years, China's population has grown astronomically from 550 million in 1950 to 1.43 billion in 2019. During the 1950s, Mao believed that China's large population could substitute for its lack of capital and encouraged people to have children. By 1980, the rapid population growth that had resulted was worrying the Chinese government, which implemented a one-child policy, limiting the majority of Chinese families (there were exceptions for those in agricultural or minority areas) to one child. The campaign was rigidly enforced, particularly in the cities. Those who had more than one child were punished through heavy fines, dismissal from their employment or reduced pay. Even more significantly, the second child would not be able to access education or health care. It was very difficult for a woman to have a second pregnancy as family planning officials in conjunction with the company work units paid very close attention to ensure unauthorized pregnancies did not occur. Those who were found to be pregnant with a second child were often forced to have abortions.

The one-child policy was relaxed in 2011 (allowing a second child under certain circumstances) and became a two-child policy in 2016. The one-child policy may have ended, but its impacts remain. Estimates are that 400 million births were prevented by the program. As boys were preferred over girls, female foetuses were aborted, and female babies were killed or abandoned. As a result, the sex ratio in China became badly skewed towards men: on average about 118 men to 100 women, but in some districts it was as high as 150 men to 100 women. In 2016, there were 33.6 million more men than women, leaving men of marriageable age with no one to marry. In Chinese, these single men are referred to as "bare branches." Brides for these men have been trafficked to China from Vietnam and other countries. In addition to upsetting the sex ratio, single-child families have also had societal impacts. Only children are the centre of the world for their parents and two sets of grandparents. They are both spoiled (nicknamed "little emperors") and the focus of enormous pressure to succeed in school and then in the job market to support their parents and grandparents in their old age. Then there are the second and third born "ghost" children who lack official registration and therefore live in the shadows of Chinese society, unable to go to school or access any kind of service. Demographically, the result of the policy has been that China's low birth and fertility rates have left the country with an ageing and soon to be declining population. A 2020 Chinese Academy of Social Sciences report states that the population is likely to begin contracting in 2027. Despite the introduction of the two-child policy, China's birth rate has continued to fall. On a positive note, the one-child policy seems to have strengthened the role of women in society, resulting in more women attending university and entering the workforce.

Related to the declining population problem is the fear that China will grow old before it grows rich, meaning that China's growth will slow before its economy has fulfilled its potential and has brought the poor portion of its population out of poverty. In the next quarter century, the percentage of China's population over 65 is projected to double to 25 percent, similar to the trajectory followed by Japan, which was much wealthier on a per capita basis when its population decline began. Because China's working age population has already begun to decline, there are now fewer workers, less consumer spending and increased funding needs for pensions and health care than was the case a few years ago. Nonetheless, China has some options for improving the situation. To begin with, as the *Economist* wrote, China can "mitigate the downside from its ageing by boosting both labour-force participation and productivity—that is, getting more people into work and more out of them." ("China's Median Age," 2019). This could be done through raising the low retirement age, making better use of underemployed university graduates and replacing or enhancing workers with technology. Other analysts point out that because the labour supply plays only a small role in China's economic growth, a decline in the working age population will have little impact on China's growth rate. As John Rich points out, the factors that will determine China's growth and future prosperity are productivity and investment (Ross, 2013). This does not mean, however, that China's ageing and declining population does not create challenges.

China-U.S. relations

The People's Republic of China and the United States did not formally establish diplomatic relations until 1979. Throughout the Cold War, most of the West officially recognized the Republic of China (Taiwan) as China. Both the Republic of China and the People's Republic of China stated that there could be only one China—not two Chinas and not one China and one Taiwan—so other nations could recognize only one or the other. Slowly, more and more countries began establishing relations with the PRC. In 1971, Secretary of State Henry Kissinger secretly visited Beijing, and on July 15, 1971, President Richard Nixon announced that he would visit the PRC the following year. It was clear that the United States would eventually recognize the PRC. But Nixon was a hard-line anti-Communist, so this new stance was a big shock to Americans and to America's allies. Nixon's sudden decision to visit China was related to U.S.-Soviet relations. An improvement in relations between the United States and China would (and did) shift the Cold War balance and drive a wedge between the Soviet Union and China. Nixon's 1972 visit to China ended a quarter of a century with no form of diplomatic connection or communication between the two countries. During the visit, President Nixon and Premier Zhou Enlai (head of government under Chairman Mao) signed the Shanghai Communique, beginning the normalization of relations between the United States and the PRC.

Entering the second decade of the 21st century, the China-U.S. relationship is a complicated one. They are the two largest economies in the world and are each other's largest trading partner. However, they have been locked in a trade war since 2018, when U.S. President Trump, accusing China of unfair long existing trading practices and the theft of intellectual property, placed tariffs on $34 billion worth of Chinese goods. The United States and other countries have serious concerns about Chinese theft of intellectual property and trade secrets, counterfeit products, pirated goods and software. China is thought to be behind 50–80 percent of global intellectual property theft cases, costing the United States and other countries billions of dollars every year.

China responded to the American tariffs with its own tariffs on U.S. goods. The trade war escalated until the United States had imposed tariffs on $386 billion worth of Chinese products and China on $100 billion of U.S. goods. In January 2020, the two countries signed a phase one trade deal in which China agreed to buy $200 billion more goods from the United States and improve its intellectual property regime, and in return the United States would

50 China (People's Republic of China)

reduce or eliminate some of its tariffs. Although the deal represents progress, it is only one step forward.

Another area of tension between the two countries is the U.S. belief that China keeps its currency, the renminbi, artificially low, thus reducing the price of its exports.[4] Exacerbating the tenuous relationship between the two countries was the U.S. decision to ban American companies from selling technology to Huawei, a Chinese multinational telecommunications company now one of the leaders in 5G technology networks, a decision that angered China. Although a private company, Huawei is believed to have close ties with the Chinese government, and there are concerns that the 5G network could contain backdoors enabling the Chinese government to spy.

When it comes to security, China and the United States often find themselves either at odds or approaching issues from different angles. These differences are evident in United Nations Security Council deliberations, in which China is usually reluctant to become involved in the affairs of other states. For example, China vetoed interventions in Syria and Darfur that the United States, France and the United Kingdom were seeking, and was also unwilling to condemn Russia's annexation of Crimea. Another point of contention between China and the United States is China's economic support for North Korea, support that has undermined the sanctions the United States and other countries have imposed to try to halt North Korea's nuclear program.

Conclusion

Over the past five decades, China has transformed itself from one of the poorest countries in the world to its second largest economy. Now the top global trader, China is the most important trading partner for more than 100 countries and, in 2018, was responsible for 12.4 percent of global trade, valued at $4.6 trillion. The country has the distinction of being the world's largest manufacturer, is the second largest recipient of foreign direct investment and holds the largest foreign exchange reserves in the world.

Individual wealth has exploded in China. In 2019, the country was home to 4.4 million millionaires and 658 billionaires, its top 1,800 earners having an average wealth of $1.4 billion. China's middle class is close to 400 million people (depending on the definition of middle class). Responsible for one-third of the global luxury market in 2018, China is predicted to soon surpass the United States as the world's largest consumer of goods. On Singles Day (November 11) 2019, a Chinese shopping holiday with online and offline deals, Alibaba and JD.com had combined revenues of $60 billion.

Much of China's wealth has been made in science and technology, fields that have seen substantial advances made possible by its vast talent pool. Every year, 4.5 million students graduate in the STEM (science, technology, engineering and mathematics) fields. Technological advances are seen across the STEM fields: China has over 200 of the 500 fastest supercomputers in the world. The country is at the forefront of high-speed trains, 5G wireless technologies and artificial intelligence. The Chinese government's Made in China 2025 strategy is intended to build Chinese expertise and leadership in 10 sectors, including aerospace, medical devices and new materials. Chinese platforms in digital commerce (Taobao, Tmall, JD), payments (Alipay, WeChat pay, Baidu Wallet), video streaming (Yukou, Tudou, iQiyi, PPS, Tencent video) and search (Baidu, Shenma) have enormous audience reach. WeChat, the Chinese social media messaging app (with shopping features), has 1.1 billion active monthly users.

China has changed geopolitics and international governance. While accepting the role of international institutions and the systems they support, China does not always share the norms and principles that underlie them. Chinese preferences and priorities are often different and gradually China has been trying to remake the rules and transform the international system. When it cannot change the system, sometimes China sets up new institutions (e.g. the Asian Infrastructure Investment Bank) or initiatives (e.g. the Belt and Road program) to achieve its agenda.

Today, China is more repressive and ideological than it has been since it began to open up under Deng in the late 1970s. The CCP's focus on stability and a fear of chaos is sometimes dismissed by the West, but, as prominent Chinese security scholar Michael D. Swaine argues,

> It is difficult to exaggerate the extent to which a proud, historically powerful, and influential people were traumatized, in the modern era, by the experience of imperial collapse, prolonged civil war, economic weakness, and victimization at the hands of Western powers and Japan. This experience, passed down to every Chinese citizen through highly nationalistic textbooks and government propaganda, has created both a strong sense of nationalism and a deep, enduring sensitivity throughout society to the fragility of political rule and the potential threat posed by external powers. Moreover, this perception was magnified during the Maoist period by the upheavals and widespread deaths caused by the Great Leap Forward and the Cultural Revolution. And this sensitivity has been worsened by the corruption and disruption generated by China's rapidly growing, outwardly extending economic system.
>
> (Swaine and Devries, 2019)

While the rest of the world talks of China's rise, China and the CCP perceive that the country has returned to its rightful place at the centre, with the rest of the world acknowledging China's interests and influences and paying it the deference its status deserves. The Party will do everything it can to complete that return and remain in power. Knowing that its legitimacy rests on economic growth, the CCP will continue to intervene to keep the economy growing at 6 percent annually, at least. But this may not be easy, as China must also deal with serious problems, including its ageing population, growing inequality, air and water pollution, the crisis in Hong Kong and a trade war with the United States.

The sheer power of the Chinese state and its authoritarian nature can impress and dismay in equal measure. At no time was this more apparent than during the 2019–2020 coronavirus outbreak. On the one hand, once the central government decided to act, within days it had quarantined 16 cities with a total population of about 50 million people, used big data to track down passengers who had shared a railway carriage with people who were infected and set up drones with speakers to tell people to wear masks and return home. New hospitals were built in less than two weeks. The World Health Organization praised China's efforts to combat the coronavirus epidemic as "extraordinary," with the WHO Director General stating that "China is actually setting a new standard for outbreak response." However, when the virus was first detected and doctors tried to draw attention to it, they were quickly silenced. Local officials in Wuhan, where the virus began, feared being punished for bringing a potential problem to their superiors, although some officials did report it to Beijing early. So, as the virus spread, officials withheld information and did nothing to warn the public. Early intervention could perhaps have stopped the virus from becoming an epidemic. The coronavirus outbreak has revealed the problems with censorship, the culture of fear and submission and the recent focus on political loyalty over skills that plague China's system of governance today.

52 China (People's Republic of China)

Notes

1 His grandson, the Qianlong Emperor, abdicated to his son so as not to reign longer than his revered grandfather. Because the Qianlong Emperor remained as the retired emperor and held ultimate power, in reality he ruled longer than the Kangxi Emperor.
2 Japan had taken over the area from Germany in 1915 and was allowed to keep it under the treaty, which angered China. The dispute was resolved in China's favour in 1922.
3 The Lunar New Year holiday in China is considered the biggest human mass migration in the world; about three billion trips are made.
4 In the 1980s, Japan was also accused of this kind of currency manipulation (see p. 76).

Bibliography

"China's Median Age Will Soon Overtake America's", *The Economist*, October 31, 2019.

"Idle Hands: The Growing Ranks of Unemployed Graduates Worry China's Government", *The Economist*, August 1, 2019.

Amighini, Alessia. 2018. "China's New Economic Powerhouse", in *China: Champion of (which) Globalization?*, Alessia Amighini, editor, Ledizioni Ledi Publishing.

Avedon, John F. 1987. "Tibet Today: Current Conditions and Prospects", *Himalaya: The Journal of the Association for Nepal and Himalayan Studies*, 7(2): 1–10.

Bloomberg. 2020. "University of Minnesota Student Jailed for 6 Months for Critical Tweets He Sent in the U.S.", *Time*, January 23.

Cook, Sarah. 2019. "The Remarkable Survival of Free Thought and Activism in China", *Freedom House*, May 28. https://freedomhouse.org/blog/remarkable-survival-free-thought-and-activism-china

Gibson, Carolyn. 2018. "Water Pollution in China is the Country's Worst Environmental Issue", *The Borgen Project*, March 10. https://borgenproject.org/water-pollution-in-china/

Graham, Edward and Erika Wada. 2001. "Foreign Direct Investment in China: Effects on Growth and Economic Performance", *Achieving High Growth: Experience of Transitional Economies in East Asia*, Peter Drysdale, editor, Oxford University Press.

Hays, Jeffrey. 2015. *Facts and Details: Chinese Society: Crowds, Individualism and Villages*. http://factsanddetails.com/china/cat11/sub70/item159.html

Hui, Echo. 2020. "Dirty Money: China's False War on Corruption", *Forbes*, January 10.

Kuo, Lily. 2018. "'My Soul, Where Are You?': Families of Muslims Missing in China Meet Wall of Silence", *The Guardian*, September 13.

Li, Cheng. 2016. *Chinese Politics in the Xi Jinping Era: Reassessing Collective Leadership*. Brookings Institution Press.

Lorentzen, Peter L. and Xi Lu. 2018. *Personal Ties, Meritocracy, and China's Anti-Corruption Campaign*. November 21. https://ssrn.com/abstract=2835841 or dx.doi.org/10.2139/ssrn.2835841

Minter, Adam. 2019. "China's Brightest Are the Trade War's Latest Casualties", *Financial Review*, May 28.

Needham, Joseph. 2013. *The Grand Titration: Science and Society in East and West*, Vol. 21. Routledge.

Nicocali da Costa, Ana. 2019. "China's Economic Slowdown: How Bad Is It?", *BBC News*, September 26.

Ross, John. 2013. "Why China Will Grow Rich Long Before it Grows Old", *China.org.cn*, December 8.

Sautman, Barry and Yan Hairong. 2019. "The Truth about Sri Lanka's Hambantota Port, Chinese 'debt TRAPS' and 'Asset Seizures'", *South China Morning Post*, May 6.

Shambaugh, David. 2016. *China's Future*. New York Polity Press.

Shepard, Wade. 2020. "How China's Belt and Road Became A 'Global Trail Of Trouble'", *Forbes*, January 29.

Sperling, Eliot. 2004. "The Tibet-China Conflict: History and Polemics", *Policy Studies*, 7, East-West Centre.

Su, Yang. 2011. *Collective Killings in Rural China During the Cultural Revolution*. Cambridge University Press.

Swaine, Michael D. and Ryan Devries. 2019. "Chinese State-Society Relations: Why Beijing Isn't Trembling and Containment Won't Work", *Commentary for Carnegie Endowment for International Peace,* March 10.

Texter, C. 2020. "Value of Foreign Direct Investment Inward Stock 2000–2019", *Statista*, May 27. https://www.statista.com/statistics/1017011/china-foreign-direct-investment-inward-stock/

Walder, Andrew G. 2014. "Rebellion and Repression in China, 1966–1971", *Social Science History*, 38(3–4): 513–539.

Wong, Joseph. n.d. *Choosing Democracy*. https://munkschool.utoronto.ca/downloads/pdfdoc/joe_wong_brief.pdf

Yongyi, Song. 2011. "Chronology of Mass Killings During the Chinese Cultural Revolution (1966–1976)", *Online Encyclopedia of Mass Violence*, 315–327.

Further Reading

Brook, Timothy. 2019. *Great State: China and the World*. Harper Collins.

Chang, Jung. 1991. *Wild Swans: Three Daughters of China*. Touchstone.

Chang, Jung and Jon Halliday. 2011. *Mao: The Unknown Story*. Random House.

Cheung, Gordon C.K. 2009. *Intellectual Property Rights in China: Politics of Piracy, Trade and Protection*. Routledge.

Coble, Parks M. 1991. *Facing Japan: Chinese Politics and Japanese Imperialism, 1931–1937*. Council on East Asian Studies, Harvard University.

Fewsmith, Joseph (editor). 2010. *China Today, China Tomorrow: Domestic Politics, Economy and Society*. Rowman and Littlefield Publishing Group Ltd.

Fong, Vanessa. 2002. *Only Hope: Coming of Age Under China's One China Policy*. Stanford University Press.

Hui, Wang. 2006. *China's New Order: Society, Politics, and Economy in Transition*, Translated by Theodore Huters and Rebecca E. Karl. Harvard University Press.

Joseph, William A. 2014. *Politics in China: An Introduction*. Oxford University Press.

Lee, Ching. 2017. *The Specter of Global China: Politics, Labor and Foreign Investment in Africa*. University of Chicago.

Pei, Minxin. 2008. *China's Trapped Transition*. Harvard University Press.

Sun, Wanning and Jingjie Guo (editors). 2012. *Unequal China: The Political Economy and Cultural Politics of Inequality*. Routledge.

3 Japan

Introduction

Something of a geographic anomaly, Japan is a string of four main islands (from south to north—Kyushu, Shikoku, Honshu and Hokkaido) and thousands of small ones that stretch over 3,000 km southwest to northeast. The Sea of Japan (East Sea) separates the Japanese archipelago from the Asian mainland. At 377,000 km^2, the country is larger than Germany and Great Britain. Japan is divided into 8 regions and 47 prefectures or administrative districts. Its northern tip lies at a similar latitude to southern Quebec, or slightly above that of Detroit, Michigan; the most southerly point is at the same latitude as the Bahamas, or central Mexico. Japan's nearest neighbours are South Korea to the west (the Tsushima Strait off Kyushu is only 200 km from the Korean peninsula), China to the west and south and Russia to the west and north (see Figure 3.1).

Over half of the country is mountainous—the Japanese Alps, a series of mountain ranges, bisect the island of Honshu—and covered with forests. As a result, the population is concentrated on the plains and along the coast. The capital of Tokyo is the world's most populous metropolitan area with more than 38 million residents. Japan has limited arable land; a good portion of the arable land it does have is on the northern island of Hokkaido. The country sits quite literally on shaky ground, at the confluence of four major tectonic plates, which created a land of mountains, volcanoes and ancient craters. Since a remarkable 10 percent of the world's active volcanoes are in Japan, it is hardly surprising that the nation has a long history of earthquakes, landslides and tsunamis.

In 2019, Japan had the 11th largest population in the world at 126.8 million. Since 2011, following years of slow growth, Japan's population began to decline sharply, caused by a low birth rate, minimal immigration and an ageing population. In 2020, about 27 percent of the Japanese population is over 65 years old. Japan is one of the most ethnically homogenous countries on the planet: 98.1 percent Japanese, 0.5 percent Korean, 0.4 percent Chinese, and 1 percent other (CIA World Factbook, n.d.). This homogeneity is maintained at least partially by the country's nationality law, which determines nationality according to that of one's parents not to one's nation of birth. Because of this law, children born to foreigners in Japan do not automatically receive Japanese citizenship. The law has major implications for the majority of the 800,000 Koreans who live in Japan who are *Zainichi* Koreans. Although *Zainichi* means "Japan resident" and implies a temporariness, *Zainichi* Koreans are long-term Japan residents who have descended from people who came to Japan before 1945, many as forced labourers during World War II. (The other ethnic Koreans living in Japan emigrated to Japan from South Korea post 1945.) *Zainichi* Koreans—second, third or later generations

Figure 3.1 Map of Japan.

56   *Japan*

of children born and resident in Japan for their entire lives—must apply to become Japanese citizens. Unfortunately, Koreans in Japan often face discrimination, racism and prejudice.

Japan has several other minority groups, including the Ainu, Indigenous peoples only officially recognized as such in 2019. The approximately 25,000 Ainu people (there are up to 200,000 people of Ainu ancestry) live in Hokkaido, the Kurile Islands and the southern part of Sakhalin Island. Other minority groups include the Ryukyuwans, who have their own language and a distinct culture, with 1.3 million living on the Okinawan islands and another 300,000 in other parts of Japan. Less well known are the *burakumin*, ethnically Japanese people whose ancestors worked as butchers or leather workers and who continue to face hostility and discrimination. In the 1990s, South Americans (mainly Brazilians) of Japanese descent came to Japan as contract workers. The government believed that their Japanese ancestry would allow them to easily integrate into Japanese society. Although this did not turn out to be the case and many returned home, approximately 275,000 Japanese Brazilians remain in Japan primarily working in automotive and electronics factories (Textbox 3.1).

Textbox 3.1 Different periods in Japanese history

- Jomon period (14,000–300 B.C.)
- Yayoi period (300 B.C.– A.D. 300)
- Kofun period (c. 300–538)
- Asuka period (538–710)
- Nara period (710–794)
- Heian period (794–1185)
- Kamakura period (1185–1333)
- Muromachi period (1338–1573)
- Sengoku or Warring States period (1467–1568)
- Azuchi-Momoyama period (1573–1603)
- Tokugawa/Edo period (1600–1868)
- Meiji period (1868–1912)
- Taisho (1912–1926) and early Showa period (1912–1945)
- Showa period (1926–1989)
- Heisei period (1989–2019)
- Reiwa period 2019–

Early Japanese history

Ancestors of the current Japanese people are thought to have inhabited the Japanese islands tens of thousands of years ago. Human fossil remains have been found that are 30,000 years old. Evidence of a more settled and organized society in what is now Hokkaido and the northern regions of Honshu dates from about 3200 B.C. These early peoples likely came to the Japanese islands from mainland Russia via Sakhalin Island and the Kurile Islands. They began cultivating rice; hunting deer, bear and boar; gathering nuts, fruit and roots; fishing; and making pots and figurines. Primary evidence of this early habitation lies in the pottery they left behind, which was made with rows of rolled clay. This first era of Japanese history was named for the pottery, which is called Jomon, meaning cord/rope pattern. The Jomon stone and clay figurines are striking: many have bulging eyes, some are pregnant females and others appear to be broken, perhaps on purpose by the artist. Stocky with broad faces, the Jomon people looked somewhat similar to the Ainu of today, and anthropologists confirm that the Ainu are descended from the Jomon.

About 300 B.C., immigrants arrived on the southern island of Kyushu, most likely from the Korean peninsula. These people were taller with more narrow faces. They were named the Yayoi after the district in Tokyo in which archaeologists first found a reddish pottery different from the Jomon. Although little is known about the Yayoi, archaeological evidence shows evidence of wet rice paddy cultivation, a style of pottery smoother and more elegant than that of the Jomon and a mastery of metalwork. Bronze and iron were used to make tools, armour, weapons and other items. The Yayoi appear to have spread from the southwest to about the middle of Honshu. Excavated Yayoi settlements show houses with thatched roofs and sunken floors. By the middle of the Yayoi period, villages had built raised wooden storehouses to protect crops from insects and rodents. The Yayoi period lasted until about the 3rd century A.D. Along with the Jomon period that preceded it and the Kofun period (A.D. 300–538) that followed, and during which the leaders of the Yamato clan began to establish control over large parts of the country, the Yayoi period made up what is considered to be ancient Japan. The Kofun period got its name from the enormous keyhole shaped Kofun burial mounds constructed for the ruling elite of the day between the 3rd and 7th centuries.

Classical Japan (538–1185) comprises three periods: Asuka, Nara and Heian. During Asuka (538–710), Japan transformed from a loosely structured tribal land into a more organized society. The Yamato clan gradually gained considerable authority over the 4th and 5th centuries, and by the early 6th century, they were the ruling family. (The Kofun and Asuka periods are collectively referred to as the Yamato period.) In the mid-6th century, Buddhism came to Japan from Korea. Prince Shotoku, who ruled from 594 to 622, was a strong Buddhist and spread Buddhism throughout the land. He commissioned the construction of many Buddhist temples in the Kansai region, including Shitenno-ji in Osaka and Hōryū-ji in Nara prefecture. Prince Shotoku established a centralized government with a merit-based civil service. He also authored a 17-article constitution that focused on the morals and virtues expected of government officials such as loyalty, harmony and dedication to government. These core values became deeply embedded in Japanese society.

Japan remained open to external influences. Confucian ideas and philosophy entered Japan from China, and in 645, Emperor Kotoku implemented a series of doctrines called the Taika Reforms. Based on Confucian beliefs and the Chinese example of a strong imperial court and centralized government, the Taika Reforms transformed land holding arrangements, produced a household registry and implemented a system of taxation. Thus, the Chinese idea of an all-powerful centralized government remained in place in Japan for the next five centuries. Interest in learning from China incorporated everything from architecture to literature. Technologies, institutions, legal systems and Chinese characters originated in China and were adapted to Japanese conditions.

A country built around a centralized political system needed a capital city. The first capital was established in Nara in 710, where it remained as the seat of government until 784. Nara was a carefully designed city, laid out in a Chinese checkerboard plan, and host to a large court bureaucracy. During the Nara period (710–794), the first Japanese histories were written: the *Kojiki* and the *Nihon Shoki*. These books chronicled Japan's early history, including legends, songs, myths and oral traditions. Japan's creation story (see Textbox 3.2) was first widely shared in the *Kojiki*. In fact, the Kojiki was commissioned in part to solidify the position of

58 *Japan*

the emperor by linking him directly to the creation story (see Textbox 3.2) and the unbroken lineage claim. The first poetry anthologies were also published in this time. The Manyōshū (Collection of Ten Thousand Leaves) is a collection of 400 poems published in 759.

Textbox 3.2 Creation story

Japan's creation story explains the origins of the Japanese islands, describes the emergence of the celestial and earthly worlds and recounts the birth of the first Gods. The Gods Izanagi and Izanami leaned down from the floating bridge of heaven and stirred the ocean with a jewelled spear. The droplets of water that dripped from their spear formed into an island and the Gods descended onto it. Izanagi and Izanami gave birth to a large number of Gods, including Amaterasu, the Sun Goddess, from whom Japan's imperial line is said to descend. The story, chronicled in the *Kojiki* (Record of Ancient Things), described how Amaterasu was sent by Izanagi to rule over the heavens. Her younger brother Susano'o was to rule over the seas but he was disobedient, so Izanagi banished him. On his way to exile, he visited Amaterasu. He teased and tormented Amaterasu so much that she hid herself in a cave, thereby plunging the world into darkness. Eventually, the other Gods enticed her out of the cave using a bronze mirror (in which she sees her reflection) and some curved beads also described as jewels. Once Amaterasu is out of the cave, the door is shut behind her. Light is restored to the world. Later, Susano'o gave Amaterasu a sword as an apology. Amaterasu sent her grandson down to earth to rule. He carried with him the mirror, the sword and the jewels, which now form the Japanese imperial regalia. Amaterasu's great-grandson, Jimmu, became the first emperor of Japan.

In 794, Japan's capital moved from Nara to Kyoto, where it remained until 1868. Heian (an early name for Kyoto) was also laid out in a Chinese grid style. The Heian period (794–1185) is celebrated as the golden age of Japanese culture. Japan's classical art, culture, poetry, music and painting all flourished, and institutions and culture borrowed from China took on a Japanese life of their own. The Japanese created two sets of phonetic *kana* syllabaries from the Chinese characters, enabling people to write in Japanese. Ladies of the Heian imperial court kept diaries. One of the most famous works of Japanese literature, and considered to be one of the world's first novels, was written at the start of the 11th century. The *Tale of Genji* was written by Murasaki Shikibu, a lady-in-waiting, and tells of the life of Hikaru Genji, the son of an emperor. The book gives great insights into the refined and gentle court life of the Japanese elite of the time.

During this time, the emperor held official sovereignty, but the Fujiwara family wielded the real power and controlled most government posts. Branches of the imperial family moved from the capital to the provinces to make their fortunes and establish political power. The guards and soldiers of imperial families and the Fujiwara and other noble families gradually formed into a warrior class, which was the predecessor of the samurai of later fame. Rivals within the imperial family, supported by military groups, the Taira and the Minamoto, pushed for control of the royal court. In 1156, a four-year civil war broke out. The Taira clan ruled the country until they were destroyed by the Minamoto clan at an epic battle in 1185. Minamoto Yoritomo[1] established military rule and became the first all-powerful *Shogun* (generalissimo) (Textbox 3.3).

> **Textbox 3.3 Shogun**
>
> *Shogun* became the word used for Japan's military dictators from Minamoto Yoritomo's rule until 1868. (Prior to this, *Shogun* had been a temporary title the emperor bestowed on a loyal military commander for the duration of a military campaign.) The Shogun was notionally appointed by the emperor and was the ruler of Japan. His officials were called the *bakufu* or tent government (implying the Shogun's role in the field doing the work of the government for the emperor) and were responsible for the administration of government. This military government is referred to as the shogunate. In the 12th century, under this first shogunate, the samurai or warrior class began to develop. The samurai would serve the daimyo or feudal lords who supported the Shogun (see Figure 3.2).
>
>
>
> *Figure 3.2* Portrait of Minamoto, Yoritomo, the first Shogun.

The Kamakura period (1185–1333) marked the beginning of Medieval Japan. Yoritomo made his base at Kamakura (about 50 km southwest of present-day Tokyo) and built a military government. (The court remained in Kyoto.) Loyal warriors from throughout the country collected taxes, administered the area under their control and maintained law and order. This was a feudal system with strong and personal lord-vassal relationships. In the late 11th century, Japan faced its first serious invasion from overseas. Twice (in 1274 and in 1281) the Mongols, under Kublai Khan, tried to invade Japan. On both occasions, the Mongol fleets were destroyed by typhoons, prompting the Japanese to call the storms *kamikaze* (or *shinpū*, which is another reading of the same kanji characters) meaning divine winds.

60 *Japan*

As military loyalties wore thin, the Kamakura military government system eventually broke down. In 1333, Emperor Go-Daigo attempted to regain control of the country. Ashikaga Takauji, a Kamakura general sent to stop him, joined him instead, and the two were able to restore Imperial rule, at least temporarily. However, Ashikaga broke with Emperor Go-Daigo (because the emperor would not grant him the title of Shogun) and set up another member of a rival branch of the Imperial family as emperor in Kyoto. This emperor anointed Ashikaga Shogun. This was the beginning of the two and a half century Ashikaga or Muramachi period (1333–1573). However, establishing lasting unity among the warrior class under one ruler did not appear possible. Instead, a ruler controlled one group of leaders and expected them to control others in their region. But the strategy often failed. Emperor Go-Daigo, for example, set up a rival imperial court in the mountains 100 km south of Kyoto, and for almost 60 years, there were two courts. Japan eventually disintegrated into what was referred to as the Warring States period (1467–1568), a time of great instability and bloody conflicts as rival daimyo fought for control of Japan.

In 1543, three Portuguese traders, the first Europeans in Japan, landed on the south coast of Japan. The Portuguese introduced the Japanese to many new things but most significantly to guns. The traders were soon followed by Society of Jesus (Jesuit) missionaries. In 1549, after successful missions in India, Francis Xavier, later sanctified, arrived. Very quickly, the missionaries won close to half a million converts to their austere version of Christianity.

In the second half of the 16th century, power gradually consolidated at the local level. Feudal lords or *daimyo* emerged. *Daimyo* formed regional alliances, castle towns were built and two warlords, Oda Nobunaga and Toyotomi Hideyoshi, gradually brought the country together. [The Azuchi-Momoyama period (1568–1600) takes its name from Nobunaga's Azuchi castle and Hideyoshi's Momoyama castle.] In 1568, Oda Nobunaga seized Kyoto, subjugating lesser lords and destroying the power of the Buddhist monasteries. Oda was making great progress towards unifying the country when he was killed by one of his own officers. By 1590, his successor, Toyotomi Hideyoshi, had established control over the whole country, including Shikoku and Kyushu. Toyotomi implemented a land survey to determine taxes, confiscated swords from the peasantry and persecuted Christians. Although Toyotomi successfully invaded Korea twice, he was unable to defeat the Chinese and Korean armies on the peninsula. When he died in 1598, war broke out between his former allies and those loyal to another leader, Tokugawa Ieyasu. Tokugawa and his daimyo coalition emerged victorious at the Battle of Sekigahara in 1600; they unified the country and launched over two and a half centuries of Tokugawa family rule.

A fun description of the role of the three main samurai (Oda Nobunaga, Toyotomi Hideyoshi and Tokugawa Ieyasu) in uniting Japan likens their roles to the making of mochi, a Japanese pounded rice cake: Oda pounds the rice cake, Toyotomi kneads it and Tokugawa sits down to eat it.

The Edo/Tokugawa era (1600–1868)

Tokugawa Ieyasu chose not to move to Kyoto, although the emperor remained there. Maintaining his base of power in eastern Japan in Edo (present-day Tokyo), he consolidated his family's supremacy, and his heirs ruled Japan until the mid-19th century. Calling himself Shogun, Tokugawa Ieyasu set up a new structure to administer the country. Roughly 25 percent of the land belonged to the Tokugawa family, amassed during their rise to power, including all the important mines, the major seaports of Osaka and Nagasaki and the city of Kyoto. The Tokugawa holdings extended throughout the country but were primarily in central Honshu; all of these were ruled by the family directly. The remaining three-quarters of the country was governed indirectly through the *daimyo* (feudal lords), all of whom swore allegiance to Tokugawa.

A *daimyo*'s domain produced a minimum of 10,000 kokus of rice. One koku was approximately 180 litres of rice, enough to feed a person for a year. A daimyo's rice production determined the tax he paid and the number of soldiers he could be required to contribute to a battle. During the two and a half centuries of Tokugawa rule, there were between 245 and 295 daimyo. The Tokugawa government maintained its power by commanding the allegiance of the daimyo, thereby avoiding the emergence of an anti-Tokugawa alliance.

The daimyo were generally left relatively autonomous, although expected to follow the shogunate's guidelines, unless they exhibited signs of disloyalty, in which case they would be punished by losing part of their domain. They had to swear allegiance to their lord and promise to keep order over their domains. In general, they managed their local affairs and retained vassals, who were paid in rice. The Tokugawa shogunate developed policies to control the daimyo. Firstly, they divided the daimyo into three categories. The first of these were the *shimpan* daimyo, members of the Tokugawa extended families. If the main line of the family died out, a Shogun would be chosen from among these 23 lords. The second category was the *fudai* lords. These daimyo had pledged their loyalty to Tokugawa prior to the Battle of Sekigahara, and so were considered trustworthy. The third category, the *tozama* daimyo, had pledged their loyalty only after the battle and thus were considered less trustworthy. Members of the *tozama* daimyo were given remote domains or domains near Edo and played no role in the Tokugawan government. The *fudai* and *shimpan* daimyo and their samurai kept watch over the *tozama* domains for possible threats to the Tokugawa authority. Interestingly, two and a half centuries later, daimyo from two of these remote domains (Satsuma in southern Kyushu and Choshu in western Honshu) would eventually be part of the successful effort to topple the Tokugawa shogunate.

The daimyo domains were carefully arranged, with potentially disloyal daimyo located in remote parts of the country or in domains surrounded by loyal daimyo. Regions in which Christianity had found converts were given to daimyo who were decidedly not Christian. To prevent alliances from forming, members of a daimyo who wished their children to marry had to ask permission from the Shogun. A daimyo believed to be amassing too much wealth would be ordered to spend funds repairing a castle, shrine or bridge.

To ensure that *tozama* lords with coastal territories far from Edo did not benefit from trading or form military alliances with foreign countries, the Tokugawa regime eliminated almost all contact with the outside world. This policy of seclusion was called *sakoku*, meaning closed country. Japanese were prohibited from travelling abroad, and foreigners could not enter Japan. Japanese who were outside the country were prohibited from returning to the country for fear that they might reintroduce Christianity or bring in foreign ideas. Ships were limited to those unsuitable for open ocean voyages. There was some limited contact, including some trade with China and Korea. The Dutch were permitted a small trading station on the island of Dejima (sometimes written as Deshima) in the Nagasaki harbour. Missionaries were expelled, and those who had converted to Christianity were persecuted and forced to convert (people were forced to step on a picture of Christ's face to test their faith.) By 1638, Christianity had been virtually eliminated. For over two centuries, Japanese society developed in almost complete isolation at a time when the rest of the world was being integrated through the intertwined processes of exploration, conquest, colonization and international trade.

A particularly effective form of Tokugawan control was the alternate attendance system (*sankin kotai*). All daimyo were obliged to move their residence between their home domain

62   *Japan*

and Edo every year. They were required to reside in Edo every other year under the watchful eye of the Shogun. When they returned to their domains, they left their wives and their children behind in Edo as hostages. Maintaining two residences and travelling back and forth (with a large entourage, of course) was a major drain on the economic resources of the daimyo. Some daimyo spent half of the taxes they collected on the alternate attendance system. This system had an enduring impact on Japan. Five major roads connecting the various regions of the country to Edo were built, with two of them, the Tokaido and the Nakasendo, stretching from Kyoto to Edo. Over time, roadside stations developed every 5–10 miles along the highways as merchants provided food, lodging, fresh horses and entertainment to the daimyo and their entourages travelling between their home domains and Edo. The daimyo travelled in processions of between 100 and 1,500 people, a large number to feed, house and generally support. There were 53 stations along the Tokaido road and 67 along the Nakasendo. Over time, regional food and craft specialities developed along the route. This regional specialization and interest in the unique products of particular areas of Japan remain today.

Tokugawan society was feudal and hierarchical, designed to prevent social chaos and rebellion. Each of the four classes—samurai, peasants, artisans and merchants—had specific rules of behaviour and dress. Tokugawa Ieyasu "is said to have defined 'rude behaviour'— for which a samurai could lop off the miscreant's head—as 'acting in an other-than-expected manner'" (Henshall, 2012, 55). There was little mobility between the classes, which was a way of enforcing stability and conformity. About 6 percent of the population was samurai. Only they were allowed to have surnames, wear their hair in a topknot and carry swords. Bushido, the unwritten code of samurai conduct, emphasized loyalty, courage, truth and honour. A samurai was to have the utmost loyalty to his lord and be willing to die for him. Samurai were required to lead frugal and disciplined lives, to be adept at martial arts (including archery and sword skills) and to appreciate literature and the arts. As the Tokugawa era was one of peace, gradually most of the samurai became bureaucrats, some of whom were involved in policing. The peasant class consisted of farmers who made up over three-quarters of the population. To ensure that there were adequate amounts of food and income for the nobility, peasants were permitted to work only in the agricultural sector and could not sell their land. They also lived frugally, wearing only cotton. Peasants were ranked higher than the artisans and merchants as the peasants produced essential goods. Coming after peasants in the hierarchy were artisans who produced needed goods such as clothes and cooking utensils. They were organized into guilds based on their craft. At the bottom of the social order were merchants, who due to their dealings with money and the belief that they contributed little to society, were at the bottom of the social order. Beneath the merchants were other small communities of outcasts such as the burakumin, whose death-related occupations (butchers, leather workers, undertakers) were considered unclean.

Over the 250 years of the Tokugawan era, society gradually changed. Artisans became well known for their beautiful silk, paper, ceramics and sake. At the bottom of the social hierarchy, merchants amassed great wealth as they sold more and more goods to the daimyo and their entourages as they trekked to and from Edo. The samurai, ostensibly warriors, had no battles to fight and instead did administrative work for their lords. Although they were paid monthly stipends of rice by the daimyo they served, agricultural production failed to keep pace with the growth in the rest of the economy, and the samurai began to suffer financially. Many samurai became indebted to the merchants. As samurai unrest and peasant uprisings rocked the country in the early 1800s, the carefully constructed feudal society began to fray at the edges.

Overall, however, the Tokugawan era was a time of remarkable stability and peace. Between 1600 and 1721, Japan's population doubled, and Edo became a city of over 1 million inhabitants, one of the largest cities in the world. (London at that time had approximately 625,000 people.) The shogunate established an effective system of government to collect taxes, manage society, develop the country and exert control over other potential competitive centres of political power, like the imperial court and Buddhist temples. The economy grew dramatically but without the intense poverty and disruptions of early stage industrialization. At the same time, the country developed a strong national identity. Numerous Japanese cultural forms—literature, poetry, *ukiyo-e* (wood block prints), *bunraku* (puppet theatre), *kabuki* (theatre)—developed and flourished. Among young men, literacy was 40 percent, higher than in many European countries.

However, by the mid-1800s, dissatisfaction within Tokugawan society had grown and festered. Young, able samurai felt frustrated by the rigidity and hereditary nature of the system and the expenses for the daimyo were soaring, cutting into their quality of life. Seeing merchants become much richer than they were added to the samurais' discontent. The system began to crack from within. It was pressure from the outside, however, that would force Japan to change. By the mid-19th century, European maritime powers controlled much of East Asia and were now in China, while Russia dominated Siberia, pushing towards islands north of Japan. Between 1791 and 1849, Russia, Britain and the United States each tried repeatedly, but always unsuccessfully, to persuade Japan to open relations. The shogunate realized that the Western powers were not going to leave Japan alone but worried by what had occurred in China (e.g. the Opium Wars), was determined to keep other countries at a distance. However, in 1853, anxious to expand its global presence having settled its North American conflicts with Great Britain, the United States sent one-quarter of its navy under Commodore Matthew Perry to try to establish relations with the Japanese government. One goal of the U.S. government was to acquire protection for shipwrecked American sailors and acquire access to ports where their ships could be supplied with provisions. Most of all, however, because they were constrained by a relatively small domestic population, the Americans were seeking trade with the heavily populated countries of East Asia.

The Japanese recognized their vulnerabilities. Perry's Black Ships—so-called by the Japanese because of the black coal smoke they emitted—with their large cannons could have destroyed Edo. Perry arrived in July 1853, made his proposal and promised to return in a year for an answer. He returned to Tokyo Bay with a larger fleet in early 1854, much sooner than promised, where he was greeted by sombre and resigned Japanese authorities. The Americans and the Japanese, the latter reluctantly, signed the Treaty of Kanagawa, ending Japan's period of seclusion by opening two ports to trade and allowing the Americans to establish a consulate in Japan. The United States paved the way for other Western countries to establish relations with Japan. Britain signed a similar treaty in 1854, Russia in 1855, followed by France and Holland. Concessions granted to one country were granted to all of them. The Westerners were granted the right of extraterritoriality, a policy in which foreigners would be tried in their own countries for crimes committed in Japan. As this implied a distrust of Japan's legal system, this concession rankled the Japanese.

Among the Japanese, popular feeling ran strongly against opening the country. Many felt that Japan was sacred ground and that the Shogun was responsible for keeping the barbarians out. "Honour the Emperor, expel the barbarians" became a popular saying. Protests erupted throughout the country, and samurai leaders, especially from the domains of Satsuma and Choshu, killed prominent foreigners, including translators and diplomats. The Tokugawan system was badly shaken by these events. In 1867, an alliance between Satsuma and Choshu

64 *Japan*

seized control of the court, and, in the name of the emperor whom they controlled, they announced direct Imperial rule. In 1868, they took the 16-year-old emperor to Edo, renamed Tokyo (Eastern Capital), where they installed him as ruler. His era was known as Meiji (Enlightened Rule). (After his death, an emperor is referred to by the name of the era of his reign.)

Meiji period (1868–1912)

The teenage emperor was installed in power, but a group of samurai, including Saigō Takamori (Satsuma), Ōkubo Toshimichi (Satsuma), Yamagata Aritomo (Choshu) and Itō Hirobumi, provided the real leadership and direction for the country. All these men were young and came from lower ranks within the samurai. They wanted to do their best for their country, and they hoped to improve their own lot in life, which had been limited under the Tokugawan feudal system, at the same time. Fortunately for Japan, these young samurai proved themselves to be wise and mature leaders as they sought to create a country that could hold its own among the Western powers.

The new government quickly worked to calm the population, which was understandably shaken by all of the changes that had occurred. Any pockets of resistance were quickly put down. The imperial court was moved from Kyoto to Tokyo, which was now officially the capital city. The city's population had declined dramatically over the previous two decades as daimyo and their families were no longer obliged to live there. Without the daimyo, those who catered to them were without work and suffered economically. The Meiji Restoration—the term for the return of the emperor to power and this time period—brought life back to the city. The government took over the samurai district, built administrative buildings and army barracks and began to transform Tokyo into a more modern city.

The Meiji leaders initially planned to expel all the foreigners, but they soon recognized that the Westerners would fight to defend their access to Japanese ports. The Meiji leaders also realized that Japan technologically lagged far behind the West. To be strong enough to oust the barbarians, Japan would first need to catch up technologically. They therefore set out to modernize Japan, launching one of the world's fastest, most intense and successful efforts at national modernization and industrialization. The old catchphrase of "Revere the Emperor, Expel the Barbarians" was replaced by a new one "Japanese spirit, Western learning."

They replaced the feudal system with more centralized rule and built a more professional administrative structure. The daimyo handed over their land to the government, and, in return, they were reissued prefectures of roughly similar size and government bonds to make up for any losses. The financial precariousness of many daimyo made this daunting task less formidable. The Meiji oligarchs also put in place a system of Western-style laws and courts. By demonstrating that Japan had a fair and open judicial system, the Japanese sought to convince Western powers to give up extraterritoriality. A modern banking system and a mint were established, as were Ministries of Finance and Army and Navy. A massive infrastructure initiative brought lighthouses, ports and railways, laying the foundation for a globally competitive industrial economy. The railway was a particularly significant and important accomplishment. The first railway (between Shinagawa and Yokohama) was completed in 1872; by 1900, the country had 8,000 km of track. The railway system had an enormous impact on the movement of people and goods. Telegraph and postal systems were put into place. National compulsory education was established up to grade 4, and by 1900 almost all primary age children were attending school. The University of Tokyo was established as Japan's first national university in 1877.

The restrictive Tokugawan class system was abolished. Most dramatically, the Meiji leaders set out to destroy their own class, the samurai. In 1871, samurai were no longer required to wear their swords in public; by 1876, they were prohibited from wearing them. Samurai rice stipends were gradually reduced, and, by 1876, almost completely eliminated. In less than a decade, the samurai lost almost all their special privileges. The transformation was all the more significant because it was led by samurai themselves. Recognizing the need to look more broadly for talent, the Meiji leaders knew they could no longer rely on a hereditary system. The separate samurai armies of the various domains were replaced with one national army, and national conscription was implemented. Many peasants resented the changes as the combination of conscription and compulsory education took badly needed help from the family farms.

Not all the samurai were happy with the situation either. Frustrated samurai launched several major uprisings, the largest of which was the Satsuma Rebellion of 1877, led by Saigō Takamori, the commander of the army that had toppled the Tokugawa shogunate and one of the Meiji oligarchs. He had resigned from the government after it had refused to agree to his plan to invade Korea. When the government abolished the right of samurai to wear swords, he led a rebellion against the government. The rebellion was decisively defeated, and Saigō committed *seppuku* (ritualized suicide) in true samurai fashion.

Meiji Japan embraced the need for Western technological skills, as well as for Western dress, hair styles, fashion, dance and ideas. Eating beef became popular, leading supposedly to the "Japanese" dish of sukiyaki. Official missions of political leaders went to Europe and America, students in the hundreds were sent abroad to study and Western experts were brought to Japan. One of the most famous proponents of learning from the West who now graces the 10,000 yen note, Fukuzawa Yukichi studied Dutch and English, travelled to the United States and Europe and wrote a series of books on Western learning. Strong interest developed in Japan on Western-style democracy, the idea that everyone was equal and that individuals could control their own destiny. Almost overnight, common people were studying translations of Western books and learning about democracy and Western ways. These ideas were a shock to people who had grown up in a fixed society in which rules prescribed how one should behave. Popular rights societies sprang up; there were about 150 of them by 1880. Soon after, two political parties (the Liberal Party and then the Constitutional Reform Party) were founded, and the idea of a national assembly gained popularity. The Meiji leadership wrestled with the push for democracy. While not unsympathetic to the ideals of democracy (and recognizing that it would impress the Western powers and placate any anti-government feelings out there), "(I)t had to be democracy on the oligarchs' terms, an 'authoritarian democracy'" (Henshall, 2012, 90).

In the 1880s, the Japanese leadership embraced the idea of a Constitution, believing it would lend credence to the notion that Japan was a "civilized country" and appease the popular rights movement. Itō Hirobumi, one of the leaders of the early Meiji government, took charge of drafting the Constitution. In 1882, he went to Europe to study constitutional systems and drew on other constitutions, particularly those of the German empire and Prussia, in drafting the Japanese Constitution. Proclaimed in 1889, the new Constitution outlined the obligations that subjects had to the nation and the emperor, who was to exercise all authority. The Constitution created the bicameral Japanese Parliament or Diet. The Lower House was elected by male taxpayers, who represented slightly more than 1 percent of the total male

66 *Japan*

population. Ministers reported to the emperor not to the Diet, and the emperor had command of the Army and Navy. (In reality, the emperor was not expected to rule but to validate decisions made by his ministers.) Certain rights like freedom of speech were guaranteed but with limits. The first elections for the Diet were held in 1890 and the first Diet assembled later that same year. Nonetheless, while the Constitution represented a step towards democracy, the oligarchs remained in charge.

In 1890, the government issued the Imperial Rescript on Education and distributed it to schools across the country and later the Japanese empire. Signed by the emperor, the Imperial Rescript was a statement of Japan's guiding principles of education. It told students to honour their parents, respect the Constitution and work hard for the state and the emperor. It was designed to build patriotism and national unity. Students were required to memorize the Rescript and it was often recited on special occasions. This continued until the Occupation at the end of World War II when the American authorities forbade it; the National Diet officially abolished the Imperial Rescript on Education in 1948.

Japan began to industrialize rapidly. The emergence of the industrial society depended on agriculture, as farming provided the foreign exchange necessary to buy industrial machinery and raw materials from abroad. Farmers also contributed money through the land tax, which funded the infrastructure necessary for industrialization. The tax was now linked to the assessed value of the land rather than, as before, the value of the harvest. Aside from agriculture, priority was given to strategic industries producing weapons and ammunition for the expanding Japanese military. Trade in silk and tea expanded. Sub-contracted to the private sector, state-built factories were subsidized until they were making money. Japan had fallen behind the West in technology, so the country imported foreign technology and consulted with Western technical experts in an effort to catch up. Japan lacked entrepreneurs at that time, so the government started industries that it then sold to individuals with entrepreneurial potential or to private companies. Meiji thus established the roots of Japan's military industrial complex and of the industrial conglomerates known as *zaibatsu* (see Textbox 3.5). After a slow start, progress was rapid but the price in human terms was high. Factory life was miserable for the workers, and pollution and urban blight were early side-effects of economic growth.

Japan's swift modernization combined with a nationalist drive to catch up with the West. This, following the European and American models, created a desire among Japan's leaders to acquire an empire. Japan needed access to raw materials and global markets, and it wanted to take its place among the great powers, a remarkable transition for a nation that only half a century earlier had blocked itself off from the world. In 1894–1895, Japan started a war with China over influence on the Korean peninsula, easily defeating the larger country. In the Treaty of Shimonoseki, which ended the conflict, China was forced to pay Japan a war indemnity (money as a form of compensation), renounce any claims to Korea and cede the Liaodong peninsula in Manchuria (although within a week Russia, France and Germany forced Japan to give it back), the island of Taiwan and the Penghu Islands, to Japan in perpetuity. (Japan occupied Taiwan from 1895 to 1945. For more information, see Chapter 5.) In response to being forced to return the Liaodong peninsula, in 1902, the Japanese leaders negotiated the Anglo-Japanese Alliance, a pact with the British to guarantee that Britain would not unite with other European powers to oppose the Japanese. This was the world's first military pact between a Western and non-Western nation. Japan was earning the respect from the West that it wanted. Britain gave up its right of extraterritoriality in 1894, for example, and other countries soon followed suit.

Japan   67

The government expanded its army and navy and raised taxes to pay for them. In 1904, Japan and Russia went to war over interests in Manchuria and Korea. Japan won and acquired the southern tip of Manchuria, the southern half of Sakhalin and complete control over Korea. However, Japan did not receive an indemnity from the Russians, which it had very much wanted to make up for the huge expenses it had incurred waging the war. In 1905, Korea became a Japanese protectorate with Itō Hirobumi as Resident-General. The Koreans assassinated Itō in 1909, but the following year, Japan annexed Korea completely. (For more on the Japanese occupation of Korea, see Chapter 4.) With the emergence of Japan as a potent international force, exemplified by the Japanese victory in the Sino-Japanese war and, even more, after the Russo-Japanese war, a growing fear of East Asia became embedded in the racist concept of the "Yellow Peril." Westerners demonized the East Asians, believing that their shockingly large populations, growing industrial wealth and military might represented an existential threat to the economic, social and political well-being of the democratic nations of the West. The cartoonish concepts of the "Yellow Peril" became imbedded in Western imagination and in immigration laws and racially discriminatory policies across the Western world.

The Meiji period came to a close in 1912 with the death of the emperor, concluding a remarkable transition from isolation to global competitiveness and demonstrating to the world the country's resilience, intensity and determination. Little known a half century earlier, Japan was now the most dominant non-Western nation, a military victor over Russia in a major war, and a rapidly expanding industrial power with ready access to hundreds of millions of Asian consumers. Moreover, Japan had learned its Western lessons well, adopting democratic institutions, the rule of law and central government programs and services. But imitating aspects of the West did not strip the nation of its inherent Japaneseness. By controlling the nature and pace of change and by adapting to the West without surrendering to a European or American colonizer, Japan stepped into the world on its terms, with its own agenda and with Japanese values, religion, language and culture intact.

Taisho period (1912–1926)

The era following Meiji was called Taisho after the new emperor. Emperor Taisho struggled with illness throughout his life. During the Taisho period, power shifted from the old world of the oligarchs to the new world of elected representatives (Diet members). During this era, often referred to as the Taisho democracy, efforts were made to build a Japanese democracy: competitive political parties emerged, public interest in democracy surged, a commoner was elected as prime minister (PM) in 1918 and universal male suffrage was granted in 1925 (women received the vote in 1947). The economy grew rapidly, and government foreign policy focused on ensuring access to markets and to the raw materials needed to fuel the fast-growing industrialization. While in 1870 Japanese imports were almost exclusively manufactured products and its exports primary products, 50 years later, the situation had reversed. Ninety percent of Japanese exports were now manufactured goods, particularly textiles.

The Great Kanto Earthquake struck Tokyo and its surrounds in September 1923. The earthquake had a magnitude of 7.9 and killed over 100,000 people. Many large fires broke out, fanned by high winds, which were responsible for many of the deaths and injuries and the loss of homes and other property. In the aftermath of the quake, false rumours spread that ethnic Koreans were looting and even that they had set some of the fires. Anti-Korean sentiment was high at that time in response to the Korean independence movement taking place

68   *Japan*

in Japan-occupied Korea. Mobs in Tokyo and Yokohama attacked Koreans and an estimated 6,000 Koreans were murdered.

Showa period (1926–1989): The militarist era—Japan's pursuit of global power

Hirohito became emperor at the end of 1926 upon the death of his father. His reign began in a time of difficulty. The Great Depression and accompanying global protectionism were challenging for Japan, which had begun to rely on international trade. Silk and rice prices fell, the economy weakened and domestic unrest grew. At the same time, tensions increased between the elected representatives and the Japanese military. As the last vestiges of samurai culture and intense nationalism clashed against the forces favouring industrialization and global integration, an all-out conflict brewed behind the scenes. Many felt that the West's influence had been bad for Japan and questioned the benefits of democracy.

The military pushed for territorial expansion. In 1931, the Japanese army brutally annexed and established a puppet regime in Manchuria, a large section of northeast China, partially to acquire Manchuria's abundant resources. The following year, the elected Japanese prime minister was assassinated by junior naval officers for failing to promote an aggressive military agenda. As democracy disintegrated, political dissent was repressed, political parties banned, the press censored and opponents of the military government imprisoned. The military steadily expanded its influence, and Japan moved progressively from a democracy towards a military dictatorship.

In 1937, Japan waged war against China, after years of working to dominate it economically and politically for its resources, agriculture and labour. From the Asian remnants of the rapidly declining post–World War 1 European empires, the Japanese military leaders intended to carve out their own empire, which they called the Greater East Asia Co-Prosperity Sphere. Japan had first sampled expansionism after World War I when it acquired Germany's Pacific colonies—the Marshall, Mariana and Caroline Islands. In 1940, Japan signed a tripartite pact with Hitler's Germany and Mussolini's Italy and formed the Axis military alliance against the Allied Powers organized by the United States and the United Kingdom. On December 7, 1941, the Japanese launched a surprise attack, which they still regard as a pre-emptive strike of protection against American aggression, on the Pacific Fleet at Pearl Harbour, Hawaii. The United States declared war on Japan, and its Axis allies launched a counteroffensive. This was the beginning of the Pacific War, the Asia Pacific theatre of World War II. The Americans were convinced by their allies to focus their efforts first on the European front while they planned for the complex challenge of retaking the Pacific Islands and pushing the war to Japan.

Why did Japan go to war? Japan wanted to be a great power. Like all the Western powers that had taken territory around the world, Japan saw its new empire as a matter of national pride and international recognition. In 1933, a Japanese diplomat described the West's response to Japanese imperialism this way: "'the Western Powers had taught the Japanese the game of poker … but after acquiring most of the chips,' as Matsuoka Yosuke, a future foreign minister put it, 'they pronounced the game immoral and took up contract bridge'" (Lamb and Tarling, 2001, 70).

The Japanese leaders desperately wanted to avoid the fate of China, which after being a formidable economic power for centuries had been reduced to widespread poverty and political powerlessness due to Europe's interventions and an increase in opium addictions. In an effort to limit Japanese aggression and force the Japanese military to withdraw from

China, the United States imposed economic sanctions and restricted access to crucial industrial supplies. With few natural resources of its own and almost no sources of energy, Japan quickly felt the pain of the sanctions. War with China had proved costly, and Japan rapidly ran out of oil, rubber and other raw materials. The only obvious way to obtain desperately needed resources was to invade Southeast Asia. Between 1941 and 1942, Japan seized or invaded Indochina (Vietnam, Laos and Cambodia), Hong Kong, Thailand, Malaya, Burma (now called Myanmar), the Dutch East Indies, most of the Philippines and parts of New Guinea, while also expanding its presence in China and in the South Pacific Islands. Well-armed, highly motivated and superbly trained, Japan's armed forces seemed unstoppable. Both Singapore and Hong Kong, the United Kingdom's strongholds in the region, fell in a matter of weeks. Australia and New Zealand prepared for an imminent invasion, while the Japanese quickly island-hopped across the Pacific.

Believing and supporting the Japanese slogan of "Asia for Asians," many people in Southeast Asia welcomed the Japanese as liberators and celebrated them for freeing the population from European colonial rule. The Japanese occupations, however, were exercises in cruelty. Tens of thousands (estimates are as high as 200,000) Korean women, along with women from other countries Japan occupied during the war, were coerced into sex slavery. Euphemistically called "comfort women," they were compelled to service Japanese soldiers both before and during World War II. Feelings that there has not been a sincere official apology and appropriate compensation for these women has remained an issue of ongoing tension between South Korea and Japan (see Chapter 9 for more information).

The sustained mistreatment of women was only one part of a horrific legacy of Japanese expansionism. Early on, the Japanese army established a pattern of brutality towards occupied lands that has few parallels in world history. In December 1937, the Japanese attacked and captured the Chinese capital city of Nanjing. Not content with a decisive military victory, Japanese troops turned their attention to the civilian population and the captured Chinese troops. What became known as the Nanjing Massacre or the Rape of Nanjing included the callous murder of thousands of civilians, the rape of uncounted thousands of Chinese women and the unprovoked destruction and theft of private poverty. Nanjing and its citizens were completely devastated, the first major victims in what would become the Pacific War.

News of the Nanjing massacre spread, creating the stereotype of Japanese military brutality, a lack of concern for civilian life and a disregard for the basic tenants of civilized warfare. Over the next few years, fuelled by aggressive American wartime propaganda, stories of Nanjing and other atrocities accelerated the demonization of Japan and, particularly, its military. In the following years, debates proliferated about the scale and severity of the Nanjing attacks, with most estimates asserting that approximately 300,000 people had died. These historical debates, fuelled by unofficial Japanese attempts to deny the events took place, created severe discord, bordering often on hatred, between China and Japan.

Although subsequent Japanese occupations were not quite as terrible as the tragic precedent set in Nanjing, Japan's presence extracted a significant price on civilian populations throughout East Asia. If the local people were believed to be disloyal to the Japanese or overly supportive of American forces and their allies, the Japanese treated them abysmally. Meeting the needs of Japan's forces took top priority, often leaving civilians with little food, medical goods or other supplies. Any signs of insurrection or interference with Japanese military operations were met with brutality. In some areas, notably the Philippines, locals launched guerrilla attacks on the Japanese, even though their actions often led to vicious

70 *Japan*

reprisals. In total, the Philippines suffered close to 1 million deaths during the Japanese occupation. Even on the Pacific Islands, where local residents were often disconnected from the politics of war and lived traditional harvesting lives, many became forced labourers and endured serious food shortages and other indignities. At the end of the conflict, as the Allies took back island after island and country after country and as the Japanese fought ferociously for each piece of land, the occupiers typically scorched the countryside, leaving little of value for the Allied troops or the local population.

One of the greatest legacies of World War II was the treatment of prisoners of war. In Japan's military culture, surrender was deemed unforgivable, a sign of personal failing. Fighting to death in aid of the war effort or committing *seppuku* (ritualized suicide) was viewed as much more honourable than surrender. When the Japanese captured Allied troops, they viewed the military survivors with contempt, basically considering them to be "non-people." The treatment of the prisoners by the Japanese ignored international military conventions and resulted in the deaths of tens of thousands. Many Allied prisoners were relocated to Japan, where they lived in squalid conditions, with many subjected to brutal treatment by their Japanese captors or starved to death. Torture was commonplace, and hundreds of thousands of military personnel and civilians endured months of forced labour, with many dying at the hands of their Japanese handlers. Of the close to 140,000 Allied troops captured by the Japanese, almost 40,000 perished before they could be liberated. In one infamous case, over 100,000 forced labourers and Allied prisoners died during the construction of the Burma Railway, immortalized in the acclaimed 1957 film *The Bridge on the River Kwai*. When the Allies rounded up large numbers of Japanese prisoners of war after 1945, the Allies resisted the temptation to match brutality with equal aggression.

Gradually, and at enormous cost, the U.S. military pushed Japan out of most of the lands they had conquered. By 1944, the aerial attacks started on the Japanese islands themselves, while the Americans and their allies prepared for a land assault. Tokyo, all the major cities except Kyoto (initially protected because the city had few military targets and then because it was on the initial list of potential targets for the atomic bombing) and most medium-sized cities were firebombed and utterly destroyed (Textbox 3.4).

Textbox 3.4 Kamikaze

Kamikaze refers to the Japanese pilots (and also the aircraft they flew) who, under orders during World War II, deliberately flew their airplanes loaded with bombs or extra gasoline into enemy aircraft and ships. The word kamikaze (divine wind) was first used in reference to typhoons that were credited with saving Japan from Mongol invasions in 1274 and 1281. Sometimes the planes used were regular planes but often they were very crude—little more than bombs with wings and steering. The planes did not have enough fuel for a return trip.

The Americans prepared for an all-out assault on the main Japanese islands, anticipating that the causalities would be counted in the hundreds of thousands. The last major conflict, the deadly Battle of Okinawa, raged from April to June 1945, providing proof that the Japanese intended to fight to the death, with a ferocity that the Allied forces found terrifying. Worried

Japan 71

Figure 3.3 Atomic bombings of Hiroshima and Nagasaki.

about the now-inevitable massive loss of life through armed combat, the United States looked to its unfolding secret weapon, developed through the Manhattan Project. America now had the world's most powerful bomb at its disposal. As the prospect of the further invasion of Japan loomed, debate about the bomb raged among leading authorities in the United States. In early August 1945, ignoring suggestions that a demonstration bomb be exploded away from settled areas or that the weapon be used only on military targets, the U.S. Army Air Force dropped atomic bombs, first on the city of Hiroshima on August 6th and then on Nagasaki three days later (see Figure 3.3). Between 130,000 and 230,000 people died in the initial explosion or later from radiation exposure. The vast majority of the victims were civilians.

All told, by the end of the Pacific War, there had been about 2.2 million Japanese military casualties, between 500,000 and 800,000 Japanese civilian casualties and 25–30 million civilian and military non-Japanese deaths (including 110,000 U.S. military deaths). On August 14, 1945, Emperor Hirohito announced on the radio that Japan had been defeated. Few Japanese had ever heard the emperor's voice before, and the formality of his speech together with the poor quality of the broadcast meant that many did not understand him. He told his people that Japan "resolved to pave the way for a grand peace for all the generations to come by enduring the unendurable and suffering what is insufferable" (Nisei Veterans Legacy, n.d.). Japan's formal surrender to the United States, Great Britain and the Soviet Union (which declared war on Japan shortly before the end of the conflict in order to gain a role in the peace negotiations that followed) took place on September 2, 1945 (see Figure 3.4). Japan was deeply broken: millions of people were dead or injured; almost all major cities lay in near ruins; the country's industrial and agricultural infrastructure was completely destroyed; starvation was widespread; and the civilian population was physically and emotionally exhausted.

72 Japan

Figure 3.4 Signing the Japanese Instrument of Surrender on the USS Missouri—September 2, 1945.

The Occupation

The Occupation of Japan began in the fall of 1945 and ended seven years later in the spring of 1952. Although officially an Allied Occupation, in reality the Occupation was almost entirely American, led by the Supreme Command of Allied Powers (SCAP) under General Douglas MacArthur. Despite their initial fears that the American occupiers would be vindictive and cruel—a fair assumption given the intensity of wartime hostilities—the Americans helped the Japanese gain a path to a better future. Ultimately, the Occupation forces helped Japan rebuild and implement a wide range of economic reforms. To encourage business activity, they disbanded the *zaibatsu* (industrial conglomerates—see Textbox 3.5), established a Free Trade Commission, implemented land reform and stripped power from absentee landlords, passed an Anti-monopoly law, supported union organizing and made education up to grade 9 compulsory.

Textbox 3.5 Zaibatsu and Keiretsu

The zaibatsu (meaning financial clique) were the industrial and financial combines that developed during the Meiji period. At that time, the government promoted industries that it then sold to private companies, which had the money and skills to operate them. As Japan was just emerging from its feudal past, there were not many potential buyers. Wealth and power therefore became concentrated in a few hands. By the time of the Pacific War, over three-quarters of the country's economic wealth belonged to just 12 families.

Japan 73

There were a number of smaller zaibatsu and four big ones: Mitsui (roots in dry goods and money lending), Mitsubishi (shipbuilding), Sumitomo (copper mining) and Yasuda (banking). The zaibatsu were controlled through a central holding company owned by the original family. The holding company controlled numerous corporations, each of which in turn controlled a series of other companies. Not all the affiliate companies were owned by those above them, but they were connected. Each zaibatsu had its own financial institution, assuring member companies preferential access to capital and thereby allowing companies to expand. Each zaibatsu also had its own general trading company (sogo shosha). During the Meiji period, the zaibatsu companies were small and had little experience with the outside world. People with international experience were concentrated in the sogo shosha, which provided services to member companies, helping them procure raw materials and sell products internationally.

By World War II, the zaibatsu had grown very large. For example, Mitsui had approximately 300 companies. The member companies were closely linked, sharing directors and executives, and prices charged within the zaibatsu were lower than those imposed on non-member companies. The family maintained tight control of the holding company and of the most important companies within the combine. Shares in the companies were not available for purchase until the Japanese went into Manchuria in the 1930s and the companies needed money for expansion.

Although the zaibatsu concentrated wealth and power in only a few hands, the system was not a monopoly because the zaibatsu competed with one another in many business fields. The concentration of capital allowed the zaibatsu to invest in and reinvest with an eye to future growth. Having developed a strong industrial base for Japan, the zaibatsu were also key players in Japan's war effort. When the war ended, the Occupation ordered their dissolution, arguing that the zaibatsu had helped the government carry out the war. Although SCAP talked a great deal about breaking up the zaibatsu, it did not actually do that much to do so. As a result, after 1945, Japanese companies were able to reorganize themselves into a different version of the zaibatsu called the keiretsu.

Like the zaibatsu, keiretsu are a group of companies across a wide range of industries from food to electronics to chemicals. The six large horizontal keiretsu are Mitsui, Mitsubishi, Sumitomo, Fuyo, Sanwa and Ikkan. The first three are former zaibatsu. The keiretsu all include a bank, allowing easier access to capital, and a trading company. There are other enterprise groups, often called vertical keiretsu, which are not based around a bank and tend to be in one industry. With their wide range of suppliers and distributors, Toyota and Sony are good examples of vertical keiretsus, which are characterized by interlocking share holdings and preferential business practices.

The presidents of the key firms within a keiretsu attend regular Presidents' Club meetings at which the strategic decisions for the keiretsu are made. These presidents represent the stock their company holds in the other member companies. In the mid-1990s, Mitsubishi, as an example, consisted of 185 companies, which produced approximately 9 percent of all Japan's corporate profits, and Mitsubishi's Presidents' Council consisted of 28 firms. Since the 1990s, the keiretsu changed and inter-firm ties weakened. Banks and other firms from different keiretsu have merged, and member companies do much more business with non-member companies than in the past.

Two fundamental beliefs underlaid the Occupation: the universality of American values and the conviction that democracy could curb militarism. Confident that the United States

Figure 3.5 Japanese war crime trials—International Military Tribal for the Far East.

was the most advanced nation in the world, the Occupation planners intended to remodel Japan (and the former Nazi Germany and Italy) in the American image. Although General MacArthur had a large staff of civilian and military personnel, few of its members had any knowledge or understanding of Japan or Japanese, making it difficult to implement reform through the Japanese government.

The first step in the Occupation was demilitarization. The Japanese army and navy were demobilized; Japanese troops and civilians from all over Asia were rounded up and brought back to Japan; and ships, weapons and tanks were destroyed. All the land Japan had taken was repatriated. At trials in Japan and overseas, thousands of members of the Japanese military were tried and convicted of committing atrocities. From 1946 to 1948, the Tokyo War Crimes Tribunal tried 28 Japanese military and political leaders, including former prime ministers, cabinet ministers and military generals, for war crimes, crimes against humanity and crimes against peace. Sixteen defendants were sentenced to life imprisonment, and seven were sentenced to death and executed (see Figure 3.5).

A key goal of the Occupation was to build a Japanese democracy. To this end, political prisoners (many whom had been Communist sympathizers) were freed, and repressive laws were rescinded. But the occupiers had to decide what to do with Emperor Hirohito. Should they try him as a war criminal? Should he be forced to abdicate? Ultimately, General MacArthur decided not to do either. The Americans kept the emperor as a constitutional monarch, the symbolic head of Japan. A crucial change eliminated the discussion of the emperor's divinity, which had been enshrined in the 1889 Constitution because of the Shinto belief that the emperor was directly descended from the Sun Goddess. The decision to exonerate the emperor and his family from responsibility for the war remains controversial inside and outside Japan.

The Supreme Commander for the Allied Powers also decided that the Meiji Constitution had to be rewritten. Initially, the Japanese government was tasked with rewriting this foundational document, but General MacArthur rejected the Japanese draft. Turning to his own inexperienced staff of young Americans who had little constitutional expertise and even less knowledge of Japan, MacArthur gave them six days to draft a new constitution. That the document they produced remains Japan's Constitution three-quarters of a century later is little short of astonishing. The most significant article in the new Constitution was Article 9, the peace clause, which forbade Japan from having armed forces with war potential (for more information on the Constitution and Article 9, see p. 78).

During the early years of the Occupation, Japan was economically extremely weak and much of the population was starving. The Supreme Command of Allied Powers initially obliged Japan to pay reparations and restricted the industries in which it could invest. However, mid-way through the Occupation, fears about the spread of communism convinced MacArthur to focus on rebuilding Japan as an economically strong ally. MacArthur and U.S. leaders were concerned about the intensifying Cold War between the United States and the Union of Soviet Socialist Republics (USSR), as well as the growing power of the Communist Party in China. The Occupiers were also concerned about the potential popularity of Communism in Japan, as the newly released Communists, leftists and labour unions created a role for themselves in business and government. As a result, the Occupiers slowed or reversed some of their democratic reforms and focused instead on Japan's economic recovery. They supplied the Japanese with substantial reconstruction aid, and Joseph Dodge, a Detroit banker, was brought to Japan to advise MacArthur on how to help Japan's economy and to control inflation. Dodge was able to reduce inflation, stabilize the exchange rate and curtail government subsidies. The government was able to present a balanced budget but bankruptcies and unemployment increased.

In January 1946, the Occupation issued a directive prohibiting anyone who had played a role in the promotion of Japanese aggression from participating in public life, making them ineligible to run for political office or run a corporation. This ruling affected about 200,000 people, many of whom had been the backbone of Japanese political and commercial leadership. The "purge," as it was called, opened the way for a new generation of leaders. However, with the onset of the Cold War, the Occupation forces became nervous when left-wingers and Communists began to gain influence. As part of a "reverse course" shift from a focus on democratization and demilitarization towards reconstruction and remilitarization, the Occupation began to soften and rehabilitate many wartime leaders. At the same time, the Occupation launched the "Red Purge," the firing of thousands of people from the government, the education system and the business sector for being "Red." The "Red Purge" occurred between 1949 and 1951 and targeted not just communists and labour union activists but also those who dared criticize the Cold War and the Occupation's reverse course. As Japanese historian Tetsuo Hirata wrote, "the event directly called into question the foundations of the freedom and democracy guaranteed by the Japanese constitution" (Dower and Hirata, 2007).

The Japanese economy received a big boost from the Korean War (1950–1952). Japanese firms supplied the United States with $2–3 billion worth of war supplies over the three years, allowing domestic companies to invest and expand. Mazda Motors, for example, made jeeps for the American forces, giving the company its start. A logistics hub for the Americans, Japan was also a prime location for American G.I.s Rest and Relocation leaves. From the Korean War onward, Japan's economy boomed. Remarkably, by 1955, only 10 years after the utter devastation of the Japanese economy, industrial production had returned to pre-war levels. As many of the Occupation forces were now in Korea, General MacArthur decided Japan needed a National Police Reserve. Given the constraints of the new Constitution, it had

76 *Japan*

to be clear that the Reserve was for self-defence. The name was changed to the Self-Defence Forces in 1954 (for more information on the Self-Defense Forces, see pp. 84–85).

Japan's sovereignty was returned, and the Occupation ended with the signing of the San Francisco Peace Treaty, which came into force in April 1952. The treaty outlined Japan's acceptance of the judgements of the various military tribunals and its commitment to compensate Allied civilians and prisoners of war and the Allied Powers for damage and suffering. At the same time the San Francisco Peace Treaty went into force, the United States and Japan signed a bilateral security treaty. Japan agreed to allow American military bases on Japanese soil in exchange for a commitment by the United States to defend Japan.

Post-war development (1950s–1980s)

Once sparked by American spending during the Korean War, Japan's economy grew rapidly. Leaders in both government and business were obsessed with catching up with other industrialized countries. Average growth rates in the 1960s were in the double digits, far exceeding even the government's ambitious five-year GDP growth plans. In 1964, the country hosted the successful Tokyo Olympics, drawing the world's attention to Japan's successful economic transition. In 1945, Japan had been a pariah state, despised for its wartime and colonial aggression and held responsible for millions of deaths and mass devastation. Less than 20 years later, in a transition rivalled only by the Allied-driven revitalization of West Germany in the same time period, Japan re-entered the circle of respected and successful nations, its wartime aggression largely forgiven but not forgotten.

Plaza Accord and the bubble economy (1980s)

As the 1970s and 1980s progressed, Japan developed a large trade surplus with the United States. In a situation similar to the Trump presidency's difficulty with China's economic role, the United States became increasingly concerned, believing that the root of this trade surplus was the strong U.S. dollar and the weak Japanese yen, which made Japanese goods relatively inexpensive. In 1985, the Americans proposed to the G5 (the United States, Japan, Germany, France and Britain) meeting of finance ministers and Central Bank presidents that the U.S. dollar was too strong, especially relative to the yen and the German mark. The resulting agreement, the Plaza Accord, signalled a commitment to funding interventions to reduce the value of the dollar and increase the value of the yen and the mark. The logic behind the agreement was that as the value of the U.S. dollar declined, American goods would become less expensive, while as the yen increased in value, Japanese goods would become more expensive as Japanese manufacturers would be forced to raise their prices. The expected result was that Japanese and U.S. consumers would buy more products from the United States and fewer from Japan. These actions, it was thought, would adjust the trade balance.

However, this was not what happened. The yen escalated dramatically in value but with no corresponding reduction in Japan's trade surplus with the United States. There were several reasons why this occurred: firstly, Japanese companies chose to take very little or no profit in order to maintain market share; secondly, the resources and other inputs for Japanese manufacturers were now less expensive; thirdly, the Japanese government made sure that its industrial sector received the financial backing it needed to remain globally competitive. Japanese companies found the adjustment difficult initially, but over time they learned how to cope with a much stronger yen.

One of the impacts of the Plaza Accord was that, in international terms, the Japanese were suddenly rich. While the yen did not buy more at home, it suddenly bought a lot more overseas.

The Japanese began buying precious art, gems and foreign real estate, especially in Hawaii, California and Australia's Gold Coast. People borrowed money using hyper-inflated Japanese real estate as collateral, and because Tokyo's property values were so high, small properties in Tokyo allowed for the purchases of huge properties abroad. Japanese homes, previously disparagingly called "rabbit hutches," were now worth more than Hollywood mansions. Commercial real estate in particular skyrocketed in value between 1986 and 1991. At the height of the bubble economy, as this period came to be called, Japanese companies and individuals owned a good portion of the Los Angeles skyline, the Rockefeller Centre in New York and MGM Studios. Stories of wild Japanese spending and excess circulated widely.

The prosperity could not last. Eventually, Japanese real estate prices peaked and fell, and the banks began to call in loans as the land held as collateral lost value. As a result, the banks found themselves holding unpaid loans worth trillions of yen. When the bubble finally burst in late 1991, Japan's economy ground to a halt. Over the next decade, Japan's GDP grew only 1.14 percent, below that of other industrialized countries.

Japan's political heritage

Japan's political culture emerged from its history, culture and values. Whereas the political system of Western countries is rooted in concepts like individual rights, the importance of representation and the rule of law, Japan's political heritage is based in Confucianism and the relationship between the lord and his retainers. Until Meiji, there was no systematic Japanese discussion of inalienable rights or representative bodies. Confucianism, though, taught the importance of formal education and the ethical basis for government, resulting in high levels of literacy and strong administrative standards. For hundreds of years Japan had been open to learning from other countries (building on writing and administrative systems from China, Buddhism from India and weaponry from the Portuguese). This openness ended during the Tokugawa era but restarted with the desperate desire during the Meiji period to learn from and catch up with the West. Tokugawan seclusion greatly contributed to the development of regional identities, and gradually as the work of philosophers, poets and playwrights spread throughout the country, a strong sense of national unity and identity developed.

Political and government structure

Government

Japan is a unitary state with most power in the hands of the national government. The country is divided into 47 prefectures, each with its own governor and legislature. These prefectural governments focus on local issues and are dependent for most of their budget on the national government.

The head of state

As Japan is a monarchy, the emperor is the country's head of state. After the adoption of the 1947 constitution, the emperor's position became symbolic but nonetheless significant. The Constitution states that the emperor is "the symbol of the State and of the unity of the People, deriving his position from the will of the people with whom resides sovereign power" (Prime Minister of Japan and his Cabinet, n.d.). A hereditary patrilineal (following the male line) position, the emperor performs ceremonial tasks such as appointing the prime minister (once he or she has been elected and selected by the Diet) and the chief justice, receiving foreign ambassadors and representing the nation abroad. The current emperor, Naruhito,

78   *Japan*

ascended to the Chrysanthemum throne on May 1, 2019 after the abdication of his father, Emperor Akihito. Emperor Naruhito is 126th in an unbroken line, which legend traces back to Emperor Jimmu in 660 B.C., a descendant of Amaterasu, the Sun Goddess. Prior to 2006 and the birth of Prince Hisato (the son of Emperor Naruhito's younger brother Crown Prince Akishino), a lack of young male heirs sparked much discussion about whether to change the laws of succession to allow a woman to ascend to the throne.

Head of government

Japan has a parliamentary system of government. The prime minister is the head of government, chosen by the elected members of both Houses of the Diet. The prime minister is almost always the leader of the majority party in the Lower House. In the case of a minority government, the PM could be the leader of the dominant party in a ruling coalition. The prime minister chooses the members of his or her cabinet, who serve as ministers and heads of agencies.

Constitution

As discussed earlier, Japan's Constitution was drawn up by the Americans during the Occupation. Traces of American values and constitutional priorities are evident. For example, the Constitution begins with "We, the Japanese people …;" it includes universal suffrage, a parliamentary legislature and an independent judiciary, and it guarantees fundamental rights such as freedom of religion, thought, assembly and residence. The Constitution's most famous and controversial clause is Article 9, the peace clause, which states that "Aspiring sincerely to an international peace based on justice and order, the Japanese people forever renounce war as a sovereign right of the nation and the threat or use of force as means of settling international disputes. In order to accomplish the aim of the preceding paragraph, land, sea, and air forces, as well as other war potential, will never be maintained. The right of belligerency of the state will not be recognized" (Prime Minister of Japan and His Cabinet, n.d.). Current Prime Minister Abe, many conservative politicians and a significant percentage of the Japanese public would like to rewrite Article 9 to allow Japan to have a military like all other "normal" nations. A constitutional amendment must pass both the House of Representatives and the House of Councillors with a two-thirds majority. It must then be approved by a majority in a national referendum and promulgated by the emperor. Even if a proposed amendment (and exactly how to revise Article 9 would first have to be decided) passed both the Houses of the Japanese Parliament, it is not clear it would pass a referendum. In the meantime, the government has been gradually expanding the boundaries of what the country's well-funded and large Self-Defence Forces (SDF) are able to do. In 2015, the government passed legislation allowing Japan to engage in collective self-defence, which means the SDF could go to the aid of Allied troops if Japan was at risk.

The legislature

The Japanese Parliament is bicameral (meaning it has two houses) and is called the Diet (from the Latin *dieta* or "assembly"). The Lower House (House of Representatives) has 465 members elected for four-year terms. It is more powerful than the Upper House (House of Councillors) which has 242 seats. Its members serve six-year terms, with half elected every three years.

Japan 79

Electoral system

Japan has a complex electoral system. The 465 seats in the House of Representatives are elected through a mixed system. There are 289 seats elected in a first past-the-post system from single seat constituencies; the other 176 seats are elected through proportional representation (a closed list system with the political parties identifying their preferred candidates in order) in 11 districts. Voters vote twice—once for their constituency representatives and once for the party of their choice. The party supplies a list of candidates ranked in order. The higher the percentage of the vote a party receives, the further down the list of candidates the party is able to go. In June 2016, the country's voting age was lowered from 20 to 18.

The electoral system for Japan's House of Representatives changed to this mixed system in 1993 when an opposition coalition was in power. Previously, it resembled the multi-member district (MMD) system used for House of Councillors elections in which multiple members were elected in a single district. Voters have one vote. Each district returns between one and five members. One of the drawbacks of the previous system was that people competed against members of their own party, leading to the creation of factions within the Liberal Democratic Party (LDP) and other larger parties and reduced party loyalty. Because they could not rely entirely on the support of their party (as it was supporting multiple candidates), politicians formed local support networks called *koenkai* to help them generate support and money. Candidates were loyal to the leader of their faction, rather than the national party. In exchange, the politicians received various forms of assistance from the faction leader.

The electoral system for the House of Councillors or Upper House is also mixed. In this case, 96 members are elected using proportional representation in a nationwide election. The other 146 are elected from 47 multi-member districts matching the nation's prefectures. Since the proportional representation system is based on an open list, it is a little different from that in the Lower House elections. Under an open list system, electors vote for either a candidate or a party. The parties receive seats based on the share of the vote received by the candidates or the party; however, the candidates who receive the most votes are prioritized in the seat allocation. To increase the votes they receive, parties often try to recruit celebrities to run.

Japan's electoral districts, especially those for the House of Councillors, are troublingly malapportioned. Some prefectures have up to three times as many registered voters as others. Japan's constitution gives the Diet the authority to determine how districts are drawn but also states that all people are equal under the law. Under the current arrangement, however, some people's votes count much more than those of others. The courts have ruled against this malapportionment and have indicated that in the Lower House, "the biggest constituency should not have more than double the number of voters of the smallest" ("Japan's electoral," 2019). Part of the challenge is the desire to have a member of both the houses of the Diet in each of Japan's 47 prefectures. As the populations of the rural prefectures are shrinking while the urban areas grow, the disparity in population among the regions is likely to increase.

Election campaigns

Japanese election campaigns are very short, usually about 12–17 days. Candidates are not permitted to campaign outside this time. Elections are always on Sundays, and there are numerous election financing and campaign restrictions designed to discourage corruption and inequities among candidates. Lawn signs, buttons and bumper stickers, door-to-door solicitation, parades or dinners and negative campaigning are not permitted. Instead, loudspeaker-equipped vans

80   *Japan*

drive around blaring out messages encouraging people to vote for their candidate. As election campaigns are so short, the *koenkai* (local support networks) play an important ongoing role by sponsoring "cultural and educational events" for their candidates.

Since the beginning of the post-war period, Japanese politics have been very personal. Historically, village groups would vote together as a block; a number of blocks would collectively elect a member to the Diet election after election. The seat might eventually be turned over to the son of the Diet member or his delegate. In return for this support, constituents expected the Diet member to bring economic development, jobs and infrastructure to the community. As block voting disappeared, the *koenkai*, personal support groups, developed. To encourage people to join their personal support groups, candidates offer favours like helping a child get accepted into a good school or secure a good job. They attend, often with a cash gift, weddings, funerals, graduations, store openings and other important events of their constituents. Some candidates attend as many as 30 such events a month. The personal nature of Japanese politics can spill into a system of money politics, with people voting in exchange for benefits. This in turn has led to numerous corruption and bribery scandals. It was public disgust with the corruption in the long dominant Liberal Democratic Party that brought an opposition coalition briefly to power in 1993. During their 11 months in power, this coalition government tried to eliminate the personalized factional nature of Japanese politics by removing the multi-member district electoral system for the House of Representatives, for example. They also started to re-engineer electoral districts, which had been designed to favour the LDP, to allow for the development of a stronger two- or multi-party system.

Japanese political parties

Liberal Democratic Party

One of the most successful democratic political parties in history, the LDP ruled continuously from 1955 until 2009, except for 11 months in 1993. In 2009, it lost to the Democratic Party of Japan (DPJ) but returned to power in 2012. Although without a well-defined unified ideology or political philosophy, the LDP is generally considered conservative, leaning to the right on economic and foreign policy issues. The LDP has numerous factions, formal subgroups of politicians organized around a senior political leader. (Factions also exist in other Japanese political parties.) These factions, usually named after the leader, try to secure power for themselves within the party. As the LDP has been in power for so long, instead of the fight for power being with other political parties, the most intense battles have been within the LDP itself. The fight is not usually over particular policy positions but for political power. There are usually 4 or 5 factions within the LDP, but, over the years, there have been as many as 13. Some factions have been as large as 120 members in both the Houses combined, bigger than the largest opposition party but not large enough not to need to form an alliance with another faction. Other factions have been as small as four members. Recently, factions have become larger and therefore more powerful. In fact, a strong faction leader can have more influence than the prime minister.

Faction leaders expect loyalty from their members and support during party elections. In return, leaders help members raise funds and build up their *koenkai* or personal support networks, offer financial assistance and assist members to obtain positions within the party and the government. The importance of factions has declined somewhat since the 1990s due primarily to electoral reforms. Nonetheless, they still play a significant role within the LDP and Japanese politics more broadly. As of 2019, there were five main factions and three smaller ones. Factions play a significant role in the selection of the party leader and, therefore, the prime minister. During the mid-2000s, factional in-fighting resulted in an almost annual change in prime minister. The most famous faction leader was Tanaka Kakuei, who served in the House of Representatives from 1947 to 1990 and as prime minister from 1972 to 1974. Even after he was convicted of bribery and put in prison, his political influence expanded, and his faction grew to 150 members. Tanaka is credited with engineering the selections of the next three prime ministers.

Former Prime Minister Abe Shinzo (2012–2020) served a one-year term as prime minister in 2006–2007 and then resigned due to ill health. Non-consecutive two-term leaders are very rare, but Mr. Abe was elected in 2012 and re-elected in 2014 and again in 2017. In November 2019, he became Japan's longest serving prime minister. Prime Minister Shinzo Abe comes from a political family; his father and grandfather were both politicians and his other grandfather, Kishi Nobusuke, was prime minister of Japan from 1957 to 1960. Prime Minister Kishi tried unsuccessfully to change Japan's Constitution, particularly Article 9, in the 1950s. Nationalistic and focused on recovering Japan's pride and dignity, Abe would have liked to accomplish what his grandfather did not: change the Japanese constitution to allow Japan to have a proper military or, as this looks unlikely, adjust the wording of the Constitution to specifically authorize the existence of Japan's Self-Defense Forces. Prime Minister Abe resigned suddenly in September 2020 due to ill health. Yoshihide Suga, former Cabinet Secretary under Prime Minister Abe, became the next Prime Minister (see Textbox 3.6 for a list of Japanese prime ministers).

Opposition parties

For nearly four decades Japan had a very stable "one and a half party system." But in 1993, the bursting of the economic "bubble" and frustration with the LDP led to a short-lived opposition coalition. This coalition used its short time in office to implement electoral reform. Until the 1990s, the Japan Socialist Party (JSP) was the largest opposition party, formed as a merger of leftist parties in 1955. In 1996, the JSP changed its name to the Social Democratic Party. Some of the JSP's more centrist members joined with some centrist politicians from the LDP to form the DPJ. Two other small parties merged with the DPJ in 1998, retaining the same name. From 1998 to 2016, the DPJ was the main opposition party. The DPJ won Upper House elections in 2004 and 2007, and, then, in response to growing voter frustration with the LDP, in September 2009, the DPJ swept to power by winning a strong majority in the Lower House.

The 2009 victory was hailed as the rebirth of Japanese democracy. It appeared that the 1993 electoral reforms had created the opening needed for a party to be strong enough to rival the LDP. There would now be two strong political parties. However, the DPJ government was plagued by numerous controversies and challenges, including the 2011 earthquake, tsunami and nuclear disaster. It suffered the same "revolving door" of prime ministers as had the LDP. Three years after they were elected, the DPJ lost badly to the LDP, first in the 2010 Upper House elections (giving Japan what was referred to as a twisted Parliament in which the LDP had a majority in the Upper House and the DPJ had the majority in the Lower House) and then in the 2012 Lower House elections.

Since then, the Japanese opposition has been fragmented with numerous smaller parties being created, merging and dissolving on a regular basis. In 2016, the DPJ merged with two smaller parties to form the Democratic Party (DP). Over the next two years, the DP merged and then dissolved, with many centre-left members forming the Constitutional Democratic Party and centre-right members forming the Democratic Party for the People. In 2019, these two parties had the largest number of seats after the LDP and in 2020 the two parties merged.

82   *Japan*

Some DPFP members reused to merge and created a new party but maintained the same name and branding as before.

Komeito, the "Clean Government Party," was started in 1964 by members of the Sokka Gakkai, a Buddhist lay organization and new religion, which claims one member in each of 8 million households across the country. A pacifist party, Komeito focuses on human rights, education, welfare and the environment. From 1999 to 2009 and again from 2012, the Komeito has been part of a ruling coalition with the LDP. Although the junior partner in the coalition with an ideological platform somewhat distant from the LDP, Komeito has managed to be independent, able to negotiate support for a series of small policies and willing to act as a brake on some LDP policies.

Textbox 3.6 Post-war Japanese prime ministers (last name first)

Yoshida, Shigeru	1946–1947, 1948–1954
Katayama, Tetsu	1947–1948
Ashida,Hitoshi	1948
Hatoyama, Ichirō	1954–1956
Ishibashi, Tanzan	1956–1957
Kishi, Nobusuke	1957–1960
Ikeda. Hayato	1960–1964
Satō, Eisaku	1964–1972
Tanaka, Kakuei	1972–1974
Miki, Takeo	1974–1976
Fukuda,Takeo	1976–1978
Ōhira, Masayoshi	1978–1980
Suzuki, Zenkō	1980–1982
Nakasone,Yasuhiro	1982–1987
Takeshita, Noboru	1987–1989
Uno, Sōsuke 1989	1989
Kaifu,Toshiki	1989–1991
Miyazawa, Kiichi	1991–1993
Hosokawa, Morihiro	1993–1994
Hata, Tsutomu	1994
Murayama, Tomiichi	1994–1996
Hashimoto, Ryūtarō	1996–1998
Obuchi, Keizo	1998–2000
Mori, Yoshiro	2000–2001
Koizumi, Junichiro	2001–2006
Abe, Shinzo	2006–2007, first time
Fukuda, Yasuo	2007–2008
Asō, Tarō	2008–2009
Hatoyama, Yukio	2009–2010
Kan, Naoto	2010–2011
Noda, Yoshihiko	2011–2012
Abe, Shinzo	2010–2020, second time
Suga, Yoshihide	2020–

Japanese political economy

In the 1980s, U.S. political scientist Chalmers Johnson labelled Japan (and South Korea and Taiwan, which followed in Japan's footsteps) a "capitalist development state," by which he meant a partnership between government and business. In using this term to describe Japan,

Johnson was arguing that Japan's government focused pointedly on economic development and the policy steps needed to achieve sustained growth. From the 1950s through the 1970s, in particular, the Japanese government played a very strong role in the development of the Japanese economy. Rather than trying to control or limit the private sector, the government worked with it, guiding businesses and industries by developing and promoting policies that support their long-term development, especially those with the most potential to create wealth and jobs. The origins of this model came from the Meiji period when the oligarchs started new industries and then sold them to private sector companies. The tight linkages between the elected politicians, the government bureaucracy and the corporate sector have been commonly referred to as the *iron triangle*. The role of the bureaucracy in the *iron triangle* is particularly significant as the Japanese bureaucracy has enjoyed greater influence and respect than its Western equivalents. Politicians, busy attending constituent events and strengthening factions, have little time for day-to-day governing. Japan's bureaucrats, selected from the top university graduates and extremely hard-working, are tasked with developing and implementing policies and programs in pursuit of economic growth.

Connections among the three groups in the iron triangle are facilitated by the education system. Graduates from Tokyo University and a handful of other well-known public and private universities that are notoriously difficult to enter dominate the leading positions in both government and business. Relationships formed at university facilitate interactions between the government bureaucracy and the corporate world. The loop closes again through a process called *amakudari* (meaning descent from heaven) by which mid-level government managers retire early and are given positions as advisors or board members of companies with which they worked while in government. The companies benefit from the skills and connections of the retired civil servants, and both the government and the corporate sector gain from an enhanced understanding of the priorities and constraints of the other.

In the latter half of the 20th century, Japan's Economic Planning Agency (EPA) and the Ministry of International Trade and Industry (MITI) (in 2001, the name changed to the Ministry for Economy, Trade and Industry or METI) were the key architects of Japan's capitalist development state model. The EPA formulated broad economic objectives and announced five-year economic plans and forecasts for the GNP growth rate. MITI was the ministry responsible for industrial policies. In the early post-war years, MITI supported industries that showed potential for quick growth and those that could employ large numbers of workers. It began by targeting iron and steel, chemicals, metals and shipbuilding and later moved to automobiles, motorcycles, computers and high technology. Using a variety of tools and policies during the high growth period from the 1950s to 1970s, MITI controlled foreign exchange and the licensing of foreign technology, supervising new technology acquisition to ensure the best deal for the country. MITI tried to steer companies into the sectors it believed would be the most productive through tax strategies and other means, at the same time working to avoid overcapacity in a sector and to prevent the creation of monopolies. The MITI bureaucrats have a great deal of power and influence because it is they, not the politicians, who develop, lead, implement and enforce the ministry's policies. When it was in power from 2009 to 2012, the DPJ intended to shift political power from the bureaucrats to elected politicians. This goal turned out to be more difficult to achieve than the DPJ had anticipated, as the bureaucrats had decades of experience and expertise on various files: alienating them had negative consequences.

A detailed study of Japan's industrial policy in action can be seen in Japan's efforts to build its own computer industry starting in the late 1950s. As Marie Anchordoguy points out in her study *Computers Inc.*, to help Japanese companies develop a computer industry and eventually compete with IBM, MITI used a variety of methods: from assisting with financing

84   *Japan*

to pressuring Japanese companies in the early days to buy inferior Japanese computers to encouraging cooperative research and development projects to establishing a computer rental company (Anchordoguy, 1989).

Proponents of Japan's industrial policy argue that Japan's economic development was extremely successful, pointing out the country's high growth rates and its success at building the sectors it selected and nurtured. However, not all analysts give credit to MITI and the Japanese government for the Japanese miracle of economic growth that took place from the 1950s to the 1980s. While the key industries grew as planned, other companies and sectors (e.g. cameras, bicycles, televisions, watches and robotics) grew and developed a strong export presence without government assistance. MITI made mistakes. For example, MITI initially planned for Japan to have one or two auto producers and intended to set standard specifications for cars. Manufacturers pushed back and numerous Japanese auto manufacturers became successful. Some economists argue that MITI actually restricted economic activity by not allowing completely free competitive markets, suggesting that Japan might have even been more successful without MITI's interference. As Japan's success grew in the late 1970s, the country's trading partners, particularly the United States, argued that Japan was protectionist and that its industrial policies were really unfair trade practices. Nonetheless, MITI/METI focused on policies and programs it considered necessary to support Japan's economic development. To this day, the government continues to fund and organize cooperative research projects that bring together scientists and technicians from a range of universities and corporations to work on cutting edge projects with commercial potential.

Over the decades, Japan's industrial policy approach changed. Throughout the 1960s, there was a "growth at all costs" mentality, resulting in environmental degradation, trade problem and other challenges. Japan's larger cities struggled with serious pollution problems. Osaka, for example, was known as the "Smoke Capital" for its pollution-producing factories. As well, many bodies of water were severely contaminated, with Kitakyushu's Dokai Bay even known as the "Sea of Death." Japan experienced four major pollution-caused disease outbreaks related to the improper disposal of industrial waste by Japanese companies. As a result of these environmental and health disasters, public concern escalated, and gradually local, prefectural and finally the national government began to enact legislation around pollution and environmental damage; this weakened the corporate-government bond. In the 1970s and 1980s, trading partners began to complain about Japan's practices, and the General Agreement on Tariffs and Trade rules were more broadly followed. As Japan's industrial sector matured, companies began moving production offshore to take advantage of lower labour costs and to deal with rising protectionism. The need for an activist industrial policy began to decline. By this time, the corporate sector was much stronger and wealthier than it had been 40 years earlier.

Japan's Self-Defense Forces

The majority of Japanese are pacifists. Article 9 of Japan's Constitution renounces war and declares that "land, sea, and air forces, as well as other war potential, will never be maintained." Japan was thereby prohibited from using force beyond the minimum required to defend itself from attack. At the demand of the United States, Japan began to rearm in 1949; in 1954, the Self-Defense Forces (Japan Ground Self-Defense Force, Japan Maritime Self-Defense Force and Japan Air Self-Defense Force) were created. Until 1992 and the passage of the International Peace Cooperation Act, which permitted Japan to participate in UN-sponsored peacekeeping missions, the Self-Defense Forces stayed home. However,

Japan did not like being criticized for sending only financial not military support to international conflicts. During the 1990 Gulf War when a coalition of countries drove Saddam Hussein out of Kuwait, Japan contributed $13 billion but no Japanese soldiers participated, for which the administration was severely criticized by the United States and other countries that supplied troops.

Since then, the SDF have participated in nine peacekeeping missions, including in Cambodia, Mozambique, the Golan Heights, Timor-Leste and Haiti. The SDF participation in these missions was constrained by several rules: there had to be a ceasefire in place; the parties to the conflict had to agree to the UN mission; the peacekeeping mission had to be impartial, and SDF members could only use force in self-defence (later expanded to include the defence of non-SDF members). After 9/11, Japan adopted the Anti-Terrorism Special Measures Law, which allowed the SDF to engage in various support activities. They dispatched the Maritime SDF to the Indian Ocean for an oil-fuelling mission supporting the United States in Afghanistan. SDF personnel were also sent to Iraq and Kuwait between 2003 and 2009 for humanitarian and reconstruction work. In 2007, the Japan Defense Agency (which has responsibility for the SDF) was upgraded to become the Ministry of Defense.

In 2015, then Prime Minister Abe, intent on changing Article 9 (see Textbox 3.7), passed new national security laws. These push the constitutional bounds of Article 9 even further by stating that SDF personnel have the right to exercise collective self-defence (defending an ally) under certain circumstances, such as when not doing so could jeopardize Japan's safety. In the past, this kind of intervention could only occur on or near Japanese territory. Examples of the kinds of activities that the SDF can now carry out include protecting vessels, removing mines and even providing munitions if a war was to occur on the Korean peninsula, thereby threatening nearby Japan.

Japan consistently spends about 1 percent of its GDP on the SDF, much less than Russia's 3.9 percent, the United States' 3.2 percent, France's 2.3 percent and China's 1.9 percent. However, as Japan's GDP is the third largest in the world, 1 percent is actually a significant amount of money. In fact, Japan's military spending in 2018 was $46.6 billion, making it the ninth highest spender worldwide, a long way behind the spending of the United States and China but not far off the United Kingdom and Germany.

Textbox 3.7 Change Article 9?

When Prime Minister Abe came to power in 2012, he campaigned to change Article 9 in Japan's Constitution. Arguing that renunciation of war does not preclude the right to self-defence, Prime Minister Abe was intent on adding a section that defines the role of Japan's Self-Defense Forces to ensure that they are constitutional, and, in fact, would prefer even more drastic changes that would allow Japan a full-fledged military. It is extremely unlikely that he or his successor would be able to garner enough political or public support for the change. However, over the past three decades, the government has been stretching the boundaries of the Article. Many constitutional scholars argue that Japan's 2015 national security changes are unconstitutional.

Japan can be considered a pacifist nation; the vast majority of its citizens are opposed to any militarization. However, some Japanese, as well as many Americans, concerned about China's burgeoning military budget and North Korea's missile tests, believe that it is time for Japan to become a "normal nation" and possess a fully developed

86 *Japan*

military. That some North Korean missiles have flown right over Hokkaido has added to the sense of unease. But if Japan were to make any steps towards a more robust military, Japan's neighbours would be deeply concerned and would likely object. Despite Abe's commitment to constitutional revision, in 2020, it still does not appear likely. A constitutional amendment requires two-thirds support in the Diet, which an LDP government could manage with the support of their coalition members, but it also requires majority support in a national referendum. A 2019 Kyodo News poll showed only 40 percent of the Japanese population is supportive of revising Article 9, with over half opposed.

North Korean abductions of Japanese citizens

During the 1970s and 1980s, North Korea abducted Japanese citizens to teach Japanese language and culture to North Korean spies. In some cases, there may have been other reasons for the kidnappings (e.g. to obtain the Japanese people's identities or have the women become wives to North Korea-based Japanese terrorists). The North Korean government has admitted to abducting 13 Japanese citizens, whereas the Japanese government has identified 17 people they believe were abducted and think there may have been many more. The abductees disappeared from Japanese coastal areas, and most were in their 20s. The youngest was Megumi Yokota, who was only 13 when she disappeared.

Until the first Japan-North Korea summit in September 2002, North Korea denied the abductions. In order to facilitate the normalization of relations with Japan, Kim Jong Il admitted to 13 abductions and apologized. The Japanese government and general public were outraged. North Korea provided death certificates for eight of the 13 people but later admitted these were forged. The five abductees North Korea admitted to be alive were allowed to go to Japan but only on the understanding that they would return to North Korea. The Japanese government agreed, but, under pressure from the families and the public, did not have the victims return. Indicating that this had broken the agreement, North Korea abruptly ended the talks. Later the children of two of the abductees' families were permitted to join their parents in Japan.

The North Korean government now claims that the issue is resolved as all the 13 abductees have been identified. The Japanese authorities, however, do not agree. They point to forged death certificates and indicate that the remains of Yokota and another abductee returned to Japan by North Korea had, according to Japanese DNA testing, been misidentified and were the remains of others. In response, in 2004, Japan restricted trade with North Korea and submitted a resolution condemning North Korea for "systematic human rights violations" to the United Nations General Assembly. In 2006, Yokota's mother testified about the abductions to a sub-committee of the U.S. House of Representatives and met with then President George Bush to ask for his help in resolving the issue. In 2013, victims' families testified at a United Nations hearing. For years, Japan has imposed sanctions on North Korea, hoping this would lead to a resolution of the abduction issue, meaning a complete accounting of the Japanese abducted, what happened to them and where their remains are. In April 2018, Prime Minister Abe asked President Trump if he would raise the issue with Chairman Kim. President Trump agreed and did so, but the issue remains unresolved.

Japanese society

Despite the relatively slow growth in the last two decades, Japan is one of the world's wealthiest countries, with the third largest economy. Both students and workers are known for their hard work and long hours at their desks. Salary men (Japanese male white-collar employees) work up to 60 hours a week on top of long commutes and frequent late nights spent drinking with customers or co-workers. As a result, men often do not see much of their families during the week.

About 70 percent of Japanese women quit working when they marry or at least when they have children and do not return to the workforce for at least 10 years. When they do return, it is usually to part-time, poorly paid jobs. As a result, for most Japanese families, the husband earns the bulk of the family income, and the wife does the vast majority of the housework and childcare. There are a variety of reasons for this situation, including lack of childcare, expectations of maternal involvement in children's education, advantages for men in promotion and opportunities and the intense work culture, which rewards the length of time a person works for a company. It is difficult to leave a job temporarily and would be very hard for both parents to work the number of hours Japan's work culture requires. Only 25 percent of mothers are employed full time, with most young women choosing instead to be full-time housewives, a more respected calling than in some other industrialized countries. In an effort to attract more women into the workforce to offset the shrinking labour force, in 2013, the Japanese government launched *Womenomics*, policies obliging large companies to outline their plans for hiring more women and raising the "dependent exemption" (the amount of money a wife can earn before the family income is taxed). *Womenomics* also involved opening up more day care places. This economic impetus may help change the deep-rooted sexism that limits female economic participation.

A record number of women, 30.03 million, are now working in Japan. However, 55 percent of women are in non-career track jobs compared with 23 percent of men (Mishima, 2019). In 2018, at medium and large Japanese companies, only 5 percent of the senior roles were held by women (Baird, 2018). Only 7.8 percent of company presidents and only 4.2 percent of the appointments to corporate boards were women (Baird, 2018; Deloitte, 2017). In the 2019 Japanese Diet, women comprised only 10.2 percent of the Lower House and 20.7 percent of the Upper House ("Gender Imbalance," 2019). And despite Prime Minister Abe's commitment to creating "a society in which women will shine," there is only one woman in his 2020 cabinet. However, the governor of Tokyo is a woman, Yuriko Koike, as is the mayor of Yokohama.

Education

Despite a difficult written language with two alphabets and Chinese characters, Japan boasts near-universal literacy and high levels of educational performance—at least on standardized tests. Interestingly, however, compared to other industrialized countries, Japan spends a smaller percentage of its GDP on education. Until middle school, children of all abilities remain in the same class. Performance differences among children are viewed by parents and teachers as due more to a lack of effort than to a lack of ability, so even weaker and less interested students feel pressured to work hard. The education system also teaches students to think of themselves as part of a group, to be aware of their impact on others and to conform, making it difficult for students who are different or do not fit in easily.

88 *Japan*

The high school system focuses on merit. The 9th grade high school entrance exam system is designed to identify the brightest and most motivated. Students can choose to take entrance exams either for an academic, vocational or comprehensive public high school or for an elite or a low-ranked private high school. Although grades and teacher recommendation letters are also required for admission, the emphasis at all institutions is on the entrance exam score. These high school entrance exams require mastery of a great deal of material. To be accepted by an excellent high school means one stands a much better chance of entering a highly ranked university, as well as securing a high-status job. Thus, students intending to attend an excellent high school must study long hours. University acceptance is also based on demanding entrance exams. The most serious students spend the better part of a year studying during almost every waking moment they are not in class. For most students (unless in medicine, engineering or the physical sciences), however, university life is much easier. During these four years, students enjoy a break before joining the working world. Japanese companies recruit students in their final year of university, and new employees begin their new jobs on April 1st.

The goal of the intense studying is to find a good position at a major Japanese corporation or within the Japanese government, both of which can mean career-long employment. In the post-war period until the bubble burst, the Japanese corporate world (primarily the large companies) was known for providing life-time employment and a seniority-based pay system. Since Japanese companies were growing rapidly during most of the latter half of the 20th century, it was relatively easy for companies to commit to their workers. Once hired, they would be employed for their career even if there was not enough work and even if they were not hard workers. Japanese companies were looking at and planning for the long term, knowing that company loyalty would serve them well. But the bursting of the bubble in the early 1990s severely tested this commitment: companies began to lay off middle managers. This came as an enormous shock for men who had devoted their whole lives to their companies and had expected to be taken care of for life.

Japan's seniority-based pay system means that employees generally move up the ranks at the same pace and pay for at least the first 10 years of their career. Only after a decade with the company are some individuals promoted over others who joined the company at the same time. Eventually, all will reach the first level of promotion but some of those promoted to the first level may be promoted to a subsequent level sooner. Because people seldom work for someone their same age or younger, nobody is forced to take orders from someone who was once their equal or junior. In the late 1990s and early 2000s, some companies experimented with changes to the seniority-based wage system, implementing various forms of merit-based compensation, but most Japanese firms today continue to have a seniority-based pay system.

Japan faces many of the same labour problems as other parts of the world. Although the ageing and declining population has kept the country's unemployment figures low (in 2018, it was 2.4 percent) ("Japan's Unemployment," 2020), over one-third of the Japanese workforce is in non-regular employment, which means in temporary, part-time or contract work. Non-regular work is clearly much less secure and usually less well paid than full-time employment. As a result, the gap between those who are well off and those who are not has been widening, and a class of working poor has emerged. In the past, those making low wages were primarily women in non-regular employment, especially those who returned to the workforce part time after their children graduated from high school. Now male workers are also part of the new precariat.

Textbox 3.8 *Nihonjinron* (theories of Japaneseness)

Nihonjinron is a genre of writing that debates the essence of "Japaneseness." *Nihonjinron* was first seen in the pre-war years, and since the 1980s, books and articles with titles like *What is a Japanese?* (Shichihei Yamamoto 1989) and *What is Japan?* (Taichi Sakaiya 1991) became very popular as they attempted to analyse and explain specific aspects of Japanese culture and ways of thinking. Nakane Chie's book *Japanese Society* discussed the strength of Japanese interpersonal relationships. *Ninhonjinron* literature covers a number of disciplines, including sociology, anthropology, psychology, history, linguistics and even biology, chemistry and physics. Although some Western authors have written books that could be considered part of the genre, most of the authors are Japanese.

The first *Nihonjinron* books were published in the early post–World War II period and discussed Japanese uniqueness quite negatively and critically. Recently defeated Japan was described as backward, if somewhat exotic. As Japan grew economically stronger in the 1960s, the writings began to discuss strengths and weaknesses in both Japanese and Western traditions. Since the 1970s, *Nihonjinron* writings have discussed Japanese uniqueness in a positive light. As Japan became the second largest economy in the world, the Japanese became more confident; at the same time, the rest of the world began to consider that perhaps there were lessons that could be learned from Japan. Japan's management programs, industrial relations and education systems were all praised. Ezra Vogel's 1979 *Japan as Number One* was one of the best known of the Western books championing Japan's unique qualities. When the economic bubble burst and Japan's economy slowed in the early 1990s, Western writers began to call instead for the globalization of Japanese society and the structural reform of Japan's corporate sector.

Japanese Nihonjinron writers focus on their belief in the uniqueness of the Japanese race: of the consequences of being an island country, of the importance of the Japanese language and, especially, of the particularities of Japanese thinking and behaviour. These authors believe that Japan is a uniquely homogenous society. Their writings dissect Japan's group orientation; hierarchical structure; belief in *ganbari* (persistence and endurance); and focus on harmony, loyalty and consensus. The Nihonjinron literature tends to assume that all Japanese possess the characteristic under discussion (and that all possess it to the same degree) and that if non-Japanese have that trait, it is only to a marginal or limited extent. At the root of Nihonjinron is the belief that there is something genuinely unique about being Japanese.

Religion

While most Japanese would say they are not religious, both Shintoism and Buddhism play a large role in Japanese life. Part of Japanese culture since ancient times, Shintoism (Shinto means "the way of the Gods") is an animistic religion whose roots lie in the worship of natural phenomena like the sun, water, rocks, mountains and even human ancestors. The spirits of these phenomenon, known as *kami*, are worshipped at 80,000 shrines throughout Japan

90   *Japan*

(see Figure 3.6). Marking the entrance to these shrines are Torii gates, usually red or vermillion, signifying the transition from the secular world to the sacred one. The Ise Grand Shrine is the most important shrine as it honours Amaterasu, the Sun Goddess.

Lacking a founder, particular theology or sacred texts, Shinto is primarily concerned with keeping away evil spirits and restoring purity through purifications, offerings and prayers. Before visiting a Shinto shrine, people wash their hands and mouths so that they are clean before approaching the kami. There is often a long rope with bells on that visitors pull to call the kami. This is followed by two bows, two claps and one bow. Shinto priests perform complicated purification rituals, often involving scattering salt and shaking sacred tree branches with white paper strips. Shrines host various annual festivals at which the kami are thanked and celebrated through dance and musical performances, and people pray for prosperity and good harvests. At many festivals, the *kami* are carried through town in an *o-mikoshi*, sacred palanquin, on people's shoulders. Shintoism deals primarily with life's happy occasions like marriages or the blessings of a child. It is not concerned with the afterlife. Buddhism generally focuses more on death, suffering and the afterlife. This difference in emphasis has allowed Buddhism and Shintoism to coexist peacefully.

Shinto was subordinate to Buddhism through the premodern period but revived during the Meiji Restoration. A key goal of the Meiji oligarchs was to create a sacred foundation for this new stage in the country's development. Shinto became the official state religion, and state financial support was given to the most important shrines. As freedom of religion was guaranteed in the Meiji Constitution, the government defined Shinto as a non-religious patriotic ideology, now sometimes referred to as State Shinto. Worship at shrines was enforced, as was reverential respect for the imperial family, particularly for the emperor. His divinity, that he was descended directly from the Sun Goddess, was emphasized.

The emperor's divinity was a particular focus for Japanese soldiers, who were expected to fight in his name. In addition to respect for the imperial family, the importance of education was also promulgated. The Imperial Rescript on Education, which had been issued during Meiji, described the central purpose of education as the cultivation of loyalty and commitment to nation and parents and was read at all school events, and students were required to memorize it. State Shinto reached a peak preceding and during World War II.

In January 1946, the emperor, at the request of SCAP, issued what has since been called the Humanity Declaration, in which he renounced his divinity. This was the precursor to the new Constitution, which would describe the emperor as the symbol of the country and the unity of the people but made him a figurehead with limited power. In Japan today, Shinto is paradoxically an important yet peripheral part of Japanese life. Few people would say they are Shintoist but almost 80 percent participate in Shinto practices. Most Japanese visit shrines for major festivals, New Year's Day and other occasions. Marriages happen at shrines as does the November 15 *Shichi-Go-San* (Seven-Five-Three) traditional rite of passage celebration for three- and seven-year-old girls and five-year-old boys. Many Japanese homes have a *Kamidana* (God-shelf), a small shrine at which offerings are made.

In around the 6th century, Buddhism was introduced to Japan from southern India via China and Korea. Buddhism teaches that life is suffering and that people can end that suffering by letting go of attachments through Buddha's teachings. The branch of Buddhism that came to Japan was Mahayana (Great Vehicle or Way) Buddhism. Mahayana emphasizes the worship of Buddha but also of Bodhisattvas, people who are on their way to enlightenment but have stayed back from Buddhahood to aid others to reach salvation. Within Mahayana Buddhism, there are a variety of schools that teach different paths to enlightenment. The three main schools in Japan are Zen, Pure Land and Nichiren. In Zen, enlightenment is

Figure 3.6 Shinto Shrine.

achieved through self-discipline and meditation. Pure Land focuses on submitting oneself to the Buddha completely, chanting the name of Amitabha Buddha and believing one will be reborn in the Pure Land where life will be easier. Based on the teachings of Nichiren, a 13th-century Japanese Buddhist priest, Nichiren Buddhism focuses on the chanting of *Nam Myoho Renge Kyo* and on the writings from the Lotus Sutra, an important Buddhist text.

At Buddhist temples, there is no clapping or bell ringing. Hands are held together in prayer, and purification is conducted with incense. People often have a *butsudan* (Buddhist altar) at home to remember a deceased relative. Some Japanese worship at Buddhist temples, and most Japanese funerals are conducted by Buddhist priests. There are special memorial services held after a certain number of days and then years after someone dies. Only about 35 percent of Japanese would identify themselves as Buddhist if surveyed, but Buddhist traditions and festivals play an important part of life in Japan (Allen, 2018).

Christianity was first introduced to Japan in 1549 by the Portuguese. Francis Xavier and his fellow missionaries quickly made close to half a million converts. However, in 1587, Toyotomi Hideyoshi banned missionaries from the country. They were not allowed back until the Meiji period, almost 300 years later. Although freedom of religion was allowed under the Meiji Constitution, the number of Christians grew slowly. Today, only about 1 percent of Japan's population identifies as Christian, most likely at least partly because of the exclusive nature of Christianity, which demands the rejection of other religious ideas and practices, specifically Shintoism and Buddhism both of which are ingrained in Japanese life. Even so, Christianity has still had a great deal of influence on Japan. There are a number of important Christian kindergartens, private high schools, universities and hospitals in Japan.

92   *Japan*

Many couples like to marry in Christian weddings even if they are not Christian. Millions of Japanese eat chicken from KFC on Christmas Day!

Japan's challenges

Japan faces a number of major challenges, including an ageing population, government debt and its relationship with the United States. These are discussed below. Other important issues for Japan are relations with China, South Korea and North Korea, which are addressed in Chapter 9.

Japan's ageing population

The percentage of Japan's population over 65 is increasing rapidly relative to the rest of its society. The percentage of seniors in 1990 was only 12 percent. It is now close to 27 percent and could climb as high as 35 percent by 2050 (see Table 3.1).

Demographers point out that by 2050, at current projections, Japan's population could decline by 30 percent, with 1 million more people dying each year than being born. There could be 1 million Japanese over 100 years old. There are implications for an ageing and declining population. People cost their governments the most during their later years as health care needs rise. Seniors generally are no longer working and paying taxes but are instead drawing pensions and using the health care system. This, however, is beginning to change in Japan. The age of retirement is increasing. For large companies, the retirement age is 60 but smaller companies are keeping staff much longer. A 2017 government survey showed that over 60 percent of Japan's citizens over the age of 65 would like to stay employed. The OECD estimates that the actual retirement age of Japanese men is closer to 70 years.

While Japan is not the only country with an ageing population and a low birth rate (Italy, Germany and some other European countries are in similar situations), the fact that Japan accepts few immigrants and has a limited number of women working in full-time career jobs has left Japan with a serious labour situation. Japan's workforce is 2 million people smaller than it was in the 1990s. New efforts to alleviate the labour shortage include Prime Minister Abe's *Womenomics* initiatives, new immigration rules allowing for the admission of 345,000 foreigners by 2024 in certain sectors (farming, nursing, construction and hospitality) and the

Table 3.1 Japanese population over age 65 compared with the equivalent population in other countries (%)

Year	Japan	United States	Germany	France	United Kingdom	China
1990	12	12	15	14	16	6
2000	17	12	16	16	16	7
2010	22.5	13	20	17	17	8
2018	28	16	21	20	18	11

encouragement of the elderly to stay employed. Technology, robotics and artificial intelligence will also be used to eliminate work currently done by people.

Government debt

After the bubble economy collapsed, the government continuously poured money into the economy to act as a financial stimulus. In the process, the Japanese government racked up enormous government debt. Japan's government debt is approximately 240 percent of annual GDP, the largest of any major economy. One advantage Japan has is that a high percentage of this debt is held domestically by the Bank of Japan and Japanese investment companies. Over the past five years, the government has begun to stabilize and even reduce the amount of debt slightly.

Japan and the United States

Japan and the United States have had a complicated relationship focused primarily on two issues: trade and security. During the Occupation and in the years afterward, it was a senior-junior relationship, which gradually became more equal as Japan's economy strengthened. By the 1970s as Japan became a powerful economic rival, tensions between the two countries escalated. There were a series of trade disputes and mounting financial frustrations. As Japanese products flooded the United States and world markets, the Americans complained about Japan's trading practices. In the 1980s, with trade tensions at their highest, Japanese auto producers agreed to voluntarily limit the number of vehicles they exported to the United States. To overcome rising trade protectionism, Japanese companies began to move their production overseas, especially to the United States. Trade relations between the two countries have generally been free of serious issues over the past two decades. However, since 2018, President Trump has been complaining about Japan's large trade surplus with the United States.

Non-trade issues are also a concern. The 1952 Security Treaty and Article 9 in the American-written Japanese Constitution set the parameters for the security relationship between Japan and the United States. The Security Treaty made Japan's military dependent on the United States, and the United States agreed to help defend Japan from outside attack in return for permission to have the U.S. military on Japanese soil. As the Constitution forbade Japan from having military forces with the potential to wage war, U.S. protection was vitally important. The Security Treaty was revised and renewed in 1960 despite major public opposition in Japan centring around fears that Japan was too dependent on the United States and the potential consequences of this dependency. The 1960 Treaty of Mutual Cooperation and Security, which included provisions for the stationing of the U.S. forces in Japan, remains in force today. Along with American troops, Japan is the home base for the aircraft carrier *Ronald Reagan*. Public opposition in Japan gradually died away (although there remains criticism of Japan's place under the U.S. nuclear umbrella rooted in Japanese efforts to rid the world of nuclear weapons). Disputes and tensions about the treaty have arisen over the years but overall both the United States and Japan have benefitted significantly from it.

When it comes to defence, there have been two main areas of friction over the decades. The first has been the United States' intention for Japan to bear the cost of more of the burden of its own defence and to participate more fully in regional and global peacekeeping operations. Through the 1980s and 1990s, critics both inside and outside Japan expressed

94 *Japan*

frustration with the country's dual personality—an economic giant but a military and political dwarf. It was time, they argued, for Japan to become a normal country. Japan, limited by Article 9, tried to compensate by contributing large amounts of money instead of soldiers to international conflicts like the 1990 Gulf War. This effort, however, did not appease the critics. In response, the Japanese government began pushing the bounds of what the Constitution would allow it to do under the rubric of self-defence. Japanese SDF troops began participating in peacekeeping operations and anti-terrorism support, and the government even passed legislation enabling collective self-defence. President Trump urged Japan to pay a higher proportion of the costs of hosting the 54,000 American troops currently stationed in Japan. He also criticized what he believes to be the one-sided nature of the security treaty, which requires the United States to come to Japan's aid but does not oblige Japan to defend the United States (because of the constitutional limits imposed by Article 9). The president raised both of these topics again at the January 2020 celebration of the 60th anniversary of the Treaty of Mutual Cooperation and Security.

The other difficult challenge in the U.S.-Japan security relationship has been the American military bases on Okinawa in southern Japan's Ryukyu Islands, one of the country's poorest prefectures. After World War II ended, Okinawa remained occupied and administered by the United States until 1972. Although it only constitutes 0.6 percent of Japan's total land area, almost 71 percent of the lands used exclusively by U.S. forces in Japan are in Okinawa. There are 25,000 American troops at 33 military installations on the island (see Figure 3.7). With such a large number of soldiers close to a civilian population, problems are inevitable. Between 1954 and 2000, over 200,000 violent crimes, including rapes and vehicular homicides, involving U.S. troops and Japanese civilians were reported. Until 1995, under an extraterritoriality agreement, all U.S. suspects were taken to the United States to stand trial. The horrific gang rape of a 12-year-old schoolgirl by three American servicemen led to a new agreement, and now members of the American military stand trial in Japan for crimes committed on Japanese soil.

A current issue for Japan-U.S. relations is the Marine Corps Air Station Futenma base currently located in the centre of Ginowan City. Thirty-eight percent of the city of Ginowan is occupied by military bases used by the United States, and the Futenma base is surrounded by a crowded residential area. Planes landing and taking off multiple times an hour shake windows and make a great deal of noise. Even worse, the presence of the military threatens the safety of the city's residents: in 2004, a military helicopter crashed onto the campus of Okinawa International University, and in 2017, a helicopter component fell onto the grounds of an elementary school. When the DPJ took power in 2009, the then Prime Minister Hatoyama tried to fulfil his election promise to move the base, but the challenges of where to move it proved insurmountable, frustrating the U.S. military leadership, who waited for months for a decision. A year later, Hatoyama resigned over his inability to move the base. Numerous subsequent prime ministers have also tried to solve the base problem without success. However, despite strong opposition from the Okinawan governor and the Okinawan public, in 2015 the Abe government began work on a replacement site at Henoko in the northern part of Okinawa. The construction of Henoko requires a great deal of land reclamation work and the creation of a runway into the sea. Many Okinawans have concerns about the environmental impact of Henoko, especially its impact on dugong (a relative of the manatee) habitat. In February 2019, a non-binding referendum was held in Okinawa asking if voters were in favour of the relocation plan, opposed it or were neutral. More than 70 percent voted against the relocation. Unfortunately for the Okinawans, the referendum results have not swayed the national government, which argues that Henoko is the only viable option and construction will go ahead.

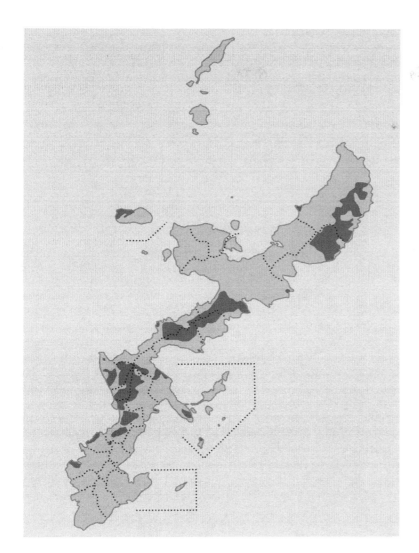

Figure 3.7 U.S. military bases in Okinawa.

Natural disasters

Japan is especially susceptible to natural disasters. In 2018 alone, Japan suffered a 6.1 earthquake near Osaka (five fatalities, many injured); Typhoon Jondari (16 injured, 37,000 evacuated); a heavy rain event (all-time precipitation records and widespread flooding, 200 fatalities); a prolonged heat wave; Typhoon Jebi (11 fatalities, 600 injured); a 6.7 earthquake in Hokkaido (40 fatalities, 400 injured); and Typhoon Trami (four fatalities, 200 injured, transportation and electricity disrupted for millions).

Seismologists indicate that there is a 60–70 percent likelihood of a major magnitude earthquake within the next 30 years along the coastal regions of western Japan and in Tokyo. The

96   *Japan*

impact of a major earthquake in such densely populated regions could be enormous in terms of casualties, property and infrastructure damage.

Despite Japan's familiarity with earthquakes and other natural disasters, the country was not prepared for the Tohoku earthquake that struck on March 11, 2011. The epicentre of the quake was 40 miles off the northeast coast of Honshu and about 20 miles under the ocean's surface. The biggest of the quake's tremors reached 9.0 on the Richter scale, making it one of the five most powerful earthquakes ever. The shaking generated waves 40 metres high, and the water travelled up to 10 km inland. The earthquake and resulting tsunami caused over 20,000 deaths and $360 billion worth of damage.

Energy

Japan has little in the way of natural energy sources and has long been dependent on Middle Eastern oil. When the price of oil rose dramatically in the 1970s, Japan became painfully aware that it needed to diversify its sources of energy and become as energy efficient as possible. The country did both, investing heavily in solar power and fuel cell technologies and constructing nuclear power plants. Although there has long been public ambivalence about nuclear power because of the atomic bombings, nuclear power offered a way for the country to gain a greater measure of energy self-sufficiency. Once the causes of global warming became better understood and the Kyoto Protocol was signed in Japan in 1997, the Japanese government saw nuclear power as a way to reach its greenhouse gas reduction targets. By 2010, Japan had 55 reactors, which produced almost 30 percent of the country's energy. Government plans called for this to reach 50 percent and Japan was on track to reach its 6 percent greenhouse gas reduction target.

The Tohoku earthquake and tsunami caused the meltdown of the Fukushima Daiichi nuclear plant, resulting in the evacuation of a 30 km zone around the plant and concerns about the threat of radiation. Japan's nuclear plants were gradually shut down for safety checks. A few were restarted in June 2012 to much protest. From 2013 to 2015, all the 54 reactors were shut down to undergo safety checks. Losing 30 percent of the country's energy supply was a major challenge. The government dramatically increased imports of natural gas and encouraged its citizens to reduce their use of electricity. A *setsuden* (power saving) campaign started in the aftermath of the nuclear disaster in March 2011 in order to prevent blackouts. Although the campaign officially ended later that year, the power saving commitment has continued.

Gradually, nine nuclear plants have been restarted as of early 2020. Many Japanese objected to a return to nuclear power, arguing that it is too dangerous in a country like Japan that is so prone to earthquakes. The government argues, however, that it has no choice in order to keep up with consumer and industrial demand. The government's target is for nuclear power to comprise 20 percent of Japan's energy supply by 2030.

Rural decline

Like much of the world, contemporary Japan has become much more urban (see Table 3.2). Combined with Japan's now declining population, many smaller and more remote parts of the country have been left with few young people or families, many senior citizens, an eroded economic base and little potential for a return to prosperity. Hundreds of thousands of private rural homes sit abandoned. A 2014 Japan Policy Council report stated that a third of

Table 3.2 Urban-rural population in Japan by percentage, 1950–2050

Year	Urban Population	Rural Population
1950	53.4	46.4
1960	63.3	36.7
1970	71.9	29.1
1980	76.2	23.8
1990	77.3	22.6
2000	78.6	21.4
2010	90.8	9.2
2020	91.8	8.2
2030	92.7*	7.3 *
2040	93.7*	6.3*
2050	94.7*	5.3*

*projected

Japan's 1,800 municipalities were at risk of collapse and that quite a few would disappear. Although concern over the collapse of villages and the declining and aging farming population has been around for decades, this concern has now spread to the small towns and cities that had prospered based on agricultural and regional industrial activity.

While much of rural Japan likely faces a future of slow and painful decline, individual communities are fighting for their futures with creative measures and investments from local entrepreneurs. One interesting government program to help struggling small towns is a hometown tax (*furusato nozei*) system. It gives taxpayers the option to direct a percentage of their tax monies to districts outside where they live. In 2017, 13 million individuals transferred $2.5 billion in tax funds to villages and towns. Local communities began to incentivize tax transfers by sending gifts in return, typically regional items like foodstuffs (e.g. meat, seafood or fruit), crafts or certificates to local attractions. However successful, this is only a small step in defeating the forces of urbanization and rural decline.

Conclusion

Japan is the third largest economy in the world. It has remade itself multiple times in the modern age from the Meiji period to post–World War II to the aftermath of the bubble economy. The country is nothing if not resilient. Over the last decade, Japan's annual GDP growth has been slow but steady, averaging 1–2 percent.

Japan is one of the largest producers of automobiles, electronics, machine tools and a range of other manufactured and processed items. Since 1995, it has been building its future on science and technology, investing heavily in innovation, new technologies and high-risk high-reward economic possibilities. Japan is a country focussed on the future. Thirty years ago, Japan was accused of being an imitator, expert at turning the ideas and products of others into commercial sectors. The country is now widely understood to be among the most technologically advanced and innovative in the world. Japan led in miniaturization; was a pioneer in the mobile Internet; has superb animation and digital content initiatives; is a world leader in products and service for the elderly; has the best industrial and service robotic

98 *Japan*

implementations; a deep interest in the Internet of Things (IoT); and extensive investments in nanotechnology, sensors, environmental technologies and integrated energy systems.

Japan was the first country to ratify the Trans-Pacific Partnership despite the political risk associated with the agricultural concessions included. When the United States withdrew from the agreement, Japan played a key role in bringing the remaining 11 countries together to ratify a renamed modified agreement (the Comprehensive and Progressive Agreement for Trans-Pacific Partnership). Japan signed an agreement with the European Union on an Economic Partnership Agreement in July 2017. Both accords should be ratified in 2020.

Japan's situation is complicated. The country's population is declining, which some believe is a crucial failing. Forty years ago, however, observers worried that the population was growing too fast and that cities were too crowded. Japan's economic growth slowed in the 1990s, seen internationally as a serious problem. But worldwide there is now discussion about the need to lower expectations for sustained economic growth as there is intense concern about the negative environmental effects of rapid growth. Looking after the elderly and paying for their health care is a significant and looming challenge. But demographic forces will lower housing prices, reduce the size of cities, lower demand for energy and lessen the cost of continual growth. Rapid technological change could replace the "missing" workers, suggesting that the technological dislocation could be less of a crisis in Japan than in other countries.

Like all nations, Japan is in transition, buffeted by global pressures and propelled by technological innovations and economic opportunities. As one of the leading countries in East Asia, deeply connected to and engaged with the other nations in the region, Japan is one of the key pillars of East Asia's emergence as the most influential area in the world. The country is rooted deeply in its past and its culture, connected to the Western industrial world but not dominated by it. Japan captured the world's attention negatively during its years of military colonialism in the 1930s and 1940s and again, more positively, during the economic boom of the 1980s and 1990s. Its global standing declined when the bubble burst, and it now attracts less international attention than in the past. But the tendency to disparage or underestimate Japan's accomplishments is wrong, for the country remains among the most creative, economically strong and culturally rich in the world.

Note

1 In Japanese, it is customary to put the family name first so this will be followed in this chapter.

Bibliography

"Gender Imbalance: Japan's Political Representation by Women Lowest in G20", *Nippon.com*, March 8, 2019.

"Japan's Electoral Map Favours the Ruling Party", *The Economist*, November 14, 2019.

"Japan Unemployment 1991–2020", 2020. https://www.macrotrends.net/countries/JPN/japan/un employment-rate

Allen, Jay. 2018. "Why are the Japanese not Religious?", *Unseen Japan*, September 18. https://unseenj apan.com/japanese-not-religious/

Anchordoguy, Marie. 1989. *Computers Inc.: Japan's Challenge to IBM*. Harvard University Press.

Baird, Cory. 2018. "Let's Discuss the lack of female leaders in Japan", *The Japan Times*, June 4.

CIA World Factbook. n.d. https://www.cia.gov/library/publications/the-world-factbook/geos/ja.html

Deloitte. 2017. *Women in the Boardroom: A Global Perspective*, Fifth edition. Deloitte Global. p. 26.

Dower, John and Tetsuo Hirata. 2007. "Japan's Red Purge: Lessons from a Saga of Suppression of Free Speech and Thought", *Asia Pacific Journal: Japan Focus*, 5(7).

Henshall, Kenneth. 2012. *A History of Japan: From Stone Age to Superpower*. Palgrave Macmillan.

Lamb, Margaret and Nicholas Tarling. 2001. *From Versailles to Pearl Harbour: The Origins of the Second World War in Europe and Asia*. Palgrave.

Mishima, Daichi. 2019. "Japan Sees Record Number of Women Working But Challenges Remain", *Nikkei Asian Review*, July 30.

Nisei Veterans Legacy. n.d. https://www.nvlchawaii.org/japan-surrenders-vj-day#:~:text=%E2%80%9CWe%20have%20resolved%20to%20pave,radio%20broadcast%20announcing%20Japan's%20surrender.

The Prime Minister of Japan and His Cabinet. n.d. *The Constitution*. https://japan.kantei.go.jp/constitution_and_government_of_japan/constitution_e.html#:~:text=The%20Emperor%20shall%20be%20the,Law%20passed%20by%20the%20Diet

Further Reading

Bix, Herbert P. 2000. *Hirohito and the Making of Modern Japan*. Harper Collins.

Booth, Alan. 1995. *Looking for the Lost: Journeys through a Vanishing Japan*. Kodansha Globe.

Dower, John. 1999. *Embracing Defeat: Japan in the Wake of World War II*. W.W. Norton and Company.

Hershey, John. 1946. *Hiroshima*. Alfred A. Knopf.

Holroyd, Carin and Ken Coates. 2007. *Innovation Nation: Science and Technology in 21st Century Japan*. Palgrave Macmillan.

Johnson, Chalmers. 1982. *MITI and the Japanese Miracle: The Growth of Industrial Policy, 1925–1975*. Stanford University Press.

Najita, Tetuso. 1974. *Japan: The Intellectual Foundations of Modern Japanese Politics*. University of Chicago Press.

Oros, Andrew. 2008. *Normalizing Japan: Politics, Identify and the Evolution of Security Practice*. Stanford University Press.

Shikibu, Murasaki. *The Tale of Genji*. (Many translations and editions)

Sugimoto, Yoshio. 2014. *An Introduction to Japanese Society*. Cambridge University Press.

Totman, Conrad. 2013. *Japan: An Environmental History*. I.B. Tauris.

4 The Korean Peninsula

South Korea (Republic of Korea) and North Korea (Democratic People's Republic of Korea)

Introduction

For the last 80 years, the Korean Peninsula has been at the front lines of international conflict, starting with the Japanese expansion into the area and extending through to the present. The actions of North Korea, one of the world's most isolated and rogue states, raise grave concerns in South Korea and Japan and create additional pressure on China's role in East Asia.

The Korean Peninsula extends southward from continental Asia 1,100 km (680 miles) into the Pacific Ocean. The north borders China, with a small portion in the northeast bordering Russia. The East Sea (Sea of Japan) is to the east, the Yellow Sea to the west. The whole peninsula is very mountainous with the highest mountains in the north. There are small arable plains between the mountain ranges. For centuries, the peninsula was one political entity, ending only with the intrusion of global geopolitics at the end of World War II.

Early Korean history

At least 30,000 years ago, the first inhabitants arrived on the Korean Peninsula. While the first Korean pottery dates from about 8,000 years ago, Chinese records date the founding of Korea as a political unit at 1122 B.C. See Textbox 4.1 for a breakdown of the different periods in Korean history. The first era about which historians are confident in their knowledge is the Three Kingdoms period (37 B.C.–A.D. 668). These kingdoms consisted of Goguryeo in the north, Baekje in the southwest and Silla in the southeast. An additional fourth state, the Kaya, lay at the southern end of the peninsula. Developed from local tribes that eventually settled in communities, the kingdoms had evolved into political entities by the 2nd or 3rd century. They had similar but unique languages, with culture and shamanistic religion in common, but relations among them were tenuous, alternating between alliances and periods of conflict. Although they fought with China and Japan, mutually beneficial arrangements emerged with time. Over the years, trade and cultural exchange between the states and China, in particular, grew: the Koreans traded iron, gold and horses for silk and tea from China. They adopted the Chinese writing system, Confucianism and later Daoism and Buddhism. Of the four states, Kaya had the strongest relations with Japan.

> **Textbox 4.1 Different periods in Korean history**
>
> - Neolithic and Bronze Age (7000–1st century B.C.)
> - Three Kingdoms period (57 B.C.–A.D. 668)
> - United Silla (668–936)
> - Goryeo dynasty (918–1392)
> - Under the Mongol-ruled Yuan dynasty in China (1270–1356)
> - Joseon dynasty (1392–1910)

Each state was ruled by a monarch with administrators from the local aristocracy. The primarily peasant population was obliged to pay taxes to the state, to fight in the army or to work on government public works' projects when required. Slaves and criminals were at the bottom of society.

The kingdoms coexisted with one another until A.D. 668, when the Silla kingdom, with help from China, conquered Goguryeo (after having conquered Kaya in 562 and Baekje in 660) and unified the Korean Peninsula. Silla promised not to join in an alliance with China's enemies if, in return, Korea would be allowed to rule itself. The Unified Silla period was a time of great prosperity and cultural development. Gyeongju, the capital, had a population of over 1 million people, making it the fourth largest city in the world at that time. Buddhism (see Chapter 8) became the major religion; Korean monks travelled to China to study, and many great Buddhist temples were built. Confucianism (see Chapter 8) also increased in importance. As in China, the study of Confucian texts became a big part of the education of government civil servants. Art and music flourished during the Silla period. Ancient records indicate that Silla artists were skilled in painting, calligraphy and architecture. Silla items created out of stone and metal, including Buddhist religious art, stone pagodas and temple bells, are still extant. Silla's apex of prosperity was the middle of the 8th century after which it steadily declined, weakened by political instability and corruption. Goryeo (established by a leader of Goguryeo descent) annexed Silla peacefully in 935 and conquered Baekje in 936, ushering in a period of unity again.

The Goryeo period lasted for four centuries. Buddhism was the main religion and helped define society. Major festivals had Buddhist origins and Buddhist temples were built throughout the peninsula. "Buddhism was the dominant religion among the officials, many of whom, including members of the royal clan, became monks. There thus grew up a monkish aristocracy parallel to that which dominated secular life. Since Buddhism was felt to be not only the refuge and salvation of the individual but also the protector of the state, the leaders of the monks became men of great influence and power. All this, plus the monks' immunity from taxation and military duty, made a religious career attractive not only to the pious but also to the ambitious" (Han, 1970, 146). In the 13th century, the *Tripitaka Koreana*, the complete Buddhist canon (a collection of over 6,500 sacred texts), was carved on to wood blocks. The carving took 60 years to finish and stimulated the development of the art of printing. Confucianism also permeated Korean society, influencing government and education. C'oe Chung (984–1068), sometimes referred to as the Korean Confucius, created a private school that trained students to pass the intense civil service exams required to secure a position in government. The success of his school led other scholars to follow his example and establish their own schools whose graduates were more successful than the graduates of the

102 *The Korean Peninsula*

government schools. In response, the government schools reorganized their curriculums and built schools throughout the country. During the late 11th and early 12th centuries, the government schools produced many scholars and government civil servants.

In the latter part of the 12th century, the Goryeo government was controlled by a series of strong warrior families in an organized military dictatorship similar to the Japanese shogunate. Between 1231 and 1270, the militaristic and expansive Mongols invaded the Korean Peninsula seven times, destroying many temples and works of art. In 1232, the Mongols burned the *Tripitaka Koreana*, a devastating loss. The Goryeo dynasty decided to have the *Tripitaka* recarved. But the task was time-consuming and onerous, prompting the dynasty to invent another way of copying: moveable metal type. In 1250, the 50-volume Buddhist text was printed using moveable type, 200 years before the printing of Gutenberg's Bible in Europe. The Koreans were unable to repel the Mongol invasion in 1270, and the Goryeo fell under the Mongol-ruled Yuan dynasty of China until it ended in 1356.

General Yi Seong-gye seized power in 1392, beginning the Joseon dynasty, one of the world's longest and most dominant governments. (Joseon has been loosely translated as "morning calm"—the literal translation is closer to morning brightness or morning freshness—from which Korea was given the epithet "Land of the Morning Calm.") The Imperial Family of Korea, the ruling family of the Joseon dynasty, was founded by King Taejo (Yi Seong-gye's name once crowned), and his descendants ruled Korea until 1910. Twenty-seven monarchs ruled over the Korean Peninsula for the more than 500 years of the Joseon dynasty. There are 40 Joseon royal tombs at 18 locations in South Korea. They were recognized as a UNESCO world heritage site in 2009.

King Taejo made Hanyang, present day Seoul, the capital city, and over the following 250 years, Chinese Confucian ideals became "Koreanized" and entrenched in Korean society. Buddhism, in contrast, was blamed as the source of corruption, and an intensely anti-Buddhist intellectual climate gradually developed. Confucian principles became the centre piece of the Joseon administrative code. Life's celebrations and rituals (e.g. weddings, funerals, coming-of-age ceremonies) were now conducted according to Confucians principles. On the cultural and intellectual front, the first century of the Joseon dynasty was a particularly exciting time as Korean artists excelled in painting, calligraphy, ceramics, poetry and other arts.

A Korean social hierarchy emerged with distinct and hereditary social classes: the *yangban* class (scholars, military officers and civil servants); professionals (doctors, lawyers, middle-ranked military); artisans, fishermen, merchants; and "unclean" professions like butchers, shoemakers, entertainers, prostitutes, and jail-keepers. The nobi, the lowest rank, were the slave class, including slaves, serfs and indentured servants. Society was highly structured with clear rules of conduct around duty and seniority. Class was hereditary and "any attempt to change one's social status was not only a crime against society but also a sin against heaven" (Han, 1970, 246).

The yangban class focussed their time on education and book-learning. Only the yangban were allowed to take the civil service exam, which would allow them to work in government. Education was therefore the key to political power. The government put a large bureaucracy in place, constructed palaces and government offices, carried out land surveys, promulgated laws, issued currency and constructed a maritime grain transportation system.

The fourth and most famous of the Yi kings was King Sejong, who ruled from 1418 to 1450 (see Figure 4.1). A progressive ruler, he promoted people outside the highest class to positions in the civil service and invested heavily in science. During King Sejong's reign, significant technological advancements like the sundial and the lunar calendar were made as were improvements in fields as diverse as firearms, musical instruments and astronomical instruments.

The king also paid particular attention to agriculture, key to the country's economic and social development, improving irrigation and experimenting with different farming techniques. Other advancements under King Sejong included the creation of Hangul, the Korean alphabet, which allowed commoners and women to read and write, skills which had before been the preserve of only the well-educated who had mastered literary Chinese. Strongly opposed to the introduction of Hangul, many Confucian scholars continued to write most official documents and literature in classical Chinese until the 20th century. Nonetheless, even today Koreans value Hangul, so much so that there is an annual national holiday in its honour.

During the late Koryo and early Joseon (Yi) periods, Korea expanded its contact with other countries, especially China, Japan and the Ryukyu chain of islands, which were somewhat independent at that time. Korea sent tributary missions to China on a regular basis. As Korean historian Han Woo-keun stated,

> The Yi dynasty shared with the Chinese government the Confucian distaste for commerce, and attempted to limit it. … The Yi rulers not only tried to prevent private trade, but disliked their subjects going abroad for any reason, fearing that they might become corrupted or betray the nation."
>
> (Han, 1970, 224 and 227)

The dynasty's policy of seclusion restricted interactions with the world to ceremonial contacts with Japan on Tsushima Island (a Japanese island about halfway between Kyushu and the southern part of the Korean Peninsula) and tributary missions with China. Contact with foreigners and outside travel was forbidden. During this period of isolation, the Korean

Figure 4.1 Statue of King Sejong.

104 *The Korean Peninsula*

Peninsula experienced over 200 years of peace, and Korean culture developed on its own away from outside influences.

In 1592, and again in 1597, the southern coast of Korea was invaded by Japanese forces under Toyotomi Hideyoshi, who had unified much of Japan and planned on conquering Korea and then China. In both invasions, the Japanese were initially successful, capturing numerous cities and leaving great damage in their wake. But both times, the Koreans, with help from Chinese forces, stopped the Japanese and forced them back to the coast. The first invasion lasted five years until 1596, at which point there was a brief truce and failed peace negotiations. The second invasion ended in 1598 with the withdrawal of the Japanese. A few decades later, in 1627, and again in 1636, the Manchus, a Tungusic nomadic people from Siberia and Northeast Asia, invaded. The Manchus established the Qing dynasty in China that same year and ruled China from 1644 until 1912. The Manchu army overwhelmed the Koreans, who were eventually forced to agree to become a tributary of the Qing.

In the early 1700s, American and European merchants arrived in East Asia, but the Joseon government continued its isolationist policies, rejecting overtures to trade or form alliances. This isolationism earned Korea the nickname of the "Hermit Kingdom." By the mid-1800s, the European powers were pressuring East and Southeast Asia to open up to trade and diplomatic relations. As the Chinese empire declined, Western powers competed for influence in the region. Western ships plied the waters near the Korean Peninsula, surveying and trying to get Korea to engage in trade and diplomacy. However, it was Japan (ironically given that a few years earlier Japan had been forced open by the Americans) that forced Korea open. In 1876, and under duress, Joseon signed the Treaty of Ganghwa (Japan-Korea Treaty of 1876), which opened three ports to Japanese ships, allowed the Japanese to survey and map in the area, granted the Japanese extraterritoriality and set out the terms of the commercial and political relationship between the two countries. Korea's signing of the Treaty of Ganghwa with Japan spurred the United States, and soon after the United Kingdom, Germany and France to initiate negotiations for their own treaties with Korea. While some of the Korean leadership believed that Korea could prosper by trading with Japan and the West and learning about Western technologies, many others were opposed to opening up the country. The opponents feared the spread of Catholicism, an inundation of the country with Japanese products and the outflow of Korean rice in return, all of which happened. Nonetheless, the government began to slowly modernize the country. In 1881, it sent a study mission to Japan to learn about Japanese government and business practices. (It is striking that the Koreans found much to learn from the Japanese early on in Japan's process of modernization.)

The Japanese occupation of Korea

Korea's entrée into diplomatic and trade relations with the West and Japan also put the country into the middle of conflicts between the various powers. Over the years following the signing of the treaty, Japan, China and Russia, all competed for political and economic control of the Korean Peninsula. Japan supported those forces within the Korean government that wanted to modernize (but Japan pushed for a modernization program that would allow it to participate and benefit economically from Korea's modernization), while China backed the more conservative officials. In 1884, a Korean independence faction supported by the Japanese attempted a coup to establish a pro-Japanese government. This was quickly thwarted by Chinese troops who were called in by conservative Korean officials. Although war was avoided and both China and Japan agreed to withdraw their forces from Korea, a decade later the first Sino-Japanese War (1894–1895) broke out. Japan won the war.

The Korean Peninsula 105

The resulting Treaty of Shimonoseki obliged the Qing government in China to pay reparations in silver to Japan and to surrender the island of Taiwan, the Liaodong Peninsula (which Japan was forced to give back within the week by Russia, France and Germany) and the Pescadores Islands (near Taiwan) to Japan.

In 1904–1905, Japan and Russia went to war over rival interests in Manchuria and Korea. To the surprise of international observers who did not believe that an Asian nation could defeat a European country, Japan won this war as well. At the Portsmouth Peace Conference, where negotiations were brokered by U.S. President Theodore Roosevelt, Japan's claims to Korea were recognized, and Russia agreed to leave Manchuria and give up its rights to the southern part of Sakhalin Island. Russia would not, however, pay Japan reparations. Believing that, as the victor, it was due reparations, Japan was not content with the outcome, which remained a source of irritation for years to come.

Even less content with the outcome were the Koreans, who were unhappy with the promise made by the United States not to interfere with Japan's ambitions on the Korean Peninsula if Japan did not interfere with U.S. rule in the Philippines. In 1905, despite Korean protestations, Japan imposed the Japan-Korea Protectorate Treaty on Korea, making Korea a Japanese protectorate. Five years later, on August 29, 1910, Japan annexed Korea completely, a day Koreans still refer to as "National Humiliation Day." The Japanese annexation of Korea lasted until 1945 and Japan's surrender at the end of World War II.

The Japanese occupation of Korea was profoundly harsh. For the first 10 years especially, Korean dissent was not tolerated, with all aspects of Korean life controlled. In the lead up to and during the Pacific War, the Japanese authorities tried to force Koreans to assimilate. Koreans were forced to take Japanese names, use the Japanese language, believe in Shinto (see Chapter 3) and pledge allegiance to the Japanese emperor. Under direct control of the emperor, the head of occupied Korea was a Japanese general who gave orders to burn books on Korean history and culture and insisted that Korean children use the same textbooks as their Japanese counterparts. Over 5.4 million Koreans were conscripted to work in factories and mines on the peninsula, in Manchuria and in Japan itself. Conditions in these workplaces were appalling and dangerous: tens of thousands of these forced labourers died. Starting in 1938, Korean volunteers were accepted into the Japanese army. Six years later in 1944, conscription began, and over the next year approximately 200,000 Koreans became soldiers for the Japanese empire.

Far from acquiescing to the occupation, many Koreans resisted and fought for an independent Korea. In 1919, early on in Japanese rule, resistance leaders read out the "Declaration of Korean Independence," but the Japanese police cracked down hard on the resistance, killing, torturing and arresting thousands of demonstrators and sympathizers. Throughout the 35-year occupation, a large Japanese police force kept the resistance under control, but the independence movement was supported by the Korean Provisional Government, a quasi-official government-in-exile in Shanghai and later in Chungking. Tens of thousands of Korean women (and women from other countries Japan occupied during the war) were forced to become sex slaves, euphemistically called "comfort women," and service Japanese soldiers both before and during World War II. Apology and compensation for these women has remained a source of ongoing tension between South Korea and Japan (see Chapter 9 for more information).

Despite the many hardships, the occupation brought some benefits. During the 35 years of colonial rule, Korea's economy grew rapidly, with agriculture, fishery and forestry sectors expanding significantly. In 1910, Korea had been primarily an agrarian society. The Japanese oversaw significant industrial development in such sectors as steel, chemicals and hydroelectric power, and they built roads, railways, port facilities and electrical facilities across the country.

106 *The Korean Peninsula*

But the effort was not altruistic: the Japanese developed Korea to benefit Japan and help the country fight its wars in China and elsewhere. Nonetheless, by the time of Japan's surrender in 1945, Korea was second only to Japan in Asia in its level of industrialization.

When Japan surrendered at the end of World War II, Korea was treated as a former Japanese asset that needed to be dealt with externally. With characteristic Western arrogance and arguing that the Korean people were not ready to govern themselves, the Allied powers divided the peninsula into two temporary occupation zones while overseeing the dismantling of the Japanese administration and preparing for the eventual establishment of an independent Korean government. Land north of the 38th parallel was to be temporarily administered by the Union of Soviet Socialist Republics (USSR). The area south of the 38th parallel of latitude (it crosses the peninsula east to west, a short distance north of Seoul) would be temporarily administered by the United States. The Soviets had only entered the war against Japan eight days before its surrender. This and the uncertainty of the USSR's commitment to the Allied Power's democratic ideals made the United States nervous. Nonetheless, the USSR occupied the north.

Civil war and the division of Korea

Soon after the division, Cold War tensions set in. The Korean population was not ideologically unified: many of the North's peasants agreed with Soviet policies, while most of the Korean middle class had fled to the South but were not strongly anti-communist. The peninsula was politically divided, and there were numerous clashes between left-wing and right-wing groups. It is not clear that an independent Korea would have been easy to establish, particularly because negotiations between the United States and the USSR on the steps needed to establish an independent unified Korea did not go well. In 1948, two separate governments were established: the Democratic People's Republic of Korea in the north and the Republic of Korea in the south. Although the United Nations tried to oversee democratic elections for the whole country, it was not allowed into the North, so United Nations-sponsored elections were held only in the south. Syngman Rhee was elected president of South Korea, while Kim Il-sung was appointed president of North Korea. The United States supported South Korea; the Soviet Union supported North Korea. Both North and South claimed sovereignty over the whole country, adding to an already tense situation.

The newly created United Nations, formed in an attempt to prevent the world from returning to armed conflict, tried to find a way to reunite the North and the South. However, no plan would satisfy both the Americans, who wanted a democratic capitalist country, and the Soviets, who wanted a communist one. Neither was willing to give way to the other. In June 1950, the North decided to reunify the country by force, invading the South and initiating the Korean War. With Soviet backing, weapons and air support, Seoul was taken in three days. Within a few weeks, North Korea controlled most of South Korea. In July, a United Nations army, led by an American general and dominated by U.S. troops, came to South Korea's aid. [The United Nations Security Council Resolution authorizing the military force had passed when the Soviet representative was absent from the UNSCR meeting, boycotting in protest of the UN's recognition of the Republic of China (Taiwan) instead of the People's Republic of China.] North Korea's army was pushed back, Seoul was retaken in September, and the war was carried over the 38th parallel into North Korea the next month. China intervened on North Korea's side, sending hundreds of thousands of soldiers into battle. The Southern forces were eventually driven back across the border. By May 1951, the war settled into a stalemate. Although ground and air fighting continued for the next two years, neither side gained any real ground.

The Korean Peninsula 107

Peace talks began in June 1951, and the Korean Armistice Agreement was signed on July 27, 1953. After more than 3 million deaths, half of them civilians, and terrible damage to the entire peninsula, the war had ended with North and South Korea divided approximately where they had been when the war started. The armistice called for the return of prisoners and created the Korean Demilitarized Zone (DMZ), a buffer zone separating the North and the South—a 160-km long, 4-km wide strip of land that runs across the peninsula along the 38th parallel. Armed troops remain stationed on each side of the DMZ, the most heavily militarized border in the world, guarding against aggression from the other. The armistice was not a peace treaty but a suspension of hostilities, so technically North and South Korea are still at war. Although the armistice was only supposed to be temporary, attempts to create a more permanent settlement have failed. The death toll from the war was enormous: millions of people died—South Korea (217,000 military; 1,000,000 civilian), North Korea (406,000 military; 600,000 civilian), China (600,000 military) and the United States (36,500 military). Millions more were wounded. The Korean War left both North and South Korea in ruins. Agriculture and industry were destroyed, and family members who were separated at the beginning of the war were never reunited.

The Korean Peninsula was one of the first battlegrounds of the Cold War. More than a civil war, the Korean War attracted the support of the United States and the United Nations because it was widely believed in the West that if the North Korean forces took over the South, the next step would be the Communization of all of Asia. Only a few years earlier (1949), the Chinese Communist Party had founded the People's Republic of China, and Americans were worried that communism would spread further. The U.S. government and military focussed on a policy of containment, preventing Communist governments from expanding their influence. The Korean Peninsula was now fully transformed from a single culture and nation into two divided and antagonistic countries, both linked to diametrically opposed super powers.

Political heritage

Korea's political foundation is rooted in authoritarian rule rather than democracy. For centuries the Korean Peninsula was ruled by kings, and power was held in the hands of a few. Korean culture was permeated with Confucian thought, with its emphasis on hierarchy, people having a pre-determined place in the social order, and all citizens owing respect and obedience to their ruler. When North and South Korea began their separate political journeys, the leaders of both maintained an authoritarian approach. Each of them "would suppress democracy in the name of national security" ("The Fight for Democracy," 1992).

Introduction to South Korea

The Republic of Korea (ROK), better known as South Korea, occupies the southern half of the Korean Peninsula. Its capital, Seoul, is about 60 km south of the Demilitarized Zone dividing North and South Korea. To the east of the Korean Peninsula is Japan across the Sea of Japan; to the west is China across the Yellow Sea. About 70 percent of South Korea is mountainous; only 20 percent of the land is arable. There are nine provinces in South Korea: North Chungcheong (Chungcheongbuk), South Chungcheong (Chungcheongnam), Gangwon, Gyeonggi, North Gyeongsang (Gyeongsangbuk), South Gyeongsang (Gyeongsangnam), North Jeolla (Jeollabuk), South Jeolla (Jeollanam) and Jeju Island. The country's main cities are Busan, Daegu, Daejeon, Gwangju, Incheon, Sejong, Seoul and Ulsan. See Figure 4.2 for a map of provinces and cities.

108   *The Korean Peninsula*

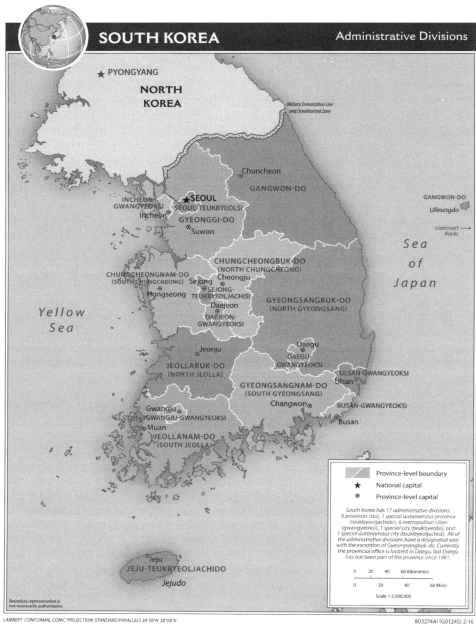

Figure 4.2 Korean provinces and main cities.

The Korean Peninsula 109

With a population of 51.3 million (2020), South Korea is both one of the world's most densely populated countries and one of the most ethnically homogenous. Over 80 percent of the population is urban, with half living in one of the six largest cities. In the past decade, new dynamics have taken hold. With the world's lowest birth rate in 2018 and an ageing population, South Korea has an urgent need for labour, particularly in certain sectors. The government has therefore begun accepting workers from overseas. As of 2016, the number of foreign migrants had reached 2 million, with over 1 million from China, half of whom are ethnic Koreans. The next largest source of migrants is Vietnam. As Koreans feel an intense pride in their Korean identity, language, culture and history, integration can be challenging for new immigrants.

South Korea is now the 11th largest economy in the world, its per capita income surpassing $31,000 in 2018. Accounting for 40 percent of the country's GDP, Korean manufacturing is among the world's most competitive and innovative, particularly in the sectors of electronics, automobiles, shipbuilding, telecommunications, steel and chemicals.

South Korea's post–World War II political evolution

U.S. Army military government

The first stage of South Korea's post-war political evolution, as with Japan's, began with the U.S. Army. From September 8, 1945, to August 15, 1948, the U.S. Army military government ran the southern half of the Korean Peninsula. A provisional government, the People's Republic of Korea (PRK), based on people's committees throughout the nation, had been organized when Japan surrendered. However, shortly after occupying the South, the U.S. military government disbanded the PRK. (North of the border, the Soviet Union merged its PRK into the new North Korean government.) During this post-war period, the South Korean economy struggled. Most of the industrial base developed under the Japanese was in the north, and the U.S. military was not well-prepared for the Occupation. Officials knew little about Korean society, and few spoke Korean. Although the Koreans strongly opposed the idea, the Americans maintained the colonial system and some of the former Japanese governors as advisors. Unsurprisingly, these decisions harmed American-Korean relations, and strong resentments developed between the Americans and Koreans. Expecting liberation, the Koreans instead found themselves with another foreign ruler and a divided country.

The First Republic

South Korea's first president was Syngman Rhee (1875–1965), who served from 1948 to 1960. Although he was from a relatively poor family, he had received a classical Chinese education and converted to Christianity while still at school. Involved politically from a young age, he was jailed for his anti-Japanese activism in 1899. After his release in 1904, he moved to the United States, where he earned a PhD in theology from Princeton University. When he returned to Japanese-occupied Korea, he became active in the independence movement and so was arrested; he fled to the United States, where he remained for decades, all the time actively supporting the fight for Korean independence. Korean nationalists who had fled to Shanghai created a government-in-exile, the Korean Provisional Government. Rhee served as president from 1919 until 1925. Upon Japan's defeat at the end of World War II, Rhee returned to Korea. Because he had lived abroad during the factionalism that had riven the Korean independence movement, Rhee was seen as a generally acceptable

110　*The Korean Peninsula*

compromise candidate for the presidency. Another point in Rhee's favour was his standing among the Americans, who approved of him because he spoke English and was strongly anti-Communist.

In 1948, Rhee was elected president of the Republic of Korea by members of the National Assembly, as per the country's new Constitution. There were two main parties on the ballot: the Nationalist Party (Rhee's party) and the Korea Democratic Party, which became the Democratic Nationalist Party and, in 1955, was renamed the Democratic Party (the opposition). Rhee's government was a strongly right wing, pro-capitalist government. Land and assets that had been owned by Japanese were returned to private Korean hands, South Koreans with large land holdings were obliged to divest some of their land and small family businesses emerged. Although educational opportunities improved and people learned about democracy, the economy was poorly managed, and corruption was widespread. Rhee and his government suppressed any left-wing opposition, including the strong Communist labour movement, passed laws curtailing political dissent and arrested opponents, some of whom were killed.

Members of the National Assembly were unhappy with Rhee's authoritarianism and corruption. As it looked unlikely that he would be re-elected in the 1952 election, Rhee forced through an amendment to the Constitution, requiring direct election of the president. To do so, he arrested Members of Parliament he thought might vote against the amendment. Subsequently, Rhee was directly elected. In 1954, he used similar means to force another amendment, allowing an incumbent to run for more than two terms in office, a common practice of strongman politicians. Opposition to Rhee's autocratic rule and corruption grew through the late 1950s. The belief that the next election would be rigged sparked student and labour protests that spread throughout the country beginning on April 11, 1960. Known as the April Revolution, the protests continued, eventually bringing down Rhee's government. He resigned and fled to the United States.

The Second Republic

In July 1960, elections brought the Democratic Party to power. The government tried to hold to account the members of the military and the police who had been involved in suppressing opponents of the Rhee regime. Under the new government, political activity by leftists, trade unions and student groups, suppressed under the Rhee regime, was now allowed. Despite the new freedoms, economic and social difficulties escalated, with soaring inflation and unemployment rates. Factional fighting escalated within the Democratic Party, weakening it. In May 1961, the army led by Park Chung-hee led a coup d'état and assumed control of the government. A military man, Park Chung-hee had served in the Japanese army during World War II and then as an officer in the Korean army during the Korean War. After the coup, Park Chung-hee became head of the military junta, the Supreme Council for National Reconstruction of the Republic of Korea. Under U.S. pressure to restore a civilian government, a presidential election was held in 1963. Park was elected president for his Democratic Republican Party.

The Third Republic

The Third Republic under Park Chung-hee emphasized economic development. With the help of aid from the United States and Japan, the government provided interest-free loans to export businesses and made major infrastructure investments. The *chaebol*, large industrial conglomerates, began to expand during this time, and per capita GDP increased.

The Korean Peninsula 111

Using Japan's highly successful export-led developmental state model, Park and his government rapidly expanded the South Korean economy. The government produced five-year plans with a focus on rapid industrialization. South Korean nurses and miners were recruited to work in West Germany. The money they sent home also contributed to South Korea's rapid economic growth.

For a time, although his government was authoritarian and suppressed resistance, the country's economic growth made Park Chung-hee popular. He was re-elected in 1967 and after a constitutional amendment allowing a third term, again in 1971. However, his 1971 victory against the New Democratic Party's Kim Dae-jung was much narrower despite the unevenness of the playing field. In 1972, facing growing opposition to his authoritarian rule, Park declared martial law and created the Yusin Constitution, which eliminated presidential term limits, implemented an indirect voting system for presidential elections and gave the president the power to appoint one-third of the legislature, thus to all intents and purposes granting himself a majority government. The Constitution also allowed the president to pass laws without ratification by the National Assembly in emergency situations, essentially granting Park dictatorial powers.

The Fourth Republic

South Korea's Fourth Republic government ran from November 1972, after the approval of the Yusin Constitution. The Yusin Constitution formalized increased presidential powers at the same time that public disappointment with Park's rule escalated. As political unrest grew, any opposition was quickly quashed. The media was heavily censored, and Park controlled the military.

Although Park Chung-hee used his new powers to crack down on dissent, protests against his authoritarianism grew in scale, intensity and violence. By 1979, massive demonstrations against his regime erupted across South Korea. After surviving several earlier attempts on his life, on October 26, 1979, Park Chung-hee, four of his bodyguards and his driver were assassinated by the head of the Korean Central Intelligence Agency inside the Presidential Blue House. The reasons for the assassination are still unclear. Park Chung-hee's legacy divided the country for years to come. Some South Koreans praised Park Chung-hee for the economic miracle he oversaw, while others abhorred his brutal authoritarianism.

By the time of his assassination, Park had ruled with absolute power for almost 18 years. His death left a political vacuum and considerable turmoil. Although the public supported free and fair elections, in May 1980, Major General Chun Doo-hwan seized power, established a military dictatorship, dissolved the National Assembly and declared martial law. In reaction, massive public protests erupted, especially in the southern part of the country. On May 18, in the city of Kwangju (formerly the capital of South Jeolla province), students and the general public demonstrated against the government and against martial law. The people from South Jeolla province were dissatisfied because their province was one of the poorest in the country, their poverty the result of a deliberate government strategy. Unhappy with the people's support of Kim Dae-jung, the most prominent opposition figure, Park had directed little of the industry or infrastructure to Jeolla. To control the demonstration, Chun's government sent in Special Forces, who clubbed, kicked and bayoneted the protestors. Rather than stopping the protests, the brutal response brought more protestors to the streets.

Over a 10-day period from May 18 to 27, 1980, the Kwangju protests grew. Many of the protestors believed that the United States, the beacon of democracy, would step in and support them. But concerned about keeping good relations with the South Korean government

112 *The Korean Peninsula*

and worried about the potential impacts of the instability, the U.S. government chose not to intervene. As the United States actually had operational control over the South Korean forces, Chun's military response implicitly came with American approval, but the Americans may not have anticipated the brutality of the crackdown. The protests and the violence continued for over a week, with protestors arming themselves with whatever weapons they could find. Gun fights, tear gas and the clubbing and bayoneting of protestors continued. Early on May 27, the military escalated the violence, sending helicopters, tanks and armoured personnel carriers to attack the protestors. Within two hours the army had crushed the uprising. The number of people killed in the Kwangju uprising has been disputed. The official government statement is about 200, but the people of Kwangju believe the number is probably 10 times higher. Although the Kwangju uprising was ultimately unsuccessful, it galvanized national support for democracy and was the precursor to the June Democracy Movement.

The Fifth Republic

Chun Doo-hwan established the Fifth Republic in March 1981. Chun and the Democratic Justice Party ran the country as a dictatorship and opposition grew. The June Democracy Movement refers to mass protests for democracy that took place across South Korea in June 1987. On June 10, President Chun announced Roh Tae-woo would be the candidate for the Democratic Justice Party and Chun's choice of successor for the presidency. This decision angered the public, who had been pressuring for the return of direct presidential elections (they had disappeared with the Yusin Constitution). Although student, labour and church groups had been protesting against the government for some time, Chun's announcement triggered massive mobilization by the opposition. On June 26, over a million people in 34 cities participated in a great national march for peace.

The Chun government was keen to suppress unrest in the lead up to the 1988 Olympic Games to be held in Seoul, Seoul's "coming out party." The government considered its options, figuring that with a fragmented opposition, Roh could win if democratic elections were held. With this in mind and to placate the country, the government agreed to the return of civil liberties and to amend the Constitution to allow for the direct election of the president. In the December 1987 elections, Roh Tae-woo ran as the government candidate against two opposition candidates, Kim Young-sam and Kim Dae-jung. The two opposition candidates agreed on almost everything except which one of them should be the president. As a result, although the opposition received a majority, the votes were split between the two candidates. Thus, the government candidate Roh won and became the democratically elected president. This was the beginning of the Sixth Republic, the current system of government in South Korea today.

Beginning of the Sixth Republic

In 1993, Kim Young Sam became the first civilian president in 30 years. All that time, Kim had been a leader of the South Korean opposition fighting against the authoritarian governments of Park Chung-hee and Chun Doo-hwan. During his one five-year term as president, Kim focussed on reforming the government and economy by combatting corruption, giving amnesty to political prisoners and challenging the power of the *chaebol*. Kim Young-sam was succeeded by Kim Dae-jung, a former political prisoner who had spent 13 years in prison or under house arrest. Kim Dae-jung promoted a policy seeking engagement and cooperation with North Korea. Known as the Sunshine Policy, the idea was to try to engage cooperatively and constructively with North Korea. Kim Dae-jung won the Nobel Peace Prize in 2000 for his efforts towards reconciliation with North Korea.

In 1996, Roh and Chun were put on trial for their role in the 1979 coup and the 1980 Kwangju massacre. They were both convicted of mutiny, treason and corruption (for receiving bribes while in office). Chun was sentenced to death, and Roh was given 22 and a half years in prison. Other military officers were also sentenced to jail for their role in the massacre. Upon taking office in 1997, in an effort to promote national reconciliation, President Kim Dae-jung pardoned both Roh and Chun.

Post-war economic development

South Korea's economic growth after the end of the Korean War has been called the *Miracle on the Han River*. (The Han River is a major South Korean river that flows through Seoul.) In the 1950s, the economy remained primarily agricultural-based. Most Korean factories and industrial facilities had been destroyed during the war, and GNP per capita was low. Beginning under the Park regime in 1960, South Korea's economy strengthened, and the country gradually transformed from a developing country into a developed one. Tremendous effort went into South Korea's economic development strategies. Because of the country's small domestic market and limited natural resources, the leaders decided to pursue export-oriented industrialization and to begin with labour-intensive light industry, specifically the textile, lumber and footwear sectors. Between 1962 and 1971, annual growth averaged 8.8 percent. By the end of the 1960s, South Korea had created a stable economic foundation for itself and was able to move away from reliance on foreign aid.

During the 1960s, South Korea developed its own version of the capitalist development state model. The South Korean government focussed on national prosperity, particularly on rapid economic growth, industrialization, support for large business and the development of national infrastructure. The Park government worked closely with South Korean companies, using persuasion and coercion to encourage them to move in the government's preferred direction, resulting in close relationships between government and business. The government implemented five-year plans that focused, like Japan before it, on export-led industrialization. Initially, South Korea focussed on expanding its agricultural production, embarking on a program of energy diversification and developing basic industries like iron and steel and chemical fertilizers. In the 1970s, the country expanded into new industries, including clothing, cars and car parts and electronics. The country's exports grew from 4 percent of GDP in 1961 to over 40 percent in 2016; average per capita income grew from $120 to $27,000 over the half century. In 2018, South Korea had the 33rd highest GDP per capita in the world, according to the World Bank—$39,600, less than $2,000 a year behind Japan.

The chaebol and the South Korean economy

Chaebol are privately owned South Korean industrial groups controlled, in most cases, by the founding family. The member companies are connected through a system of interlocking share holdings. With firms across a range of sectors, chaebol are similar in structure to the Japanese pre-war zaibatsu. In fact, chaebol and zaibatsu are the Korean and Japanese readings of the same Chinese characters, which translate into English as "financial clique." Some of the largest chaebol include Samsung, Daewoo (which went bankrupt in 1999), LG, SK Group, Hyundai and Lotte.

During the Japanese Occupation, few Koreans owned any large companies. When the Japanese withdrew, Korean entrepreneurs obtained the assets of their firms, several of which grew into the chaebol. As part of rebuilding the economy, the government used some of

114   *The Korean Peninsula*

the international aid provided to South Korea after the war to give loans and other forms of financial assistance to the chaebol. These actions proved crucial in highly capitalized sectors like shipbuilding, construction and steel. In the late 1960s and the 1970s, efforts to move the economy towards heavier industries and export-led growth needed the cooperation of the chaebol. Over the decades, the chaebol moved into other industrial sectors and expanded into more foreign markets. In fact, the chaebol led South Korea into the global marketplace.

Although chaebol-led industrialization was a success, it resulted in the concentration of capital and economic activities in a small number of hands. The chaebol became enormous commercial empires that spanned a large range of industries and sectors and crossed all stages of production. Sales of the top 10 chaebol are equal to three-quarters of South Korea's GDP. Engaged in more than two-thirds of the business categories in South Korea, the chaebol are responsible for 12 percent of South Korean employment and 77 percent of the market capitalization of South Korean firms (Albert, 2018).

The most profitable and successful chaebol is Samsung, which alone has been responsible for as high as 20 percent of the country's GDP. Sometimes called "The Republic of Samsung," the company began by exporting foodstuffs and now has more than 80 subsidiaries in sectors as diverse as insurance, shipping and luxury hotels. The largest and most famous subsidiary is Samsung Electronics, one of the world's main manufacturers of consumer electronics (televisions, mobile phones, tablet computers, flash memory devices), lithium-ion batteries and semiconductors. Although Samsung is the most successful chaebol, Lotte may be the most ubiquitous, with firms in retail, tourism, petrochemicals, construction and finance. As Daniel Tudor, author of *Korea: The Impossible Country*, writes, South Koreans "can buy Lotte chocolate bars, enjoy a film at a Lotte cinema, shop at a Lotte Mart, pay with one of the group's credit cards and return home to a Lotte flat protected by Lotte insurance. Even outside its amusement parks, South Koreans can live in a Lotte world" ("Corporate Armistice," 2013).

Unsurprisingly, this level of corporate dominance has negative consequences. Dominance allows firms to stifle competition, squeezing small- and medium-sized companies out of the market. Chaebol have been accused of waiting for an innovative new firm to prove itself, then offering to buy it out for a low price. If the firm refuses, the chaebol drives it out of business. This kind of chaebol behaviour has a chilling effect on budding entrepreneurs. As the preponderance of power rests with the chaebol, it is difficult to be a chaebol investor (unless you are one of the insiders), supplier or competitor. The chaebol also dominate the market for top talent as most young South Koreans want to work for one. In 2010, representatives of the chaebol and numerous small firms formed a National Commission for Corporate Partnership. The Commission reached an agreement to limit the presence of the chaebol in approximately 100 sectors of the economy, including restaurants and bicycles.

Traditionally, the relationship between the chaebol and the government has been close, but critics point out that this close-knit relationship has created a culture of corruption. Incidents of price-fixing, collusion, embezzlement, bribery and tax evasion are commonplace, and the public is becoming increasingly angry about the advantages given to the chaebol by government, often in return for money. As the chaebol began to move more of their manufacturing overseas and as South Korea's economy has slowed, the anger has grown. Over the past 10 years, senior executives from Samsung, Hyundai, Lotte and SK have been found guilty of corruption, fraud or tax evasion. Three chaebol chairmen have received presidential pardons following their convictions; others paid fines or received suspended sentences. Former President Lee Myung-bak was arrested on charges of bribery (one charge was for accepting $5.4 million in return for pardoning Samsung executives, including the chairman), embezzlement and tax evasion in March 2018 and was sentenced to 15 years in prison. His successor,

Park Geun-hye, was impeached, fined $17 million for taking bribes from the chaebol and sentenced to 24 years in prison.

South Koreans regularly discuss reforming the chaebol. Some changes to corporate management and ownership structures have been made, and President Moon Jae-in has promised to break the close ties between government and the chaebol. His ability to usher reforms through the National Assembly, however, depends on support from members of other parties, some of whom have personal chaebol connections. Changing the chaebol system will not be easy unless the culture that ties the chaebol and their stakeholders together changes first.

Beginning in the 1980s, South Korea developed a successful heavy industry export economy. The country became a major producer of cars, steel, semiconductors and electronics. South Korean companies like Hyundai Heavy Industries, Samsung Heavy Industries and Daewoo Shipbuilding and Marine Engineering became some of the leading producers of ships, including supertankers, container ships and oil drilling platforms. In 2008, Korea had a full 50 percent share of the shipbuilding market. However, 10 years later, it had lost much of that market share to Chinese firms. In 2018, President Moon committed to supporting the industry by ordering icebreakers and patrol vessels. South Korean manufacturers have also moved into high technology in fields like new materials, aerospace and industrial robots. South Korea has also been successful in the digital content field, particularly in video games, building on the international fascination with Korean popular culture (see Chapter 8 for more details).

Republic of Korea Armed Forces

In 1953, shortly after the signing of the Korean Armistice Agreement, South Korea and the United States signed a Mutual Defense Treaty. The two countries agreed to come to each other's aid if either were attacked. The treaty also stipulated that the United States has permission for stationing military forces in South Korea, subject to South Korea's agreement. In 1978, the United States and South Korea Combined Forces Command was created. The CFC was headed by a U.S. military officer who answered to the United States, as well as to South Korean national authorities. All South Korean forces did not come under the control of the South Korean government until 1994.

Since the signing of the treaty in 1953, the United States has had a sizeable military presence in South Korea. In 2019, approximately 28,500 American ground, air, naval, marine and special operations forces were based in South Korea at 15 bases around the country, much lower numbers both of personnel and bases than in the past. Arrangements for the bases have been renegotiated frequently. In 2019, South Korea paid $923 million of the approximately $1.5 billion cost of hosting the U.S. troops. However, in late 2019, President Trump demanded that Seoul quintuple its contribution to $4.7 billion in 2020. This increase could have serious repercussions, as some in South Korea have suggested that, in exchange for increased defence funding, it be permitted to develop its own nuclear weapons. This would have negative implications for the attempts to denuclearize North Korea and could encourage Japan to develop its own nuclear weapons. The Americans decreased their demand after South Korea agreed to purchase more U.S. weapons and expand its efforts to protect oil shipments in the Strait of Hormuz.

The South Korean government and general public have an ambivalent view of the United States' presence in their country. Some Koreans derive comfort from the presence of the American military, believing they are a deterrent to North Korea. However, the Americans are not universally embraced: the role of the United States in supporting the Chun government during the Kwangju massacre disturbed many South Koreans. Led

116 *The Korean Peninsula*

by university students, thousands of South Koreans have taken to the streets on multiple occasions to protest the U.S. military presence. They argue that in its fight against communism, the United States has suppressed democracy in many places around the world. Despite this ambivalence, a January 2019 Asian Institute for Policy Studies and Council on Foreign Relations survey of South Korean attitudes towards U.S. Forces in Korea showed that the majority in every age cohort believe that U.S. Forces is a good partner that helps ensure South Korean security ("South Korean Attitudes," 2019). Most analysts agree and believe that the U.S.-South Korean alliance is of benefit beyond the peninsula, ensuring peace throughout Northeast Asia.

South Korea lives a precarious existence. North Korea, a rogue and hostile state, lies on its northern border. South Korea's next closest neighbour is China with its military strength and commercial aggressiveness. Buttressed by the United States, which uses the country as a key East Asia base, South Korea has the world's seventh largest army, with 599,000 active military personnel and 3.1 million reservists. South Korea spends 2.6 percent of its GDP on its military and has the 10th largest military budget ($43 billion in 2019) in the world. Although South Korean troops participate in peacekeeping and humanitarian missions, concerns over North Korea understandably contribute to this intense military commitment.

Starting in 1957, South Korea implemented conscription for men over 18. Conscripts must perform approximately two years (depending on the branch of the military) of military service, although the Moon government has promised to decrease this to 18 months, still one of the world's longest periods of military conscription. Conscription is rigorously enforced and military training is tough. Although women may enlist voluntarily, they are not required to do so. Few South Korean men want to enter the army. Over the past decades, there has been increased debate about mandatory military service, the rights of conscientious objectors and exemptions granted to star athletes. Those who support conscription argue that mandatory military service protects the country, particularly in the context of North Korea. They also claim that it supports national identity by building connections and national pride, that military service changes boys into men, preparing them for South Korea's intense work culture. Critics argue that compulsory military service is outdated and ineffective and that it hinders change in national attitudes towards diversity, inclusion and gender equality. They also have serious reservations about the intense training methods and the nature of exemptions. Other countries with conscription allow exemptions for conscientious objectors, but, to date, South Korea has not done so. The granting of exemptions seems unfair: star athletes and classical musicians and artists have been granted exemptions, whereas K-pop musicians have not.

Political structure, parties and behaviour

South Korea is, in international terms, an ancient civilization and a young country, created out of what was, confusingly, a post–World War II civil war fomented by superpowers looking for strategic advantage in East Asia. The country's political system reflects this complicated origin story, the ideological tensions of East Asia and the interventions of external powers, particularly the United States. But in its flexibility, competitiveness and aggressiveness, it is a made-in-South Korea political system.

The government

South Korea is a unitary state. Administratively, it is divided into nine provinces and eight first-level cities, the latter with powers equal to those of a province. Each of these provinces and cities has a local assembly, but they have limited policy-making ability. The chief executive of each district is elected locally, but his or her deputy is appointed by the national government.

Head of state and head of government

In the Republic of Korea, the president is the head of state and head of government. The president resides in the Blue House, the official residence, which also houses the executive offices (see Figure 4.3). The current president is Moon Jae-in is, who was elected in 2017 in a special election called after Park Geun-hye, his predecessor, was impeached and removed from office on charges of abuse of power, bribery and coercion. The daughter of former authoritarian President Park Chung-hee, Park Geun-hye was the first female South Korean president. In 2018, she was sentenced to 24 years in prison.

Representing the centre-left Democratic Party, Moon Jae-in ran as its candidate (then called the Democratic United Party) for president against Park Geun-hye in 2012 and served in the National Assembly from 2012 to 2016. He was a student activist and was arrested and imprisoned in the 1970s after protesting the Yusin Constitution. Moon became a human rights lawyer and later from 2003 to 2008 served as chief of staff to the former president Roh Moo-hyun. Moon promised a transparent government, reform of the chaebol, a hike in the minimum wage and a move away from coal and nuclear energy. He also strongly supported more peaceful interactions with North Korea.

Constitution

South Korea's first Constitution was promulgated in July 1948. Since then the Constitution has been revised five times, an extraordinarily high number for a modern democracy. Each revision signalled the beginning of a new republic. In October 1987, after the pro-democracy protests that occurred in June of that year, South Korea's Constitution was amended to take effect on February 25, 1988. The Constitution has 130 articles, which define the rights and

Figure 4.3 Reception Center at Cheongwadae or "Blue House", the South Korean presidential residence in Seoul South Korea.

118   *The Korean Peninsula*

duties of citizens, followed by sections on the national assembly, the executive, the courts, election management, local government and the economy. The first article declares South Korea to be a democratic republic.

Legislature

South Korea's National Assembly, the *Gukhwe*, is a unicameral (one level of government) 300-member assembly. Members are elected for four-year terms.

Electoral system

The National Assembly is elected through a mixed electoral system. A large majority, 246 members, are elected through a first-past-the-post system in single member districts, while 54 members are elected through proportional representation. The South Korean president is directly elected and serves one five-year term. Each voter (over 19 years old) in a national election votes for a presidential candidate, a political party (represented as a list of preferred party candidates) and a local candidate.

Election campaigns

South Korean election campaigns are, like those in Japan, comparatively short: 14 days for National Assembly elections and 23 days for presidential elections. Making the campaign time frames short was an attempt to lower campaign spending and prevent over excitement, but the short time frame makes it difficult for new candidates to become known. Television advertising is permitted but with tight limits on how much a party can spend. The voting age in South Korea is 18.

Political parties

Over the past decades, South Korean political parties have been changing names and merging, making politics hard to follow. Between 2016 and 2019, for example, all the main parties changed their names. The names change so rapidly that it is not worthwhile including a description of the values and program priorities of each party.

In the 2020 legislative elections, President Moon Jae-in's Democratic Party witnessed a major victory securing 163 seats, 180 seats when the seats of its satellite party, the Platform Party, are included, of the 300 seats. The United Futures Party won 103 seats.

Mass mobilization—popular protest

Popular protests have been a major part of South Korean politics since before democracy. In fact, enormous pro-democracy protests were a significant feature of South Korean life in the 1980s. Mobilization—in which hundreds to hundreds of thousands of people gather— is a common way South Koreans engage politically. A 2009 study of popular protests by Sunhyuk Kim reported that Korea recorded an average of 372 protests a year and that most of these targeted the government. According to Jennifer Oh of Ewha Women's University in Seoul, "During the candlelight vigils that occurred during the 2000s, hundreds of thousands, even a million protestors gathered to protest government action and policies. The candlelight vigils were a powerful demonstration of public opposition and dissatisfaction with government decisions and policies" (Oh, 2012).

South Korean society

South Korean society is based on Confucian values. As in other societies rooted in Confucianism, good behaviour is that which benefits the group, not the individual. For Koreans, good behaviour means following the rules, working or studying hard and living modestly. Also important in Korean society is harmony, as is the concept of *kibun*, meaning face. To maintain harmony, Koreans make an effort to avoid conflict and, as in other Confucian societies, order and hierarchy are valued as means of maintaining harmonious relations. In Korea, it is important to know where a person ranks on the hierarchy—in other words, the person's status, which is typically based on age, occupation, level of education and gender. Those who are younger are expected to respect and obey their seniors. In return, seniors must guide, protect and look after their subordinates. The importance of status is evident in the workplace, where employees are expected to treat their supervisor and senior employees with the utmost respect.

Gender roles and work

The Confucian positioning of men above women has created a sexist and gender-bound society. Even though South Korean women are well educated, they face rampant discrimination in hiring and at work. Most men assume that women will leave the workplace when they marry and that, if they do keep working, their wives' commitment to their work will be less than their own. These views are shared by employers, most of whom are unwilling to hire or continue to employ a woman with a child, doubting that she would make a full commitment to her job. As a result, women are poorly treated at work with few opportunities for advancement. Additionally, working hours are extremely long (approximately 18 percent above the OECD average) at South Korean companies (Ock, 2015; "A pram too far," 2013), so a working mother would find it very challenging to fulfil a company's expectations and be able to look after her child.[1] At home, South Korean women do almost all of the housework and childcare. South Korea ranks lowest among OECD countries for the amount of time their men spend caring for children (Hong, 2020; Brunhuber, 2018).

In a self-fulfilling prophecy, many women do leave the workforce in their 30s, marry and raise children, although they sometimes return in their mid-40s to less corporate jobs. Recently, however, more women have been forgoing marriage and concentrating on their careers. According to Statistics Korea, in 2017 only 47.5 percent of women surveyed agreed with the statement "marriage is a must." This view may be largely due to the attitudes of Korean men, many of whom are still very traditional, particularly if their mothers were. In other words, there may "not [be] enough modern men for newly educated women to marry" ("Women in South Korea," 2013). As single women almost never have children in South Korea, a declining marriage rate guarantees a declining birth rate. In 2018, South Korea's fertility rate fell to 0.98, the lowest in the developed world. South Korean women have been speaking out and arguing for change on issues ranging from beauty standards to changing

120   *The Korean Peninsula*

South Korea's national assembly, which many would like to see 50 percent female. South Korea's #MeToo movement has exploded. Thousands of Koreans have marched in protest, and numerous prominent men have been forced to apologize for sexual misconduct. Some have been prosecuted.

Textbox 4.2 Korean names

Most Koreans have three characters in their names: two in their given names and one in their surname. When written in Chinese or Korean, the surname always comes first. There are about 285 family names in use in South Korea, but most Koreans use only half a dozen surnames. About 22 percent of the population uses the last name Kim, about 15 percent uses Lee or Yi and about 9 percent Park or Pak. In other words, 45 percent of the population has one of three last names. This is the case because for centuries, surnames were only granted to royalty and a few members of the aristocratic (yangban) class. Kim and Lee were among the names used by the royalty. Since it was not until 1894 that those at the very bottom of society were allowed to adopt a surname, many took a popular name or the name of their master.

Concerns about North Korea

Anxiety about North Korea has been a continual part of South Korean life, occupying the minds of both public officials and private citizens. The division of the peninsula left families unable to visit or communicate with other family members (see Family Reunions on p. x). The threat of a military invasion from the north has been a constant background worry, leading South Korea to spend large sums of money on its military, and there are understandably particular concerns about Pyongyang's nuclear weapons program.

Education and career prospects

"The fundamental problem of child-rearing in South Korea is too few children, too much rearing" ("Women in South Korea," 2013).

South Koreans have a passion for education. Linked to socio-economic success, status and the desire for social mobility, societal emphasis on education dates back more than 1,000 years when the South Korean civil service exam began in 958. Only legitimate members of the *yangban* class (those who could prove their lineage on both their paternal and maternal sides) were permitted to write the exam. Becoming a civil servant guaranteed a good life, a stable income and respect from all, and to reach this goal, education was the key. A thousand years later, education is still revered as the means to a prestigious, well-paid career in the government, bank or chaebol companies. To this end, South Korean children are expected to study extremely hard and for long hours, with the goal of doing well on the national College Scholastic Ability Test and gaining entry to one of South Korea's three most prestigious universities: Seoul National University, Korea University and Yonsei University. To boost their children's test scores, families spend about 20 percent of their income on tutoring at cram schools called *hagwon*, and mothers devote their lives to navigating the educational journey of their children. The huge amounts of time and money devoted to a child's education are daunting for prospective parents, so many young couples will not even think about having children until or unless they have sufficient income to help them become successful. Under these conditions, it is little wonder that South Korea has an extremely low birth rate. As a result, South Korea suffers "from a shortage of happy mediocrities, countercultural rebels, slackers, dropouts and eccentrics. These people, in effect, remain unborn" ("Snake Heads," 2013).

The focus on education boomed in the post-Korean War period. Competition escalated to such an extent that the government began to take steps to curb it. In 1971, middle school entrance exams were cancelled, but that shifted the focus to high school entrance exams. The government later replaced the high school exams with a lottery, leaving all the competition for the university entrance exams. More recently, Seoul placed a 10 p.m. curfew on the *hakwon*, but students have circumvented this by continuing to study online. A key element of the university entrance exams is English, which therefore plays an important role in exam preparation. The emphasis on learning English is so strong that some families move their children, with or without their mothers, to English speaking countries in an effort to improve their English abilities.

This complete commitment to education bears results. South Korea is one of the most educated countries in the world, with 70 percent of 24- to 35-year-olds having finished post-secondary education. In a key international test (Trends in International Math and Science Study) conducted every four years, South Korean students finish near the top. In 2016, South Korea placed third after Singapore and Hong Kong and slightly above Taiwan and Japan. However, there is a cost to this ultracompetitive education system. OECD studies show South Korean children and adolescents to be among the least happy in the developed world. They rank at or near the bottom of the 22 surveyed countries for life satisfaction. Students cite academic stress, a lack of leisure time, sleep deprivation and long hours spent studying as reasons for their dissatisfaction with their lives.

South Korean children and adolescents spend 14 hours a day studying. Young South Koreans are very concerned about their futures as there is intense competition for good jobs, especially those with the government or a chaebol. This competition and anxiety about the future has placed enormous pressure on this generation, sometimes referred to as the three-renunciation generation because its members do not have the time or money for dating, marriage or children. The renunciations are sometimes increased to five, to include housing and skill building, or seven, adding hobbies and hope. The goal of all this hard work is a good job (better paying and more prestigious) in the government, a bank or one of the chaebol companies.

Religion

Buddhism had an early influence on Korean culture and remains the most significant religion in South Korea. About half of South Koreans practise a religion, and almost half of those practising are Buddhists. Korea also has a sizeable Christian population—11 percent of the population is Catholic, and 18 percent is Protestant. Confucianism, with its emphasis on the harmony of the group, the importance of education and respect for ancestors, continues to have a big impact on Korean society (see Figure 4.4).

Figure 4.4 Jogyesa Buddhist temple, Seoul.

Textbox 4.3 Asian financial crisis

Between June 1997 and January 1998, a financial crisis swept through Asia. While in retrospect signs of looming problems were evident, at the time it came as a big shock. There were some differences in the causes, responses and impact of the Asian financial crisis on the main countries it affected: Thailand, Malaysia, Indonesia and South Korea. All, however, had been economic powerhouses in the previous decade (South Korea's growth rate averaged about 12 percent between 1990 and 1996), fuelled by inexpensive and educated workforces producing increasingly higher-value exports. These conditions sparked an investment boom, both foreign and domestic, in commercial and residential property, and in industry and infrastructure, leading eventually to a significant amount of excess capacity. In addition, some of the investments were quite dubious. Excess capacity led to falling prices and companies suddenly had huge debts they could not service.

The roots of the 1997–1998 financial crisis in South Korea were the macroeconomic conditions that had deteriorated in 1995–1996, as well as the accumulation of short-term foreign debt. Demand for semiconductors, a major South Korean export at the time, had fallen. Export growth had declined, causing a decrease in industrial production. Because Korean banks had borrowed extensively from overseas and had funded questionable loans to the chaebol for a number of years, many of the biggest South

Korean companies were heavily overextended. When the economy slowed, companies were unable to pay their debts and/or obtain new loans. Eight major chaebol companies, including Hanbo Steel and Kia Motors, suddenly went bankrupt. In November 1977, the value of the Korean won fell, worsening the situation for banks as much of the short-term borrowing had been in U.S. dollars.

To ameliorate the situation, the South Korean government applied for a financial bailout from the International Monetary Fund (IMF), which provided a $57 billion bailout. But difficult conditions were attached: Korea was required to increase taxes, cut public spending, raise interest rates, admit foreign banks and privatize some state-owned businesses. South Koreans resented the IMF's terms and were embarrassed about asking the IMF for help, so much so that the day the agreement was signed with the IMF (December 3, 1997) was named National Humiliation Day. (The same name had been given to the first day of the Japanese occupation of the peninsula in 1910.) In the wake of the agreement, unemployment tripled as corporate restructuring led to large-scale layoffs. South Koreans remained angry at the IMF both because of its imperious attitude and a sense of injustice that irresponsible international lenders who had made the risky loans were not forced to bear any responsibility.

The country's response to the humiliation was quite remarkable. In January 1998, the Korean Broadcasting System (the country's national broadcaster) in conjunction with a number of banks launched a gold gathering campaign that ran for four months. Citizens were encouraged to collect any gold they might have in their homes and donate it to collection centres. The gold would be exchanged for money to pay off the IMF loan. Millions of South Koreans donated 227 tons of gold valued at over $2 billion.

Challenges facing South Korea

Like all East Asian countries, South Korea is facing a series of significant social and economic challenges, many shared with neighbouring nations.

Demographics

South Korean society is rapidly ageing. While 10 percent of the population was over the age of 65 in 2008 and 15.5 percent in 2019, predictions are that this will reach more than 20 percent in 2026 and to 30 percent in 2041 ("Aging Population," 2020). Caring for the elderly is likely to be a significant challenge as only one-third of the older population currently receives a pension. At present, only about 25 percent of people over 70 live with their children. South Korea has the lowest birth rate in the developed world, falling to 0.98 in 2018. (To put how low this is in perspective, Japan, also concerned about its low birth rate, had a rate of 1.42.) Because it is so expensive to raise a child, many women have intentionally decided not to have a child until economic and social conditions are more favourable. Their actions are often referred to as a "baby strike."

Since 2005, the South Korean government has spent $120 billion on campaigns to encourage couples to have more children, but the continuing low birth rate indicates that these initiatives have not been successful. Critics argue that the reason these campaigns fail is that

124 *The Korean Peninsula*

they reward couples with more than one child rather than making it easier for women to have their first child. In 2018, benefits were added, including monthly child subsidies and the right to work an hour less a day for parents with children under eight. Additionally, optional paternity leave has now been increased to 10 days from 3. Undermining this increase, however, is the lack of consequences for employers who choose not to offer their workers the benefits. Until South Korean societal attitudes and realities change, it is unlikely that these state policies will affect the birth rate.

A rapidly ageing population and an extremely low birth rate mean that South Korea's population is projected to flatten around 2023 at approximately 52.6 million people and then begin to decline. As a result of this projection, South Korea has begun to look more closely at immigration. Traditionally, nearly all Koreans prided themselves on their pure blood and saw themselves as part of a distinct culture with a shared bloodline. Textbooks and national imagery have reinforced this belief. The obsession with *minjok*, meaning race nation or ethnic group, grew in response to the years of attempted assimilation under the Japanese occupation. At the end of Japanese rule, academics and activists continued to write about *minjok* and to build national pride by emphasizing the unique racial and cultural heritage of Koreans.

As a result of these beliefs, immigration to South Korea has been limited. Some foreign women have been sent to South Korea through international marriage brokers to become wives for farmers. Over the past few decades, most of the foreign workers from China and South and Southeast Asia have come to South Korea primarily to do the dirty or dangerous jobs South Koreans avoid. In the mid-2000s, South Korea signed agreements with some Southeast and Central Asian countries to allow their citizens to apply for time-limited work visas for low-skilled jobs. As a result, the number of foreigners living in South Korea doubled from 1.2 million in 2009 to 2.4 million in 2018. Also gradually increasing is the number of naturalized South Koreans. Since 2013, over 10,000 people annually have become naturalized South Koreans. (To put this number in perspective, since 1948, only 190,000 people have become naturalized South Koreans.) The first foreign-born South Korean to win a seat in the National Assembly was Jasmine Lee, in office from 2012 to 2016. Originally from the Philippines, Ms. Lee married a South Korean man she met at university in Davao City and became a popular actress and television personality in South Korea. However, when she won her seat in the National Assembly (she was on the Saenuri Party's proportional representation list so was not voted for directly), she received a strongly negative reaction because she was not ethnically Korean. Jasmine Lee was excluded from the Saenuri's Party list in the 2016 election.

Most of the recent naturalizations have come through marriage. Over 10 percent of all marriages are now international, with the majority of mixed marriages between a South Korean man and a foreign woman. Those marrying foreign brides tend to be poorer South Korean men from rural areas. Having been brokered by a third party, many of these marriages are between two people who have not met before the wedding. The largest number of foreign wives comes from China (including women from the 5 million ethnically Korean Chinese). Others come from Vietnam, the Philippines, Japan, Taiwan, Mongolia, Uzbekistan and a number of other countries. These non-Korean wives are often poorly treated; the victims of prejudice, discrimination and abuse; and their mixed-race children bullied. Although the government was unprepared for the big increase in mixed families, it is now offering support to these mixed couples and encouraging public acceptance of multicultural families through poster campaigns and children's books featuring mixed-race families.

Frustration with the elite

Immediately prior to the impeachment of former President Park Geun-hye, hundreds of thousands of South Koreans took to the streets to protest against her continued occupancy of the presidency. As many as a million people attended one of these marches in Seoul. The scandal revolved around the accusation (later proved in court) that Park had shared government secrets with her friend and spiritual advisor Choi Soon-sil. With Choi, Park was accused and later convicted of bribery, extortion and abuse of power for collecting millions of dollars in bribes from big companies. Park is not the only South Korean president to be jailed. Park's predecessor Lee Myung-bak was sentenced to 15 years for bribery, embezzlement and abuse of power. Two former presidents were imprisoned for the Kwangju massacre, although they were later pardoned, and another previous president was investigated for corruption.

The Park scandal, however, hit a particular nerve with the South Korean public. Park had seemed to govern from on high, remaining distant from voters. As in other parts of the world, South Korean frustration had been mounting, centred on the belief that the system is designed to benefit the elite—those with connections and money—while the average South Korean struggles. Choi is said to have used some of the funds extorted from the companies to pay for horseback riding lessons for her daughter. She then convinced the prestigious Ewha Womans University to add dressage to the special criteria for admission in order to help her daughter get a place. Merit-based university admission is important to South Koreans, as it is a route through which people from less-privileged backgrounds can advance and families make enormous sacrifices to give their children a chance for success. This scandal therefore infuriated South Koreans.

Growing inequality

Inequality is becoming an increasingly significant issue in South Korea. The top 10 percent of South Koreans hold about two-thirds of the country's wealth, while the bottom half of the population holds only 2 percent of the wealth. Lack of social mobility—of a chance for the poor to better themselves economically—entrenches inequality. As they have been for years, career opportunities are often still tied to a person's family background and/or connections. In the last decade, people have grown bitter and frustration has exploded, seen in the new slang phrases referring to those who have made it as "gold spoons" and those who have not as "dirt spoons." This theme of the haves versus the have-nots has been embraced in recent Korean films. The 2019 film *Parasite* follows the destitute Kim family as it tries to improve its lot in life by taking advantage of the wealthy Park family. *Parasite* won four awards at the 92nd Academy Awards, including the Best Picture award.

Conclusion

In a few decades, South Korea rose from being one of the poorest countries in the world to the 11th largest economy. Through the "miracle on the Han River," GDP growth continues

126   *The Korean Peninsula*

at approximately 3 percent annually. Unemployment is low, although, as in much of the world, part-time and more precarious employment has increased, and there is stiff competition for well-paid careers. South Korea remains a manufacturing powerhouse, producing cars, chemicals, ships and steel, and spends 4.6 percent of its GDP on research and development, the highest percentage in the world. This investment has clearly produced dividends, as over one-third of South Korea's manufacturing exports are high-technology products, especially in electronics and telecommunications. Trade also continues to increase. In recent years, South Korea has signed 15 free trade agreements, including with the United States, China and the European Union. These agreements will loosen the chaebol's grip on the South Korean economy.

Since the 1990s, South Korean culture has become popular internationally, particularly within Asia. Dubbed Hallyu or the Korean wave, first South Korean television dramas and then Korean pop music (K-pop), movies and fashion inundated Asia and spread globally. Recording artist Psy's 2012 hit *Gangnam Style*, which parodies the lifestyles of the wealthy people who live in the Gangnam neighbourhood in Seoul, was a global sensation. The South Korean government has committed to supporting its cultural industries and has begun to use the Korean Wave as a form of soft power.

South Korea's strengths were revealed in the country's response to the COVID-19 pandemic in 2020. The size and efficiency of South Korea's testing, tracing and quarantine system—it was the first country to launch drive-through testing facilities—earned the country international praise and was credited with rapidly limiting the number of new cases appearing each day. All this was done without shutting down the South Korean economy or creating mass buying of staples like toilet paper, as was seen in other countries. Despite fractious politics (in the middle of the pandemic the Korean Medical Association was demanding that the government dismiss the health and welfare minister and the presidential advisory panel), the South Korean leadership was quick to act and to act competently, inspiring trust from the general public.

Introduction to North Korea

North Korea occupies the northern part of the Korean Peninsula, bordering China and Russia to the north. As the country is mountainous, the majority of the population of 25 million lives in the southern coastal plains. Over 3 million people live in the capital city Pyongyang, which is situated on the Taedong river just over 100 km from the river's mouth on the Yellow Sea (the name for the northern part of the East China Sea). North Korea's government is based in Pyongyang; the city is also the industrial centre of North Korea.

At the end of World War II and the Japanese occupation of the Korean Peninsula, Korea was divided into two zones. The north was occupied by the Soviet Union under the Soviet Civil Administration from October 3, 1945, until the Democratic People's Republic of Korea (DPRK) was established in 1948. The Soviet Union had entered the war only eight days before Japan surrendered, but this last-minute engagement left them in the position to be one of the occupying armies. Highly suspicious of the West's intentions, the Soviet Union intended to create a buffer zone between itself and the West, so it embraced the opportunity to make the region north of the 38th parallel a separate political entity. When in 1948 United Nations representatives arrived on the peninsula to oversee democratic elections, the Soviet Union did not admit them and selected Kim Il-sung to be the leader of the Democratic People's Republic of Korea (see Textbox 4.4).

Textbox 4.4 The Supreme Leaders of North Korea

Kim Il-sung (1912–1994)

Many of the details of Kim Il-sung's life remain unclear as the truth has been embellished by the personality cult that developed around him (see Figure 4.5). It is known that he was born near Pyongyang under the birth name of Kim Song-ju and moved to Manchuria, perhaps because his parents were active in the anti-Japanese resistance. In China, he became a member of the Communist youth league and later of the Communist Party itself. Active in the Korean guerrilla resistance against the Japanese occupation, he took the name of a famous guerrilla fighter. In World War II, Kim crossed from Manchuria into Russia and joined the Soviet Red Army, fighting as the commander of one of two Korean units. According to mythology, Kim is said to have fought from secret bases around Mount Paektu, a revered mountain believed to be the birthplace of the Korean people. However, although he was a guerrilla fighter, Kim actually fought in Manchuria not on Mount Paektu. When Japan was defeated, Kim was with an army unit in the Russian Far East and did not take part in the liberation of the Korean Peninsula in 1945. Although Kim did not enter Korea until a month after the Japanese were defeated, North Korean books praise his role in the defeat, giving only some of the credit for the defeat of the Japanese to the Soviets. On July 8, 1994, Kim Il-sung died suddenly of a heart attack.

Figure 4.5 Official North Korean portrait of Kim Il-sung (posthumous).

Kim Jong-il

Kim Jong-il succeeded his father as Supreme Leader of North Korea (see Figure 4.6). Records show that he was born in a Russian military camp in the Russian Far East. His official biography, however, has him born on sacred Mount Paektu and maintains that a shining star allegedly appeared in the sky on the night of his birth. In 1980, he had been named the successor to his father and began being groomed for the role. Upon his father's death, he was given the title Dear Leader, and the government began to build a personality cult around him. Kim Jong-il had a special passion for film, theatre and art. To improve the North Korean film industry, he kidnapped a South Korean actress and her film producer/ex-husband in 1978. After making many films, the two escaped in 1986. Kim Jong-il ruled North Korea until his death in 2011.

Figure 4.6 Official North Korean portrait of Kim Jong-il (posthumous).

Kim Jong-un

The third son of Kim Jong-il and the grandson of Kim Il-sung, Kim Jong-un became the Supreme Leader of North Korea in 2011 and Chairman of the Workers' Party of Korea the following year. In his youth, he attended a private school in Switzerland. One of his early acts as Supreme Leader was to have his uncle Jang Song-thaek arrested and executed for treachery. He is also suspected of having arranged the murder of his older half-brother Kim Jong-nam in Malaysia in 2017.

In 2019, as negotiators for the United States failed to reach an agreement with North Korea over its nuclear program, Kim Jong-un began preparing the North Korean citizenry for potential hard times ahead. To do so, his underlings circulated images of Kim Jon-un astride a white horse on Mount Paektu, a reminder of his sacred roots. The commentary that accompanies the image emphasizes how Kim Jong-un's grandfather conquered enemies on the battlefield, just as his grandson will do in battle against the Americans and their sanctions.

The Post-war transformation of North Korea

Once the Soviets had chosen Kim Il-sung as leader, they helped create his credentials and build the base for the mythology that now surrounds him, his son and grandson. On September 9, 1948, with the backing of the Soviets, Kim Il-sung was declared premier of the Democratic People's Republic of Korea. In 1950, with the goal of unifying the Korean Peninsula and with the reluctant backing of the Soviet Union and China, Kim led an invasion into the South. The Kim regime, however, tells its citizens that North Korea was attacked by the United States and its South Korean "puppet" government.

After the conclusion of the Korean War, Kim transformed North Korea into a highly controlled totalitarian state. Kim introduced the Juche ideology of self-reliance, focussing domestic policies on militarization and industrialization. His exploits as a guerrilla fighter against the Japanese were extolled and formed the basis of the cult of personality that surrounded him. As early as 1949, statues were being built of him, and Kim Il-sung had started referring to himself as the *Great Leader*. There are now over 500 statues of Kim Il-sung in North Korea, and his birthday is still celebrated as a national holiday, known as the Day of the Sun. Portraits of him and of his son and grandson hang in every home, and all citizens are expected to wear patriotic pins on their chests. During his rule, children were taught that it was because of Kim Il-sung that they had food and were clothed. The preamble of the North Korean Constitution concludes by stating that Kim Il-sung and his son and successor Kim Jong-il are eternal leaders of North Korea and the Constitution would now be the Kim Il-sung Kim Jong-il Constitution as it is based on their ideas and achievements.

After the Korean War (see pp. 106–7), the North Korean leaders established a Communist single-party state with a planned economy. Industries were nationalized and farms collectivized. At the time of the division, the North had a significant economic head start over the South as the majority of industrial development under the Japanese had been in the North. As it began to rebuild its economy, North Korea focussed on heavy industry. With financial and technical aid from the Soviet Union and China, North Korea invested in iron and steel, cement and machine tools.

North Korea became a political dictatorship run by an extremely repressive government, with a unicameral legislature known as the Supreme People's Assembly (SPA). One person from each of the country's 687 constituencies is "elected" to a five-year term. According to its Constitution, North Korea is a democratic republic: the SPA's representatives are directly elected by all North Koreans aged 17 and over. However, in reality, the elections are in name only, as one candidate runs in each riding. To be elected, the candidate must be a member of the Democratic Front for the Reunification of the Fatherland, in which there are three political parties: Workers' Party of North Korea, the Korean Social Democratic Party and the Chondoist Chongu Party. The Workers' Party of North Korea is led by a member of the ruling family and is recognized by the Constitution as the main state party. The Workers' Party of North Korea is the ruling political party of North Korea, and the other two parties are minor and subservient to it. Seven mass organizations (e.g. the Korean Children's Union, the Kimilsungist-Kimjongilist Youth League, the General Federation of Trade Unions of Korea, the Union of Agricultural Workers of Korea and the Socialist Women's Union of Korea) also form part of the Democratic Front for the Reunification of the Fatherland, which holds mass meetings at which candidates are selected to run in the elections. The name of the selected candidate for the district appears on the ballot. While a voter could cross off a candidate's name in front of election officials, this would be considered a treasonous act with serious personal consequences.

Although the SPA is the country's main legislative body, it only sits a few days a year. Authority is delegated to the much smaller Presidium, which is elected from the SPA and

130 *The Korean Peninsula*

has about 15 members, including the president, two vice presidents and a secretary general. North Korea is, however, actually a one-man dictatorship, with power firmly in the hands of the national leader. The founder and first president was Kim Il-sung, who governed from 1945 to 1994 and was given the title Eternal President. He was followed by his son, Kim Jong-il (1994–2011), and his grandson, Kim Jong-un (2011 to present) (see Textbox 4.4). Complete loyalty and obedience to the leader is expected, and leader-focused propaganda is intense and commonplace. The citizenry truly believe that their leader is embedded with special powers.

North Korea's economy

North Korea is governed according to Juche, an ideology of self-reliance, which was first presented in the mid-1950s by Kim Il-sung and enshrined in the country's Constitution in 1972. The official state policy, Juche, advocates that true socialism can only be achieved through economic self-sufficiency, military independence and political independence. On the economic front, this means that the state controls the economy. Capital goods are all owned by state-owned enterprises and agriculture is collectivized. Following the Soviet model, North Korea's initial focus was on heavy industry, and industrial input therefore increased in the 1960s. However, in the 1970s, the economy suffered from problems with centralized planning, including supply shortages, poor infrastructure and ageing equipment. North Korean had taken on foreign loans to buy machinery and other industrial equipment and then had difficulty servicing its debt payments. The oil shocks of 1973 and 1979 followed, leading to a dramatic increase in the price of oil, a major import.

By the 1990s, the North Korean economy had edged towards collapse. The break-up of the Soviet Union in 1991 cost North Korea its main source of foreign aid, trade and technology transfer. Between 1990 and 1993, the value of trade between North Korea and the Soviet Union plummeted from $2.4 billion to $222 million, and the transfer of military technology also evaporated. A series of natural disasters, beginning with hailstorms in 1994, ravaged the country. Catastrophic floods destroyed crop lands, harvests, emergency grain reserves and infrastructure across almost a third of the country. Further flooding occurred in 1996, followed by a serious drought the following year. As a result, North Korea suffered a major famine between 1994 and 1998, which killed 600,000 to 1 million people (access to information in North Korea is unreliable, so estimates vary widely) ("How Did the North Korean Famine Happen?," 2002). These hardships are continuing: every year, thousands of people are at risk of starvation or malnutrition. In 2019, for example, the United Nations World Food Program estimated that over 10 million North Koreans out of a population of 25.5 million were food insecure.

Since Kim Jong-un took power in 2011, there has been some economic liberalization. However, North Korea still ranked last in the 2019 Heritage Foundation's Economic Freedom Rankings. GDP per capita is approximately $1700, and poverty and hardship are widespread. Reliable North Korean economic statistics are hard to obtain, but in the last decade there appears to have been some economic growth. Pyongyang, in particular, appears to have prospered, evidenced by an increase in high-rise buildings, vehicles and a better dressed and well-fed population. The city even boasts a dolphinarium and a water park. The growth may be attributable to a shift towards a more market-based economic system in which households are now responsible for their own farming. After giving the state about one-third of their production, they are able to keep the remainder. For industry also, centralized planning appears to have been relaxed and a more free market system embraced. Since the collapse of the Soviet Union, China has been North Korea's main ally and trading partner.

According to the *CIA World Factbook*, in 2017, China was the source of 92 percent of North Korean imports and the recipient of 86 percent of its exports.

North Korea follows a military-first policy called *Songun*. Absolute priority is placed on the development of a strong military, and major investments are made in the military despite the country's poverty. Estimates are that about one-quarter of the national budget is devoted to military expenditures, with a significant amount spent on the country's nuclear program. North Korea has the fourth largest active duty army in the world with 1.2 million active military members and a total of close to 7.5 million military, reserve and paramilitary personnel out of a population of 25 million (Albert, 2019). This represents 30 percent of the total population of the country.

One of the world's most repressive states, North Korea ranks at the bottom of Freedom House's *Freedom in The World Index*. North Korean citizens have very few civil or political rights and freedoms. Freedom of expression, speech, assembly, association and religion are restricted, and political opposition, independent media and labour unions are prohibited. The government is brutal in its suppression of dissent. In 2014, a United Nations special commission of inquiry published a 400-page report of atrocities occurring in the DPRK and stated that "crimes against humanity have been committed and continue to take place in the Democratic People's Republic of Korea" ("North Korea: UN Commission," 2014). Arbitrary arrest, torture and execution instil fear in the population. Amnesty International's 2017–2018 report on North Korea cites "systematic, widespread and gross human rights violations" (Amnesty International, 2018). An estimated 200,000 people are incarcerated in North Korean prison camps, and over the years, hundreds of thousands have died in them (The Committee for Human Rights in North Korea. n.d.; Rendler, n.d.). Prisoners are subjected to forced labour, on infrastructure projects for example, and other forms of physical abuse. Capital punishment is still practised in North Korea. Amnesty International estimates that 105 people were executed between 2007 and 2012. (Numbers for more recent years are not available.)

Many North Koreans have attempted to defect, so the government tightly restricts contact with the outside world and prohibits almost all crossings of the border into China or South Korea. However, thousands have defected successfully, some through safe houses in China. The Chinese government considers North Korean defectors as illegal economic migrants and refuses to grant them refugee status. If they are caught trying to cross the border or in China, they are captured and returned to North Korea, where they face years of harsh punishment. According to South Korea's Ministry of Unification, over 31,000 North Koreans, three-quarters of them women, have defected to South Korea. Despite the shared cultural heritage, North Korean defectors have not found it easy to settle in South Korea. They report experiencing discrimination and poor treatment, and many struggle with mental health issues.

North Korean society

North Korean society is based on traditional Korean culture and emphasizes nationalism and equality. Since the vast majority of North Koreans have practically no contact with the outside world, they have extremely limited exposure to foreign influences. Although North Korea was established as a classless society, a privileged elite consisting of the highest echelon of the military and the Korean Workers' Party has emerged. As the government has devoted a significant part of its budget to the military, the provision of health care, housing and social services have been limited. In the large cities, most North Koreans live in

132 *The Korean Peninsula*

small apartments in high-rise buildings. The ideology of Juche (now often referred to as Kimilsungism-Kimjungilism) emphasizes self-reliance and Korea's cultural distinctiveness.

North Korea-South Korea relations

The border between North and South Korea is one of the most tense and potentially volatile places in the world. Large numbers of troops guard both sides of the line, and there have been numerous shootings and other incidents in the demilitarized zone (DMZ) over the decades. Between 1953 and 2004, both sides broadcast propaganda over loudspeakers towards the other. Both have also sent propaganda leaflets in balloons to the other side. In 1974, the South Koreans discovered the first of four tunnels the North Koreans had dug across the DMZ, most likely to facilitate a military invasion.

In 1971, the first reunification talks between North and South Korea began and continued intermittently over the next decades. During the 1970s and 1980s, relations between North and South Korea were extremely changeable. A positive step was the first reunion of families separated by the war, which took place over three days in September 1985 (see Textbox 4.5). Another was discussions about co-hosting the Seoul 1988 Olympics and about various forms of economic cooperation. However, these rapprochements were far from smooth, tending to start, stop and then start again. In 1991, both North and South Korea were granted seats in the United Nations, and the two countries signed the Agreement on Reconciliation, Non-Aggression, Exchanges and Cooperation. This agreement was to be a step towards an eventual peace treaty, which, however, has still not materialized. Officially, North and South Korea remain at war.

Textbox 4.5 Family reunions

The Korean Red Cross estimates that approximately 10 million families were affected by the division of the peninsula at the end of the Korean War (Foley, 2001). Family members who found themselves on opposite sides of the border have lived for decades unable to have any contact with one another. Reuniting divided families has been a longstanding humanitarian issue. The first Korean family reunion took place in 1985 when approximately 150 Koreans were able to meet family members they had not seen in 30 years. Sadly, it was to be 15 years before another reunion was held. After the historic Kim-Kim summit in 2000, a commitment was made to hold more reunions. This was especially urgent as many of the affected family members were ageing and could die before seeing their family members again. Approximately 21,000 people have participated in over 20 rounds of reunions since 2000. To put this in perspective, however, 57,000 South Koreans who applied for the most recent reunion in 2018 were not chosen. Many of them were over 80 years old. Thousands of others have died without ever being selected.

The nuclear issue

Early in 1992, South and North Korea signed the Joint Declaration of the Denuclearization of the Korean Peninsula, in which they agreed to the following: (1) not to test, manufacture, possess or use nuclear weapons, (2) to use nuclear energy only for peaceful purposes, (3) not to have either uranium enrichment or nuclear reprocessing facilities, and (4) to allow inspections to verify the denuclearization. However, the words did not translate into verifiable action. North Korea had been pursuing a nuclear weapons program since the 1980s, operating uranium processing facilities and conducting high explosive tests. Although it acceded to the Treaty on the Non- Proliferation of Nuclear Weapons (the NPT, an agreement to prevent the spread of nuclear weapons) in 1985, North Korea was never in compliance. Within a year of signing the Joint Declaration, North Korea refused to allow International Atomic Energy inspectors to visit its nuclear sites and threatened to withdraw from the NPT. Tensions rose as the rest of the world, particularly South Korea, the United States and Japan, remained convinced that North Korea was developing a nuclear bomb. After diplomatic talks, North Korea backed down and allowed inspectors to visit in March 1994. In June of the same year, U.S. President Jimmy Carter made a goodwill visit to Pyongyang and met with Kim Il-sung, which paved the way for the Agreed Framework between North Korea and the United States. In the Agreed Framework, North Korea agreed to dismantle its nuclear reactors and remain party to the NPT. In return, the United States would provide oil and two light-water reactors. At the Carter-Kim meeting, North also promised to hold the first summit meeting with South. However, a few weeks later, Kim Il-sung died of a heart attack; the summit was cancelled as the country plunged into a period of mourning.

In 1998, North Korea launched its first ballistic missile, the Taepodong-1 missile, over Japan (see Figure 4.7). Tensions increased until the following year when North Korea declared a moratorium on missile testing in exchange for the easing of American sanctions. (The United States first imposed sanctions on North Korea in 1950 and has tightened them numerous times since then.) Suddenly, the North agreed to a summit with the South. In June 2000, North Korea's President Kim Jong-il and South Korea's President Kim Dae-jung met in Pyongyang. The summit was a success, and the two leaders agreed to reunions for separated families and various economic development projects.

Figure 4.7 North Korean ballistic missile.

134 *The Korean Peninsula*

In 2001, American President George W. Bush took a hard-line position on North Korea, calling it part of an "axis of evil" (along with Iran and Iraq) and putting new sanctions in place. In October 2002, the U.S. confronted North Korea with evidence it had been running a clandestine uranium-enrichment program in clear violation of the Agreed Framework, the Joint Declaration and the Non-Proliferation Treaty. North Korea admitted to the program, prompting the United States to halt its energy assistance. In retaliation, Pyongyang expelled the IAEA inspectors, withdrew from the NPT and restarted the Yongbyon nuclear plant.

In August 2003, North Korea agreed to participate in multilateral talks with the United States, Russia, Japan, China and South Korea. These Six-Party Talks proceeded in a series of rounds that lasted until 2009. The first round of talks took place later in August 2003 in Beijing, ending with a few points of consensus but no breakthroughs. The second and third rounds of talks were in 2004, but it was not until September 2005 in the fourth round that the first breakthrough in resolving the North Korean nuclear crisis was achieved. The six parties issued a joint statement outlining the agreed upon steps, with North Korea committing itself to abandoning nuclear weapons, allowing inspections and returning to the NPT. The other five countries would supply North Korea with energy, including a light-water reactor at some point. The United States and South Korea promised they also would not use nuclear weapons on the Korean Peninsula.

The breakthrough did not last long. The fifth round of negotiations in November 2005 was only three days. Although there were discussions on how the details of the joint statement would be implemented, no major steps were achieved. In the following months, tensions rose over U.S. sanctions on the Banco Delta Asia of Macao, which froze $25 million in North Korean funds. North Korea boycotted the next proposed talks and, in July 2006, conducted seven short-medium and long-range ballistic missile tests. On October 9, 2006, the North Koreans conducted an underground nuclear test. In response, the United Nations Security Council passed a resolution unanimously condemning the tests and requiring North Korean to stop further testing and join the Six-Party Talks. The $25 million was released and North Korea committed to stopping its nuclear operations at Yongbyon. Talks resumed in September 2007, and in exchange for 900,000 tons of oil and an American commitment to remove North Korea from its state sponsors of terror list, North Korea agreed to disable its facilities. Talks continued in June 2008 after North Korea delayed implementing its commitment to end its nuclear facilities. Reaching an agreement on a verification system proved difficult. On April 5, 2009, Pyongyang tested a Taepodong missile, arguing it was part of the country's space program. In response, the UN Security Council expanded sanctions on North Korea, prompting North Korea on April 14 to indicate that it would no longer participate in the Six-Party Talks, nor be bound by any of the former agreements. On May 25th, Pyongyang conducted a second nuclear test.

North Korea's missile and nuclear tests are designed to test the capabilities and range of its weaponry and prove its ability to inflict damage on South Korea, Japan and the United States. Over the years, it appears to have often used these tests as a way to increase tension and force the United States and/or South Korea to engage with it and offer assistance. South Korean leaders have tried different approaches to improving relations with the North, particularly over the nuclear issue. Kim Dae-jung's famous Sunshine Policy was an attempt to engage with the North and improve relations and understanding between the two countries. Although the policy resulted in increased contact through summits and joint economic development projects, despite its promises, the North's nuclear program has continued. Subsequent South Korean presidents have adopted a more hard-line approach (waiting to engage until North Korea makes some kind of concession). President Park Geun-hye even

The Korean Peninsula   135

tried a middle approach that she called *Trustpolitick*, which used both carrots and sticks in interactions with the North. However, North Korea's steps towards building a nuclear arsenal continued unabated. Some analysts argue that the legitimacy of the North Korean regime with its citizens rests upon it being in a continual state of confrontation with the United States and South Korea. The North Korean public is aware that South Koreans are better off economically but believes they are unhappy because they are subjugated to the Americans. According to one journalist, "Giving up nuclear weapons would spell the end. So he negotiates with America not to end tensions, but to manage them: neither all-out war nor all-out peace" ("The mother of all," 2010).

Over the decades, differences between the North and South have widened as South Korea has modernized and its economy expanded. One way in which the two countries differ is in the health of their populations. Men in North Korea on average measure 8 cm less and die 12 years sooner than their counterparts in South Korea. Another example is technology: the North is using technologies the South has not used in decades. Since trade between the two Koreas has been limited to basic goods, usually carried through China, it has not extended to technology and consumer goods. Even the language spoken in the two countries differs, likely because they have been apart so long. In fact, scholars say that almost one-third of the commonplace words used are different. In the South, this is partly due to the influence of English and American culture, while the North, under the self-reliance ideology, bans words with foreign origins. Language differences could be seen in the experience of the unified hockey team that South Korea and North Korea fielded at the 2018 Winter Olympics. The Canadian/American coach noted on television that overcoming the language difference between the two groups of players had been challenging as they use very different ice hockey terminology.

While still a topic of discussion and debate and even a long-term dream for many, the possibility of reunification—of uniting North and South Korea into a single sovereign state—remains unlikely. The financial cost of reuniting the two countries, as happened between East and West Germany, would be enormous. The economic gap between the two is staggering: South Korea's GDP per capita was $39,500 in 2017, while the most recently available GDP per capita figure for North Korea was $1,700 (2015). Southern young people feel little connection to the people in the north. They are not consumed with hatred nor do they romanticize the simple lifestyle, as some older leftists used to do. A December 2017 Korea Institute for National Unification survey showed that 71 percent of South Koreans in their 20s and 42 percent of all South Koreans saw reunification as unnecessary (Park and Rhee, 2017).

Two economic initiatives to bring North Korea and South Korea together were developed over the past quarter century: the Kaesong Industrial Park and the Mount Kumgang tourism project. In September 2018, the Inter-Korean Liaison Office was established to facilitate direct communication between the two Koreas and function as a de facto embassy. In June 2020, however, North Korea blew up the building, ending what had been a two-year period of improved relations.

Kaesong Industrial Park

Kaesong Industrial Park was set up in 2002 as an economic development project between North and South Korea. Kaesong is about 10 km north of the Korean demilitarized zone with road and rail access into South Korea. The purpose of the park is to attract South Korean companies to set up there and employ inexpensive North Korean labour. For South Korean companies, this would reduce costs while giving them access to an educated Korean-speaking workforce. The North in return received valuable foreign currency.

136 *The Korean Peninsula*

At its height in 2013, about 125 companies with 55,000 North Korean workers and 800 South Korean staff were based at Kaesong Industrial Park. The South Korean companies were making clothing, textiles, electronics, chemical products and metals and machinery. Approximately $120 million in annual wages was paid directly to the North Korean government, which took about 30 percent in taxes and then paid the workers the remainder in food and coupons for government stores.

However, when tensions between North and South escalated, North Korea restricted access to the industrial park for periods of time. The longest closure began in April 2013 when North Korea recalled all its workers from Kaesong and lasted until mid-September, when the two countries reached an agreement to reopen it. In February 2016, in retaliation for a North Korean nuclear test and rocket launch, the South Koreans unilaterally closed the park. The South Korean government argued that it did not want the money the North Koreans earned from Kaesong used to fund the North's weapons program. The Kaesong Industrial Park remains shut although when relations between the two countries warm, the possibility of reopening Kaesong goes back on the table.

Mount Kumgang (Diamond Mountain) tourism project

On the eastern coast of North Korea north of the border with South Korea lies Mount Kumgang. With its steep cliffs, sharp ravines and lovely waterfalls, the mountain and surrounding area has been renowned for its beauty for centuries. Mount Kumgang has been the subject of many poems and works of art and is considered a sacred site by Korean Buddhists. When the peninsula was divided, South Koreans no longer had access to this important and scenic spot. In 1989, the CEO of Hyundai, originally from the North, proposed a joint tourism project to Kim Il-sung. Nine years later, during the time of improved relations between the North and South under Kim Dae-jung's Sunshine Policy, the Kumgang area was opened to South Korean and other foreign visitors. The tourism project gave North Korea access to much needed foreign currency, and the proximity to the border meant South Koreans could reach the area without meeting many North Koreans, a goal of the North Korean government, which did not want its citizens to see how much better off the South Koreans were. The North Korean government made sure that few North Koreans were allowed in the area, and only ethnic Koreans from China were hired as staff.

The area was organized as a special tourist region. A Hyundai subsidiary built hotels, restaurants, a golf course, a spa and hospital and organized tours. Foreign visitors, mainly South Koreans, visited Mount Kumgang on tours by cruise ship and later by bus through the Demilitarized Zone. However, in 2008, a North Korean soldier shot and killed a South Korean tourist when, according to the North Korean government, she walked into a military area and did not respond to warnings. The incident and resulting tensions brought tours to a halt. North Korea took over the resort. In the 10 years Mount Kumgang was open, just under 2 million South Koreans visited the region. Both governments indicate that they would like the area to reopen, but as of 2020, it remains closed.

Relations between North Korea, South Korea and the United States

Testing missiles, conducting nuclear tests, building a uranium-enrichment facility and other provocations—all have continued since 2009. In March 2010, a South Korean warship, the *Cheonan*, was hit by a torpedo, resulting in the death of 46 seamen. An international investigation into the accident led by South Korea concluded that a North Korean

The Korean Peninsula   137

torpedo sank the *Cheonan*. North Korea vehemently denied involvement. Later that same year, as South Korean troops were beginning their annual military drills, North Korea fired artillery and rockets at Yeonpyeong Island, killing four, injuring 19, and causing widespread damage. North Korea claimed that it was responding to South Korea firing into North Korean waters.

In 2012, North Korea committed again to suspend its missile and nuclear testing and stop the uranium-enrichment program in exchange for American food aid. But this deal also collapsed after another North Korean rocket launch. More North Korean nuclear tests took place in February 2013 and in January and September 2016, and more short-, medium- and long-range missile tests were also carried out in 2015 and 2016. The motivation for the missiles was multi-level: to show North Korea's military capabilities, increase the pride and confidence of the people of North Korea, to push for greater concessions from the United States and to demonstrate and exercise Kim Jong-un's power as a military leader. In 2015, responding to North Korea's missile and nuclear tests after months of China-U.S. negotiations, the United Nations agreed to the strongest sanctions yet imposed on North Korea. These included an arms sales embargo, an export ban on coal, iron and other minerals (North Korean's main exports) and an inspection of goods entering and leaving the country. The effectiveness of the sanctions depended on China's commitment to enforcing them, an uncertainty given that it had not strictly enforced previous sanctions.

U.S. President Donald Trump took office in January 2017. In July, North Korea successfully tested its first intercontinental ballistic missile and, later that year, held its sixth nuclear test, announcing that it had tested a thermonuclear weapon (hydrogen bomb). Since thermonuclear weapons are even more destructive than first-generation atomic bombs, this test greatly concerned the international community. In November, North Korea tested a missile, which it claimed could carry a nuclear warhead and reach anywhere in the United States. Following this test, relations between the United States and North Korea plummeted, as their leaders exchanged insults and threats. Trump called Kim Jong-un "Little Rocket Man" and threatened North Korea with "fire and fury like the world has never seen" (Stevens, 2018). In return, Pyongyang referred to Trump as a "mentally deranged U.S. dotard" (Stevens, 2018). As tensions escalated between the two leaders in early January of 2018, Trump tweeted "North Korean Leader Kim Jong-un just stated that the 'Nuclear Button is on his desk at all times.' Will someone from his depleted and food starved regime please inform him that I too have a Nuclear Button, but it is a much bigger & more powerful one than his and my Button works" (Trump, 2018). Fortunately, relations between the United States and North Korean improved subsequently.

In 2018, South Korean and American relations with North Korea started to improve. South Korea and North Korea agreed that their athletes would march in the opening ceremony for the 2018 Pyeongchang Winter Olympics together and compete in women's ice hockey as a joint team. For South Korea's President Moon, this was a step towards reconciliation and potentially a more peaceful future for the Korean Peninsula. Kim Jong-un saw the Olympics as a chance to raise the profile and improve the image of North Korea internationally, while shoring up his image and legitimacy as a leader with his domestic audience. This rapprochement led to an inter-Korean summit between South Korea's President Moon Jae-in and North Korea's President Kim Jong-un on April 27, 2018. (This was the third inter-Korean summit; the first had been in 2000 between Kim Dae-jung and Kim Jong-il and the second was in 2007 between Roh Moo-hyun and Kim Jong-il.) The meeting was held on the South Korean side of Panmunjom, but President Moon stepped over the demarcation line into North Korea. The two leaders discussed the improvement of relations between their two countries, including potentially formally ending the Korean War.

Surprisingly, President Trump and Chairman Kim also agreed to a summit, which took place in Singapore on June 12, 2018. The summit almost did not take place as President Trump withdrew in late May due to anger and hostility over North Korean statements. The summit emerged from President Trump's desire to distinguish himself from President Obama and the Democrats' approach to North Korean and to demonstrate his abilities as a negotiator and a dealmaker. For President Kim, the opportunity for a summit was too good to squander. He hoped to capitalize on Trump's newness as president to create new options for North Korea. Both leaders hoped for a breakthrough in a relationship that had festered for decades. After the summit, the leaders signed a joint statement in which they committed to work towards denuclearization of the peninsula and lasting peace and prosperity. The statement pledged a commitment to recovering the remains of American prisoners of war and those missing in action from the Korean War. Separate from the joint statement, President Trump announced that the United States would suspend the joint military exercises it annually undertakes with South Korea (apparently without consulting South Korea or the U.S. forces in South Korea). But he did not follow through with his commitment, and five months later, limited joint military exercises resumed.

A second Moon-Kim summit—a two-hour meeting in the Joint Security Area of the Demilitarized Zone—took place on May 26, 2018. A more substantial third summit between President Moon and Chairman Kim took place in Pyongyang from September 18 to 20, 2018. At the end of the third summit, the leaders signed a joint declaration that outlined plans for reducing tensions and expanding cooperation on the peninsula. President Trump and Chairman Kim met again, this time in Vietnam in February 2019 (see Figure 4.8), but this summit ended early without a deal as the leaders disagreed over denuclearization and

Figure 4.8 Kim-Trump summit in Hanoi, February 2019.

sanctions relief (the United States wanted North Korea to disarm before America would lift sanctions, while North Korea claimed it has already made significant steps towards denuclearization and would not do any more without sanctions relief). However, President Trump stated that relations remain friendly. At the end of June 2019, Trump and Kim met at the DMZ and agreed to restart negotiations over denuclearization. Trump stepped across the border into North Korea, and both leaders talked to the press about their "great" relationship. But North Korea soon indicated it was no longer interested in future talks and, worryingly, undertook a series of short-range missile tests.

Conclusion

The Korean Peninsula has emerged as one of the most important places on the planet. Situated between Japan and China, two of the world's economic superpowers, its position is highly strategic. Unlike other places where relations between countries formerly divided by the Cold War have improved, the division between North and South Korea remains extremely sensitive. As they have for decades, negotiations over denuclearization continue. But the normalization of relationships founders as the belligerence of Chairman Kim and President Trump's non-conformist approach to regional relations lowers the prospects for a quick resolution. Although relations between the two Koreas warmed in 2018 with their joint participation in the parade of athletes at the Winter Olympics and a series of meetings between Chairman Kim and President Moon, since then little progress has been made on North Korean denuclearization. Indeed, North Korea has resumed short-range missile testing, leaving the possibility of improved relations on the peninsula in doubt.

Note

1 In July 2018, the government implemented a 52-hour maximum work week, which has improved people's work-life balance.

Bibliography

"Aging Population", *Korean Herald*, January 15, 2020. http://www.koreaherald.com/view.php?ud=2 0200115000621
"Corporate Armistice: Can South Korea's Big and Small Countries Thrive Together?", *The Economist*, October 28, 2013.
"How did the North Korean Famine Happen?", *The Wilson Centre*, April 30, 2002. https://www.wil soncenter.org/article/how-did-the-north-korean-famine-happen
"North Korea: UN Commission Documents Wide-Ranging and Ongoing Crimes Against Humanity, Urges Referral to ICC", *United Nations Human Rights Office of the Commissioner*, February 17, 2014. https://www.ohchr.org/EN/NewsEvents/Pages/DisplayNews.aspx?NewsID=14255&LangID=E
"South Korean Attitudes Toward the U.S.-ROK Alliance and USFK", *The Asian Institute for Policy Studies, Issue Briefs*, February 22, 2019. http://en.asaninst.org/contents/south-korean-attitudes-toward-the-u-s-rok-alliance-and-usfk/
"Snake Heads and Dragon Tails", *The Economist*, October 28, 2013.
"The Mother of All Dictatorships", *The Economist*, February 27, 2010, p. 52.
"Women in South Korea: A Pram Too Far", *The Economist*, October 28, 2013.
Albert, Eleanor. 2018. "South Korea's Chaebol Challenge", *Council on Foreign Relations*, May 4. https://www.cfr.org/backgrounder/south-koreas-chaebol-challenge#:~:text=Introduction,of%20 the%20world's%20largest%20economies

140   *The Korean Peninsula*

Albert, Eleanor. 2019. "North Korea's Military Capabilities", *Council on Foreign Relations*, December 20. https://www.cfr.org/backgrounder/north-koreas-military-capabilities

Amnesty International. 2018. *Amnesty International Report 2017/18 - Korea (Democratic People's Republic of)*. February 22. https://www.refworld.org/docid/5a9938d74.html

Brunhuber, Kim. 2018. "South Korean Women on 'Birth Strike' as Children Come With Too High a Cost", *CBC News*, February 25. https://www.cbc.ca/news/world/fertility-rate-south-korea-1.4540398

Foley, James A. 2001. "'Ten Million Families': Statistic or Metaphor?" *Korean Studies*, 25(1): 96–110.

Han, Woo-keun. 1970. *The History of Korea*. Eul-Yoo Publishing Co. Ltd.

Hong, Seung-Au. 2020. "Gendered Politics of Work-Life Balance in South Korea", in Jieyu Liu and Junko Yamashita, eds., *Routledge Handbook of East Asian Gender Studies*, Routledge.

Ock, Hyun-ju. 2015. "Koreans' Average Work Hours Still Second-Longest in OECD", *Korean Herald*, November 2.

Oh, Jennifer S. 2012. "Strong State and Strong Civil Society in Contemporary South Korea: Challenges to Democratic Governance", *Asian Survey*, 52(3): 528–549.

Park, Juh-wa, MinKyu Rhee and Won-Bin Cho. 2017. *2017 Survey of Inter-Korean Integration*. Korean Institute for National Unification.

Rendler, Jack. n.d. *North Korean Prison Camps Grow Larger*. Amnesty International. https://www.amnestyusa.org/north-korea-the-last-worst-place-on-earth/

Stevens, Matt. 2018. "Trump and Kim Jong-un, and the Names They've Called Each Other", *The New York Times*, March 9.

The Committee for Human Rights in North Korea. n.d. https://www.hrnk.org/about/about-hrnk.php

Trump, Donald. 2018. *Twitter*. https://twitter.com/realdonaldtrump/status/948355557022420992?lang=ga

Further Reading

Korean Peninsula

Eckert, Carter, Ki-baik Lee, Young Ick Lew, Michael Robinson and Edward W. Wagner. 1957. *Korea Old and New: A History*. Harvard University Press.

Halberstam, David. 2008. *The Coldest Winter: America and the Korean War*. Hachette Books.

Hastings, Max. 1987. *The Korean War*. Simon and Schuster.

Kim, Richard. 2011. *Lost Names: Scenes from a Korean Boyhood*. University of California Press, (first edition 1971).

South Korea

Breen, Michael. 2017. *The New Koreans*. Thomas Dunne Books.

De Mente, Boye Lafayette. 2012. *The Korean Mind: Understanding Contemporary Korean Culture*. Tuttle Publishing.

Hong, Euny. 2014. *The Birth of Korean Cool: How One Nation is Conquering the World Through Pop Culture*. Picador Paper.

Kang, Han. 2017. *Human Acts*, Translated by Deborah Smith. Hogarth.

Lee, Krys. 2012. *Drifting House*. Viking Adult.

Tudor, Daniel. 2012. *Korea: The Impossible Country: South Korea's Amazing Rise from the Ashes: The Inside Story of an Economic, Political and Cultural Phenomenon*. Tuttle Publishing.

North Korea

Cha, Victor. 2012. *The Impossible State: North Korea, Past and Future*. Ecco.

Demick, Barbara. 2009. *Nothing to Envy: Ordinary Lives in North Korea*. Spiegel and Gau.

French, Paul. 2014. *North Korea: State of Paranoia*. Zed Books.

Harden, Blaine. 2012. *Escape from Camp 14: One Man's Remarkable Odyssey from North Korea to Freedom in the West*. Penguin Books.

Jang, Jin-sung. 2015. *Dear Leader: My Escape from North Korea*. 37 Ink.

Lankov, Andrei. 2013. *The Real North Korea: Life and Politics in the Failed Stalinist Utopia*. Oxford University Press.

Martin, Bradley K. 2004. *Under the Loving Care of the Fatherly Leader: North Korea and the Kim Dynasty*. St. Martin's Griffin.

Myers, Brian. 2010. The Cleanest Race: How North Koreans See Themselves and Why it Matters. Melville House Publishing.

5   Taiwan (Republic of China)

Introduction

Taiwan, formerly known as Formosa, is an island about 145 km off the coast of China in the west Pacific Ocean, south of Japan and north of the Philippines (see Figure 5.1). Taiwanese jurisdiction includes numerous islets and the archipelagos of Penghu, Kinmen and Matsu. Including the outlying islands, Taiwan's total land area is approximately 36,000 km^2 (slightly smaller than the Netherlands, slightly larger than Massachusetts). The island itself is just under 400 km long and 145 km wide. Over 70 percent of Taiwan is mountainous with five major mountain chains running through the centre of the island. In fact, there are 286 mountains over 3,000 m in Taiwan, with the highest being Yushan (Jade Mountain) at just under 4,000 m.

Early history

The island was originally inhabited by Malayo-Polynesian Aboriginal peoples from Southeast Asia. There were sporadic visits of people from China from the 7th century on; however, prior to the arrival of the Dutch, there were no permanent settlements on the island, only stateless Austronesian groups. Tonio Andrade, whose book is the most authoritative history on this period, describes Taiwan in 1600 as "a wild land, inhabited by headhunters and visited mainly by pirates and fishermen" (Andrade, 2010).

Taiwan was "discovered" by Portuguese sailors in the early 1500s; they named it Formosa meaning "beautiful island." In the early 1600s, the Dutch East India Company set up a trading post on the Penghu Islands off Taiwan's southwest coast, but China's Ming government stepped in and pursued the Dutch until they left the island. Undeterred, the Dutch returned in 1624 and established Fort Zeelandia on the coast of southwestern Taiwan, now part of the city of Tainan. Fort Zeelandia soon became an important trading colony and transit site. The Dutch East India Company employed Chinese people to farm rice and sugarcane, which along with tea, deer hide and other products were exported. The Dutch retained control of a significant portion of southwestern Taiwan until 1662. In 1642, the Dutch pushed out the Spanish, who had established a small colony on the northern part of the island 16 years earlier. During the 17th century, in the central west part of Taiwan, an alliance was formed among Taiwanese Aboriginal peoples. Known as the Kingdom of Middage, the alliance ruled about 27 villages.

In China, the Manchus brought an end to the Ming dynasty in 1644 (see Chapter 2). Ming loyalists led by Zheng Chenggong, better known by his Romanized Dutch name *Koxinga*, laid siege to Fort Zeelandia on April 30, 1661, and within a year had driven the Dutch out of Taiwan. With Koxinga came tens of thousands of mainland Chinese who would remain in Taiwan.

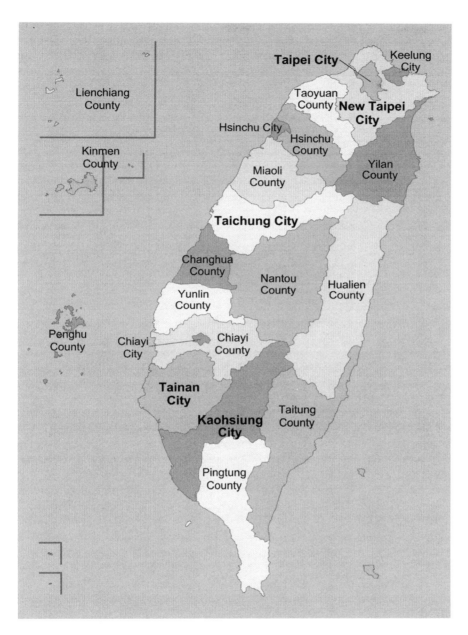

Figure 5.1 Map of Taiwan.

More Chinese followed, resulting in a population boom that allowed for increased development of the island. Koxinga himself died soon after the Dutch exodus. His son and grandson initially ruled the island, but in 1683, the Qing (Manchu) government took over and made Taiwan part of Fujian province. Once that was established, however, the Qing paid little attention to the island. In fact, the Qing left the indigenous areas entirely alone, putting over

144 *Taiwan (Republic of China)*

half the island outside of Qing jurisdiction, until the 1871 Mudan Incident in which 54 ship-wrecked Ryukyuan sailors who, having made their way inland to central Taiwan, were massacred by local indigenous people.[1] In 1885, Taiwan was declared its own province of China, but a decade later Taiwan fell under Japanese control. Upon its loss in the 1894–1895 First Sino-Japanese War, China was forced to sign the Treaty of Shimonoseki, which ceded the Pescadores Islands, the Liaodong Peninsula (soon after reversed) and the island of Formosa (Taiwan) to Japan. Japan ruled Taiwan from 1895 until the end of World War II in 1945.

Japanese administration of Taiwan

Initially, the Japanese met fierce resistance to their administration. It took them years to subdue and control many parts of the island. A group of Taiwanese intellectuals declared the island the Taiwan Democratic Republic, a sovereign nation, and even wrote a Declaration of Independence. Those dreams were quickly crushed, however; the Japanese remained in charge for the next 50 years. After 90 days of resistance from May to August 1914, the Truku indigenous group was the last of the indigenous groups to surrender. The unrest and armed uprisings peaked with the Tapani Incident of 1915, when both Chinese and Aboriginal fighters stormed police stations. Chinese violent resistance stopped after Tapani, but the Aboriginal peoples continued to fight against the Japanese and their harsh policies of assimilation and forced relocation. The October 1930 Musha Incident, also known as the Wushe Rebellion, is the best known and last act of Indigenous rebellion. Three hundred Seediq Indigenous warriors attacked the village of Musha, killing 134 Japanese. The Japanese counterattack killed more than 600 Seediq.

Once the Japanese were fully in control, they began to modernize the island. They built and improved roads and railways, opened up remote areas, constructed schools and hospitals, developed Taiwan's resources and agriculture and established financial and educational systems. All of these changes allowed the Japanese to create a modern economy on the island, and Taiwan soon became the second most economically advanced country in East Asia after Japan itself. However, although less brutal than the Japanese occupation of South Korea, the Japanese in Taiwan nonetheless forcefully suppressed dissent, limited personal freedoms and made the population speak Japanese rather than their native languages.

For Taiwan, the years between 1915 and 1937, after the Tapani Incident and before Japan's entry into World War II, was a period of integration which corresponded with the Taisho period of democratization in Japan and growing anti-colonialism worldwide. In the spirit of democracy, the Japanese in Taiwan allowed for more local government; however, they continued to enact a policy of assimilation, whose goal was to have the Taiwanese see themselves as Japanese subjects. Partly due to the influx of labourers from the Chinese mainland, the population of Taiwan, 3 million people in 1905, doubled to 6 million by 1945.

With the rise in Japanese militarism and the beginning of World War II, this drive for assimilation intensified. Because the Japanese government needed Taiwanese cooperation to make the best use of local resources and personnel, the Taiwanese were strongly encouraged to adopt Japanese ways (clothing, language, Shinto religion) and even to take Japanese names. In 1940, the Taiwanese were encouraged to volunteer for the Japanese army, and, in 1945, a full draft was put in place. An estimated 30,000 young Taiwanese died serving in the Japanese military in World War II.

During the war, Taiwan was the base for Japan's invasion of southern China, and many Taiwanese worked in defence and war-related industries based on the island. As a result, they often fell victim to U.S. bombing attacks targeting oil storage depots and other strategic areas.[2]

The bombings damaged Taiwan's industrial and agricultural production, with both at under half their pre-war levels by the end of the war.

Return to China's rule as part of the Republic of China

The Republic of China (ROC), which had been established on the Chinese mainland in 1912, assumed control of Taiwan from the Japanese in 1945. When World War II ended, the government of the ROC led by Chiang Kai-shek and the Kuomintang (KMT or Nationalist Party) accepted the surrender of the Japanese in Taiwan and returned the island province to ROC rule. Very quickly, however, the local population was angered by the corrupt and imperious attitude of the KMT officials, whose focus was primarily on the civil war occurring on the mainland and not on governing Taiwan. Private property was seized arbitrarily, and the economy was poorly managed. On February 28, 1947, an anti-government uprising—now referred to as the February 28 Incident/February 28 Massacre—was violently put down by the government's armed forces. Thousands of civilians died, including some of the island's political and academic establishment. This was the lead up to nearly four decades of martial (military rule) law. The massacre marked the beginning of the period of White Terror, in which tens of thousands more Taiwanese would be killed or imprisoned.

While the Nationalists were officially ruling the ROC, Mao Zedong and the Chinese Communist Party (CCP) were gathering support for the revolutionary overthrow of Chiang Kai-shek's government. (The KMT and the CCP had been engaged in a civil war since 1927. See Chapter 2 for details.) The KMT and the CCP had united to fight against Japan, but as soon as the Japanese were defeated and their troops demobilized, Chiang Kai-shek turned his attention to defeating the Communists. The civil war resumed and raged until 1949.

After China's civil war

By 1949, the KMT Nationalist forces led by Chiang Kai-shek were facing defeat by Mao Zedong's Communist forces. Chiang and 1.2 million of his military, political and commercial elite fled to Taiwan, bringing with them many treasures of imperial China.[3] Once in Taiwan, they ran the government. The KMT's view was that the island province of Taiwan would be a temporary location for the Government of the ROC, which was the legitimate government of all of China. Concerned about an invasion by the Chinese Communists or some form of domestic subversion, the KMT suppressed all Communist or Taiwanese independence activities. Under martial law, opposition parties were not tolerated, the media was sharply curtailed and individual liberties were limited. Until his death in 1975, Chiang Kai-shek passionately believed that the KMT would one day return to the Chinese mainland and, with the support of the Chinese population, defeat the Communist government. His son Chiang Ching-kuo succeeded his father as premier in 1972 and then as president in 1978, until his death in 1988. Under Chiang Ching-kuo's leadership, Taiwan's economy grew and strengthened. Especially near the end of Chiang Ching-kuo's life, the government became more open and tolerant of dissenting views. Controls on the media and free speech were gradually relaxed, and, in 1987, martial law began to be lifted and opposition parties legalized. Chiang Ching-kuo also groomed a native Taiwanese, Lee Teng-hui, as his successor. Eight years after succeeding Chiang as president in 1988, Lee was elected president in Taiwan's first direct presidential elections in 1996. The first legislative elections took place in 1992. Establishing a critical foundation for economic and social development, the democratization

146   *Taiwan (Republic of China)*

of Taiwan and centrality of these democratic values would clearly differentiate Taiwan from mainland China in the late 20th century and decades to come.

International recognition of the Republic of China/Taiwan

Once the civil war had ended and the KMT Nationalists had arrived in Taiwan in 1949, under the name of the Republic of China, the KMT insisted it had the right to rule all of China—Taiwan and the mainland. The Communists on the mainland renamed China the People's Republic of China (PRC) and stated that Taiwan was a renegade province of the People's Republic of China; they, the Communist Party, ruled all of China, including Taiwan. This issue of Taiwan's relationship with the People's Republic of China has thereafter dominated Taiwanese politics, international relations and society. Due to disagreements over who represented the Chinese people, the Republic of China or the People's Republic of China, neither was invited to sign the 1952 San Francisco Peace Treaty, which marked the end of the Allied Occupation of Japan. The Japanese government and the ROC instead signed a separate but similar peace treaty, commonly known as the Treaty of Taipei, on the same day the San Francisco Peace Treaty was signed. In the Treaty of Taipei, Japan officially renounced all claims to the island of Taiwan, the Pescadores and the Spratly and Paracel Islands.

For many years after the KMT arrived in Taiwan, most countries sided with the ROC's claim to be the legitimate government of all of China. This was the Cold War, and the West's focus was on combatting communism. The Americans supported any Asian governments that were not Communist. Following suit, many Western nations granted the ROC diplomatic recognition, and Taiwan held the China seat at the United Nations until 1971. (The ROC was one of the founding members of the United Nations.) In 1950, the Korean War broke out. In response, the United States gave military and economic aid to the ROC and moved the U.S. 7th Fleet into the Taiwan Strait to prevent any potential invasion of the ROC by the PRC. The Sino-American Mutual Defense Treaty was signed in December 1954, committing the United States (and the Republic of China in return) to provide aid and military support if under attack. The treaty remained in effect until 1979.

During the Cold War, Western countries recognized the ROC, while Communist countries and many in the developing world recognized the PRC. Gradually, more and more nations started recognizing the PRC, realizing it was somewhat absurd that a country as large as the PRC was without representation or recognition. In 1971, Secretary of State Henry Kissinger visited Beijing secretly, and on July 15, 1971, President Richard Nixon announced that he would visit the PRC the next year, shocking Americans and America's allies. These overtures made it clear that in the foreseeable future, the United States would recognize the PRC. Because both the Republic of China and the People's Republic of China stated that there could only be one China—not two Chinas and not one China and one Taiwan—as countries recognized the PRC, they were forced to stop recognizing the ROC. The ROC could have put forward a claim to be recognized as an independent sovereign nation, but it had put itself in a bind by continuing to insist that there was only one China and that it, the ROC, was the legitimate government.

In 1971, the 21st time the UN had voted on the PRC's application, the country was finally admitted into the United Nations. The vote was still divided—76 in favour, 35 opposed and 17 abstentions. In 1972, U.S. President Richard Nixon visited China and signed the Shanghai Communiqué, beginning the normalization of relations between the United States and the PRC. Seven years later, the two countries formally established diplomatic relations.

After this international recognition of the PRC, the ROC gradually moved away from the position that recognition cannot be given to both the PRC and the ROC. It has consistently applied for a seat at the United Nations but has been denied because of PRC opposition. In 1995, the then President Lee Teng-hui offered the United Nations $1 billion for a seat for the ROC, but this was rejected because the world had succumbed to Beijing's pressure to exclude Taiwan.

In international organizations in which the PRC is a member, such as the Olympics, Taiwan participates under another name, such as Chinese Taipei. Although the Taiwan government disapproves of this name, it can accept it, but this is not the case for the other names approved by the PRC such as Taipei, China or Taiwan, province of China. If those names are used at a meeting that representatives of the Taiwanese government are supposed to attend, they refuse to participate and instead send private sector or non-governmental representation. With regard to Taiwan's participation in other international organizations, the rules can vary. For the World Health Organization (WHO), Taiwan was permitted to participate as an observer from 2009 to 2016, but since 2017, Beijing has blocked the invitation for Taiwan to do so.

During the 2020 coronavirus pandemic, Taiwan was excluded from participating in WHO emergency meetings despite its highly regarded health care system and leading-edge health technologies. The WHO even listed Taiwan's reported coronavirus cases under China's, although the two health care systems are administered by independent health authorities. As the pandemic progressed, Taiwan revealed itself to be one of the most successful countries at containing the virus while managing to maintain the economy and keep life close to normal. Indeed, Taiwan's speedy preparation for the virus and Taiwanese expertise at expanding testing and tracking offered valuable lessons to other countries (see Figure 5.2).

Instead of embassies, Taiwan has established offices around the world to handle all diplomatic, commercial and cultural relations. Similarly, countries without official diplomatic

Figure 5.2 Taiwan's COVID-19 response.

148 Taiwan (Republic of China)

Figure 5.3 Canadian trade office in Taipei.

relations with Taiwan cannot have embassies so they have established offices with a different name. For example, Canada has the Canadian Trade Office in Taipei while the American Institute in Taiwan represents the United States. Countries use different logos from those used in their embassies around the world (see Figure 5.3). The most senior person at the office is called the Head of Mission rather than the Ambassador, and signed agreements are called arrangements instead of the more official Memoranda of Understanding. In April 2020, after the Netherlands decided to change the name of its office from the Netherlands Trade and Investment Office to the Netherlands Office Taipei, the Chinese Embassy in The Hague immediately expressed concern and asked for clarification from the Dutch government. Chinese media and netizens also reacted with talk about boycotting Dutch products or travel to Holland.

Over the years, the number of states officially recognizing the Republic of China has declined. In 2020, only 14 out of 193 United Nation member states recognized the Republic of China: Belize, Eswatini, Guatemala, Haiti, Honduras, the Marshall Islands, Nauru, Nicaragua, Palau, Paraguay, Saint Kitts and Nevis, Saint Lucia, Saint Vincent and the Grenadines and Tuvalu. The Vatican also recognizes Taiwan. Those recognizing the ROC are small countries, primarily Pacific and Caribbean Islands and central American states. The PRC has been actively pursuing those that remain loyal to Taiwan, and Taiwan has been working hard to keep them as diplomatic allies. Since 2017, six countries have switched their recognition from the Republic of China to the People's Republic of China.

Current political structure

Government

The Republic of China (Taiwan) is a unitary state divided into 22 subnational divisions of three different types: special municipalities, cities and counties. The six major Taiwanese cities (New Taipei, Taichung, Kaohsiung, Taipei, Taoyuan and Tainan) fall under the special municipality classification. Each subnational division has an elected local government with responsibility (or partial responsibility) for a number of areas, including social services, water, transport, public safety and urban planning. Respect for local government is high, and local politicians often move into the national arena.

Power in Taiwan is divided among five different yuan (branches) of government: the Executive Yuan, the Legislative Yuan, the Control Yuan, the Judiciary Yuan and the Examination Yuan. The Executive Yuan is responsible for the creation and implementation of government policy and consists of the premier, vice premier, cabinet ministers, ministers without portfolios and commission chairs. The president appoints all of these positions on the recommendation of the premier. The Legislative Yuan is Taiwan's unicameral legislature, which reviews and enacts legislation. The Control Yuan oversees and audits other government agencies, the Examination Yuan manages the civil service system and the Judicial Yuan oversees the nation's court system.

Head of government and head of state

Taiwan has a semi-presidential system. The president and vice president are directly elected together, and the president serves as Taiwan's head of state. The president selects the premier, who is both the head of government and the president of the Executive Yuan. The president and vice president serve for four years and can serve two terms. Elected in January 2016 and re-elected in January 2020, the current president is Tsai Ing-wen of the Democratic Progressive Party, the first woman to be elected president, the second president from this party, and the first president of partial Aboriginal descent. Tsai was a law professor before holding a series of high-level governmental positions. Her vice president is William Ching-te Lai, who was sworn in on May 2020. He was Taiwan's premier from September 2017 to January 2019, a member of the Legislative Yuan for 11 years and the mayor of the Tainan for 7 years.

Constitution

The Constitution of the Republic of China was promulgated on January 1, 1947. However, it was not until 1987 when martial law was lifted that it truly became the basis for a democratic rule of law-based government. The Constitution has been revised seven times since 1947. The 1991 amendment acknowledged that jurisdiction of the ROC extends only to the land it controls (the island of Taiwan and the Penghu, Kinmen and Matsu Islands). Prior to that, the ROC had claimed jurisdiction over all of China, which would have made holding elections difficult.

Legislature

The Legislative Yuan, or Parliament, is a unicameral legislature with 113 seats. Members serve four-year terms. Since 2012, legislative elections have been run at the same time as the presidential election.

Electoral system and election campaigns

Of Taiwan's 113 seats, 73 are elected through a first-past-the-post system in single-member constituencies, and 34 seats are elected through proportional representation with a 5

150 *Taiwan (Republic of China)*

percent minimum threshold. The final six seats are Aboriginal seats in two three-member constituencies. Voters cast one ballot for their district and one for the proportional representation seats.

The Taiwanese political scene includes parties that lean towards being pro-China and see potential unification with China somewhat favourably; these parties are referred to as Blue parties or are considered to be part of a pan-Blue coalition. Parties that favour a more independent Taiwan are referred to as Green or are considered to be part of a pan-Green coalition. Elections are emotional affairs as opinions are very divided. Even families are often split. Approximately one-third of the population identifies themselves as pan-Blue, another third as pan-Green and the remaining third as centrist, although this breakdown is ever-changing. Support for the pan-Blue parties tends to come from mainlanders (those who came to the island after 1949), Taiwanese Aborigines and Hakka people. Blue supporters are prominent in northern and eastern Taiwan. Support for the pan-Green parties is very strong in southern Taiwan and among the young.

Political parties

Launched in 1986, the Democratic Progressive Party (DPP) is one of the two main political parties in Taiwan. The DPP is a centre-left, pan-Green party with a Taiwanese nationalist, strongly anti-Communist focus. Its first president was Chen Shui-bian, a native-born Taiwanese who was elected in 2000, and its second president was Tsai Ing-wen, elected in 2016 with 56 percent of the vote. In the 2016 election, the DPP also gained control of the legislature for the first time, winning 68 of the 113 seats. It held on to its majority in the 2020 election. In 2020, the only other pan-Green party to win any seats was the new State Building Party which won one seat.

The Kuomintang of China (KMT), or Nationalist Party of China, governed China (or most of it) from 1928 to 1949 under Chiang Kai-shek. Upon losing the Chinese Civil War to the Communist Party, Chiang Kai-shek and the KMT fled to Taiwan. The KMT ruled Taiwan from 1949 to 2000, first as a single-party state and then as an elected party, and again from 2008 to 2016. Until the mid-1970s, the KMT was run by mainlanders (those who came from mainland China at the end of the civil war in 1949), and the native Taiwanese population had little voice. The KMT is a conservative pan-Blue political party and is in favour of closer ties with China.

Other much smaller pan-Blue coalition parties include the People First Party and the New Party, but neither won any seats in the 2020 legislative elections. Both these parties have their roots in the KMT, and, although they cooperate as part of the pan-Blue coalition, the parties are also competing for the same voters. In the 2000 presidential election, James Soong, who went on to create the People First Party, ran as an independent and split the Blue vote, resulting in the election of the DPP, the main Green party, for the first time.

The New Power Party was launched in 2014; the party won five seats in the 2016 election and three seats in the 2020 election. Centre left with a focus on civil and political rights, the New Power Party advocates for Taiwanese independence but has kept itself separate from the pan-Green coalition. The New Power Party's roots are in the 2014 Sunflower Movement, which refers to three weeks of huge protests, including the occupation of the legislature, triggered by the passage of a bill on a services trade agreement with China. Protestors were concerned about the lack of transparency around the KMT government's negotiation of the bill with China and

Taiwan (Republic of China)   151

the impact of the bill on Taiwan's economy. Underlying the protests was an enormous distrust of China. The New Power Party was started by numerous Sunflower Movement activists.

The new Taiwan People's Party, created by the mayor of Taipei, won five seats in the 2020 election. Having deliberately chosen turquoise and white as its colours, this party has signalled that it is outside the Green-Blue divide.

Political situation: 1987 to the present

The first elected president in Taiwan was Lee Teng-hui of the KMT party. After having been appointed president in 1988, he served for six years and then ran for election in 1996. Lee was the first native-born Taiwanese to serve as president. Although he was the incumbent and part of the pro-China KMT party, Lee's desire for greater international recognition of Taiwan angered China. In the weeks prior to the election, China amassed 200,000 troops in Fujian province across the Strait from Taiwan and fired missiles near Taiwan's coast in an unsuccessful attempt to intimidate the electorate into choosing one of the more pro-China independent presidential candidates. Nonetheless, Lee won with 54 percent of the vote.

In 2000, Chen Shui-bian of the DPP was elected. This was the first time since 1949 that there was a non-KMT president. The Legislative Yuan, however, was still controlled by the KMT. Chen won with only 39 percent of the vote because the KMT split the vote between two candidates: the official KMT candidate Lien Chan, who had been the vice president under Lee, and James Soong, who ran as an independent. Chen campaigned on a pro-independence platform, but having been elected without a majority of the popular vote and concerned about China's threats that talk of Taiwanese independence would trigger a war, Chen calmed down his rhetoric and adopted a more conciliatory approach for a while. Relations between Taiwan and China settled down but remained tense. In Chen's inauguration speech, he pledged the Four Noes and One Without policy. The Four Noes was a promise that as long as the PRC did not attack Taiwan, President Chen would not declare Taiwanese independence, change the national name from Republic of China to Republic of Taiwan, include "state to state relations" in the constitution or initiate a referendum on Taiwan's political status. The One Without policy was a pledge not to abolish the National Unification Council, whose aim was to promote the reunification of the mainland and the Republic of China. (Nonetheless, the National Unification Council ceased to exist in 2006.) Under Chen, the government did move in a nationalist direction through actions like making the school curriculum more Taiwan-centric, increasing the use of the Taiwanese dialect for official events and printing Taiwan as well as the Republic of China on the front of passports.

In November 2003, Chen announced that a nationwide consultative referendum would be held in March 2004, at the same time as the 2004 presidential election. The referendum asked two questions:

1. The People of Taiwan demand that the Taiwan Strait issue be resolved through peaceful means. Should the Communist Party of China refuse to withdraw the missiles it has targeted at Taiwan and to openly renounce the use of force against us, would you agree that the Government should acquire more advanced anti-missile weapons to strengthen Taiwan's self-defence capabilities?
2. Would you agree that our Government should engage in negotiation with the Communist Party of China on the establishment of a "peace and stability" framework for cross-strait interactions in order to build consensus and for the welfare of the peoples on both sides?

152 Taiwan (Republic of China)

The pan-Blue coalition indicated that, while they were in favour of the proposals, they opposed the referendum, concerned that it could have negative consequences. As a result, the KMT and other parties encouraged their supporters not to vote, so the 50 percent registered voter threshold would not be met. Indeed, although about 92 percent of those who voted were in favour of the proposals, voter turnout was only 45 percent, so the results were invalid.

In the 2004 election, however, Chen Shui-bian was re-elected president by a very narrow margin. Days before the election, Chen and his running mate Annette Lu were reportedly shot at, although the KMT continues to believe that the incident was staged. Soon after Chen finished his second term as president, he was arrested and convicted in 2009 of embezzlement, bribery and money laundering. He was sentenced to 19 years but released on medical parole in 2015. Chen supporters believe that the charges and conviction were politically motivated and engineered by the KMT.

Power returned to the KMT when its candidate Ma Ying-jeou won the 2008 and 2012 elections. During the eight years of Ma's presidency, relations between Taiwan and China grew more friendly and cooperative. In this time, Taiwan signed 23 pacts with the mainland, including an Economic Cooperation Framework Agreement (quasi free trade agreement) in 2010, an investment protection pact in 2012 and the controversial (opponents worried about the impact on small- and medium-sized Taiwanese enterprises facing increased competition and feared the impact on free speech of the increased presence of Chinese companies in Taiwanese publishing and media) Cross-Strait Service Trade Agreement in 2013. After these agreements were signed, direct sea links and cargo and passenger flights between Taiwan and the mainland sharply increased, as did the number of destinations in both places to which flights travelled. Now approximately 60,000 flights with a total of 10 million passengers fly between Taiwan and China annually. Partially as a result of increased connections, the number of tourists surged. Chinese companies were permitted to invest in Taiwan and Taiwanese companies in the PRC. Taiwanese students and businesspeople also moved to mainland China, and cross-strait marriages increased. In 2014, the *Taipei Times* reported that approximately 1 million Taiwanese were living in the PRC.

Diplomatic relations between the two countries also relaxed. Significantly, the PRC did not block Taiwan's participation in the World Health Organization between 2009 and 2016 or in the United Nations Civil Aviation Organization meeting in 2013. In 2015, Ma Ying-jeou met Xi Jinping in Singapore, a meeting of party leader to party leader that marked the first time political leaders from Taiwan and the PRC had met since the end of the Chinese Civil War (see Figure 5.4).

However, in 2016, the KMT lost both the presidency and its majority in the legislature. Tsai Ing-wen of the DPP won the presidential election with 56 percent of the vote. The DPP won 68 of the 113 seats in the legislature, the first time the KMT had lost its hold on the legislature. In 2020, Tsai won re-election as president with 57 percent of the vote. This was the biggest election victory since the first presidential elections in 1996. In the 2020 election, the DPP lost seven seats in the legislature but held onto its majority with 61 seats; the KMT won 38 seats and the New Power Party won three seats. Two new centrist parties, the Taiwan People's Party and the Taiwan State Building Party, won five and one seat, respectively. Five independents were also elected.

In 2016, much of the support for Ms. Tsai and the DPP was not related to the China issue but rather to hopes that she would improve life for the average Taiwanese. Youth unemployment has been increasing in Taiwan, and Taipei is an expensive city relative to incomes. However, in 2020, while Tsai and the DPP campaigned on cost of living issues, pension reform, LGBT rights and renewable energy, escalating tensions with China meant this election was much more about the defence of Taiwan's sovereignty and democracy.

Taiwan (Republic of China) 153

Figure 5.4 Ma Ying-jeou and Xi Jinping meeting on November 7, 2015.

Taiwanese society

Much of Taiwan's current population of 23 million people is descended from people who emigrated from the southern part of the Chinese mainland prior to 1895 when Taiwan was ceded to Japan. These people were referred to as Taiwanese to distinguish them from the Chinese who fled to Taiwan during and after the civil war and were referred to as mainlanders. Taiwan is also home to over 570,000 Aboriginal people. There are 16 officially recognized tribes with a variety of languages and customs. Most live in the eastern half of Taiwan in the mountains.

Prior to the arrival of the mainlanders, the Taiwanese had developed their own culture, much of which survives today in the form of folk arts and festivals. Traditional Chinese religious and cultural festivals no longer celebrated on the Chinese mainland are still celebrated in Taiwan. Taiwan has its own dialect, which is gradually being used more on television and in the legislature. During Chen Shui-bian's presidency, the government de-Sinicised Taiwan by replacing the word China with that of Taiwan in the names of state-owned companies and government agencies (e.g. China Post became Taiwan Post, although this was later reversed under the Ma government and now is called Chunghwa Post as a compromise) or simply eliminating the reference to China (e.g. Chinese Petroleum Corporation became CPC Corporation). Memorials and statues to Chiang Kai-shek were also gradually removed, and the Chiang Kai-shek airport in Taipei was renamed the Taiwan Taoyuan International Airport.

In 1992, 18 percent of the population of Taiwan identified themselves as Taiwanese only, 46 percent identified as Taiwanese and Chinese, while 36 percent identified themselves as only Chinese. By 2019, this breakdown had changed dramatically. A full 58.5 percent identified themselves as Taiwanese, and the percentage identifying as Taiwanese and Chinese

154 *Taiwan (Republic of China)*

(sometimes referred to as "blue skin, green bones") had dropped to 34.7 percent, while those identifying as only Chinese was 3.5 percent (Election Study Centre, 2019).

Religion

The main religions followed in Taiwan are Buddhism and Daoism, with over 85 percent of the population practising one or both religions. Most people worship both Buddhist and Daoist gods. Chinese folk religion (a broad term for a variety of spiritual beliefs and practices) is also widely practised. About 4 percent of the population is Christian, including almost all the Indigenous peoples. The Taiwanese worship the spirits of their ancestors and pray to them for help. Many homes and businesses recognize a variety of deities by erecting altars at which people pray for health and fortune and make offerings of food. Throughout Taiwan are temples dedicated to an enormous number of deities. While some temples are only Buddhist, many places of worship include Buddhist, Daoist and folk religious traditions. Numerous festivals honour these gods and deities. At the annual Tomb-Sweeping Festival, families clean up ancestral grave sites, burn incense and make offerings to honour their ancestors. In Ghost Month (the seventh month of the lunar calendar), businesses sell paper facsimiles of a wide variety of items (including cars, houses and computers), which people buy and bring to a temple to burn so that their ancestors are able to use the items in the afterlife. If ancestors are neglected, they may come back and haunt their living relatives.

Like the other East Asian countries, Confucianism is a significant part of Taiwanese values (see Chapter 8).

Taiwan's economy

Over the past 50 years, Taiwan's industrial and economic structure has evolved dramatically. In the aftermath of World War II, and the Chinese Civil War, Taiwan became a low-cost manufacturing economy. During their occupation, the Japanese developed Taiwan's physical and economic infrastructure. Although a small, resource-poor island, Taiwan had a good base from which to develop its economy. It began by investing in agriculture, and in the 1950s, Taiwan was producing food and textiles, gradually moving into labour-intensive light industries. By the 1980s, the Taiwanese were finding success in strategic and high-technology industries, particularly semiconductors. Taiwan focussed on expanding exports by using tariffs, import restrictions and the control of foreign exchange to help protect and develop its domestic industries. It followed the capitalist development state model pioneered by Japan and copied by South Korea.

Today, Taiwan's economy consists of 1.4 million small- to medium-sized enterprises (SMEs) (98 percent of the private sector), which employ 80 percent of the labour force. A significant number of these SMEs are high-technology companies in a wide range of sectors. According to media and information firm Thomson Reuters, Taiwan has 13 of the world's leading technology companies (Chou and Kao, 2018). Taiwan's information and communications technology (ICT) sector is one of the largest in the world. Taiwanese ICT plays a major role in global technology supply chains and the country has developed a commanding global market share position for a wide range of ICT high-technology components. In 2014, for example, Taiwan had an 85 percent market share for motherboards and notebook personal computers, 66.5 percent for LCD monitors and 88 percent for wireless LAN (Hsiao, 2015). Taiwan is also dominant in custom IC fabrication, personal navigation devices, IC testing and packaging and high-end bicycles. With the exceptions of Acer and Foxconn, few of the companies producing these components are well known, as most are SMEs. This specialization in intermediate goods—"Taiwan Inside" as Taiwan's Institute for Information Industry describes it—has served Taiwan well, but the financial margins have declined. As a result, some Taiwanese companies are aiming to develop their own brands and to be at the forefront of high-end, higher value-added products.

In addition to ICT, Taiwan's semiconductor production industry has also been successful, achieving sales of $4.4 billion in 2017. Taiwan is now the second largest semiconductor foundry (meaning it makes chips for third parties) manufacturer in the world. Although ICT and semiconductors are two of the main sectors contributing to Taiwan's economic growth, Taiwan is also branching out into other sectors such as biotechnology, digital content, Internet of Things (IOT) and artificial intelligence.

Central to Taiwan's present and future economic development are science and technology. Taiwan spends over 3 percent of its GDP on research and development, placing it in the world's top 10 spenders as a percentage of GDP, and the government generously supports and funds applied scientific development. Taiwan is home to three large science-based industrial parks which, with their research and development facilities and access to the talent pool from Taiwan's top universities, are a base for the island's high-technology industry. Hsinchu Science Park in northern Taiwan focuses on semiconductors and optoelectronics but is moving into advanced IC fabrication, high-end medical and IOT devices. The Central Science Park in Taichung specializes in precision machinery, optoelectronics, biotechnology and computers and peripherals. The Southern Taiwan Science Park's areas of specialization are green energy and medical devices. In 2018, revenue from the three science parks was over $84 billion.

Taiwan also has some real strengths in digital content, including computer animation, digital gaming, e-learning and mobile applications. It is the world capital of Mandarin pop music (Mandopop) and a major production base for high-quality Chinese movies. Taiwan offers the movie industry free speech, rich traditional Chinese culture (much of which was destroyed in China during the Cultural Revolution) and local Taiwanese culture. Taiwan now boasts a number of internationally renowned movie directors such as Ang Lee and Tom Lin.

One of the Tsai government's goals is to become more independent of the Chinese market and strengthen regional connections. Its New Southbound Policy is a market diversification strategy aimed at expanding economic and social connections with Southeast Asia, South Asia, Australia and New Zealand.

ROC/Taiwanese Armed Forces

There are approximately 300,000 members of the ROC Armed Forces and 3.8 million reservists. Taiwan has conscription for men over 18, but the time of mandatory service was significantly reduced from two years to four months in 2013. The option of alternative civilian duties for six months is also possible. Limited conscription has meant that the Taiwanese armed forces are facing a serious shortage of manpower.

The ROC Armed Forces work closely with the U.S. military and depends upon the United States for the purchase of arms. Since President Tsai's election in 2016, Beijing has been increasing military pressure on Taiwan by conducting drills nearby and flying aircraft overhead. China has not ruled out the use of force if Taiwan were to make any move towards independence.

Taiwan-U.S. relations post-1979

In 1979, the United States granted the People's Republic of China full democratic recognition and terminated diplomatic relations with the Republic of China. Shortly thereafter, the U.S. Congress passed the Taiwan Relations Act (TRA), which governed unofficial cultural and commercial ties between the United States and Taiwan going forward. The TRA replaced the Mutual Defense Treaty and obligated the United States to help Taiwan increase its capacity to defend itself if an invasion was threatened by China. The TRA states that the United States would refer to the island's leadership as the governing authorities on Taiwan, rather than as the Republic of China. In 1979, the American Institute in Taiwan became the de facto American embassy, and the TRA recognized Taiwan as a sovereign entity.

The United States is Taiwan's main supplier of arms. Over the years, the Americans have sold Taiwan billions of dollars' worth of military equipment, including tanks, frigates, military aircraft, helicopters, missiles, mine-hunting ships and various weapons. Whenever the sale of American military equipment to Taiwan occurs or is even broached, the PRC makes its strong disapproval known. As China's economic importance to the United States has increased, the United States has justified and balanced its obligations, selling weapons to Taiwan while carefully choosing what it sells to offend China as little as possible. In 2011, for example, the Obama administration decided not to sell Taiwan the F16 fighter jets it had requested, instead offering to help Taiwan refurbish the jets it already had.

Some American analysts have suggested that perhaps the United States should rethink the Taiwan Relations Act since the actions it condones upset the Chinese government (Hsiao and Borsoi-Kelly, 2019). President Donald Trump, however, has been extremely pro-Taiwan. While still president-elect, he took a congratulatory phone call from President Tsai, the first time since 1979 that a U.S. president spoke directly to the president of the ROC. The Trump administration has made numerous major arms deals with Taiwan and has increased the presence of American patrol ships in the Taiwan Strait. The Taiwan Travel Act, which encourages engagement between American and Taiwanese officials, was passed in 2018. The following year, the House unanimously passed a non-binding resolution reaffirming America's commitment to Taiwan and the Taiwan Assurance Act, which affirms American support for Taiwan and the United States' commitment to enhancing Taiwan's self-defence capabilities.

Taiwan-China relations

For many years, there was very little contact or communication between Taiwan and the mainland. Because no treaty or agreement was signed when the civil war ended in 1949, the two governments remained in a state of war. Any trade that took place between the two was shipped through a third country. In 1979, after the United States ended its diplomatic ties with the Republic of China, the PRC government believed it now had the advantage in terms of its relationship with the ROC and put forward proposals to develop postal, transportation and trade links between the two. The then President Chiang Ching-kuo, however, refused and gave his "three noes": there would be "no contact, no compromise and no negotiation."

In 1992, a meeting took place between semi-official representatives of the PRC government led by the Chinese Communist Party and the ROC government led by the KMT. Later, the idea that an agreement was reached—later referred to as the 1992 Consensus—was frequently mentioned, although it is clear now that no such agreement was achieved. The 1992 meeting was, however, a new start as both sides sat down and spoke peacefully after decades of hostility. This would pave the way for the beginning of engagement between the two sides.

The PRC and the ROC did not have the same interpretation of the so-called 1992 Consensus. The ROC claimed that the agreement was that "There's only one China, but each side can interpret whether the ROC or the PRC is the legitimate government of this China." The PRC's position was that "There is only one China. Both sides will make efforts together to pursue the unification of China. During non-political and business engagement, the political interpretation of China can be put to the side." When relations were good, the ROC and the PRC had a tacit understanding that they would avoid the topic and allow business and civil engagements to continue. When their relationship was not good, they argued about the 1992 Consensus. Underlying the 1992 Consensus was the KMT agreement not to push for independence, but, even when relations between the CCP and the KMT government in Taiwan were at their best, the two parties did not have the same interpretation of the 1992 Consensus.

Taiwan and China view the island's status in different ways. Beijing asserts that there is only "one China" and that Taiwan is an inviolable part of it. The KMT's long-standing position was that while Taiwan belongs to China, the ROC government is the legitimate governing body of all of China. Focussing on the absence of an agreement on what is meant by China, the DPP argues that, in fact, there is no consensus at all.

Over the decades since the 1992 Consensus meeting, contact between Taiwan and the mainland slowly increased. Incremental change was evident as more family reunions took place, trade and investment increased, more Taiwanese students began studying at Chinese universities, and direct flights between the two countries were allowed during major holidays and later more frequently. However, it was not until President Ma's tenure from 2008 to 2016 that links between Taiwan and the PRC really expanded. In his augural address, Ma stated that during his time as president, there would be no unification, no independence and no use of force. Ma spoke of mutual "nonrecognition and nondenial," meaning that each side refrains from repudiating the other's jurisdiction, as the best foundation for Beijing-Taipei relations. Soon after Ma assumed office cross-Strait relations began to warm considerably. Trade and investment boomed; commercial and cargo flights increased dramatically; and students, tourists and businesspeople travelled in large numbers back and forth. Through these softer economic means, the Chinese government made significant progress improving relations with Taiwan's political and corporate leadership, media and general public. Hu Jintao (former general secretary of the Communist Party and president of the PRC) is reported to have said that it is easier and less expensive to "buy Taiwan" than to conquer it militarily.

Tsai Ing-wen was elected president of Taiwan in 2016 and re-elected in 2020. As a member of the DPP, which has a more Taiwanese nationalist and independence leaning outlook than does the KMT, Tsai's election immediately made the PRC nervous. Although Tsai has continually indicated her desire to have stable and positive relations with Beijing and not to implement significant changes to Taiwan's cross-Strait policy, she has rejected the 1992 Consensus saying that the Republic of China has never accepted it. Since Tsai's election, tensions between Beijing and Taipei have escalated, and relations have deteriorated. In August 2019, for example, the PRC suspended the solo traveller program, which had allowed mainland tourists to visit Taiwan on their own, not as part of a tour. In the first half of 2019, visitors from the PRC constituted about one-quarter of Taiwan's tourist arrivals, 40 percent of whom were independent travellers. The loss of Chinese tourists through the solo traveller program will clearly have an economic impact on Taiwan unless this loss is compensated by the arrival of tourists from elsewhere. In ending the program in the lead up to the January

158 *Taiwan (Republic of China)*

2020 presidential and legislative elections, China was likely trying to send Taiwanese voters a message. Since Xi Jinping became General Secretary of the CCP, the PRC has taken an even tougher line toward both its potentially restive regions like Tibet and Xinjiang and towards Taiwan. The election of Tsai has increased China's scrutiny of cross-Strait relations and the pressure China is willing to exert on Taiwan.

In 2018, Taiwan-China bilateral trade was $150.5 billion. China is Taiwan's largest export destination, receiving close to 40 percent of Taiwanese exports, and its largest source of imports. Additionally, China is the top Taiwanese investment destination. As of September 2017, Taiwanese firms employed 10 million workers in the PRC. (However, the tariffs imposed by the United States on Chinese exports in 2019 appear likely to result in an exodus of Taiwanese companies from China.) There are approximately 400,000 cross-Strait couples, mainly Chinese women and Taiwanese men, and about 300,000 Chinese come to Taiwan annually on medical tourism visits. The number of tourists from China to Taiwan peaked in 2015 at 4.18 million, dropping to 2.7 million in 2018. Since the DPP's election, the Chinese government has pressured its citizens not to visit Taiwan. If they do visit, they are encouraged to visit the cities and counties with KMT mayors.

In November 2019, the Chinese government announced a range of measures to strengthen economic ties between Taiwan and China. Included among them was a measure that permitted Taiwanese companies to invest in airlines and in 5G mobile networks; another measure allowed Taiwanese abroad to seek assistance from Chinese consulates. Additional measures to simplify life for Taiwanese living in China had been announced the previous year, but members of Taiwan's Mainland Affairs Council believed these measures were attempts to influence the then upcoming January 2020 presidential elections. China has actively interfered in Taiwan's elections through aggressive campaigns of disinformation (planting fake news stories by using bots and false social media accounts), cyberattacks and increased control over the Taiwanese media.

As the 2020 presidential election approached, incumbent president Tsai's polling numbers improved. Six months earlier she had been neck-and-neck with her KMT opponent, Han Kuo-yu, but by the week prior to the January 2020 election, Tsai Ing-wen was polling well ahead of him. A significant reason for President Tsai's improved polling numbers appears to be the Communist Party's hard-line response to the 2019 Hong Kong protests, which marred the potential for closer relations between Taiwan and China. As the KMT is seen as pro-China (despite its roots in opposition to the Communist Party), the DPP, which is much more anti-Beijing, has encouraged the Taiwanese public to protect their democracy. As part of its election campaign, the DPP launched a video contrasting the peace of Taiwan with the riots occurring in Hong Kong. On January 11, 2020, Tsai Ing-wen won a second term as Taiwan's president with over 57 percent of the vote, signalling strong support for her tough stance on China. Her victory has increased tensions with Beijing as she continues to refuse to endorse the position that Taiwan and the mainland are part of one China. In response to Tsai's victory, China's top diplomat, State Councillor Wang Yi, said that the principle of "one China," which includes Taiwan, is the international consensus and that reunification is inevitable. Separatists "will be doomed to leave a stink for 10,000 years," Wang said, meaning they will go down in infamy.

China has approximately 2,000 short-, medium- and long-range ballistic missiles deployed along the Taiwan coast that could be used to attack the island. China's military, the People's Liberation Army, conducts military drills in the Taiwan Strait, and fighter jets frequently fly through the Strait as a show of force. In 2005, the PRC passed the Anti-Secession Law, thus formalizing the country's policy that in the event Taiwan declared independence, the PRC would be willing to use "non-peaceful and other necessary means" in response. In his January 1, 2019, new year speech, China's President Xi Jinping told Taiwan that the objective of any cross-Strait discussions must be unification and that any serious steps towards independence could be met with force. A 2018 U.S. Department of Defense report noted that the People's Liberation Army has "continued to develop and deploy increasingly advanced military capabilities intended to coerce Taiwan, signal Chinese resolve, and gradually improve capabilities for an invasion."

Although Taiwan's legal name is still the Republic of China, it increasingly uses the name Taiwan (.tw is its Internet domain) or the Republic of China (Taiwan). The removal of China from Taiwan's official name would anger the PRC, which is largely why Taiwan has not done so. Yet, as Salvatore Babones writes in *Foreign Policy*, "Slowly but inexorably, Taiwan is going its own way" (Babones, 2020). Over 90 percent of the Taiwanese population was born after 1949, and only a tiny number of people were adults when the KMT fled to the island.

The most recent (February 2020) National Chengchi University Taiwan Independence versus Unification Survey asked if Taiwan's citizens supported unification with China, independence or the status quo. Only 1.4 percent indicated support for unification as soon as possible and another 7.5 percent supported maintaining the status quo while moving towards unification. Support for independence as soon as possible was 5.1 percent, while 21.8 percent supported maintain the status quo while moving towards independence. The vast majority—57.6 percent—wanted to keep the status quo indefinitely or keep the status quo and decide at a later date (Election Study Center, 2020).

In the wake of what has occurred in Hong Kong in 2019–2020, anti-China or anti-CCP feelings may have increased. While most people in Taiwan want to be allowed to live their lives in peace, it is clear that Taiwan is not going to choose to become a province of China.

Conclusion

Taiwan's transformation since the end of World War II is one of the most impressive in world history, but the country nonetheless struggles with national uncertainty and profound threats. Over the past four decades, Taiwan shifted from its rural, agrarian roots to contemporary industrial and technological development. "Taiwan Inside"—which refers to the fact that many of the internal components of digital devices are either made in Taiwan or by Taiwanese firms—is an apt symbol for a nation of almost 24 million that has created for itself a central role in the technology-based 21st-century economy.

Taiwan's uncertainty rests on its relationship with the People's Republic of China. For good reason, the Taiwanese watch the political struggles in Hong Kong with trepidation, discovering how weak the "One Country, Two Systems" approach is in practice. Taiwan's leadership understands their vulnerability and knows, with sorrow, that the world community will not likely stand with them in the face of China's assertiveness.

Notes

1 Three years later, Japan sent a retaliatory military force to Taiwan that killed 16 aborigines.
2 Toward the end of the war, Allied strategists considered an invasion of Taiwan but ultimately decided against it.
3 Many of these treasures of imperial China can be seen at the beautiful National Palace Museum in Taipei.

160   *Taiwan (Republic of China)*

Bibliography

Andrade, Tonio. 2010. *How Taiwan Became Chinese: Dutch, Spanish, and Han Colonization In the Seventeenth Century*. E-book, New York: Columbia University Press.

Babones, Salvatore. 2020. "Taiwan Deserves to be a Normal Country", *Foreign Policy*, January 15.

Chou, Li-fang and Evelyn Kao. 2018. "13 Taiwanese Companies Ranked Among Top 100 Global Tech Leaders", *Focus Taiwan CNA English News*, January 18. https://focustaiwan.tw/business/201 801180009

Election Study Center, National Chengchi University. https://esc.nccu.edu.tw/page1/news.php?class= 601

Hsiao, Meili. 2015. "Taiwan ICT Outlook and Software", *Institute for Information Industry Presentation*, November 20. https://www.slideshare.net/agencedunumerique/taiwan-ict-develop-outlook

Hsiao, Russel and Marzia Borsoi-Kelly. 2019. "The Taiwan Relations Act at 40: Reaching a New Equilibrium in U.S.-Taiwan Policy, Foreign Policy Research Institute, April 8. https://www.fpr i.org/article/2019/04/the-taiwan-relations-act-at-40-reaching-a-new-optimal-equilibrium-in-u-s-taiwan-policy/

https://esc.nccu.edu.tw/course/news.php?Sn=166

U.S. Department of Defense. 2018. *Annual Report to Congress: Military and Security Developments Involving the People's Republic of China 2018*. May, p. 106. https://media.defense.gov/2018/Aug/ 16/2001955282/-1/-1/1/2018-CHINA-MILITARY-POWER-REPORT.PDF

Further Reading

Brown, Kerry and Kalley Wu Tzu Hui. 2019. *The Trouble with Taiwan: History, the United States and a Rising China*. Zed Books.

Liao, Ping-hui and David Der-wei Wang. 2006. *Taiwan Under Japanese Colonial Role, 1895–1945: History, Culture and Memory*. Columbia University Press.

Manthorpe, Jonathan. 2008. *Forbidden Nation: A History of Taiwan*. St. Martin's Griffin.

Rigger, Shelley. 2011. *Why Taiwan Matters: Small Island, Global Powerhouse*. Rowman and Littlefield.

Roy, Dennis. 2002. *Taiwan: A Political History*. Cornell University Press.

Tsang, Steve (editor). 2012. *The Vitality of Taiwan: Politics, Economics, Society and Culture*. Palgrave.

6 Hong Kong, Special Administrative Region of the People's Republic of China

Introduction

Hong Kong is located on the south-eastern edge of China. It comprises Hong Kong Island, the Kowloon Peninsula and the New Territories, which stretch from Kowloon to the border with Shenzhen province, and over 200 islands and islets (see Figure 6.1). Hong Kong was under British rule from 1842 to 1997 when it returned to Chinese sovereignty and was renamed the Hong Kong Special Administrative Region (SAR). About three-quarters of the size of the Hawaiian Island of Oahu, Hong Kong has a population of 7.5 million people.

Hong Kong's reputation has been one of a capitalist free market economy with low taxes and minimal government interference in the market. One of the world's most important international financial centres, an international commercial port and an international business hub, Hong Kong has the second highest number of corporate headquarters in the Asia-Pacific region.

History

In the 1780s, the British began selling opium to China, and within 25 years, American and British traders were competing to satisfy the rapidly increasing demand for the drug. Trade between China and Great Britain had grown over the previous century, but it had been one-sided. The British bought tea, silk and porcelain from China, but the Chinese were not interested in buying many items from Britain (this was rooted in a sense of superiority, the belief that China did not need anything from Britain) and so the Chinese were paid instead with silver. Opium was one thing the Chinese would buy and the British were able to produce it cheaply in India, a British colony at the time. Britain flooded China with opium, and much of the population became addicted. The Chinese government passed a series of decrees making the opium trade illegal, but foreign merchants, particularly those of the British East India Company, continued to smuggle it in. Most of the opium came through Canton, present-day Guangzhou, the main port open to foreign traders.

In 1839, the emperor ordered the seizure of all opium in Canton, including that held by foreign governments, and put the imperial Commissioner Lin Tse-hsu in charge of carrying out those orders. Lin detained the British in Canton and confiscated approximately 1,300 tons of opium before publicly destroying them. The Chinese authorities then tried to persuade foreign companies to exchange their opium for tea, but this attempt was unsuccessful, so they raided the Western merchants' part of the city and took all the opium they could find. A blockade of foreign ships was then set up to force them to surrender the opium they carried.

162 *Hong Kong*

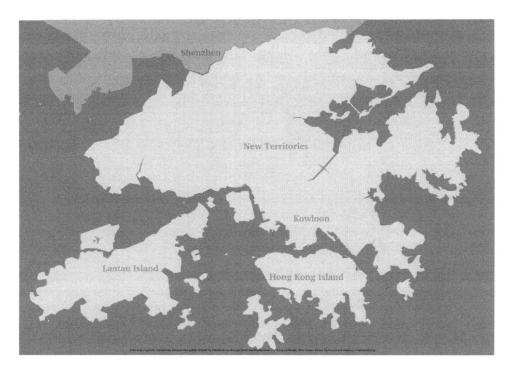

Figure 6.1 Map of Hong Kong.

The British trade commissioner brazenly recommended a military response to force China to reimburse the British smugglers for their economic losses and protect them in the future. In 1839, fighting broke out between British and Chinese ships in Kowloon harbour, and in 1940, the British government sent in troops and attacked and occupied Canton. This defeat was the first in a series that the British inflicted on the Qing Empire in China. In August 1842, the British seized the city of Nanjing, which ended the war.

In reality, the war for the British was not about opium. The Chinese government's attack on the British opium smugglers was merely an excuse for Britain to declare war on China. The real reason for this war was the British government's aspirations for free trade with China, its goal being to persuade China to open up its ports (at the time, only Canton was open to foreign trade) and to allow an equal diplomatic and trading relationship between the two nations to develop. To this point, China had considered itself culturally superior to other countries, and the Chinese demanded that foreigners kowtow to the Chinese emperor.

The 1842 Treaty of Nanjing that concluded the war was the first of what the Chinese refer to as the unequal treaties between China and foreign imperial powers. (These treaties are only part of a series of what China saw as humiliations. The Chinese government has used these humiliations to politically and diplomatically justify a range of aggressive measures to project Chinese interests onto the international stage.) The Treaty of Nanjing called for China to cede Hong Kong "in perpetuity" and required the Chinese to pay Britain $21 million. It also opened up five Chinese ports to British trade (Shanghai, Canton, Ningpo, Fuzhou and Amoy). The following year the British Supplementary Treaty of the Bogue was signed, which granted Britain most favoured nation status (meaning it receives any rights that might be granted to any other country) and extraterritoriality (the right of British citizens to be tried by British courts). Almost 20 years later in 1860, China lost to the British in battle a second time. The result of this second Opium War was that the Chinese ceded to Britain Stonecutters Island in Hong Kong harbour and the Kowloon Peninsula, the land facing Hong Kong Island. In the future, the Kowloon Peninsula would become an important part of Hong Kong.

The third and largest part of today's Hong Kong is the New Territories, a large area of agricultural land leased by Britain in 1898 for 99 years and returned to Chinese sovereignty in 1997. While Hong Kong and Kowloon were ceded in perpetuity, the lease on the New Territories ended in 1997. Hong Kong and Kowloon were closely integrated with the New Territories and dependent upon the agricultural products grown there. Knowing that the New Territories' lease would soon come to an end prompted the British to begin negotiating Hong Kong's future with China in 1982. They initially hoped to renew the lease for the New Territories when it ended in 1997, but Deng Xiaoping, the paramount leader of the People's Republic of China (PRC) at the time, threatened to send troops into the rest of Hong Kong if the New Territories were not returned.

Hong Kong was administered as a British colony from 1842 to 1997, with the exception of the Japanese occupation (1942–1945) during World War II. At the end of the war, the U.S. ordered the Japanese forces in Hong Kong to surrender to Chiang Kai-shek and his Nationalist troops (the government of the Republic of China), but since Chiang did not hurry to Hong Kong, the British arrived there first and accepted the Japanese surrender. The British and their leaders were determined to hold on to Hong Kong.

Although the Communist army did not attempt to force Britain out of Hong Kong, either during the civil war or after, Beijing never accepted that British rule of Hong Kong was legitimate. The Chinese Communist Party (CCP) always insisted that Hong Kong was a part of China that had been stolen by Britain, protesting the description of Hong Kong and Macao (a Portuguese colony) as colonies. If Hong Kongers had attempted to declare independence from Britain, China made it clear that it would have immediately stepped in.

Hong Kong under the British

British Hong Kong was primarily ruled by the colonial government of Hong Kong with little interference from either London or China. Although the Chinese government was uncomfortable with the existence of capitalist Hong Kong controlled by a foreign power, it did not step in to challenge the situation. The Hong Kong colonial government reported to the British parliament but was generally left to handle its own affairs. The governor, appointed by the British King or Queen, was the head of government and appointed the members of the Legislative and Executive Councils. While the local population was heavily involved in running the colony, the British still controlled the major levers of power, although they consulted widely with the population through a variety of consultative committees, advisory groups and local councils.

In 1967, a labour dispute turned violent, unleashing months of unrest, demonstrations and rioting across the territory. A spillover from the Cultural Revolution underway in China, pro-Communist demonstrators protested against the Hong Kong government. In response, the government arrested leftist activists, banned leftist publications and gave the police special powers to bring the unrest under control. Over time, these demonstrations coalesced into enormous protests against colonial rule by the British, which had long been seen as being out of touch with the local population. Riots and bombings killed 51 people, including 10 police officers, and injured over 800 more. The British authorities finally brought the situation under

164   *Hong Kong*

control by implementing a number of significant political reforms, the first of which was the creation of District Council offices that would allow for improved communications between the citizens and the government. Other important changes as a result of the 1967 Hong Kong protests were the opening of the Mass Transport Railway (the MRT), Hong Kong's subway and the implementation of universal education, healthcare, and a large public housing program.

Under the British, there was never universal suffrage in Hong Kong. Once the CCP took control of the mainland after the civil war, it had threatened repercussions if Britain were to take any steps toward the development of democracy in Hong Kong. Some democratic reforms did begin in the 1980s, but the Basic Law required that the British seek approval from Beijing before changing laws or policies governing Hong Kong. Nonetheless, the final British governor of Hong Kong, Chris Patten, did in fact carry out a series of democratic reforms to broaden the electorate for the colony's three levels of government without the consent of the CCP and the Chinese government. Infuriated by these changes, the PRC responded by indicating that after the handover, it would immediately nullify any of the political liberalization provisions that went beyond what was agreed to in the 1990 Basic Law (details below).

From the post-war period on, Hong Kong flourished as a centre for international trade and finance. Hong Kong's political stability meant that the colony's citizens could focus on making money, which they did with enthusiasm. Since Britain had recognized the PRC in early 1950, trade between Hong Kong and southern inland China expanded, although Britain's economic blockade of China during the Korean War temporarily decreased this trade. Towards the end of China's civil war, money, gold, commodities and talents fled China for Hong Kong. Many corporations also moved in, enabling industries like textiles, rubber and chemicals to take root in Hong Kong and play a key role in the city-state's industrialization in the 1950s and 1960s. Other sectors were also quickly established, including clothing, electronics, plastics, toys, games and watches. In the 1990s, Hong Kong became the third most important global financial centre after New York and London. The majority of the world's largest banks in the world have operations in Hong Kong, and the city is known for initial public offerings and mergers and acquisitions.

As the end of the New Territories' lease grew closer, the domestic and international business community became increasingly nervous. Much of the New Territories consisted of residential or commercial properties, which were leased to expire three days before the New Territories' lease itself expired on July 1, 1997. As that date grew closer, the leases became shorter, which were unattractive to investors. Eventually, taking into account the complicated political and economic situation, the British government took the initiative to launch negotiations with China over the future of Hong Kong.

Negotiations over the status of Hong Kong

Long negotiations between Great Britain and the PRC over the future of Hong Kong began in 1982. Both sides recognized that China's sovereignty over Hong Kong would restart in 1997 when Britain's lease for the New Territories expired. The three main districts (Hong Kong Island, Kowloon and the New Territories) comprising Hong Kong would of necessity stay together, but Britain and the PRC did not agree on how post-1997 Hong Kong would be governed. Citing their "moral commitment" to the Hong Kong people to ensure that the city remain stable and well off, the British intended their involvement with the administration of Hong Kong to continue after 1997, hoping that Chinese sovereignty over the territory would be somewhat symbolic. The PRC, however, was adamant that the country's sovereignty over Hong Kong would be far more than symbolic; Hong Kong would be under Chinese control. Hong Kong citizens themselves were not part of the negotiations about the future of their home. The PRC's position was that it spoke for all Chinese, including the Chinese of Hong Kong.

In 1984, the governments of the PRC and Great Britain signed the Sino-British Joint Declaration, which stated that as of July 1, 1997, Hong Kong would become a Special Adminnistrative Region (SAR) under the PRC. The United Kingdom would cede control of Hong Kong to China, which would assume sovereignty over the city-state. It was agreed that Hong Kong would be administered under "One Country, Two Systems" for 50 years. This meant that with the exception of foreign policy and defence, Hong Kong would remain fairly autonomous, keeping its legal, economic and political systems.

The Basic Law

The Basic Law is the document that transformed the Sino-British Joint Declaration into a legal document. The law was drafted by a working group under China's National People's Congress and consisted of members from both Hong Kong and mainland China. Although the British were not involved, there was a public consultation process in Hong Kong. Passed in 1990, the Basic Law became a mini-constitution for Hong Kong. As per the Joint Declaration, the Basic Law affirmed the One Country, Two Systems arrangement, which would mean that, except for foreign policy and defence, Hong Kong would have a large degree of independence until 2047. The city would have its own currency, status as a free port, and capital would be allowed to flow freely in and out of Hong Kong. Additionally, Hong Kong would be permitted to be an independent member of various international organizations like the World Trade Organization. Hong Kong's chief executive would be selected by an Election Committee appointed by the Standing Committee of the National People's Congress.

The Basic Law (Article 27) stated that "Hong Kong residents shall have freedom of speech, of the press and of publication; freedom of association, of assembly, of procession and of demonstration; and the right and freedom to form and join trade unions; and to strike." The Basic Law also indicated that "the ultimate aim is the selection of the chief executive by universal suffrage upon nomination by a broadly representative nominating committee in accordance with democratic procedures." What exactly this meant and how Hong Kong-China relations would evolve over the 50 years of One Country, Two Systems was left somewhat ambiguous. Many Hong Kong citizens were optimistic that, by 2047, China itself might be a democracy or moving in a democratic direction and that, in the meantime, Hong Kong would be left to operate as it had under the British. At the same time, some in the PRC perhaps envisioned that over the decades, Hong Kong would merge gradually into China, so that at the end of 50 years it would be just another Chinese city. The Chinese people were delighted about the return of Hong Kong to China. In the years leading up to the handover, a large clock in Tiananmen Square counted down the days, hours and minutes until the return.

The Basic Law was promulgated by China's National People's Congress in 1990. While the Hong Kong business community was generally supportive of the Basic Law, many Hong Kong residents were not. Protests broke out on the streets, and some people burned their copies of the Basic Law. Concerned about the handover, some Hong Kong residents claimed to want to leave. In the preceding years, many of those who were able to do so obtained overseas citizenship, particularly to Britain, Canada and Australia, as an "insurance policy"

166   *Hong Kong*

in case things did not proceed as they hoped. While some people moved or planned to move to their new country, most returned quickly to live in Hong Kong once they had obtained the new passport.

On July 1, 1997, the ceremony transferring sovereignty over Hong Kong from the United Kingdom to the PRC took place at the Hong Kong Convention and Exhibition Centre. In attendance were Secretary General of the CCP and President of the PRC Jiang Zemin, Premier Li Peng and Hong Kong Chief Executive Tung Chee-Hwa. Great Britain was represented by Prince Charles, Prime Minister Tony Blair and Hong Kong Governor Chris Patten. The official ceremony began at 11:30 p.m. on June 30 with the Prince of Wales reading a farewell speech on behalf of the British Queen. Just before midnight, the Union Jack and the British colonial flag of Hong Kong were lowered while the British national anthem, God Save the Queen, played. After 12 seconds of silence, the flag of the PRC and the new flag of Hong Kong were raised, while the Chinese national anthem, March of the Volunteers, was played.

After the handover—Hong Kong's relations with the mainland

The initial years after the handover were calm and uneventful. There was not a great deal of change in how the government functioned. Under the colonial system, a great deal of power had rested with the governor; under the Chinese, power was centralized in the executive branch, specifically with the chief executive. In the second five-year post-handover period, however, a few changes were implemented that caused some concern. In 2002, for example, the chief executive was given the authority to appoint all 14 policy secretaries within the 20-person cabinet. In years previous, those positions were held by senior civil servants and were theoretically politically neutral.

Changes in National Security legislation

In 2003, the Hong Kong government put forward National Security legislation to outline the specifics of Article 23 of the Basic Law. Article 23 states that Hong Kong should enact laws to prohibit treason, secession, subversion and sedition and the theft of state secrets. It also prohibits foreign political organizations from conducting political activities in the Hong Kong SAR or from establishing ties with domestic political organizations. The National Security legislation was met with a public outcry as many feared that the legislation would be used to limit the rights of the Hong Kong people. Many Hong Kong citizens were worried by how treason and subversion might be interpreted and what this could mean for journalists. As rule of law, freedom of speech and other civil rights do not exist in mainland China (and Hong Kong's government is subordinate to the central government in Beijing and the CCP), this fear was well founded. The CCP has a history of using these kinds of laws to violate the human and civil rights of its citizens, and Hong Kong residents were not eager for Beijing to use this law to tighten control over Hong Kong and its people. At the annual July 1 anniversary handover protest march in 2003, half a million people demonstrated against the bill. Demonstrations continued, prompting the Hong Kong government to withdraw the bill because it considered the unrest and anger directed toward Beijing to be destabilizing. In July 2020, however, China, tired of waiting for Hong Kong to pass national security legislation, imposed its own legislation on the territory deeply upsetting many in Hong Kong and around the world. Hong Kong's new National Security legislation was written in secret with little input from Hong Kong authorities. The law gives Beijing sweeping powers to arrest even the most peaceful protesters and impose tough penalties, including life in prison. Beijing's now extensive authority to intervene in Hong Kong's legal system has led many people fearing that this spells the end to One Country, Two Systems.

Moral and national education

Since 2007, the Hong Kong government has been trying to put moral and national education classes into the school curricula. The goal of these classes would be to foster a sense of national identity, patriotism for China and the PRC and loyalty to the PRC regime. Hong Kong residents started numerous groups in protest, the most significant of which was Scholarism—The Alliance Against Moral and National Education started by a group of secondary school students in 2011. (Core members of Scholarism formed the political party Demosisto in 2016.) Scholarism and other groups opposed to the moral and national education classes marched, wrote petitions and even occupied the Hong Kong government headquarters. After three months, Chief Executive Leung Chun-Ying announced that he would not continue with the national education courses for the time being. In 2017, the secretary for education indicated that national education was being included within different courses and school activities. Junior secondary schools, he went on to say, are now required to teach the Basic Law.

Suffrage and the Umbrella Movement

Articles 45 and 68 of Hong Kong's Basic Law indicate the aim of future universal suffrage for the chief executive and the Legislative Council (LegCo), respectively. In the first decade after the handover, selection of the chief executive and members of the LegCo had been controlled tightly by Beijing. In 2007, the CCP National Party Congress Standing Committee announced that there would be universal suffrage for the chief executive in 2017 and following that for the LegCo. Over the following years, Hong Kong pro-democracy politicians and citizens continued to push for these democratic reforms, including through a 2013 consultative process Beijing initiated. However, in 2014, Beijing announced that in the 2017 chief executive election, voters would be able to select between two or three candidates approved by a 1200-member nominating committee. While there would be universal suffrage, it would only be to vote on pre-screened pro-Beijing candidates.

This was far from the universal suffrage Hong Kong citizens had envisioned, and the city erupted in protests. This was the beginning of the Umbrella Movement (named for the umbrellas protesters used to protect themselves from pepper spray used by police). Tens of thousands of protestors (see Figure 6.2) occupied numerous central Hong Kong districts between September and December 2014. In June 2015, the LegCo voted against the reform plan, so the electoral system for the chief executive electoral system remained as before. Three of the young pro-democracy protest leaders were arrested for their role in the protests. Initially, two of the three were given community service sentences and the third a suspended sentence, but the Hong Kong government appealed for tougher sentences and won. (The impression that the judges may have given in to pressure created a loss of confidence in the rule of law.) The three men were sentenced to between six and eight months and released in just under five months.

The leaders of the Umbrella Movement had chosen the name and objectives carefully to avoid giving the impression that the movement had a separatist focus or was designed to overthrow the government. Beijing, however, remained deeply concerned and feared that a

Figure 6.2 Umbrella Movement protests 2014.

peaceful movement in Hong Kong demanding government change could infect mainland China. The Chinese leadership, therefore, led a campaign on the mainland to paint the protests as an anti-China separatist movement. In fact, while in Hong Kong the protests were called the Umbrella Movement, on the mainland they were referred to as the Umbrella Revolution. This terminology was meant to directly link these protests to the colour revolutions of the Middle East and Eastern Europe (e.g. Rose Revolution in Georgia, Green Revolution in Iran, Orange Revolution in Ukraine). Hong Kong had specifically chosen the word "movement" to intentionally delink its protests from those revolutions.

Booksellers' disappearance

Over the next few years, Hong Kong's autonomy and civil rights continued to be eroded. Between October and December 2015, five booksellers from Hong Kong's Causeway Bay Books disappeared. Causeway Bay Books sells political books, many of which are banned in China, making them popular with mainland visitors and local people. Three of the booksellers vanished from mainland China, one from Thailand and one from Hong Kong. Many believe the five were kidnapped by Chinese agents. One of the men was rumoured to be writing a book about President Xi Jingping's love affairs, a possible reason for the disappearances. Each of the booksellers has since reappeared, but stories of what occurred and why are complicated and confusing. One of the men did state that he had been abducted by Chinese officials at the Hong Kong-China border, held against his will for eight months and accused of selling banned books to the mainland.

Transportation links between Hong Kong and China

The Chinese and the Hong Kong governments have recently built two major infrastructure projects. The first is the Hong Kong-Zhuhai-Macau Bridge (HZMB) opened in 2018. The longest sea crossing in the world, it includes a 55-km road, an undersea tunnel, three bridges, and four artificial islands linking Hong Kong with Macau and Zhuhai, a manufacturing city, in Guangdong province. The second infrastructure project, also extremely expensive and challenging, was a high-speed railway from Hong Kong to Guangzhou, the capital of Guangdong, shortening a two-hour train ride to 50 minutes. Also opened in 2018, the high-speed railway runs 34 trains between the two cities each day. The mainland's goal is to eventually create a megacity of over 40 million people in the Guangdong Pearl River delta. Many in Hong Kong have been unhappy with the investments in infrastructure, criticizing the enormous costs and unsure if more links to the mainland benefit Hong Kong.

The improved transportation links seem likely to boost what is already a burgeoning tourism industry in Hong Kong. The past two decades have seen a massive increase in mainland visitors to Hong Kong, from 2 million in 1997 to 50 million in 2018. There has also been a huge jump in immigrants to Hong Kong from the mainland. Under the Hong Kong Basic Law, 50 mainland Chinese can immigrant daily to Hong Kong. Mainlanders who studied in Hong Kong are allowed to stay, and there are also a variety of work schemes under which they can stay.

This large influx of mainlanders has resulted in increased congestion and escalating prices on everything from daily goods to luxury goods to property. Mainlanders come to Hong Kong to take advantage of the low prices due to the city's tax-free status. Many are known as "parallel traders," meaning they buy large quantities of items that they repackage into smaller parcels and resell across the border. Concern over counterfeit products on the mainland also means Chinese mainlanders prefer to purchase items such as baby formula, cosmetics, luxury goods and medicines in Hong Kong.

The 2019 protests

In February 2019, the Hong Kong government introduced the Fugitive Offenders and Mutual Legal Assistance in Criminal Matters Legislation, which allows for the transfer of fugitives to and from Hong Kong, Taiwan, Macau and mainland China. The bill was in response to a case in which a Hong Kong man killed his girlfriend in Taiwan and returned to Hong Kong. Although he admitted to the murder, the lack of an extradition treaty between Hong Kong and Taiwan meant that the police were unable to charge him. The bill's objective was to allow for the transfer of fugitives to those areas with which Hong Kong did not have an extradition treaty.

The bill's introduction created immediate concern and criticism. Opponents feared that if the bill passed, mainland Chinese authorities would be able to arrest people in Hong Kong and bring them to mainland China for trial, away from Hong Kong's legal system with its safeguards. Gradually Hong Kong's independent legal jurisdiction, a key cornerstone of Hong Kong autonomy, could disappear. Protests against the bill erupted, increasing in size as the weeks went by. The first of the 2019 protests against the extradition bill began in March; on June 9, 2017, over a million people marched in the streets, calling for the Chief

170 *Hong Kong*

Executive Carrie Lam to resign and the bill to be completely withdrawn. By the time Chief Executive Lam agreed to withdraw the extradition bill in September, that concession was no longer enough. For the protestors, it was too little too late: the extradition bill protests had now merged into something larger.

Following orders from the Hong Kong government and supported by Beijing, the Hong Kong police retaliated harshly against the protesters, using large quantities of tear gas, water cannons, pepper spray, plastic bullets and even live ammunition. The protesters became increasingly disappointed in the Hong Kong government, frightened by Beijing's hard stance and depressed about the prospects of achieving their demands. The protests gradually turned into a fight for the future of Hong Kong, building on the 2014 Umbrella Movement. Tens of thousands of protestors took to the streets across Hong Kong on an almost nightly basis month after month (see Figure 6.3). Intentionally largely leaderless (a lesson learned from the Umbrella Movement), the protest movement was coordinated on social media. Early in August, protestors occupied the Hong Kong airport in a peaceful sit-in in an effort to secure international support for their movement. Later that same month, on both sides of Hong Kong Harbour, tens of thousands of people formed a 50-km human chain perhaps inspired by a similar human chain formed by two million protestors in Estonia, Latvia and Lithuania in 1989 in their fight for independence from the Soviet Union.

The protestors had five key demands: the withdrawal of the extradition bill, an investigation of police abuse of force during the protests, the retraction of the "riot" designation to describe the protests, the release and exoneration of all the arrested protesters and the

Figure 6.3 2019 Hong Kong anti-extradition bill protest.

resignation of Chief Executive Carrie Lam and universal suffrage for the next chief executive and Legislative Council. "Five key demands, not one less" became the rallying cry.

Months of unrest have not helped Hong Kong's economy, which fell into a recession in the second half of 2019. Business and employment slowed. Protests or the anticipation of protests meant that many people stayed home. Young people with work offers elsewhere moved away without plans to return to Hong Kong.

Hong Kong government

Chief Executive and executive branch

Hong Kong's chief executive is the head of the government of Hong Kong. After sovereignty was transferred to China, this position replaced the governor of Hong Kong. The chief executive, in consultation with his or her cabinet (the executive branch), introduces bills to the Legislative Council. He or she conducts foreign relations (although only some, as the rest is done in Beijing), appoints judges and signs bills and budgets. According to the Basic Law, the chief executive has the power to dissolve the Legislative Council and to veto bills.

The term of the chief executive is five years, and there is a two-term maximum. Interestingly, remuneration for the Hong Kong chief executive is the second highest in the world after Singapore. The chief executive is chosen by an Election Committee of approximately 1,200 individuals and special interest groups (functional constituencies, see below). To be elected, an individual must have a majority of the votes of the Election Committee, so a run-off may be necessary. The current chief executive is Carrie Lam who was elected in March 2017. She is the fourth chief executive and the first woman.

Constitution

Hong Kong's Basic Law is the SAR's mini-constitution.

Legislative Council (LegCo)

Hong Kong's Legislative Council (LegCo) is unicameral, with a total of 70 seats. The LegCo is responsible for debating the laws and budgets submitted by the executive branch. Elections take place every four years in years evenly divisible by four. (The 2020 elections were postponed for a year because of the COVID pandemic). The electoral system is complicated. Of the 70 seats, 40 are elected by popular vote: 35 in geographical constituencies and 5 in the District Council (Second) functional constituency (explained below). The other 30 seats are elected by what are called functional constituencies. Functional constituencies are professional or special interest groups such as insurance, real estate, law, agriculture and fisheries, engineering, information technology and health services.

Functional constituencies do not all elect representatives in the same way. In some each member votes, and in others membership organizations vote. Most of these functional constituency voters have traditionally tended to be pro-Beijing. As a result, the functional constituency system has basically ensured that the pro-Beijing parties win a majority of seats in every LegCo since the 1997 handover.

The significance of the functional constituencies is that only a small number of people vote for each functional constituency representative. Over 4.1 million voters are registered to vote in the geographic constituency elections to elect 35 representatives, while only about

172   *Hong Kong*

230,000 are registered to vote for the 30 functional constituency seats. The functional constituency system gives a minority of people significantly more influence than everyone else. That corporations and legal bodies have a vote also means that one person (e.g. someone whose corporate interests in one functional constituency control a sizeable portion of the vote) can have a disproportionate amount of voting power.

In 2012, in response to pressure to create a more democratic system, five District Council (Second) functional constituency seats were added. (One of the regular functional constituency seats is District Council—First.) Candidates, and nominators of candidates, for these five seats must be elected members of District Councils, which are the local councils for the 18 districts of Hong Kong. However, all registered voters who do not vote in any other functional constituency election are eligible to vote.

District Councils

District Councils are local councils for Hong Kong's 18 districts under the supervision of the Hong Kong government's Home Affairs Bureau. They advise the government on issues in their area and use public money for local public infrastructure and community activities. District Council elections have been held every four years since 1982. In 2019, 452 members were elected in the 18 District Councils. Each council has between 11 and 37 elected representatives. The November 2019 District Council elections took on unprecedented significance when, after seven months of serious unrest and mass protests, pro-democracy candidates took control of 17 of the 18 councils and won 389 of the 452 District Council seats contested. Record numbers of people voted. The pro-democracy movement considered these elections to be an endorsement of the protests and a repudiation of the argument that the silent majority was not in support of the protesters and their demands. The one district won by pro-Beijing parties was the Islands District.

Electoral system

The 35 geographical constituency seats are elected by proportional representation. A successful candidate can be elected in one of two ways: he or she receives the quota of votes, the total number of votes divided by the total number of seats (e.g. if there were a million voters and five seats, a candidate would need to receive 200,000 votes). If not enough candidates reach the quota to fill the available number of seats, the votes over the quota of the successful candidates are transferred to the next candidate from the same party. Then those candidates with the largest number of votes are elected.

Judiciary

Hong Kong's judiciary was independent under the British, and under the "One Country, Two Systems," it has generally remained so. English common law with certain adaptations is in place, and judges are appointed for life. Mindful of what attracted business in the past, China has permitted Hong Kong's legal system to be based on legal concepts not in place on the mainland. The important reasons that people are attracted to live and build businesses in the territory are Hong Kong's stability, the integrity of its judiciary and the territory's adherence to the rule of law. However, on political matters, the Basic Law states that the National People's Congress in Beijing interprets whether laws passed by the Hong Kong legislature are in conflict with the Basic Law. The power of the chief executive, who is basically selected by Beijing, to dissolve the legislature and veto bills also ensures this to be the case.

Hong Kong courts have stated that Hong Kong's judicial independence means that its citizens cannot be tried in China for any crimes committed in Hong Kong, even if the person was apprehended in mainland China. However, mainland China's criminal code states that the country has the right to prosecute a Chinese citizen who commits a crime anywhere if that crime has an impact on China. This broad jurisdiction, which clearly puts the two systems in conflict, is particularly significant as there is great mobility across the Hong Kong-mainland China border, and Hong Kong's criminal gangs also operate in mainland China.

During the 2019 protests, the independence of Hong Kong's judiciary was again tested when the government introduced a ban on the wearing of face masks at public gatherings. Protestors had been wearing a variety of face coverings to avoid the ubiquitous face recognition technology and protect themselves from the pepper spray used by the police. Hong Kong's High Court, however, struck down the anti-mask law as unconstitutional. The next day, the Chinese Central Government retaliated, saying that under the Basic Law, Hong Kong courts do not have the power to rule on the constitutionality of legislation.

Defence

Prior to the handover, the British Forces overseeing Hong Kong were responsible for the defence of Hong Kong. Britain stationed a military force of approximately 12,000 in the territory. In 1997, the People's Liberation Army took over the British military installations with their own forces of approximately 10,000–12,000 military personnel.

Political parties

Hong Kong has numerous political parties, and there are alliances among many of them. Overall, they fall into three camps: pro-Beijing parties, pan-Democratic parties and localist parties.

Pro-Beijing parties

Also referred to as the pro-establishment camp, pro-Beijing parties generally support the policies of the PRC towards Hong Kong. They have roots in the pro-Communist organizations that began when the CCP was founded in the 1920s. Supported by Hong Kong's political and business elite for whom a good relationship with Beijing brings business opportunities and political advantages, these parties tend to be conservative and emphasize social stability and economic prosperity. Some of the pro-Beijing party members are mainlanders who moved to Hong Kong after the handover.

Since the 1997 handover, these parties have been in control of the Hong Kong Legislative Council, partly because of their advantage in the functional constituency elections. In the 2016 election, the pro-Beijing parties won 40 seats. The Democratic Alliance for the Betterment and Progress of Hong Kong currently holds 12 seats in the LegCo, the largest number of seats of any party. Other major pro-Beijing parties include the Business and Professionals Alliance for Hong Kong (currently with seven seats), the Federation of Trade Unions (with five seats), the Liberal Party (with four seats) and the New People's Party (with three seats). There are also a range of other minor parties that also hold a seat each.

174   *Hong Kong*

Pan-democratic parties

Pan-Democratic parties support increased democracy for Hong Kong, specifically universal suffrage and direct elections for the chief executive and all members of the LegCo. With roots in the 1970s social activist youth movements and in the push for democracy during the lead-up to the 1997 takeover and after, members of these parties believe that only democracy can safeguard Hong Kong's civil liberties. Although they universally embrace liberal values such as human rights and social justice, their views on how best to achieve democracy vary, as do their economic approaches. The pro-democracy camp has received over 50 percent of the popular vote in LegCo elections, but the nature of the electoral system means that this majority has not been reflected in the number of seats they have received. In the 2016 election, the pan-democracy camp won 23 seats. (This is down from the 27 seats the pan-democrats won in the 2012 elections.) Some of the traditionally pan-democratic voters supported localist (see below) candidates in 2016. The two pan-democratic parties with the most support are the Democratic Party (currently with seven seats) and the Civic Party (currently with six seats). Others include Professional Commons, the Labour Party, People Power and the League of Social Democrats.

Localist parties

The localist political movement emerged as a serious political force after the 2014 Umbrella Movement. Although different groups with disparate goals are part of this movement, they share a concern about Beijing's encroachment on the life of Hong Kong and a desire to preserve the city's autonomy and local culture. Some organizations are focused on land development or cultural heritage or concerns over the influx of mainland tourists into Hong Kong. Some parties advocate for increased self-determination for Hong Kong; some even argue for independence. In the 2016 LegCo elections, localist parties won six seats, however, four of those elected were subsequently disqualified (see Hong Kong Legislative Assembly oath-taking controversy). Civic Passion currently has a seat in the LegCo and Demosisto. It opposes China's interference in Hong Kong, including the increased use of the Mandarin language. Demosisto won a seat in 2016 but was disqualified. It advocated for civil disobedience and supported a referendum on independence after the 50 years One Country, Two Systems agreement ends. Demosisto disbanded hours after the new national security law was passed. In November 2020 Beijing imposed a new law on Hong Kong allowing the disqualification of legislators deemed to be unpatriotic. Four sitting legislators were almost immediately dismissed and shortly thereafter the remaining 15 pro-democracy legislators resigned.

Hong Kong Legislative Assembly oath-taking controversy

To be sworn into the Hong Kong LegCo, elected members must take the oath of office in which they swear allegiance to the Hong Kong SAR of the PRC. This ceremony has been the site of protests in the past. At the October 12, 2016, oath-taking ceremony, five localist and eight pan-democracy representatives protested by intentionally saying the words of the oath incorrectly or saying something in advance of or after the oath, shouting slogans or displaying a banner reading "Hong Kong is not part of China." At the end of the subsequent government response and judicial review, six elected legislators (four localist and two pan-democrat) were disqualified and removed from office.

Hong Kong society

Ninety-two percent of Hong Kong's population is Chinese. The other 8 percent comes from around the globe but is primarily Filipino, Indonesian, Vietnamese, Indian, British and French. Immigrants from the Chinese mainland, primarily from China's southern provinces, have been coming to Hong Kong since 1842, particularly during and after the Chinese Civil War (1945–1949), following the Great Leap Forward (1959–1962) and during the Cultural Revolution (1966–1976). Many mainlanders fled to Hong Kong to escape poverty and to try to build a better life for themselves. Hong Kong also received many ethnic Chinese refugees from Vietnam in 1975 at the end of the Vietnam War. As China's economy has improved over the last 30 years, the flow of illegal immigrants has subsided. Since the handover, however, over 1 million mainland Chinese have moved to Hong Kong and become permanent residents. Unlike in the past, many of these new residents come from more distant provinces of China.

In 1996, just prior to the handover, the Chinese University of Hong Kong began conducting an annual telephone survey on Identity and National Identification of Hong Kong People. Respondents were asked how they identified themselves and given the options of Hong Kongese, Hong Kongese but also Chinese and Chinese but also Hong Kongese or Chinese (see Table 6.1). In 1996, about one-quarter of the population identified itself as exclusively Hong Kongese and another quarter as exclusively Chinese. Within the first decade of Hong Kong's handover to China, the percentage of the population who saw themselves as exclusively either one declined to about 17 percent. Gradually more and more Hong Kong citizens, possibly because of pride in the 2008 Beijing Olympics, saw themselves as Hong Kongese but also Chinese or Chinese but also Hong Kongese. However, by 2016, the survey results show that, as had been the case before the handover, almost one-quarter of the Hong Kong respondents saw themselves as only Hong Kongese, while the percentage who saw themselves as only Chinese continued to drop. The Chinese government's efforts to instil national pride worked for a few years, but Hong Kong's identity is rising again (Centre for Communication and Public Opinion Survey, 2017).

Hong Kong's two official languages are Chinese/Cantonese and English. Although a wide range of Chinese dialects are spoken in the city, approximately 80 percent of Hong Kong Chinese speak Cantonese as their mother tongue. As part of an effort to tie Hong Kong more closely to the mainland, the Chinese and Hong Kong governments have been promoting Mandarin, China's national language. Perhaps, as a result of these efforts, Mandarin is increasingly being used, and it is spoken daily by many of the mainlanders who have moved to Hong Kong in recent years. (The PRC calls Mandarin Putonghua, which means common speech. Putonghua was adopted in 1956 by the government to refer to the standardized form of Mandarin officially used in the PRC.) Mandarin is now used as the language of instruction

Table 6.1 Hong Kong identity survey

Year	Hong Kongese	Hong Kongese but also Chinese	Chinese but also Hong Kongese	Chinese	Other/No Answer
1996	25.2	32.9	14.7	25.7	1.5
2008	16.7	39.8	24.9	17.7	0.8
2016	24.0	42.8	19.9	12.2	1.1

176 *Hong Kong*

by the majority of Hong Kong primary schools and over one-third of secondary schools. When parents consider the growth of China's economy, they generally support the use of Mandarin in schools, believing that knowledge of the language will improve their children's job prospects. All Chinese languages use the same characters, but written Chinese is basically Mandarin in grammar and syntax with some adjustments. It can be pronounced with Cantonese or Mandarin (or other Chinese language) sounds. Cantonese language activists are fighting back to protect the language, hosting a Cantonese writing competition and developing the first ever Cantonese language dictionary.

In a 2014 Gallup International and the WI Network of Market Research survey, 70 percent of Hong Kongers indicated that they were either not religious or atheist (Noack, 2015). Nonetheless, about half the population identifies with Chinese folk religions, while 21 percent is Buddhist, 14 percent Taoist and 12 percent Christian. Smaller numbers of people are Hindu, Muslim, Sikh and Jewish. Confucianism, with its emphasis on hierarchy, the value of education and respect for parents, plays a major role in Hong Kong society. Falun Gong, the Chinese religious practice that combines slow exercises with qigong breathing, meditation and a philosophy of compassion, tolerance and truthfulness, has been banned in China but is still practised in Hong Kong.

Although one of the world's richest cities, Hong Kong is increasingly becoming a city of income inequality. The 2016 median monthly income of those at the top was 43.9 times those at the bottom (Wong, 2018). Extremes of wealth and poverty are widely evident. The rich have chauffeurs, maids and cooks to take care of them. In 2017, there were 370,000 foreign domestic workers in Hong Kong, almost all from the Philippines or Indonesia. The Hong Kong wealthy use their money to buy luxury cars (Hong Kong has the highest number of Rolls Royces and Mercedes Benz per capita in the world, often paying thousands of dollars for a personalized license plate), property, jewellery, collectibles, pets to pamper and unique experiences. Hong Kong's 21 wealthiest business people have assets equal to Hong Kong's US$166 billion fiscal reserves. Nine of Asia's 50 richest families are in Hong Kong. There are 93 U.S. dollar billionaires. Kevin Kwan who wrote the book *Crazy Rich Asians*, which was turned into a 2018 Hollywood film, is reportedly now working on a television series for Amazon that will be set in Hong Kong and focus on one of the city's richest and most powerful families.

Poverty, however, is a serious problem in Hong Kong. According to the annual Hong Kong Poverty Situation report, approximately 1.37 million of the city's 7.39 million people are poor. Twenty percent of the population, one in five people, survives on less than US$510 a month in one of the world's most expensive cities (Chiu, 2018). Exorbitant property prices and rent make the stark inequality in the city most obvious in housing. For half of the city's citizens, monthly rent is 70 percent of their median household income. Many in Hong Kong live in crowded high-rise apartment buildings; sometimes multiple families occupy one small apartment. The average living space per capita in Hong Kong is about 16 m^2 (172 ft^2), and in public rental housing it is only 12 m^2 (130 ft^2). Approximately 200,000 people live in "coffin homes," also called "cage homes," which are only 4.5 m^2 (48 ft^2), barely the size of a table tennis table. Multiple coffin homes made of stacked shoddily constructed wooden beds or metal cages are in one apartment with shared washrooms and kitchens. They are home to drug addicts, retirees without pensions and some of the city's working poor.

Hong Kong's economy

As a decidedly free market, Hong Kong has been at the top of the Index of Economic Freedom since the index was started in 1995. With its strong banking and legal systems,

Figure 6.4 Hong Kong Central and Victoria Harbour.

Hong Kong is considered a highly favourable place in which to start a company. Hong Kong has traditionally seen very little government intervention in the economy, making it different from the rest of East Asia. The seventh largest trading economy in the world, Hong Kong is extremely dependent on international trade and finance. Its main trading partner is mainland China, which receives about half of Hong Kong's exports and imports. Hong Kong's main exports include electrical machinery and appliances, textiles, clothing and watches. The city is also a major service economy with links to China and the rest of East and Southeast Asia. Hong Kong's currency, the Hong Kong dollar, is pegged to the U.S. dollar. One American dollar is worth HK$7.80.

Conclusion

Many Hong Kong citizens are fearful of what is ahead for the future of the territory. If the Chinese government is too disruptive of Hong Kong's political and economic system, then the international business community and local citizens who believe in Hong Kong's future prosperity may lose confidence in Hong Kong. As this could mean a loss of talent, investment, tourism and trade, many in Hong Kong and outside used to not believe Beijing would put that at risk. Hong Kong's integration with the mainland was also supposed to be a bellwether for the Taiwanese about how any potential future reunification might unfold. The CCP intended to make Hong Kong an example for Taiwan on how positive unification with the mainland under the "One Country, Two Systems" policy could be.

In 2020, however, the Chinese government's nervousness about the territory's potentially disruptive impact on the mainland outweighed these concerns. As the emergency measures to address the COVID-19 pandemic gradually lifted, popular protests returned to the streets of

178 *Hong Kong*

Hong Kong. And while the city and the rest of the world were distracted by the pandemic, China pressured the Hong Kong government to take a much harder line against the democracy movement and its supporters. It is hard to feel optimistic about the future of democracy in Hong Kong.

Bibliography

Centre for Communication and Public Opinion Survey. 2017. *Chinese University of Hong Kong*. http://www.com.cuhk.edu.hk/ccpos/en/tracking3.html

Chiu, Peace. 2018. "Record 1.37 Million People Living Below Poverty Line in Hong Kong as Government Blames Rise on Ageing Population and City's Improving Economy", *South China Morning Post*, November 19.

Noack, Rick. 2015. "Map: These Are the World's Least Religious Countries", *The Washington Post*, April 14.

Wong, Michelle. 2018. "Explainer | Why the Wealth Gap? Hong Kong's Disparity Between Rich and Poor is Greatest in 45 Years, so What Can be Done?", *South China Morning Post*, September 27.

Further Reading

Dapiran, Antony. 2017. *City of Protest: A Recent History of Dissent in Hong Kong*. Penguin Specials.

Dapiran, Antony. 2020. *City on Fire: The Fight for Hong Kong*. Scribe Publications.

Dimbleby, Jonathan. 1997. *The Last Governor: Chris Patten and the Handover of Hong Kong*. Pen and Sword History.

Kong, Tsung-Gan. 2017. *Umbrella: A Political Tale from Hong Kong*. Pema Press.

Ng, Jason Y. 2015. *Hong Kong State of Mind: 37 Views of a City That Doesn't Blink*. Blacksmith Books.

Tsang, Steve. 2003. *A Modern History of Hong Kong*. Hong Kong University Press.

Welsh, Frank. 1993. *A Borrowed Place: The History of Hong Kong*. Kodansha.

Xi, Xu. 2017. *Dear Hong Kong: An Elegy to a City*. Penguin Random House Australia.

7 Macau (Special Administrative Region of the People's Republic of China)

Introduction

The Special Administrative Region of Macau (also spelt Macao) is located across the Pearl River Estuary from Hong Kong (see Figure 7.1). Consisting of a peninsula and two small islands (Ilha da Taipa and Ilha de Coloane) now linked by an artificial landfill, Macau is only 28 km² with a population of 670,000 people (see Figure 7.2). This makes it the most densely populated place on the planet.

Macau history

Macau was colonized by the Portuguese in the 16th century, making it the oldest European settlement in Asia. In fact, Macau was actually the first *and* last European outpost in Asia. A Portuguese explorer, Jorge Alvares, was the first European to reach China, setting foot on what is now Macau in 1513. There was a small village with some Cantonese-speaking farmers and fishermen in the area at the time, but Alvares saw the location's potential as a port between the West and the East. Portuguese merchants soon followed and established a trading colony. Because Chinese traders were prohibited from private foreign trade by the laws of China's Ming dynasty, the Portuguese took on the role of middleman. They took Chinese goods, including tea, silk and lacquerware to Goa, a Portuguese colony in India. Some products were transported to Lisbon, while others were exchanged for cotton and textiles, which went to Malacca (in Malaysia) and were traded in turn for spices and sandalwood. The Portuguese took the spices and sandalwood to Japan and exchanged them for silver, swords and fans to trade in Macau for more Chinese products. The Portuguese middlemen would place large mark-ups on these exchanges and grew wealthy in the process.

Under the Portuguese

In 1557, China agreed to allow the Portuguese to settle in the area in exchange for an annual payment of 500 taels (about 19 kg) of silver. A permanent settlement was established with basic stone houses within a walled village. Although the territory was under Portuguese administration, China continued to have sovereignty over Macau, which was proclaimed a city (previously it was called a settlement) by the Portuguese crown in 1586. A municipal council was established and a Catholic Bishop installed. Chinese and Portuguese traders

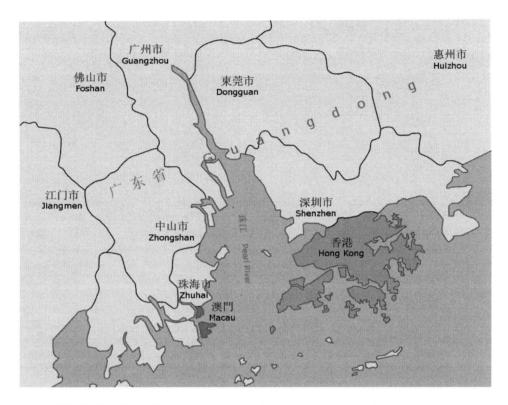

Figure 7.1 The Pearl River Estuary—Eastern portion, in Guangdong Province.

flooded into Macau, and by the beginning of the 17th century, Macau had several thousand permanent residents, including 900 Portuguese and slaves from colonial outposts. Throughout the century, thousands of Chinese workers, craftspeople and traders moved into Macau. During this period of prosperity, Macau found itself a target of the Dutch, who were fighting for independence from Spain, to which Portugal was aligned. In 1622, in an attempt to capture the city and establish their own base in China, the Dutch attempted a full-scale invasion, which Macau successfully defeated.

Along with its growth as a trading centre, Macau also became an important centre for Christianity in Asia. In the 1560s, Jesuit missionaries arrived, followed in the 1580s by the Dominicans, both of whom built churches and schools. Not particularly interested in converting the local population to Christianity, the Catholic church used Macau as a base for converting the large populations of China and Japan. The Jesuit Church of St. Paul known as the "Vatican of the Far East" was, for a time, the largest church in Asia. On the same site was St. Paul's College of Macau, in which missionaries were taught Chinese language and culture. A fire in 1835 destroyed both the buildings, leaving only the stone façade of the church, which remains a major tourist attraction today. The beautiful Saint Dominic's Church built by the Dominicans in 1587 (but restored later) still stands, as do a number of other large Catholic cathedrals (see Figure 7.3).

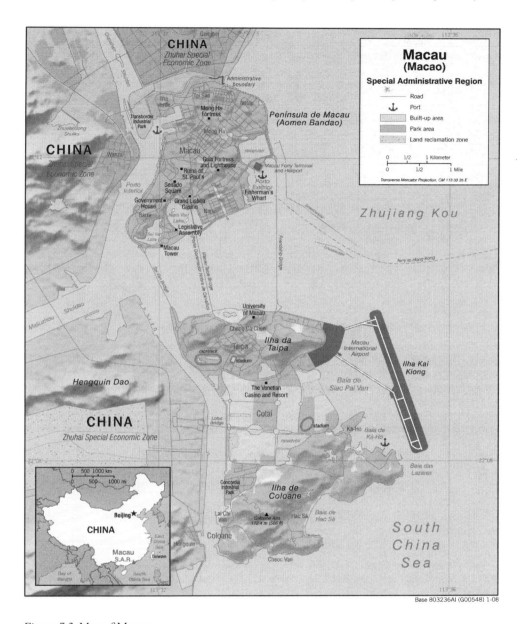

Figure 7.2 Map of Macau.

In 1849, Portugal declared sovereignty over Macau, which was made official by the signing of the Sino-Portuguese Treaty in 1887. The Second Opium War had just ended and Portugal agreed in the treaty to help curtail the smuggling of opium. During the Japanese occupation of parts of China in the 1940s and again at the end of the Chinese Civil War in 1949, many Chinese sought refuge in Macau.

Figure 7.3 Saint Dominic's Church—St. Dominic's, Macau.

Negotiations for the handover of Macau to China

In 1987, after over a year of negotiations, China and Portugal signed an agreement to end Portuguese rule and make Macau a special administrative region of the People's Republic of China on December 20, 1999. Interestingly, Portugal had offered to return Macau to China in 1967 (after demonstrations against Portuguese rule inspired by the Cultural Revolution), 1974–1975 and 1977 (when Portugal was divesting itself of its overseas territories), but China had refused the offer for various reasons, particularly because it did not want to upset Hong Kong (Edmonds, 1993, 879; Edmonds, 2002, 112).

The agreement to end Portuguese rule was similar to that signed between the United Kingdom and China over Britain's withdrawal from Hong Kong. In the agreement, China agreed to a "one country, two systems" arrangement in which local elections would be permitted, residents could travel freely and Macau's capitalist economic system and way of life could continue for 50 years. Macau would be allowed substantial autonomy outside of foreign affairs and defence for the same period of time. From the signing of the agreement until the handover (1987–1999), the transition was uneventful. Since a significant proportion of Macau's citizens were openly pro-Communist or at least had Communist sympathies and much of the control of Macau had already been ceded to China, Macau residents were unconcerned, an optimism not shared by their Hong Kong counterparts, many of whom were apprehensive about the transition to Chinese rule. The Macau handover ceremony was similar to the 1997 handover of Hong Kong: the Portuguese flag was lowered and the Chinese flag raised to signal the end of 442 years of Portuguese control over the city.

Macau government

Head of government

The chief executive of Macau is the head of the government. The position is elected by 400 members of the Chief Executive Electoral Commission. Three hundred and forty-four of the Chief Executive Electoral Commission members are elected by approximately 5,000 people from a range of sectors (e.g. industrial, commercial and financial; sports; education; labour and culture). The other 56 spots on the Commission are filled by local members of China's National People's Congress, representatives from Macau's Legislative Council and Municipal Council, members of the Chinese People's Political Consultative Conference and religious sector representatives.

The chief executive serves for a five-year term, which is renewable once. Current Chief Executive Ho Iat Seng, former president and member of the Legislative Assembly, is the third chief executive of Macau since the transition to Chinese rule in 1999. He was the sole candidate for chief executive.

Constitution

The Basic Law of the Macau Special Administrative Region of the People's Republic of China is Macau's mini constitution. Along with describing the chief executive and legislature, the Basic Law states that Macau has special administrative region status; that Portuguese remains an official language of Macau; that the legal system is separate from that of the People's Republic of China and is based on the Portuguese civil system; and that freedom of speech, of the press, of association and assembly and the right to join trade unions and strike are all protected.

Legislature and electoral system

Macau has a unicameral legislature with 33 seats. Fourteen members are directly elected by proportional representation, 12 are elected indirectly by an electoral college composed of representatives of functional constituencies (various professional and industry sectors) and 7 members are appointed by the chief executive. The members serve five-year terms. The next election will be in 2021. Unlike in Hong Kong, no promise was made for future universal suffrage in Macau.

Political parties

Rather than political parties, a wide variety of organizations representing business, labour, civic and social welfare constituencies submit a list of candidates for the proportional representation seats. More than 20 organizations participated in the 2017 legislative elections. The civic organizations fall into two main camps: pro-Beijing and pro-democracy. In 2017, of the 14 proportional representation seats, pro-Beijing organizations won 9 seats, pro-democracy groups 4 seats and a centrist organization 1 seat. The functional constituency seats and those appointed by the chief executive are all pro-Beijing people.

Defence

The People's Liberation Army (PLA), the Chinese armed forces, has had a garrison with approximately 500 troops in Macau since the handover on December 20, 1999. The other half of the Macau garrison is based just outside Macau in Zuhai, China (see Figure 7.1). In

184 *Macau (Special Administrative Region of the People's Republic of China)*

accordance with the Basic Law, the garrison does not participate in internal security, but it can be called on by the Macau government to help when necessary. In the aftermath of Typhoon Hato in August 2017, the garrison was asked to help with disaster relief and clean up.

Macau society

Today, the population of Macau is almost 89 percent Chinese, between 1 and 2 percent Portuguese, with the remaining 9 percent primarily Macanese, people of mixed Portuguese and Asian ancestry. The two official languages are Chinese and Portuguese; 80 percent of the population has Cantonese as a mother tongue, 5.5 percent has Mandarin and the rest has a variety of other Chinese dialects, Tagalog, English and Portuguese. The Macanese even have their own dialect, Patuá, which blends Malay, Sinhalese, Cantonese and Portuguese, and their own distinct culture with its own food, festivals and traditions. After the transition, Macau kept the pataca as its currency. The pataca is pegged to the Hong Kong dollar, which is tied to the U.S. dollar.

The people of Macau follow a variety of religious faiths. Almost 60 percent of the population practises various Chinese folk religions, 17 percent are Buddhist and 7 percent Christian. The Roman Catholic church's Macau diocese has 30,000 members. Along with Christian churches, Buddhist temples also abound. In fact, Macau has potentially the highest number of churches and temples per square kilometre of anywhere in the world.

The economy

Casino gambling is Macau's largest industry, accounting for approximately 40 percent of the territory's GDP and about one-third of its direct employment. In 2016, gaming-related taxes were three-quarters of the total government revenue. Gambling has been legal in Macau since the 1850s when Portuguese administrators watched foreign traders moving out of Macau and into Hong Kong and started looking for new sources of revenue. (In 1841, Hong Kong had been ceded to the British, soon growing into an important financial hub and surpassing Macau.) At that time in Macau, Chinese games such as Fan Tan, a pure chance game like roulette, were primarily played. In the early 1960s, Stanley Ho and his STDM (Sociedade de Turismo e Diversões de Macau or Macau Travel and Amusement Company) was granted the monopoly rights on all gambling in the territory. STDM introduced Western style casino games and improved marine transportation between Macau and Hong Kong, bringing millions of Hong Kong gamblers to the territory every year. During the STDM monopoly, Macau's casino industry expanded substantially, but the monopoly also brought violence as rival street gangs strove to gain control over part of the business.

In 2002, the government ended Ho's monopoly and opened up the gambling sector to overseas investors. Casino-operating concessions were granted to Wynn Resorts, Las Vegas Sands, Galaxy Entertainment Group and others. As a result, tens of billions of dollars in foreign investment flowed into Macau. Around the same time, the Chinese government relaxed its travel restrictions on Chinese citizens who wanted to travel to Macau. Macau gradually became known as the gambling capital of the world. In 2007, it surpassed the Last Vegas strip in gambling revenues, and, in 2019, Macau's gambling revenue was three times bigger than that of Las Vegas ("Macau vs. Las Vegas," 2019). The territory has about 40 casinos, a horse track, a greyhound track and thousands of slots and table games. Of the 10 largest casinos in the world, six are in Macau (see Figure 7.4).

Figure 7.4 Casino lights in Macau.

Over 35 million people visited Macau in 2018. Visitors are mainly Chinese, with two-thirds coming from mainland China and another 25 percent from Hong Kong and Taiwan. Since gambling is illegal in China, Hong Kong and Taiwan, Macau is an enormous attraction to a vast number of Chinese people. Macau's gambling industry was hit hard by China's anti-corruption campaign, which started in 2013. (The PRC was concerned that high rollers were using Macau to launder money.) Spending in casinos contracted sharply for the next few years, but, by early 2020, spending had rebounded until the coronavirus hit. Macau has made steps to diversify its gambling customers beyond just the high-end market by reaching out to middle-class gamblers.

Recognizing the vulnerability of an over-dependence on the casino sector, Macau has also begun to appeal to a wider demographic by adding non-gaming attractions and by promoting Macau's historic streets, churches and temples and architectural and aesthetic influences from East and West. The number of visitors from Hong Kong to Macau increased when the Hong Kong-Zhuhai-Macau bridge opened in 2018, cutting car travel time between Hong Kong and Macau from four hours to 45 minutes.

Macau's other main industries are clothing, textiles, electronics and footwear. Its three main export markets are China, Italy and Hong Kong. Interestingly, for much of the 20th century, Macau was the largest exporter of fireworks in the world. At one point, Macau had seven firecracker factories. The largest of these factories, Kwong Hing Tai, alone employed

186 *Macau (Special Administrative Region of the People's Republic of China)*

one-third of the population and produced 3 million firecrackers daily. In the 1980s, firework production slowed as employees began to move to better paying and less dangerous jobs (Keegan, 2017).

Casino revenues have made Macau and many of its inhabitants enormously wealthy. As well as having no public debt, the territory has foreign exchange reserves of US$22 billion (2020) (CEIC, 2020). GDP per capita is very high—adjusting for purchasing power parity, it was US$122,000 per person in 2018—and unemployment very low. Additionally, in 2008, the government launched a Wealth Partaking Scheme (WPS), under which Macau residents are paid an annual cash dividend—permanent residents US$1,200 and non-permanent residents US$670.

Nonetheless, many Macau residents feel they do not fully benefit from the territory's economic success. They complain about the cost of housing and the lack of social housing, poor public transportation and expensive medical fees. Growing inequality is a serious problem. At the most recent large protest in Macau—as there is no universal suffrage, protest is the main way to make discontent heard—protesters objected to proposed extravagant retirement packages for former chief executives and ministers. The chief executive withdrew the proposal.

Conclusion—Macau today

While Hong Kong has been rocked by months of protest centred on the city's relationship with China, Macau remains untouched by the political turmoil. Attempts in 2003 in Hong Kong to pass National Security legislation as required by Article 23 of its Basic Law (mini constitution) were met with such serious protest and pushback that no subsequent chief executive attempted to put forth the legislation again. Hong Kong had national security legislation imposed on it by China in 2020; Macau, on the other hand, passed its own national security legislation back in 2009. Macau's chief executive has vowed to make Macau a poster child for "one country, two systems," which can serve as an example for Hong Kong and Taiwan.

To address why Macau's relationship with China has been so much calmer than Hong Kong's, some analysts point out that Macau's civil society and sense of local identity are weaker than those of Hong Kong. More than half of Macau's residents were born in China and, as a 2018 University of Hong Kong survey showed, strongly identify as citizens of the PRC. Macau also has a history of support for Communism and the Communist Party. However, there are those in Macau who would like to express dissenting views. Local activists have tried numerous times to hold rallies in support of Hong Kong but have been banned from doing so. Academics, journalists and lawyers describe being scared to criticize either their local government or the one in Beijing.

Bibliography

"Las Vegas vs. Macau: Which Is the Capital of Casino Gambling?", *Business Matters*, May 16, 2019. https://www.bmmagazine.co.uk/business/las-vegas-vs-macau-which-is-the-capital-of-casino-ga mbling/

CEIC. 2020. *Macau SAR, China Foreign Exchange Reserves 1984 – 2020*. eicdata.com/en/indicator/ macau/foreign-exchange-reserves

Edmonds, Richard Louis. 1993. "Macau and Greater China", *The China Quarterly*, 136, Special Issue: Greater China. p. 879.

Edmonds, Richard Louis. 2002. "Hong Kong and Macau", in Richard Louis Edmonds, editor, *China and Europe Since 1978: A European Perspective*, The China Quarterly Special Issues New Series No. 2, Cambridge University Press, p. 112.

Keegan, Matthew. 2017. "A Brief History of Fireworks in Macau", *Culture Trip*, January 18. https://theculturetrip.com/asia/china/articles/a-brief-history-of-fireworks-in-macau/

Further Reading

Gunn, Geoffrey (editor). 2016. *Wartime Macau: Under the Japanese Shadow*. Hong Kong University Press.

Hao, Zhidong. 2011. *Macau: History and Society*. Hong Kong University Press.

Porter, Jonathan. 1999. *Macau: The Imaginary City: Culture and Society, 1577 to Present*. Westview Press.

8 Connections and commonalities in East Asia

Introduction: A shared culture and history

The countries of East Asia have much that binds them together. Over their 2,000-year histories, the Chinese, Japanese and Koreans have fought, traded and learned from one another. As a result, they share a common cultural foundation. In the 3rd, 4th and 5th centuries, the use of Chinese characters spread gradually from China to the Korean Peninsula and Japan. By the 8th century, literary Chinese was used for formal writing, literature and government in both countries. While Japan and Korea developed their own writing systems, they continued to use Chinese for formal writing until the late 1800s.

Rice growing has been central to the East Asian region for millennia. Rice farming has influenced the languages, customs and festivals across the region. Some sociologists have proposed that rice growing has created a collectivist mindset in East Asia. If farmers do not work collectively to create proper irrigation systems, one family's fields will have too much water, while others will not have enough. Rice preparation methods are similar: Japanese and Koreans both eat similar rice rolls (maki sushi for the Japanese, kimpap for Koreans), rice with fillings wrapped in seaweed and made into a roll. (There are differences as the Korean rice is mixed with sesame oil, while the Japanese is mixed with vinegar, and Korean kimpap contains kimchi, marinated meat or ham and cheese rather than raw fish.)

People throughout the region cook with soybeans, tofu, ginger, garlic, mung beans, wheat noodles, sesame seeds, sesame oil, soy sauce and seafood. Tea is also popular across East Asia. Tea ceremonies, stylized ways of preparing and serving tea, are traditional arts in Korea, Japan and China. Across the region, people have been eating with chopsticks for centuries. The chopsticks vary a little by country: Chinese chopsticks are longer (easier to reach a communal platter), thicker and not as tapered as Japanese and Korean ones. Korean chopsticks are usually made out of stainless steel; in Japan, most are made from wood or bamboo. Korean chopsticks are usually paired with a spoon.

East Asian cultures also share an interest in traditional East Asian medicine (TEAM). Although TEAM varies by country, the main therapeutic methods include acupuncture, cupping, moxibustion, herbal medicines and various forms of massage. TEAM originated in China and spread to Korea and Japan in the 6th century. The underlying philosophy centres on looking after the whole patient rather than focussing on a particular symptom. In the process of diagnosis, the doctor looks at the patient's tongue and complexion and checks other physical signs, particularly multiple pulse points. Although each country's traditional medical system has developed separately and has distinctive characteristics, traditional medicine is a significant part of the health care systems in China, Japan, South Korea, North Korea, Taiwan, Hong Kong and Macau.

Figure 8.1 Ink wash painting.

On the artistic front, much borrowing occurred over the centuries among the East Asian countries. An aesthetic sense emerged that is unique to the region and very different from Western traditions. For example, East Asian dance is much more rooted to the floor without the leaping and jumping seen in other forms of dance. Dancers move more slowly, and the movements of their arms and hands have significance. In all of the East Asian arts, there is an emphasis on, and a beauty found in, form. Even speech in theatre is delivered in a stylized way. An appreciation of correct form binds the performers and the audience.

Another shared art form is ink wash painting, which emerged during the Tang dynasty in China and spread across East Asia. Called *shui-mo-hua* in Chinese, *sumukhwa* in Korean and *sumi-e* in Japanese, this kind of painting on silk or paper uses black ink made from carbon sticks. The artist grinds the carbon sticks with a stone, mixes in water to achieve the shade and density desired and places varying amounts of ink on special brushes with tapered fine tips to create different shades. The brushwork requires great skill and thousands of hours of practice as only one brushstroke is used for each mark. Rather than trying to paint an exact representation of a subject, the artist tries to capture its spirit or soul (see Figure 8.1).

The East Asian countries also share religious and philosophical roots, which have underpinned each nation for close to 2,000 years. Each country's culture is rooted in Confucian and Buddhist thought, intellectual foundations that continue to shape how people think and live.

Confucianism

All of the East Asian countries share Confucian roots, which have greatly influenced national values and economic development throughout the region. A form of political thought and ethical teaching with a religious foundation, Confucianism takes its name from Confucius, a Chinese philosopher and politician who lived from 551 to 479 B.C. Confucianism spread from Han dynasty China (206 B.C. to A.D. 220) to the Korean Peninsula and then into Japan in the latter half of the 4th century.

190 *Connections and commonalities in East Asia*

Confucianism is not concerned with gods or faith but is more of an ethical system for human relationships, both among individuals and between the governing and the governed. The writings of Confucius focused on individual morality, ethics and the proper exercise of power by the government. Society should be governed by a paternal leader who looks after the people he/she rules. In return, those who are governed are expected to give respect and obedience to the leader. This hierarchical structure—protect the ones below, serve the ones above—is seen as the basis for all relationships and not just those between the ruler and the ruled. Society's most fundamental relationships are captured in what is known as "the Three Bonds": ruler and subject, husband and wife, parent and child, which set the structure for all human social interactions. (Further two bonds include the relationships between elder sibling and younger sibling, and between friends.) In each relationship, a person is either a senior or a junior. (Sometimes the friend-to-friend relationship is more equal, but even here age and rank within school, work or club usually puts one friend in a more senior position to the other.) While juniors owe their seniors respect and obedience, seniors must look after their juniors with kindness and generosity. Social harmony comes from each person knowing his or her place in society and acting accordingly.

The husband and wife relationship clearly puts the woman in the junior position, offering respect and obedience in return for benevolence and care. This teaching produced a culture in which women were legally and socially inferior to men, which has had a major impact on East Asian societies. In Confucian philosophy, filial piety (respect for one's parents and one's ancestors) is an important virtue. Many Chinese, Japanese and Korean stories emphasize being good to and respecting one's parents and not bringing shame or disrepute to the family. This value is inculcated into children. The concept of rituals, beyond formal ceremonies and social conventions, was part of Confucian teachings. Social rituals are ways of behaving, common courtesies that Confucius believed form the basis of a civilized and stable society.

Confucianism also emphasizes respect for education and the importance of literacy and book learning. The authority of rulers stems from their greater knowledge and superior moral insights. The Confucian canon consists of the Five Classics (*Book of Odes*, *Book of Documents*, *Book of Changes*, *Book of Rites* and *Spring and Autumn Annals*) and the Four Books (*Doctrine of the Mean*, *Great Learning*, *Mencius* and the *Analects*). For centuries, these books formed the subject matter for Chinese and Korean civil service exams and were also studied by the samurai during the Tokugawa era (1600–1868). As seen in the development of Confucianism in East Asia, the belief system is not monolithic but has varied across time and in different countries.

When China's imperial system collapsed in 1911, many of China's elite began to question Confucianism. During Mao's Cultural Revolution, the Chinese Communists rejected Confucianism completely, perceiving it as a contradiction of Marxism, and desecrated many Confucian sites. They rejected its emphasis on education and on a system that gave officials the right to expect obedience from their subordinates. In the 1980s, the Confucian values of hard work, education and family gradually regained importance, and Confucianism has since seen a strong revival. Since he became China's president in 2012, President Xi has praised Confucianism and emphasized its relevance for today. Qufu, the birthplace of Confucius, now hosts an annual ceremony honouring his birth with ceremonies and prizes for excellence in Confucian culture and literature. Although Confucius lived over 2,000 years ago, Confucian values continue to influence thought and behaviour across East Asia.

Buddhism

Buddhism came to China from India. By the 1st century A.D., there was a small community of Chinese Buddhists in China. (Siddhartha Gautama who later became known as the Buddha lived between the 6th and 4th centuries B.C. in what is now southern Nepal.) In the following centuries, Buddhism spread throughout China, becoming by the 7th century A.D. a significant part of Chinese culture, influencing art, literature and philosophy. A Chinese monk first introduced Buddhism to the Korean Peninsula in the 4th century, but Buddhism did not become widely practised in Korea until the 6th and 7th centuries, after a group of Korean monks went to China to study Buddhism. Towards the end of the 7th century in Korea, Buddhism became the national religion of the Silla kingdom, prompting the construction of beautiful temples and the carving of the complete Buddhist canon on to wooden blocks. Buddhism also arrived in Japan in the 6th century, spreading throughout the county under Prince Shotoku (594–622) and flourishing until the 16th century when it fell out of favour with the military rulers. In all three countries, Buddhism was actively suppressed for long periods, but it never disappeared entirely.

The Four Noble Truths of Buddhism are that life is full of suffering, anguish and pain; that this suffering is brought upon people by their attachments and desires; that the end of suffering can be attained if people let go off these desires; and that individuals can learn how to let go off these desires through Buddha's teachings. The branch of Buddhism that spread to East Asia was Mahayana (Great Vehicle or Way) Buddhism. Mahayana emphasizes not only the worship of Buddha but also of Bodhisattvas, people who are on their way to enlightenment but have stayed back from Buddhahood to aid others to reach salvation. Within Mahayana Buddhism, there are a variety of schools that teach different paths to enlightenment through reading certain texts or sutras, seated meditation or chanting.

There are numerous Buddhist universities in South Korea, China, Taiwan and Japan. Across East Asia, people visit Buddhist temples to pray for their own health and happiness and for their ancestors. In Japan, most homes have small Buddhist altars at which people pray for deceased family members.

Shared values

To some extent, the people of East Asia and Southeast Asia share a number of values, some of which have their roots in Confucian teachings. According to Confucian values, hierarchy is embedded in almost all relationships: one person is "higher" than another by virtue of age or status, and this hierarchy determines the nature of the interaction between the two. This hierarchy is reflected in speech. The Japanese and Korean languages use honorifics, a specific speech that shows respect. The way one speaks changes quite dramatically depending on who is being addressed. Someone older, in a position of authority, a customer or a guest is always shown greater respect than those who are younger, more junior or more familiar. In business settings, the most senior person is given the best seat, sits down first and begins eating first. In East Asia, there is a greater comfort with hierarchy than there is in the West.

East Asian cultures are collectivist, with the group taking precedence over the individual. From a young age, children are taught that they are part of a group or groups, including their family, school, club, workplace and country—and that they have responsibilities to these groups. These responsibilities include maintaining harmony within the group and being careful not to cause others embarrassment. People are expected to subjugate their feelings to the

192   *Connections and commonalities in East Asia*

will of, or for the good of, the group. Thus, it is the team player who is most appreciated. A sense of belonging is fostered by schools, clubs and companies, using uniforms, songs and group activities. One downside of the emphasis on the group is the behaviour often demonstrated towards those who are different or who do not fit in: they can be bullied or ostracized.

This focus on obligations to the group means that people feel a strong sense of duty to their colleagues and expect that all members will do their share of any collective work. As a result, according to the International Labour Organization, Asians work longer hours than residents of other countries, with South Koreans working the longest hours in any developed country. In 2018, South Korea reduced its maximum working week to 52 hours from 68. Long working hours are also common in Japan, China, Taiwan and Hong Kong. There is even a word in Japanese (*karoshi*) for "death by overwork." In 2015, South Korea had about 600 compensated cases of work-related cerebrocardiovascular diseases and Japan had over 200. (This is down from over 1,500 cases in 2006 for South Korea and 400 for Japan.) In 2015, China had over 8,000 cases of disease-caused sudden death at work (Wang and Hancock, 2019). Hierarchy and social obligation make it difficult for staff members to leave work before their boss or to refuse after-work activities, such as drinking with clients. Importantly, the incidence of death from overwork has dropped by close to two-thirds in South Korea over the past 15 years and has levelled off in the other East Asian countries. In China, in sharp contrast, the incidence of such deaths has increased over three times in the same time period, which coincides with the expansion of capitalist-style commerce in the country.

Relationships and connections among people are important in East Asian life. Business is conducted among people who have built relationships with one another. The Chinese term "*guanxi*" means connections or networks. Guanxi opens doors; people with guanxi are better able to generate business than those without. As a result, people take care with their relationships, to build and nurture reciprocity and trust. In addition to valuing relationships and connections, East Asian societies also place a high value on education. For centuries, these societies have revered knowledge and learning and appreciated poetry and literature. There is a strong focus on education, teachers are accorded a great deal of respect and young people are pushed hard to succeed at school. School days in Japan, China, South Korea and Taiwan are longer than those in other parts of the world. Most East Asian children attend school for between 210 and 222 days a year compared with between 180 and 200 in Australia, Canada, the United Kingdom and the United States. School days are also longer for East Asian students, starting earlier and ending later. In addition, many East Asian students, particularly high school students in large cities, regularly attend afternoon and evening cram schools. East Asian students in high school are expected to study hard as their goal is to be accepted by a good university, seen as the gateway to a good job with a major corporation or in government.

All this study produces impressive results. As an illustration, the countries of East Asia topped the comparative educational rankings in the 2018 OECD Programme for International Student Assessment (PISA). Table 8.1 presents the average scores in three combined subjects—math, science and reading—of the top performers. On this test, which is administered to 15-year-olds around the world, all the East Asian countries placed in the top 10. East Asian dominance is even more striking if one looks only at the math test. In math, the top six countries in order were China, Singapore, Macau, Hong Kong, Taiwan, Japan and South Korea.

Another shared East Asian trait is long-term focus. Companies and the government plan for the long term. Panasonic, for example, is famous for having corporate plans of 100 years or more. For decades, governments across East Asia set themselves series of five-year economic plans with growth rate targets and other goals. Not all were achieved but the purpose

Connections and commonalities in East Asia   193

Table 8.1 Programme for international student assessment (PISA) 2018—average score of mathematics, science and reading

1. China (Beijing, Shanghai, Jiangsu, Zhejiang)	578.7
2. Singapore	556.3
3. Macao	542.3
4. Hong Kong, China	530.7
5. Estonia	525.3
6. Japan	520.0
7. South Korea	519.7
8. Canada	516.7
9. Taiwan	516.7
10. Finland	516.3

of the plan was as much about having the targets and calculated hopes as it was about actually achieving them.

It is important to note that, like all societies, those in East Asia are continually changing. Although all the values discussed above continue to be important in contemporary East Asia, over the post-war decades, there have been changes. Individualism, for example, plays a larger role than in the past. Many young people have decided that they do not necessarily want the same lives as their parents, delaying or forgoing marriage and/or childbearing and selecting jobs or careers that allow them to pursue their own dreams rather than succumbing to societal pressures.

East Asia and popular culture

Over the past four decades, there has been a huge growth in popular culture exports—fashion, video games, television shows, musical acts, animation and comics—within East and Southeast Asia and around the world. Japanese cultural products first started to become popular within the region in the 1980s. Oshin, a 1983 NHK (Japan Broadcasting Corporation) television drama, was an enormous hit in East Asia; it's a story of a girl born into poverty, who overcomes hardships through perseverance. The storyline resonated with East Asian audiences. Subsequent Japanese dramas with similar themes of staying strong and determined in the face of difficulty were also very popular. In the 1990s, Japanese pop culture products grew in popularity throughout East and South East Asia, specifically television dramas, fashion magazines, comic books, karaoke, digital pets (like the tamagotchi), video games, animation and anime. Japanese comic books/graphic novels were translated into Korean, Thai and Chinese, and they dominated the regional markets. Animated characters like Hello Kitty, Sailor Moon, Doraemon Pikachu and Pokemon became ubiquitous on licensed and unlicensed toys and products throughout the region. Animators across the region were influenced by Japanese animation, which began with shows like *Astro Boy* and *Sailor Moon* and skyrocketed in popularity. *Cool Japan*, the coordinated promotion of Japanese popular culture exports, captured the hearts and pocketbooks of millions of South Korean, Taiwanese and Chinese consumers.

Figure 8.2 Japanese pop group AKB48.

Another example of a popular culture success is AKB48, a Japanese idol girl group that began in 2005 (see Figure 8.2). (AKB is short for Akihabara, the Tokyo district where the group's theatre is located; 48 is the number of original members.) The idea behind AKB48 was to create a roster of performance teams that would be accessible to fans because these teams would perform live at the same time in different locations across the region. This "idol you can meet" philosophy has been a huge success, with AKB48 selling tens of millions of records, regularly topping the Oricon Weekly Singles Chart and becoming one of Japan's highest earning musical acts. As of 2020, AKB48 had 115 members, divided into teams. It has spawned five sister groups in different locations in Japan and seven sister groups in cities throughout Asia (Jakarta, Bangkok, Manila, Shanghai, Taipei, Chiang Mai, Ho Chi Minh City, Delhi and Mumbai). AKB48 is a classic example of regional integration through popular culture.

Korean popular culture launched in Japan with the success of a television drama called *Winter Sonata* in 2003. The show and its male star, Bae Yong Joon, attracted a large audience among middle-aged Japanese women who even took tours to visit sites where the show was filmed. *Winter Sonata* was followed by another successful historical drama, *Dae Jang-geum*. Around the same time, Korean pop music, or K-Pop, burst into popularity first across Asia and then around the world. The first K-Pop idol group, a five-member boy band called H.O.T, achieved great success in South Korea, China and Japan. Along with BoA, a South Korean singer-actress who was the first individual to become well known in Japan, H.O.T.'s success was the beginning of what became known as *Hallyu* or the "Korean Wave." Other Korean

Connections and commonalities in East Asia 195

dramas and musical acts debuted to immense popularity across Asia. With the increase in social media and video sharing, the Korean Wave spread to Western and global audiences. Psy's hit *Gangnam Style* solidified K-Pop's international status. BTS, a South Korean seven-member boy band replicated its domestic success around the world, its albums topping U.S. charts in 2018, 2019 and 2020. *Love Yourself: Answer* became the first Korean album certified Platinum in the United States. On a smaller scale, Mandopop, Mandarin language popular music from Taiwan and China, has grown in popularity. Taiwanese Mandopop has tended towards sad ballads with subtle meaning and has not yet made major inroads into South Korea or Japan.

East Asia and the 21st-century economy

For parts of their histories, each of the East Asian countries resisted efforts to form close ties with other nations. Each country restricted the entry of outsiders, limited the influence of foreign powers, closed themselves off from much of the world and reluctantly lowered barriers to integration. This isolationism had profound impacts on how each country saw outsiders, fostering an unease that lingers to this day. In the 21st century, however, the East Asian countries are very significant members of the global community and major trading economies. They are particularly economically integrated with each other.

On the trade front, the East Asian countries are closely connected. In 2018, China's largest export markets after the United States (19.2 percent) were Hong Kong (12.2 percent), Japan (5.9 percent) and South Korea (4.4 percent), with the country's trade with its East Asian neighbours standing at over $559 billion. In the same year, China's largest source of imports were South Korea (9.6 percent) and Japan (8.5 percent). For South Korea, China is its most important export market. In 2018, almost 27 percent of South Korean exports went to China, its other large export markets being the United States, Vietnam, Hong Kong and Japan. Almost 20 percent of South Korean imports come from China and over 10 percent from Japan (World Integrated Trade Solutions, 2018).

In 2018, 19.5 percent (US$144 billion worth of goods) of Japan's exports went to China, with 7.1 percent (US$52 billion) going to South Korea, its third largest export market after the United States (World Integrated Trade Solutions, 2018). Over 23 percent of Japanese imports came from China, with 4.3 percent coming from South Korea, Japan's fifth largest source of imports (World Integrated Trade Solutions, 2018).

For Taiwan, China is by far its most important trading partner, accounting in 2019 for almost 28 percent of Taiwan's total exports at a value of US$91.9 billion (Workman, 2020). Hong Kong, Japan and South Korea are all among Taiwan's top six trading partners. Since 2013, South Korea, Japan and China have been in free trade negotiations but, in the long shadow of historical and territorial disputes among the three and amid tensions compounded by the U.S.-China trade war, significant progress has not yet been made.

The East Asian economies are clearly strongly intertwined. For each of the East Asian countries, the others are important trading partners. China is now a vital market for Japan. Companies from Sony to Honda to Uniqlo desperately need Chinese consumers to buy their electronics, cars and clothing. Chinese consumers fed up with safety-related scandals at home now prefer Japanese snacks, drinks and medical products. For China, Japan (and South Korea and Taiwan) offers machinery, high-tech components and badly needed industrial equipment. Japan's special expertise in energy efficiency and air, water and waste management technologies can help China deal with its environmental problems. In 2019, Toyota sold electric-car technology to Singulato, a Chinese company that makes

196 *Connections and commonalities in East Asia*

low-emission cars, and it entered into a partnership with the Chinese companies CATL and BYD to build batteries.

A critical part of the economic reality in the region is foreign direct investment between East Asian countries, with the most significant investments involving China. To illustrate, over 30,000 Japanese companies had cumulative investments of US$117 billion in China in 2017 ("Neighbourly love-in," 2019) and about 10,000 Taiwanese firms have operations in China (Dasgupta and Phartiyal, 2019) despite the political tensions between the nations. Many of these Taiwanese companies are small- and medium-sized enterprises, mostly producing electronic component parts. Trade statistics, however, only show part of the economic picture and can even be misleading. Many of the products exported to Hong Kong, for example, do not necessarily stay there as it is a major port and transshipment hub. In addition, in the 21st century, products are produced through integrated production networks. The entire range of a company's business activities no longer take place in its home country. Often component parts are manufactured in a variety of countries and assembled in a different location, while the design, marketing and research and development are done in yet another country or countries. For many Chinese, Japanese, Taiwanese and South Korean companies, these different business activities are all happening within East Asia. A very significant segment of East Asia intra-regional trade is in parts and components that are assembled in China and then exported to a third country, often the United States. China does an enormous amount of the assembly work for East Asian multinational companies.

Students, tourists and foreign workers

On the people-to-people front, the connections in East Asia are also strong and becoming stronger. In China, by far the largest number of international students are from South Korea, and in both South Korea and Japan, Chinese students comprise approximately 40 percent of international students. Substantial numbers of South Korean and Taiwanese students also study in Japan, while several thousand Japanese study in South Korea and Taiwan. About one-quarter of the international students in Taiwan are from China; another 21 percent are from Japan, Hong Kong, Macau and South Korea. Clearly, a significant portion of the international students studying in the East Asian countries are from their East Asian neighbours.

Tourism shows a similar pattern. In 2019, Chinese tourists comprised about 33 percent of the total number of foreign tourists visiting Japan and 37 percent of the total spending by foreign tourists ("Chinese Visitors," 2020). South Korea is Japan's second largest source of tourists. China has supplied the largest group of tourists to South Korea for years. Over 6 million Chinese tourists, 3.2 million Japanese (the second largest sending country), 1.3 million Taiwanese (third largest) and over 694,000 Hong Kong visitors visited South Korea in 2019 ("Visitor Arrivals, 2020). The largest number of visitors to China come from Taiwan, Japan and South Korea. Of Japan's 1.6 million foreign workers in 2019, the largest group, one-quarter of the total, were Chinese. Both Japan and South Korea have Chinese immigrant populations of over 700,000 people. Tourism and migrant worker numbers can fluctuate dramatically, tied to flare-ups in political tensions, trade conflicts or, as in 2020, an epidemic.

Challenges facing East Asian countries

The East Asian countries are facing many of the same challenges. Each struggles with demographic transitions. Low birth rates, ageing societies, and ambivalence about immigration contribute to declining populations. How to manage this decline, the role of technology in work and human services, the impact on health care and pensions, are all shared concerns. These countries are also facing serious issues with climate change and the environment. Although these issues are global, the technological expertise in the region could be the source of some of the adaptation or mitigation solutions. As neighbours, one country's problems affect the rest. Seasonal dust storms, where winds pick up clouds of fine particular matter and spread them from Mongolia, Kazakhstan and northern China across China to North and South Korea and Japan, have become a very serious problem over the past 15 years. These storms have become more frequent with increased desertification. Of most concern is the increase in the industrial pollutants in the dust, which contains everything from sulfur to pesticides and heavy metals. The dust plumes can also move viruses and bacteria from one place to another, and dust dramatically decreases visibility, degrades the soil, affects wildlife and makes people ill.

Another shared challenge is relations with the North Korean regime. All North Korea's neighbours, and indeed the whole world, are greatly concerned about the North's development of nuclear weapons. South Korea is obviously particularly worried, prompting South Korean's President Moon to make major diplomatic overtures. In 2018, he and North Korean President Kim held three inter-Korean summits but tensions remain. Moon expressed his concerns in a January 2020 speech: "In a time of deadlock in U.S.-North Korea talks—and where we are even concerned about a step backward in inter-Korean relations—we are in desperate need of practical ways to improve inter-Korean cooperation" ("South Korea's Moon, 2020). Japan is also concerned about North Korea, and with good reason: North Korean missiles have passed over the northern Japanese island of Hokkaido more than once. The fear is so prevalent in Japan that NHK television once mistakenly announced an incoming North Korean missile attack. Another major Japanese priority is resolving the issue of the abduction of Japanese citizens by North Koreans in the 1970s and 1980s. Meanwhile, China is North Korea's biggest trading partner and arguably has the most influence on Kim Jong-un's regime. Beyond North Korea's denuclearization, China's primary concern is simply stability and peace on the peninsula.

Conclusion

East Asia is a region bound by history, religion, tradition and culture. Despite the serious tensions and conflicts that continue to rip the region apart, the countries of East Asia have much in common. In the 21st century, it is economic integration that most closely binds the individual countries in the region together.

It is important to place the current state of East Asian regional integration against the situation a quarter of a century ago. Over the past 25 years, the countries in the region have been brought together by a combination of intra-regional trade, the "soft power" of cultural exchange, billions in East Asian direct foreign investment and large-scale international student enrolment. Consider tourism alone: Chinese visits to Japan jumped from around 352,000 in 2000 to over 9.6 million in 2019 ("Visitor Arrivals to Japan," 2020). In 2019, approximately 70 percent of the 32 million foreign visitors to Japan came from East Asia, with almost half from China and South Korea ("Japan-bound Statistics," 2020).

198 *Connections and commonalities in East Asia*

Contact has accelerated cross-cultural understanding, and business connections have reduced the potency of political tensions. Despite the divisions of history, culture and language, East Asia has become a complex, interconnected and globally powerful region.

Bibliography

"Chinese Visitors Spend ¥1.8 Trillion in Japan in 2019", *Nippon.com*, February 12, 2020. https://www.nippon.com/en/japan-data/h00646/chinese-visitors-spend-%C2%A51-8-trillion-in-japan-in-2019.html#:~:text=Preliminary%20figures%20show%20that%209.6,significant%20rise%20from%202014%20onward.

"Neighbourly Love-in Japan Inc. Has Thrived in China of Late", *The Economist*, November 9, 2019.

"South Korea's Moon: 'Desperate Need' to Improve North Korea Ties", January 6, 2020. https://www.aljazeera.com/news/2020/01/south-korea-moon-desperate-improve-north-korea-ties-200107020137522.html

Dasgupta, Neha and Sankalp Phartiyal. 2019. "Taiwanese Businesses Look to India as Alternative to China", *Business News*, September 20.

"Japan-bound Statistics". 2020. *JTB Tourism and Consulting Company*. https://www.tourism.jp/en/tourism-database/stats/inbound/#annual

"Visitor Arrivals." *Korea Tourism Organization*. https://kto.visitkorea.or.kr/eng/tourismStatics/keyFacts/KoreaMonthlyStatistics.kto

"Visitor Arrivals to Japan". 2020. *Japan National Tourism Organization, Japan Tourism Statistics*. www.statistics.gnto.go.jp

Wang, Xueqiao and Tom Hancock. 2019. "Overdoing It: The Cost of China's Long Hours Culture," *Financial Times*, January 17.

Workman, Daniel. 2020. "Taiwan's Top Trading Partners", World*'s* Top Exports, March 24. http://www.worldstopexports.com/taiwans-top-import-partners/

World Integrated Trade Solutions. https://wits.worldbank.org/CountryProfile/en/Country/KOR/Year/2018/TradeFlow/EXPIMP/Partner/by-country

Further Reading

Fallows, James. 1994. *Looking at the Sun: The Rise of the New East Asian Economic and Political System*. Vintage Books.

Schuman, Michael. 2009. *The Miracle: The Epic Story of Asia's Quest for Wealth*. Harper Business.

Wan, Ming. 2007. *The Political Economy of East Asia: Striving For Wealth and Power*. CQ Press.

9 Security and regional tensions in East Asia

Introduction

In Chapter 8, the close economic and cultural connections in the East Asian region were explored. However, while there is much that binds East Asian countries together, there are also many tensions and historical grievances that make the region home to some of the most potentially serious conflicts in the world (see Figure 9.1). Some of these conflicts have been discussed within the individual country chapters: the Taiwan-China relationship, tensions on the Korean Peninsula and North Korea's nuclear weapons program and the resolution of the issue of the abducted Japanese citizens by North Korea in the late 1970s and early 1980s. This chapter will explore the additional hot spots and issues of conflict in East Asia.

Japan and Russia: Northern Territories/Kuril Islands dispute

Since the end of the World War II, territorial relations between Japan and Russia have centred around three islands and one group of islets northeast of mainland Japan. The islands (Habomai islets, Shikotan, Kunashiri/Kunashir and Etorofu/Iturup) form the southern part of an archipelago, known as the Kuril Islands, which stretches from Hokkaido in northern Japan to the Kamchatka Peninsula in Russia. At dispute are only the three islands and the one group of islets, which Japan refers to as the Northern Territories. (Kunashir and Iturup are the Russian names for the larger two islands. Both the Russians and the Japanese use Shikotan and Habomai for the other two.)

The history of the dispute is somewhat complicated. The Shimoda Treaty of 1855 (the first treaty between the Japanese Empire and the Russian Empire after the Americans began opening up Japan) defined the border between the two countries to be between the islands of Etorofu/Iturup and the Uruppu/Urup islands north of it (see the 1855 line on the map in Figure 9.2.) However, the status of Sakhalin Island was left undefined, prompting sporadic conflicts between settlers on Sakhalin. To remedy the situation, the two countries negotiated the Treaty of Saint Petersburg in 1875, stipulating that Japan would cede Sakhalin in its entirety to Russia and that, in exchange, the entire Kuril archipelago would be Japanese territory. After the Japanese victory in the Russo-Japanese War of 1904–1905, the southern half of Sakhalin was ceded to Japan.

At the end of World War II, shortly after the atomic bombing of Hiroshima, the Soviet Union declared war on Japan. The Soviets invaded Manchuria and took control of Sakhalin and the Kuril Island chain. At the time, about 17,000 Japanese lived on the Habomai islets, Shikotan, Kunashiri/Kunashir and Etorofu/Iturup. Some fled immediately after the Soviet invasion, while others remained for a time, living alongside the Russians. However, by 1948, all the Japanese were forced to leave.

Figure 9.1 Japan, its neighbours and territorial disputes.

The San Francisco Peace Treaty, which officially ended the American/Allied occupation of Japan in 1952, discussed what was to happen to Japan's overseas territories. The treaty stated that Japan renounce all claims to the Kuril Islands. However, the treaty did not define which islands made up the Kuril chain, nor did it indicate to whom the islands should be surrendered. Japan claims that the disputed islands are not part of the Kuril Island chain, pointing to the 1855 Treaty of Shimoda, which depicted the four islands as being on the Japanese side of the border. (Interestingly, the official text of the Treaty of Shimoda is in Dutch, and the Russian and Japanese translations give different impressions of where the Kuril Islands begin.) Russia argues that the Yalta Agreement (the outcome of the Yalta Conference attended by the leaders of the United States, the United Kingdom and the Soviet Union held during February 4–11, 1945) promised all the Kuril Islands to Stalin in exchange for the Soviet Union's promise to enter the war against Japan after Germany's defeat.

The Soviet Union did not sign the San Francisco Peace Treaty, but in 1956 Japan and the Soviet Union ended their state of war by signing the Soviet-Japanese Joint Declaration. This agreement restored diplomatic relations and stated a commitment to reach a peace treaty. However, as of 2020, a peace treaty has not been reached between the two countries because of the territorial dispute over the islands. In its Article 9 on the continuation of peace negotiations, the 1956 Declaration stated that Moscow would hand over two of the islands in question—the Habomai islets and Shikotan—after the conclusion of a peace treaty. However, the crux of the impasse even at the most recent 2018 Summit between Russian President Putin and Japanese Prime Minister Abe is that Russia will not sign a peace treaty unless Japan recognizes Russian sovereignty over the islands, while Japan continues to maintain that the islands are an inherent part of Japanese territory. Russia's position is that although it is open to a negotiated resolution, the legality of Russian possession of the islands is not open for discussion.

Security and regional tensions in East Asia 201

Some historians and analysts who have looked at the documentary evidence are convinced that Etorofu and Kunashiri were parts of the territories Japan was required to renounce under the San Francisco Peace Treaty. Towards the end of the 1956 talks, there were hints that Japan might be willing to settle for the return of just Shikotan and the Habomai islets in exchange for a peace treaty. However, by this time, the Cold War was building, and the United States wanted Japan as an ally. Determined not to let Tokyo become too close to Moscow, the United States pressured Japan not to sign a peace treaty and even warned that if Tokyo gave up on its claims to Kunashiri and Etorofu, then the United States would not return Okinawa (Clark, 2005, Hara 2012).

Prime Minister Abe was intent on having the Northern Territories returned to Japan. Although he met with President Putin more than 27 times, he did not resolve the territorial issue. (Putin has, however, strongly hinted that he might be willing to return the Northern Territories to Japan if Japan abrogated the U.S.-Japan Security Treaty.) Abe even offered Japanese investment in the Russian Far East and the possibility of shared sovereignty over the islands as inducements, but, if anything, recent events suggest that the Russian approach to the Kuril Islands is hardening. In August 2019, the Russian prime minister visited Etorfu, much to the dismay of the Japanese. The following month Putin sent greetings to the opening of a seafood processing plant on Shikotan.

Meanwhile, the former Japanese residents of the Northern Territories are ageing, and their desire to return to their island homeland looks likely to remain unfulfilled. Ancestral visits to the islands without a visa have been permitted since 1991. (If Japanese citizens visited with a Russian visa, it would imply Japanese acceptance of Russian sovereignty over the islands.) Being able to visit is of particular importance for Buddhists who must tend the graves of their ancestors. Every February 7th is Northern Territories Day in Japan in which people gather to call for the return of the islands.

Japan and South Korea: Takeshima/Dokdo Island dispute

The island grouping at the centre of a dispute between Japan and South Korea is called Dokdo (meaning solitary islands) in Korean and Takeshima (bamboo islands) in Japanese. Although everyone speaks of Dokdo/Takeshima as "an island" (singular), it is actually a group of islets also referred to as the Liancourt Rocks, named after a French whaling ship that was almost shipwrecked there in 1849. Located in the Sea of Japan/East Sea, the islets are almost equidistant between the South Korean mainland and Japan's main island of Honshu. There are two small islands and about 35 surrounding rocks in an area of approximately 230,000 m^2.

Occupied by South Korea since 1954, these islands have long-standing historical ties to both Japan and South Korea, both of which claim the islands belong to them. South Koreans believe that the rocky islets are an integral part of Korean territory and that their ownership was recognized by the Japanese after a confrontation between Japanese and Korean fishermen in 1696. In 1900, the Dokdo Islands became part of Uldo county in Korea prior to Japan's annexation of the Korean Peninsula. At the end of World War II following Japan's surrender, the islets were therefore, in the eyes of the Koreans, rightly restored. These tiny, rocky islands are virtually uninhabited, although there is a coast guard garrison on the eastern islet and an elderly widow still lives on the western islet. Yet the islands are a point of great civic pride for South Koreans, many of whom in the summer take a boat ride of more than two hours to fulfil their patriotic duty by visiting them, even though there is little to do upon

Figure 9.2 Korean tourists visiting Dokdo/Takeshima Islands, 2009.

arrival (see Figure 9.2). Propaganda about Dokdo is ubiquitous in South Korea, including in a video on a train from the airport.

Japanese also claim sovereignty over these islets that they call Takeshima. According to the Japanese government, during the Meiji period, the Japanese were fishing in the area and docking at the islets. The islands were terra nullius (nobody's land) at that time the Japanese claim, as the Koreans were doing nothing (e.g. sending survey ships) to maintain a territorial claim. Japan incorporated the islands into its Shimane prefecture in 1905. Although the islets were not included in the list of territories to be returned to Korea in the final version of the San Francisco Peace Treaty, the early drafts of the Treaty indicated that Takeshima/Dokdo "was Korean territory, then transferred ownership to Japan (1949), then omitted any designation of this area (1950)" (Hara, 2006, 2).

Why are these small, barren islets and rocks in the middle of the Sea of Japan of such importance? On the surface, the reason is that the surrounding waters are rich fishing grounds and there may be a good natural gas deposit beneath them. The real answer, however, has more to do with the historical grievances that still linger about Japan's colonization of the Korean Peninsula. Tensions flare up easily, as in 2005 when Shimane prefecture (the prefecture that claims the islands) announced a Takeshima Day. In response, Korean protestors burned Japanese flags, and a Korean mother and son cut off their little fingers. In 2012, a South Korean man drove his truck into the gates of the Japanese embassy in Seoul to protest Japan's claims to the islands. During a women's hockey game at the Pyeongchang Winter Olympics in 2018, the Korean unification flag, which shows a blue map of the peninsula and includes a dot for the Dokdo islets, was flown. When Japan launched a protest, the South Korean government promised not to use that version of the flag during the Olympics; North

Koreans, however, continued to wave it. The Japanese government has proposed taking the dispute to the International Court of Justice for resolution, but South Korean officials have so far refused. The weight of international legal opinion favours the Korean claim.

South Korea-China tensions

In 2017, the government in Seoul decided to permit the Americans to deploy a Terminal High Altitude Area Defense (THAAD) anti-missile system in South Korea. While the South Koreans saw THAAD as a defensive weapon to be used against potential nuclear missiles from North Korea, the Chinese government believed that THAAD could also monitor Chinese military activities and responded with anger. South Korean companies were forced to leave the Chinese market, Chinese tourists were discouraged from visiting South Korea, various South Korean brands were boycotted, and K-pop and Korean dramas were banned for two years. From THAAD's deployment to the end of 2019, the Hyundai Research Institute estimated that South Korea suffered economic losses of over $9 billion (Kim Yoo-chul, 2019). The South Korean government is intent on convincing China to end the retaliatory measures and relations appear to be gradually improving.

China and Japan: Diaoyu/Senkaku Islands dispute

The Diaoyu (Chinese name)/Daioyutai (Taiwanese name)/Senkaku (Japanese name) Islands are five small islands and three rocky outcrops in the East China Sea, approximately 145 km north of Japan's Yaeyama Islands (part of Okinawa) and 193 km northeast of Taiwan. Japan has administered the archipelago since 1895, except from 1945 to 1972 when the Senkakus were under American jurisdiction as part of the Ryukyu Islands at the end of World War II.

China's claim to the islands is based on historical evidence showing that the Chinese discovered and named the Diaoyu Islands around the 14th century and that the old maritime boundary put them on the Chinese side. Official maps and documents show that the Qing court (1644–1912) put the islands under the jurisdiction of the island of Taiwan.

The Japanese government bases its claim on the rule of effective control in international law, arguing that when the government of the day surveyed the islands in 1894, it found them unoccupied and with no evidence of Chinese ownership. It therefore went ahead and annexed them in 1895. A Japanese businessman, Tatsuhiro Koga, began developing some of the islands, first hunting albatrosses for their down and then establishing a bonito (young skipjack tuna) processing plant. The last employees of that business left during World War II.

While the Chinese believe that the territory was seized by Japan and should be returned as other lands were in 1945, the Japanese make several arguments for why the islands belong to Japan. First, they point out that under the San Francisco Peace Treaty, the islands were placed with the Ryukyu Islands under American jurisdiction and that the Chinese did not protest at that time. Second, they argue that China and Taiwan's claims on the islands did not begin until after a 1969 United Nations Economic Commission for Asia and the Far East report was released, indicating the possible existence of oil and gas reserves. Third, they maintain that on more than one occasion, Chinese officials and Chinese publications have acknowledged the Senkaku Islands as Japanese and that under international law, these actions constitute relinquishing a claim.

Three of the Diaoyu/Senkaku Islands were privately owned by a Japanese family, the Kogas. In 2012, the Koga family decided to sell their islands. Initially, the governor of Tokyo, a known ultranationalist, announced plans to buy them, but the national government,

204 *Security and regional tensions in East Asia*

hoping to avoid angering the Chinese, stepped in to buy the islands instead. This move did not appease the Chinese government, and Sino-Japanese relations deteriorated badly, with anti-Japanese protests erupting across China.

The Diaoyu/Senkaku Islands dispute is the most serious of the territorial disputes and the one most likely to lead to military conflict. The surrounding waters are valuable fishing grounds and strategically important for control of the sea lanes. To back up the Chinese government's sovereignty claims, Chinese fishing trawlers, Coast Guard patrol boats and naval vessels are frequently seen in the vicinity of the islands, where they have clashed with Japanese Coast Guard patrol boats numerous times. In 2010, a Chinese fishing trawler collided with two Japanese patrol vessels. After the Japanese detained the Chinese boat's captain and took him back to Japan for three weeks, an angry Chinese government responded by blocking rare earth exports to Japan. (Rare earth metals are used to make electronics and China controls almost the entire production of these minerals.). Another confrontation occurred when in 2013 the Chinese government declared an Air Defense Identification Zone (ADIZ) over the islands, requiring foreign aircraft flying through the zone to identify themselves to, in this case, Chinese authorities and to follow Chinese rules about the islands. Japanese and American aircraft ignored the ADIZ, but the situation increases the possibility of dangerous near misses or serious accidents or conflicts. One of the reasons why these territorial disputes are such significant foreign policy issues is that if a government chooses to compromise or indicate flexibility, nationalist groups are often provoked to protest in full force putting the government in a difficult position.

China and the South China Sea

The South China Sea is a critical international waterway situated between the Pacific Ocean and the Indian Ocean. Every year, approximately one-third of global shipping, with goods valued at an estimated US$3.4 trillion, passes through the South China Sea, making it one of the world's main shipping routes (China Power Team, 2019). These goods include massive amounts of oil destined for China, Japan and South Korea. The South China Sea is also home to a rich fishery and unexplored oil and gas potential of up to US$2.5 trillion.

The South China Sea has been the target of maritime and territorial claims by the governments of Brunei, China, Malaysia, the Philippines, Taiwan and Vietnam. Many of these claims overlap, and they all overlap with the Chinese government's expansive claim based on the country's long-time historical activities in the area. Although its maritime claims are somewhat ambiguous, the government has used a nine-dash demarcation line on maps to denote the territorial features and "associated waters" that it claims. (The government did not indicate what it meant by "associated waters," and it stopped referring to the nine-dash line after the 2016 UNCLOS ruling described below.) First used by the Chinese Nationalists (KMT) in 1947, the nine-dash (then eleven-dash) line is used by the Taiwanese government as the basis for its claim to land features in the South China Sea. The Chinese public has always been taught that the whole South China Sea belongs to China, and many become emotional if anything else is suggested. However, as a party to the United Nations Convention on the Law of the Sea (UNCLOS), which the Chinese government ratified in 1996, China is bound to follow the rules, rights and obligations of the Convention. According to UNCLOS, China cannot claim an open water sea as historic waters.

UNCLOS was at the centre of a dispute between the Philippine and Chinese governments, when the former grew frustrated with the Chinese blocking access to what had been traditional Filipino fishing grounds near Scarborough Shoal. In 2012, Manila took Beijing to

Security and regional tensions in East Asia   205

the Permanent Court of Arbitration (PCA). The Philippine government asked the tribunal to investigate China's maritime claims: was the nine-dash line legitimate? Did the Chinese have the right to deny Filipino fishermen access to certain fishing grounds? Did they have the right to build artificial islands in the South China Sea, as they were doing? The Manila government also asked the tribunal about the status of the territorial features (which were rocks, islands etc.?) in the South China Sea. These distinctions are important under UNCLOS because the extent of maritime rights depends on the territorial features. Although the Chinese government refused to participate in the tribunal proceedings, the tribunal did make every effort to take Chinese views into account.

In 2016, the tribunal announced its findings, ruling almost completely in support of the Philippines and dismissing any expansive Chinese claim. The tribunal also ruled that there are no islands in the South China Sea, or, technically, at least, that none of the geographic features the Philippine representatives inquired about could be considered islands. Notably, the tribunal was not asked about the Paracel archipelago, around 130 tiny islets and reefs in the north-east of the South China Sea and claimed by Vietnam, Taiwan and China, although it is doubtful that the tribunal would have ruled them to be islands. Under UNCLOS, to be classified as an island as opposed to a rock, the land must be able to support human habitation in its natural condition by having freshwater, among other elements. Nobody had ever lived on these geographical features in the South China Sea because they were barren, exposed rocks, incapable of supporting human habitation without outside supplies. The tribunal decision was significant because, under UNCLOS, islands are given a 200-nautical mile Exclusive Economic Zone (EEZ), while rocks are only entitled to a 12-mile territorial sea and an additional 12-nautical mile "contiguous zone" (Welch, 2016). (An EEZ is the area to which a country has exclusive rights to fishing, harvesting, drilling, etc.) This ruling means that the only EEZs that can be claimed in the South China Sea are those from a country's coastline and not from any islands within the Sea. This simplified things considerably.

Since 2012, the Chinese have been building artificial islands on which they have constructed airbases to be used to patrol the South China Sea in the area of the Spratly Islands, but these plans have been put aside. The tribunal ruled that artificial islands can be built upon features over which a country already has jurisdiction and that are within a country's EEZ. However, an artificial island does not confer on the country any additional maritime rights above those they would have had if the island was in its natural condition. (One of the islands the Chinese built is actually within the Philippine's EEZ.)

Unsurprisingly, the Chinese government was displeased with the tribunal's rulings. In addition to being embarrassed that its official position was rejected as illegal, the government was aware the decision had domestic implications. Chinese public opinion was firmly behind the government's position that the South China Sea belonged to China, and citizens were deeply angered by the tribunal's decision. Despite the vitriol, the government proceeded cautiously, officially rejecting the tribunal's findings but doing nothing to contravene the ruling. The way forward was made easier by the Philippine government, which made overtures to China and worked to build cooperative ties between the two countries.

Nonetheless, many observers are concerned that China has not abandoned its aggressive and expansionist behaviour in the South China Sea, pointing to the sophisticated airfields being built on a number of artificial islands in the Spratly Islands. These airfields include runways, aircraft hangers, radar installations, warehouses and military buildings. David Welch of the University of Waterloo argues that these airfields were intended as part of China's plans to create an Air Defense Identification Zone over the South China Sea. Although, these

206 *Security and regional tensions in East Asia*

plans have been deferred or abandoned, the Chinese are now simply completing the building they had already begun.

Despite the Chinese relinquishing their original plans for the islands, the South China Sea remains an area with potential for conflict. In 2020, the Council on Foreign Relations' Preventive Priorities survey, which consults foreign policy experts about possible discord, put the potential for an armed clash between China and one of the other countries with a claim in the South China Sea as one of the top disputes to monitor (Centre for Preventive Action, 2019). A confrontation could occur if U.S. ships taking part in American Freedom of Navigation exercises, intended to underscore that the South China Sea is an international waterway, venture too close to one of China's artificial islands.

Historical memory in East Asia

Yasukuni Shrine visits

Although it has been 75 years since the end of World War II, tensions from Japanese actions during and before the war linger in the region. Japan's relations with its East Asian neighbours, particularly China and South Korea, remain scarred despite the existence of close economic ties. Certain issues bring the anger and outrage to the surface, particularly when Japanese politicians visit the Imperial Shrine of Yasukuni, a major Shinto shrine in the heart of Tokyo. Built in 1869 by the Emperor Meiji, the shrine was intended to enshrine the souls of those who died fighting in Japan's civil conflicts and then in later wars, and the names and birthplaces of almost 2.5 million deceased are inscribed on the shrine. Among those listed are over 1,000 war criminals, including 14 Class A war criminals (those who were convicted of preparing or waging war) who were enshrined in 1978. One of those enshrined war criminals is wartime Prime Minister General Hideki Tojo.

Visits to the shrine by Japanese politicians—particularly on significant dates like August 15, the anniversary of Japan's surrender at the end of World War II—have caused great controversy. The Chinese and South and North Koreans all react with anger and outrage, believing these visits are indicative of Japan's unapologetic and revisionist approach to its militarist past. Domestically many agree, arguing that the Yasukuni Shrine glorifies the country's military past for which it has not adequately apologized, whereas others believe that Japan has the right to pay tribute to its citizens who died in war, the same as any other country does. Public opinion polls on whether Japanese politicians should visit the shrine show varied results. A 2013 *Asahi* newspaper poll found that 56 percent of the respondents supported prime ministerial visits to Yasukuni Shrine, while 31 percent did not agree with them (Fukuoka, 2019). Certainly, the strongly nationalist component of the population supports the visits.

Emperor Hirohito chose not to visit the Yasukuni Shrine from 1978, when the war criminals were interred, until his death, and his son Emperor Akihito did not visit either. Emperor Naruhito has not visited since his 2019 ascension to the throne. Former Prime Minister Junichiro Koizumi (2001–2006) made annual public visits to the shrine, stating that he was making these visits as an individual citizen expressing his respect to the people who lost their lives in the war and not to honour war criminals. Nonetheless, each visit provoked a great outcry. Prime Minister Abe visited the shrine on August 15 when he was not prime minister or in cabinet. As prime minister, he visited Yasukuni Shrine in December 2013, infuriating the Chinese and the Koreans. To avoid any controversy, he has not visited since then.

To add to the controversy around the Yasukuni Shrine is the Yūshūkan War Museum, the shrine's war museum that sits next door. Visitors point out that the museum presents a revisionist interpretation of Japan's war history—"a retelling of the war from the perspective of the ultra-right wing" (Fallows, 2014), as author James Fallows put it, which omits any discussion of the atrocities committed by the Japanese army and describes Japan as being forced into World War II by economic and military pressures from the West.

Japanese history textbooks

What and how much Japanese middle and high school students are taught about Japan's military actions before and during World War II is an issue of serious concern to the country's East Asian neighbours. Japanese schools are required to use Ministry of Education approved textbooks, although each local school board selects textbooks from an approved list. The history textbooks in general have been criticized for spending too little time on the war and on Japan's invasion and annexation of vast parts of Asia. Most controversial is that on the list of approved history textbooks are usually a few that supress or justify Japan's actions. Japan's invasion of China, for example, is described in some books as an "advance." Barely mentioned is the Rape of Nanjing, at which the Imperial Japanese army murdered an estimated 40,000–300,000 people, and looting and rape were widespread.

The content of school textbooks matters. As Mark Selden and Laura Hein write so passionately,

> People fight over textbook content because education is so obviously about the future, reaches so deeply into society, and is directed by the state. Because textbooks are carried into neighborhood schools and homes, and because, directly or indirectly, they carry the imprimatur of the state, they have enormous authority.
>
> (Hein and Seldon, 2000, 3–4)

Chinese and North and South Koreans, and many in Japan as well, fear what will happen if Japanese are not taught their history. Without knowing the history, how can they understand the feelings of their East Asian neighbours and how can they commit to never returning to militarism?

Comfort women

The term comfort women is a euphemism for the women and girls who were forced—by Japanese military officers, human traffickers and/or desperate circumstances—into prostitution before and during World War II. Conscripting comfort women was never a national policy, but the practice was widespread in the 1930s and 1940s among Japanese military units throughout the Pacific theatre. Between 1932 and 1945, estimates are that between 80,000 and 200,000 women were coerced to work in brothels called "comfort stations." The brothels were ostensibly designed to improve soldiers' morale and curtail sexual misconduct, the spread of venereal diseases and fighting. The establishment of comfort stations in all Japanese occupied areas occurred after the Nanjing Massacre (December 1937–January 1938) during which mass rape occurred. Wartime government documents reveal that the army asked the government to provide "one comfort woman for every 70 soldiers" ("One

208 *Security and regional tensions in East Asia*

Comfort Woman," 2019). The vast majority of the women were Korean, although women from Taiwan, China, the Philippines and other parts of Asia also worked in these brothels.

The testimony of former comfort women reveals that some were abducted and taken to the brothels, while others were sold or lured by the untrue promises of jobs. The women lived lives of sexual servitude and were expected to serve about 30 men a day. Beatings and other forms of violence were common. Many comfort women were killed or committed suicide. Others became addicted to narcotics or became mentally or physically ill. When Japan was defeated, some of the comfort women were killed to hide evidence of the comfort women stations. Most survivors were left infertile due to sexual diseases or trauma.

Whether Japan has adequately apologized and financially compensated for the suffering of the comfort women (and of those forced into other forms of wartime labour) remains an issue today. Beginning in 1951, South Korea and Japan entered into bilateral discussions towards a normalization of diplomatic relations, including compensation for Koreans who had suffered under Japanese military rule, particularly those who had been conscripted into the military or into the wartime labour force for Japanese companies. In 1965, the Treaty on Basic Relations between Japan and the Republic of Korea was signed. In the treaty, Japan agreed to provide an $800 million economic aid package; $300 million was a grant and the rest was a low interest loan. (This was a large amount of money, equivalent to $6.5 billion in 2019 and about 25 percent of South Korea's GDP at the time.) In 2005, declassified documents revealed that Japan had intended to compensate individuals. However, the Korean government pressed to receive the funds itself, which it then invested in the nation's economic development. This lack of transparency combined with the imprecise language used in the treaty, which indicated that the funds were a gesture of goodwill rather than compensation for Japan's wartime actions, meant that the South Korean public was left believing that the victims had not been compensated.

In 1991, the Association of Korean Victims filed a lawsuit against the Japanese government in Tokyo District Court. The 35 plaintiffs from the Association, including three former comfort women, alleged that the Japanese government had violated their human rights and demanded a thorough investigation of their case, an apology, compensation of 20 million yen (approximately US$154,000), a commitment that a memorial museum be built and the amendment of Japanese textbooks to include a discussion of what occurred. The following July, Chief Cabinet Secretary Koichi Kato acknowledged responsibility for the comfort women system that forced tens of thousands of Korean and other women to provide sexual services to Japanese soldiers. On behalf of the Japanese government, Kato expressed

> its sincere apology and remorse to all those who have suffered indescribable hardship as so-called "wartime comfort women," irrespective of their nationality or place of birth. With profound remorse and determination that such a mistake must never be repeated, Japan will maintain its stance as a pacifist nation and will endeavour to build up new future-oriented relations with the Republic of Korea and with other countries and regions in Asia.
>
> (Japanese Ministry of Foreign Affairs, 1992)

A few days later, Prime Minister Kiichi Miyazawa apologized about the comfort women in a speech to the South Korea National Assembly. Kato's successor, Yōhei Kōno, released a statement in August 1993 specifically acknowledging that the Japanese army had coerced women to work in military brothels in which conditions were miserable. The Kōno statement is seen as one of Japan's landmark apologies.

Security and regional tensions in East Asia 209

However, in March 2001, the Tokyo District Court dismissed the 1991 claims for compensation from the Association of Korean Victims, stating that the 1965 Treaty had settled all war debt. Appeals to the High Court and then the Supreme Court were also rejected. Other victims and victims' groups have also sued for compensation, largely to no avail. In December 1992, 10 South Korean women, including 3 comfort women, filed a lawsuit asking for an apology and compensation from Japan for the suffering they incurred during the war. In 1998, the court ruled that the Japanese government must compensate the women, but the amount of compensation awarded was only about US$2,300 for each woman. Still fighting for a proper apology and compensation, the women appealed, but the appeal was rejected by the High Court and then the Supreme Court, and the 1998 compensation decision was nullified. Song Shin-do, a former comfort woman, was the only Korean resident of Japan to file a lawsuit on the comfort women issue. The Tokyo District Court also dismissed her claims, stating that an individual cannot sue the nation for damages.

In 1993, the Liberal Democratic Party lost the legislative elections. For the first time since 1955, Japan had a non-LDP prime minister, Tomoichi Murayama. The following year, Murayama established the Asian Women's Fund (AWF) to provide financial compensation to former comfort women, with most of the funds provided by the Japanese government and the remainder from private donations. Three hundred and sixty-four women from South Korea, the Philippines, Taiwan and the Netherlands (from Japan's occupation of the Dutch East Indies) received 5 million yen (approximately US$42,000) each and a signed letter of apology from the prime minister. However, the South Korean government and some of the Korean former comfort women expressed unease about the private sources of some of the funding, believing that only compensation from the Japanese government could be considered official. The Korean government gave its own compensation to 142 former Korean comfort women who did not accept the AWF monies.

In 1995, on the 50th anniversary of the end of the war, Prime Minister Murayama released what is considered the second landmark apology. In his statement, approved unanimously by his cabinet, Murayama apologized unequivocally. He acknowledged that Japan had caused "tremendous damage and suffering" to its Asian neighbours during World War II through its "colonial rule and aggression." Murayama's spoke of "deep remorse" and included the word "owabi," a formal, unambiguous word for apology. On the 60th anniversary of the war in 2005, Prime Minister Koizumi upheld the Murayama statement. On the 70th anniversary, Prime Minister Abe expressed his deep remorse and offered sincere condolences but stopped short of an apology. He has also said that future generations should not have to continually apologize for events that occurred before they were born.

At the end of 2015, the governments of South Korea and Japan reached a "final and irreversible" agreement on the comfort women issue. The agreement included a commitment by the Japanese government to give $8.3 million to a South Korean foundation for survivors to be established by the South Korean government. To avoid the problem with the origins of funding that beset the Asian Women's Fund, resources came only from Japan's national budget. The agreement also called for Prime Minister Abe to issue sincere apologies as prime minister of Japan, as some critics felt the Kōno and Murayama statements were personal rather than official apologies. Although this final agreement was supposed to end years of tension and mistrust between Japan and South Korea, public opinion opposing the deal remained in segments of both countries.

This mistrust had been exacerbated by an incident that occurred four years before the signing of the agreement: the Korean government had allowed a statue of a young girl commemorating the comfort women to be erected in front of the Japanese embassy in

210 Security and regional tensions in East Asia

Seoul, as well as a replica in the city of Busan. Both statues were the source of much anger in Japan, particularly the statue outside the embassy, because it was constructed without the Japanese government's approval. As part of the 2015 agreement, the South Korean government agreed to consider removing the statues, but this never happened. When Moon was elected president of South Korea in 2017, he expressed his opinion that the agreement was flawed and attempted unsuccessfully to persuade the Japanese government to renegotiate the agreement. In 2019, the South Koreans closed the Japan-funded foundations office from which most of the comfort women and their families had received compensation.

Japan-South Korea: war time labour compensation and apologies

Also affecting South Korean-Japanese relations is the issue of compensation for South Koreans forced to work for Japanese companies during Japanese colonial rule. In 2018, South Korea's Supreme Court ruled that Japanese companies must compensate wartime workers and ruled that individual claims are invalid. The Japanese government argued in response that the 1965 bilateral agreement settled all compensation completely. Relations between the two countries spiralled down in 2019. Tensions over Dokdo/Takeshima reignited, Japan removed South Korea as a most favoured trading partner, and South Korea announced it would withdraw from an intelligence sharing agreement with Japan, although at the last moment it did not.

Conclusion

The biggest challenge in the relationship between Japan and South Korea and between Japan and China is that, at root, neither the South Koreans nor Chinese believe that Japan has really properly "owned" or atoned for its aggressively militarist past. This grievance is made worse when right-wing Japanese scholars or politicians make statements denying or excusing historical events, claiming that the comfort women were simply prostitutes or denying the Nanjing Massacre, as did the then Justice Minister Shigeto Nagato in 1994. Jennifer Lind, in her book *Sorry States: Apologies in International Politics*, captured the ongoing mistrust between Japan and the other East Asian countries when she wrote:

> the world criticizes Japan for failing to come to terms with its past. Tokyo's apologies have been perceived as too little, too late. Even worse, its politicians repeatedly shock survivors and the global community by denying past atrocities; its history textbooks whitewash its wartime crimes. Japan sees itself as a pacifist, cooperative, and generous global citizen, with a strong antiwar and antinuclear identity. But after sixty years, Japan's neighbors still see bayoneted babies. Relations between Japan and its former victims remain fraught with distrust.
>
> (Lind, 2008, 2)

Although Japanese polls show that most Japanese are remorseful about the country's past, at the same time, they feel that Japan has apologized enough and that the country's global citizenship and good behaviour over the past 75 years should have earned it some measure of absolution. Many in Japan are resentful and angry because China and Korea refuse to recognize Japan's remorse and apologies and to move on from the past.

Security and regional tensions in East Asia   211

Bibliography

"'One Comfort Woman for Every 70 soldiers' Japanese Records Show", *Reuters News Agency*, December 7, 2019.

Centre for Preventive Action. 2019. "Conflicts to Watch in 2020: Preventive Priorities Survey Results", *Council for Foreign Relations*, December 18. https://www.cfr.org/report/conflicts-watch-2020

China Power Team. 2019. "How Much Trade Transits the South China Sea?", *China Power*, August 2. Updated October 10, 2019. https://chinapower.csis.org/much-trade-transits-south-china-sea/

Clark, Gregory. 2005. "Japan-Russia Dispute Over Northern Territories Highlights Flawed Diplomacy", *Asia-Pacific Journal: Japan Focus*, 3(4), 1–5.

Fallows, James. 2014. "Stopping Talking About Yasukuni, the Real Problem is Yūshūkan", *Atlantic*, January 2.

Fukuoka, Kazuya. 2019. "Commemorating and Othering: A Study of Japanese Public Opinion on Prime Minister Abe's 2013 Yasukuni Pilgrimage", *East Asia*, 36, 349–368. https://doi.org/10.1007/s12140-019-09322-w

Hara, Kimie. 2006. "Cold War Frontiers in the Asia-Pacific: The Troubling Legacy of the San Francisco Treaty", *The Asia Pacific Journal: Japan Focus*, 4(9), September 4. https://apjjf.org/-Kimie-Hara/2211/article.pdf

Hara, Kimie. 2012. "The San Francisco Peace Treaty and Frontier Problems in the Regional Order in East Asia: A Sixty Year Perspective", *The Asia Pacific Journal: Japan Focus*, 10(17/1), April 22. https://apjjf.org/-Kimie-Hara/2211/article.htmlc

Hein, Laura and Mark Selden. 2000. "The Lessons of War, Global Power, and Social Change", in *Censoring History: Citizenship and Memory in Japan, Germany, and the United States*, ed. Laura Hein and Mark Selden, Armonk: M.E. Sharpe, 3–4.

Kim, Yoo-chul. 2019. "Seoul Will Ask Beijing to End 'THAAD Retaliation'", *Korean Times*, November 28.

Lind, Jennifer. 2008. *Sorry States: Apologies in International Politics*. Ithaca: Cornell University Press.

Ministry of Foreign Affairs. 1992. *Statement by Chief Cabinet Secretary Koichi Kato on the Issue of the so-called 'Wartime Comfort Women' from the Korean Peninsula, July 6*. https://www.mofa.go.jp/policy/postwar/state9207.html

Welch, David. 2016. "The Hague's South China Sea Ruling: Implications for East Asian Security", *Asia Pacific Foundation of Canada*, November 29. https://www.asiapacific.ca/canada-asia-agenda/hagues-south-china-sea-ruling-implications-east-asian

Further Reading

Emmers, Ralf. 2012. *Geopolitics and Maritime Territorial Disputes in East Asia*. London: Routledge.

Hara, Kimie. 2007. *Cold War Frontiers in the Asia-Pacific Divided Territories in the San Francisco System*. London: Routledge.

Hasegawa, Tsuyoshi and Kazuhiko Togo, eds. 2008. *East Asia's Haunted Present: Historical Memories and the Resurgence of Nationalism*. Westport: Greenwood Publishing Group.

Hyun, Dae-song, ed. 2008. *The Historical Perceptions of Korea and Japan: Its Origins and Points of the Issues Concerning Dokdo-Takeshima, Yasukuni Shrine, Comfort Women, and Textbooks*. Paju: Nanam.

Kaplan, Robert, 2014. *Asia's Cauldron*. New York: Random House.

10 21st-century political economy in East Asia

National science, technology and innovation strategies

Introduction

High-intensity scientific and technological advances have put Japan, China, South Korea and Taiwan at the cutting edge of global innovation. China is a world leader in supercomputing, which enhances the ability to do research on everything from climate modelling to information systems and pharmaceutical design, and has over 200 of the 500 fastest supercomputers in the world (Wiggers, 2019). The country is at the forefront of high-speed trains, drone technologies, mining machinery, 5G wireless, and artificial intelligence (AI). Japan has the best industrial and service robotic implementations (see Figure 10.1) and extensive investments and expertise in nanotechnology, Internet of Things (IoT), medical devices, sensors, environmental technologies and integrated /smart energy systems. South Korea is one of the world's largest manufacturers of consumer electronics, lithium-ion batteries, mobile phones and semiconductors. With extensive manufacturing in new materials, aerospace and industrial robots, South Korea topped the Bloomberg Innovation Index in 2019 as the world's most innovative country for the sixth year in a row (Jamrisko, Miller and Lu, 2019). Taiwan dominates the market for a wide range of ICT high-technology components, has a significant semiconductor production industry, massive high-technology investments in China, and is investing heavily in biotechnology, digital content, IoT and artificial intelligence.

In a number of patent applications, one of the main markers of innovation, China leads the world. World Intellectual Property Organization (WIP0) figures for patent applications for the top 10 patent offices in 2018 showed China had filed over 1.5 billion applications, followed by the United States at approximately 600,000. In the third and the fourth spots were Japan (300,000) and South Korea (200,000) (WIPO 2019). Although Taiwan was not included in this ranking, other WIPO information shows Taiwan to have had four companies among the top 100 patent applicants between 2003 and 2012. During this period, Taiwan's Honghai Precision Industry was the 19th largest patent applicant (WIPO, 2015, 3).

This level of science, technology and innovation (STI) leadership did not arise overnight. Working in conjunction with its corporate sectors, and to a lesser extent its universities, each government has made a strategic commitment to science, technology and innovation. The whole region believes STI to be the key to future prosperity. The initiatives and policies undertaken by governments in Japan, China, Taiwan and South Korea demonstrate the importance they attach to the commercialization of science and technology. The STI-based approach to economic planning, along with how best to manage the flow of information and ideas among the people and institutions involved, is called national innovation systems (NIS). This chapter offers a brief look at national innovation systems and their part in East Asia's 21st-century political economy.

21st-century political economy in East Asia 213

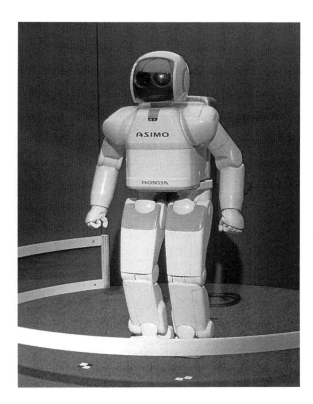

Figure 10.1 Honda's Humanoid Robot Asimo.

Background on national innovation systems

From Kenya to South Korea and from Canada to Taiwan, national and sub-national governments wrestle with the difficult problems associated with promoting commercial innovation and creating an environment for scientific and technological competitiveness. Governments uniformly accept the idea that a combination of research and commercialization are key elements in national prosperity. However, it is challenging for governments to determine which sectors to support and how to support them. National innovation systems—the study of how to support innovation by looking at technology, information flows and relationships among government, industry and academia—is an attempt to develop the structures, systems, programs and policies that support effective innovation. The primary 21st-century twist in NIS has been the addition of the environmental imperative, looking to create economic growth by producing technological solutions to climate change and environmental sustainability.

The debate about the role of governments in promoting innovation touches on one of the central issues in the field of political economy—the role and effectiveness of governments in shaping national economic activity. For decades, a professional and political emphasis on Keynesian economics supported the idea that governments could and should play an active,

214 *21st-century political economy in East Asia*

if not an activist, role in managing economic developments and priorities. The neoliberal revolution, represented intellectually by Milton Friedman and politically by Margaret Thatcher and Ronald Reagan, challenged belief in the efficacy of national leadership and favoured reduced taxes, fewer regulations, limited trade barriers and the removal of other areas of government interference from the economy. During the same period, however, South Korea, Taiwan, Malaysia and Singapore modelled themselves after the activist model of post-war Japan.

Academic interest in state industrial policy came primarily from scholars interested in the growth of the East Asia economies—Chalmers Johnson (Japan), Robert Wade (Taiwan), Alice Amsden (South Korea), Alexander Gerschenkron (latecomer nations)—and then others who, in the 1980s, were interested in Japan's remarkable rise and its impact on the United States, including William Dietrich, Clyde Prestowitz and James Fallows. (See the Further Reading list at the end of this chapter for the references to some of these books.) While the free market emphasis was credited with sparking a period of global economic prosperity, it also undercut the economic stability of many countries and forced governments to reconsider their role in providing economic leadership and guidance.

Japan has been a key player in national innovation systems. In fact, the book that launched the burgeoning academic and policy field centred on Japan. Chris Freeman, who along with Bengt-Åke Lundval is seen as a parent of the national innovation systems research, published *Technology Policy and Economic Performance: Lessons from Japan* in 1987 (Freeman, 1987). Freeman pointed out the importance of an active role for government in promoting technological change.

National innovation and science and technology— how does East Asia stack up?

Today, many countries highlight scientific and technological innovation as the cornerstone of long-term economic success and as an appropriate locus for government engagement. Much is debated about how to successfully mobilize human and financial resources in the interests of national economic success and how to determine the drivers and actions needed to accelerate innovation. The literature on innovation emphasizes several factors: major policy statements by government; private sector support; sizeable public research and development funding, especially in basic sciences; improvement of educational systems, including the engagement and reorganization of the university system; industrial clusters; and the selection of key sectors for substantial support. Public and private sector spending on research and development is one of the most important comparative input indicators. Among the 36 developed countries of the Organization for Economic Cooperation and Development (OECD), the average national spending on research and development in 2018 was 2.4 percent of GDP, with China spending 2.4 percent, Taiwan 3.5 percent, Japan 3.3 percent and South Korea 4.5 percent (OECD 2019a).

Being competitive in technological fields like biotechnology, nanotechnology, environmental technologies, information technology and artificial intelligence requires governments to make major investments in both basic and applied research and related infrastructure, often in partnership or collaboration with key business sectors. Financing high-risk, high-reward research falls to government as the investments are beyond the capacity of all but the largest companies. The innovation risk then transfers from companies to governments. The science and technology economy put governments back into a central economic role as they

21st-century political economy in East Asia 215

experiment with policies and programs to help the private sector develop and commercialize new science and technology-based products and services.

Japan, China, Taiwan and South Korea are all characterized by strong central governments that have the authority and predilection to impose dramatic policies on the country. In the era of green growth and national innovation systems, which benefit from consistent and substantial government investment and policy support, East Asia, already the world leading region in the creation of the 21st-century economy, is determined to hold and expand its current standing.

National plans and policies

Japan, China and South Korea demonstrated to domestic and international audiences their belief that science, technology and innovation will be the bedrock of their 21st-century economies. They then took steps to make that a reality. Even in democracies, governments have a lot of power to signal the direction in which they want the economy to go. They have a "bully-pulpit," a commanding position from which to speak and be heard and from which they can promote their plans and priorities. Government money can be used to support research and development programs in areas they deem important. The East Asian national governments have used these opportunities over the past 30 years to make powerful leadership statements about the importance of science and technology in economic planning and development. An overview examination of the high-level national strategies in Japan, China and South Korea demonstrates the scale, detail and long-term focus of Asian national innovation.

Japan was early to peg its economic future on science and technology, proclaiming itself to be a science and technology nation in the mid-1990s. After the passage of the Science and Technology Basic Law in 1995 (the objective of which was to improve the level of science and technology and thereby help the country's economy and society), the country developed and implemented a series of five-year Science and Technology Basic Plans and put in place a Council for Science and Technology Policy led by the prime minister to select the sectors it planned to encourage as the basis for Japan's 21st-century economy. The Basic Plans, developed in conjunction with the Japan Business Federation (the *Keidanren*), provided the financing and the broad outline of a five-year strategy. The First Science and Technology Basic Plan (1996–2001) cost approximately US$180 billion, funded 10,000 PhD and post-doctoral positions and expanded academic-business collaboration. In Japan's Second Science and Technology Basic Plan in 2001, the government announced its goal of having Japanese scientists win 30 Nobel Prizes over the next 50 years. Japan had long been embarrassed by its poor Nobel Prize winning record of only nine (six in the sciences) Nobel wins in the past 100 years and the country's unfair reputation for imitation as opposed to innovation. Japan's pledge was met with criticism and some ridicule both inside and outside of Japan. However, between 2001 and 2019, Japanese creators won 19 Nobel Prizes, 18 of them in the sciences ("Japan's Nobel Laureates," 2019). (This number includes three Japan-born Nobel laureates who subsequently acquired foreign citizenship.)

Each Basic Plan built on the one before it but also stepped in new directions. The Third Science and Technology Basic Plan (2006–2010) chose priority sectors in life sciences, information technology, environmental research and nanotechnology/material science; emphasized promoting science among youth and women; recruited more foreign researchers; and continued efforts began in the Second Plan to reform national universities. The Fourth Science and Technology Basic Plan (2011–2015), coming in the wake of the Great Tohoku

216 21st-century political economy in East Asia

Earthquake, focused on disaster recovery and revitalization. Other priorities were green innovation, life innovation and science, technology and innovation system reform.

In the Fifth Science and Technology Basic Plan (2016–2020), Japan took an even bolder approach, outlining its vision of Society 5.0. In this "super smart society," ICT, Internet of Things, big data and artificial intelligence would be interconnected to help address international and domestic economic and social challenges and to deliver the services and products people need as they need them. To lead the creation and implementation of a super smart society, the plan argues, Japanese technological strengths must be enhanced, including robotics, sensor technology, actuator technology and materials nanotechnology, cybersecurity, Internet of Things, big data analytics, artificial technology and network technologies. Plans call for extensive collaborations across industry, government and academia and within and across ministries, agencies and departments to find the funding and create the research and commercialization opportunities to realize this super smart society. The Japan Business Federation (Keidanren) is a key player in Society 5.0, recognizing that expertise in these technologies will give Japan both an economic edge and the ability to address some of its greatest challenges, including those of an ageing society and a vulnerability to natural disasters. A key part of Society 5.0 is the funding of high-risk high-impact research collaborations in a wide range of fields. The objective is to bring together researchers from a variety of corporations and universities to investigate technologies and create products that have substantial potential but would be too expensive and risky for a company to undertake on its own.

Since the late 1990s, and starting well after Japan, China has poured huge amounts of financial and human capital into almost every scientific and technological field imaginable. As an authoritarian government, China can move quickly to mobilize innovation in a desired direction. China turned to the corporate sector (major parts owned by government) to become a central participant in its innovation agenda. State-owned enterprises as well as private companies were required to establish technology centres. High-technology companies were told to spend at least 5 percent of their annual sales on research and development in order to build in-house capabilities. A Technology Innovation Fund for Small and Medium-Sized Enterprises was launched in 1999. China encouraged the flow of foreign direct investment into certain industries and restricted it in other sectors, depending on the country's strengths or needs. The government would give foreign companies access to the Chinese market in return for sharing their technology with a Chinese firm or establishing a research and development centre in the country. (This is one of the tensions underlying the U.S. trade dispute with China.)

In 2006, China implemented its National Medium-to-Long-Term Plan for Science and Technology Development (2006–2020), a national innovation plan designed to make China a world leader in science, technology and innovation. China increased the percentage of its GDP spent on research and development from 1.37 percent in 2006 to 1.91 percent in 2012 to 2.4 percent in 2018 (OECD, 2019b). Programs, policies and new research institutions, like the Shanghai Industrial Technology Institute, were established to facilitate connections between government research institutes, companies and universities.

Starting in 2012, China shifted its focus to "frontier" technologies, innovations that have been researched and even somewhat developed but not yet mass marketed or adopted. Expecting the corporate sector to be the main source of innovation, the Chinese government focussed particularly on smart manufacturing, big data and artificial intelligence. Through this emphasis on science, technology and innovation, the government expects the country to maintain economic growth and develop more sustainably. In 2015, the government launched Made in China (MIC) 2025, a comprehensive state strategy to shift China from a

21st-century political economy in East Asia 217

manufacturing economy to a producer of high-value-added products (Institute for Security and Development Policy, 2018). According to documents on MIC 2025, its objective is to make China a "manufacturing superpower" (Kania, 2019). The plan focuses on ten priority sectors, including new-generation information technology, robotics, advanced machine tools, aerospace and high-performance medical equipment. The government itself makes major investments in these fields, while allowing firms in these sectors preferential access to credit from state banks; it also helps with the acquisition of intellectual property.

The MIC name comes from its stated goal of increasing the domestic content of core components in the prioritized sectors to 40 percent by 2020 and 70 percent by 2025. MIC 2025 provoked an international reaction, particularly from the United States, which is unusual for an industrial policy plan. As one analyst thoughtfully summarized, the reason for this reaction is that "implicitly and often explicitly, China's objective to become a manufacturing superpower implies the ambition not merely to catch up with other advanced economies but to surpass and displace them to achieve a dominant position in these industries worldwide" (Kania, 2019).

Artificial intelligence is one of the sectors China hopes to dominate. In 2017, the country's New-Generation Artificial Intelligence Development Plan was launched, outlining China's plans to become the leading AI global power by 2030. The main sections of the plan concern creating sufficient funding support from government, companies and industry alliances to support everything from start-ups and small- and medium-sized enterprises to the venture capital investments or private-public partnerships needed for larger projects or companies. AI innovation clusters with incubators and makerspaces are being created around key national laboratories. Chinese companies are encouraged to cooperate with foreign firms, universities and scientists and to recruit them to establish joint research projects or institutes in China. China is ranked as one of the top nations in the world in AI research and application. To the degree that AI has broad commercial applications, China is well-placed to maintain a substantial global lead over other technology-rich nations. It has focused its efforts on deep societal learning, which allows government monitoring and oversight of the economy, society and politics. The country is remarkably data-rich, drawing on extensive use of cell phones, the power of an authoritarian state and a willingness of the national government to use the collected information and analytical power of AI. Other nations are constrained by democratic values and limits on the authority of the state; China faces no such barriers.

South Korea began expanding its national research and development system in the late 1980s by founding industrial technology research associations in different industrial sectors that would allow the member firms to share technology, research facilities and funding. This expansion led to the development of a number of technologies, including semiconductors, which would eventually become a South Korean success story. The Basic Research Promotion Law (1989) made basic research a priority and established science and engineering research centres to improve university research and increase the number of well-trained scientists. Over the 1990s, the percentage of South Korean research funded by the private sector soared. By 1999, almost 5,000 company-affiliated research institutes had been established. Once the research and development capabilities of the private sector had grown, the government promoted large-scale national R&D projects. Launched in 1992, the Highly Advanced Nation (HAN) project aimed to make South Korea one of the world's seven most technologically advanced nations. The government strategically selected and funded sectors in which it believed the country had the capacity to compete, including agrochemicals, biomaterials and next-generation vehicles and semiconductors. The 21st-century Frontier R&D

218 *21st-century political economy in East Asia*

National Project followed in 1999 as did Biotech 2000 and Korean Bio-Vision 2010, the latter two aimed at making Korea a world leader in biotechnology.

By the beginning of the 21st century, South Korea had narrowed the technological gap between it and other advanced industrialized countries. The government developed a national innovation system that would create better linkages between industry, academia and government. In 2004, the South Korean government launched its IT 839 policy, which outlined the eight services, three infrastructure initiatives and nine products on which Korea would focus. Under its Framework Act on Science and Technology (2001), South Korea launched a series of Science and Technology Basic Plans. In the latest of these plans (2018–2022), the government committed to strengthening the role of companies in directing innovation and ensuring that research results reach new industries. South Korea followed through, spending a higher percentage of its GDP on research and development than almost any other country in the world. Like Japan, South Korea's new 21st-century science and technology planning is focussed on using science and technology to solve or improve social and environmental problems while developing a growth industry for the country. The South Korean government has made major investments in green technologies and in areas such as food safety, cybercrime and chronic diseases.

Supporting a key sector—digital content

National governments cannot support all emerging technology sectors. Available investment funds and the need to select sectors of national specialization force governments to choose investment and support opportunities. This section will provide a brief overview of how South Korea, Japan, Hong Kong and Taiwan have supported the development of their digital content sectors.

The key element is the range of policies and programs these East Asian governments and their corporate partners have undertaken in support of the sectors. Other countries have comparable policies and not all the East Asian policies or programs have worked perfectly. The effort, however, showcases the focus and commitment East Asian governments put into developing, supporting and promoting an emerging economic sector, such as digital content.

Japan, South Korea and Taiwan were quick to see the economic potential of the digital content sector. The rapid expansion of wireless technologies, an innovation led more by Japan's NTT DoCoMo than, as most people believe, Apple or Research in Motion/Blackberry, sparked an early realization of the commercial potential of digital content. Whole new sectors—video games in Japan, massive online gaming in Korea, animation in China—emerged in fairly quick order. Asian companies realized, too, that they had significant advantages in language and cultural understanding in reaching into the fast-growing Asian markets, particularly the underdeveloped Chinese-language sector. Governments thus became enthusiastic about the prospects of digital content. Taiwan launched extensive content development strategies, while Japan, Korea and Hong Kong promoted video, art, music and other digital products. Government policies focused on everything, from skills training and talent promotion to marketing support.

Governments set up central agencies to coordinate the development of the digital content sector. Taiwan established the Institute for Information Industry (Triple I) in 1979 with the goal of developing a world-class Taiwanese information industry. Beginning in 2002, the government, led by Triple I, began focusing on developing a globally competitive digital content industry. The Digital Content Industries Promotion and Development Office was established and charged with the development of policies for the industry. Triple I encouraged university-business collaboration, talent cultivation and market promotion and supported the country's aggressive e-economy strategies. Korea created a similar organization, the Korea Creative Content Agency, in 2009, bringing together five existing organizations into one charged with expanding the national presence in global digital content. Korea's ambitious aspiration was to have the country ranked among the five top digital content countries.

East Asian governments also recognized the importance of drawing attention to the digital media field and highlighting its increasing economic importance. To this end, the creation of flagship facilities—high-profile digital content showcases—provide tangible evidence of what the government believed would be the scale and significance of the content industry. In South Korea, Songdo inside the city of Incheon was designed as a demonstration project for all manner of digital content and connectivity initiatives. Songdo's U-City (the "U" symbolizing ubiquitous computing) model illustrated how work, personal life, government and recreation could be bundled together through digital technology, providing residents and visitors alike with a window on the digital future. Seoul's Digital Media City (DMC), planned and funded by the Seoul City government, brings together researchers, companies and digital content creators to become a hub for research and development, production and marketing of digital content (see Figure 10.2). In 2020, a complex of 500 companies, DMC has a goal of growing to 800 firms. Most DMC companies are in three main industry fields: media and entertainment (broadcasting, game, film/animation, music and digital education); software related to media and entertainment; and IT-related to media and entertainment. DMC also holds events, including virtual reality content competitions, film festivals and street festivals at which firms display elements of their digital content on outdoor LED media installations.

Figure 10.2 Digital Media City—a sign of Digital Media City Station on Seoul Subway Line 6, 2019.

Hong Kong has invested $2 billion in Cyberport, a collaborative centre that educates young people and supports entrepreneurs with a focus on digital content. The goal is to establish Hong Kong as a leading digital content centre, incubating new companies and creating jobs. Equipped with cutting-edge infrastructure and hardware, software and technical support, Cyberport is home to a digital creative cluster of over 1,000 companies in financial tech, IoT/wearables, e-commerce and big data/artificial intelligence. Cyberport provides excellent infrastructure (from the broadband network to intelligent office buildings to hardware, software and technical support) conducive to the development of a strategic small and medium IT enterprise cluster.

On the policy front, the various East Asian countries have approached development of their digital content sectors in different ways. Japan identified the content industry as a key national strategy in 2002. The government launched a Japan Brand Strategy with the slogan "Cool Japan" to promote Japanese popular culture exports and then passed the Content Industry Promotion Law, allowing the government to expand support. Japan has developed a large domestic market for digital content. Its challenge was not so much building the digital content sector as it was increasing digital content exports (see Figure 10.3).

Building off Japanese domestic success in animation, video games and apps and using the Cool Japan branding, Japan slowly built a global market for the country's digital production. The government put in place a variety of promotional and support activities designed to increase international sales of its digital content products. Given the domestic success of the digital content sector, some critics questioned the need for the Cool Japan strategy. In response, the Ministry of Economy, Trade and Industry (METI) pointed out that most of the

Figure 10.3 Cool Japan Fest, 2018.

21st-century political economy in East Asia   221

creative companies are small or medium sized and lack the funding to establish themselves globally. To help these firms branch out internationally, the Cool Japan Fund was launched in 2013. A public-private sector partnership, the fund provided risk capital and support for the international promotion of uniquely Japanese products and services, including digital content. Companies could also apply to another fund for assistance with the costs of localizing (subtitling, dubbing and/or translating) their products.

CoFesta (the Japanese International Content Festival) was created by the METI in 2007. Each year since, the government has co-sponsored numerous events showcasing Japanese content to the world. Four of the main events are the Tokyo Game Show, the Japan Content Showcase, the Tokyo International Film Festival and Anime Japan. The Japan Content Showcase, as an example, is an international content fair held annually in Tokyo and includes animation, music, film and television. CoFesta ambassadors, international students who love Japanese content, have been enlisted to help promote it overseas.

Hong Kong's digital content support centres around Cyberport and has three main priorities. The first is to encourage young people to become coders, programmers and digital entrepreneurs. To this end, the centre hosts several thousand youth visits annually. Young people participate in hands-on workshops and in competitions on coding, robotics, animation, etc. Students are also eligible for six months of seed funding to take a project from idea to concept. Cyberport's second focus is the support of entrepreneurs. Hong Kong companies with a compelling business plan are eligible for Cyberport office space at much reduced rates. Support for the entrepreneurs includes on-site talks, pitching sessions, product trials, networking events with investors, marketing support and business matching. Meeting and conference rooms are available for free, and production, training, trade fair/exhibition and professional services (e.g. legal, advertising) are all generously subsidized. Cyberport also offers financial assistance to its entrepreneurs. Cyberport's third pillar is partnerships; it believes that it is crucial to assist start-ups and established companies to grow, and to promote connections to investors and others in the industry. To that end, Cyberport offers networking opportunities, with 150 events at Cyberport annually, and helps facilitate connections in other parts of the world, particularly China.

The Korea Creative Content Agency (KOCCA) is the main South Korean government office, tasked with expanding Korea's digital content presence. Its Contents Korea Lab supports prospective creators and start-ups by allowing participants to use shared working and creative space. The motto of the Contents Korea Lab is "sparkling small ideas can become global contents." Available equipment/spaces include a green studio, a recording studio, video editing suites, a sound editing suite, 3D printers, a pitching room, lecture rooms, meeting rooms, conference rooms, a library, a product showcase, lounges and a Content Job Counselling Centre to provide more detailed business development advice. These centres support the government's desire to boost "the start-up scene" by helping entrepreneurs turn their ideas into viable businesses through mentoring, funding, marketing and networking. KOCCA is also tasked with helping companies sell creative products and content internationally, with offices overseas that offer business consulting and localization support. The agency also hosts international events to showcase Korean content to investors, partners and licensing companies.

To promote the development of creative talent for the digital media industry, South Korea holds a national storytelling competition as storytelling is an important part of successful multi-player games. Animators are offered content production assistance and technical support for original animation and webtoons. There is also marketing and pitching support available and assistance with entry into overseas markets or international trade shows. Seoul's

Figure 10.4 Seoul Animation Centre, 2015.

Animation Centre has an animation cinema and various spaces for students, content businesses and creators to learn and create (see Figure 10.4). Near the museum is Seoul Comics Road, which showcases Korean cartoons and animation and is host to parades, art markets and cosplay events. The East Asia nations, to put it simply, understand the commercial and economic potential of the digital content industries.

Conclusion

The digital content sector is a small, but critical, example of East Asian innovation strategies. Over the past 40 years, and following Japan's impressive lead in consumer technologies, automobiles and digital entertainment, East Asia has worked to reinvent itself. The region dominates the digital technology sector in hardware, software and digital content and leads in many industrial and manufacturing fields. Many of the world's largest research institutes and most effective scientific commercialization centres are in East Asia. But while the East Asian countries produce a disproportionate percentage of science, engineering and technology graduates—a major advantage during periods of rapid technological change—they produce fewer social science and humanities specialists. The expertise and social value of those in the social sciences and humanities is more clearly revealed when nations are struggling with "wicked" social problems like climate change, globalization and technological transitions. This may be an area in which East Asia will have to change. Japan has decided to include social sciences and humanities in its Sixth Science and Technology Basic Plan at the same time, however, that the support for these disciplines at universities within the country is declining.

The regional effort is supported by a large and increasingly prosperous regional consumer market. Twenty years ago, East Asian firms looked firstly to the United States and secondly to Europe for sales and commercial credibility. With Japan emerging as one of the most

21st-century political economy in East Asia 223

demanding and high-priced consumer markets, the country has supported hundreds of innovative companies on the basis of domestic sales alone. The growing Chinese middle class started to compete in size with both the American and Japanese markets, allowing East Asian firms to develop viable products (Asian-themed video games) and services (like WeChat) that sold primarily in the region and that were little known in the rest of the world. East Asia's innovation economy is focused, primarily but not exclusively, on the regional market.

East Asian innovation has rested, further, on the combination of centralized government coordination and subsidies and the deep scientific and mathematical education systems in the region that have proven so important in sustaining a technology-centred economy. When these attributes are combined with major investments and coordination between national governments and the business sectors, East Asia's innovation system built on and modernized the region's model of state-directed post-war economic development. In the process, East Asia has shifted in less than three decades from an economy focused on heavy industry to a high-technology, science-based economy based on creative adaptation and government-business collaboration. East Asian accomplishments set the competitive bar for countries aspiring to 21st-century national economic success.

Bibliography

"Japan's Nobel Laureates", *Nippon.com*, October 10, 2019. https://www.nippon.com/en/japan-data/h00304/japan%E2%80%99s-nobel-laureates.html

Freeman, Chris. 1987. *Technology Policy and Economic Performance: Lessons from Japan*. London: Pinter Publishers.

Institute for Security and Development Policy. 2018. *Made in China 2025*. Institute for Security and Development Policy.

Jamrisko, Michelle, Lee J. Miller and Wei Lu. 2019. "These are the World's Most Innovative Countries", *Bloomberg*, January 22.

Kania, Elsa B. 2019. "A Deep Dive Into China's Techno-Strategic Ambitions for 2025 and Beyond", *The Diplomat*, February 1.

OECD. 2019a. *Main Science and Technology Indicators*. http://www.oecd.org/sti/msti.htm

OECD. 2019b. *Gross Domestic Product on R&D % of GDP 2000 – 2019*. https://data.oecd.org/rd/gross-domestic-spending-on-r-d.htm

Wiggers, Kyle. 2019. "Top500: China Has 219 of the World's Fastest Supercomputers", *Venture Beat*, June 17.

WIPO. 2015. *Special Section The Top 100 Global Patent Applicants*, p. 3. https://www.wipo.int/edocs/pubdocs/en/wipo_pub_941_2015-section1.pdf

WIPO. 2019. *Facts and Figures 2019*. https://www.wipo.int/edocs/infogdoc s/en/ipfactsandfigures2019/

Further Reading

Amsden, Alice. 1992. *Asia's Next Giant: South Korea and Late Industrialization*. Oxford University Press.

Anchordoguy, Marie. 1989. *Computers Inc.: Japan's Challenge to IBM*. Harvard University Press.

Coates, Kenneth and Carin Holroyd. 2012. *Digital Media in East Asia: National Innovation and the Transformation of a Region*. Cambria Press.

Fallows, James. 1994. *Looking at the Sun: The Rise of the New East Asian Economic and Political System*. Vintage Books.

Johnson, Chalmers. 1982. *MITI and the Japanese Miracle: The Growth of Industrial Policy 1925–1975*. Stanford University Press.

Wade, Robert. 1990. *Governing the Market*. Princeton University Press.

11 East Asia in the 21st century

East Asia has emerged as a dominant and influential region, in ways and to a degree that is little understood. It is home to more than 1.6 billion people, 22 percent of the world's population, and responsible for almost one-quarter of the world's GDP. China, Japan and South Korea have greatly expanded their economic presence around the globe, particularly through overseas direct foreign investments in natural resources, manufacturing and services. With the largest economy in the world, China has become the epicentre of the world's economy, with Japan not far behind at third position. Yet the trajectory is uneven, with regional leadership in technological innovation offset by demographic challenges and many strategic and environmental issues in need of urgent attention.

The region is famous for its economic booms, in which countries forced to restructure and reorient themselves have in the process achieved enormous and rapid growth. The first boom was Japan's rapid emergence from a feudal state into an industrial power during the Meiji Restoration. After the country's complete devastation and defeat at the end of World War II came its economic miracle: by the 1980s, five-year economic plans, industrial policy and double-digit growth had underpinned Japan's transformation into the world's second largest economy. Using Japan's playbook, South Korea followed with the "Miracle on the Han River," its transformation from a developing country with a GDP of US$2.4 billion in 1961 to a developed country with a GDP of US$598.1 billion in 1996 (World Bank, n.d.). South Korea was joined by Taiwan and Hong Kong as three of the four Asian Tigers, so named for their rapid industrialization and high growth rates from the 1960s to the 1990s (Singapore was the fourth.) All four became high-income economies and continue to serve as role models for developing countries. China's economic rise began later but has been just as spectacular. From the late 1970s to 2005, China's average annual GDP growth rate was about 10 percent, making it the fastest growing economy in the world over those decades.

With the notable exception of North Korea, the nations of East Asia have successfully navigated the transition from industrial to high-technology economies, establishing the region as the global leader in the technology sector. People outside the region typically underestimate East Asia's electronic and digital dominance in large measure because many of the key elements—social media, online shopping, specialized consumer products, video games, animation and the like—are nation and region specific. Many of the region's most important contributions, like Taiwan's superconductors, are either hidden inside consumer and industrial products or buried in the complicated supply chains of the modern electronics manufacturing industry. High technology is the most public manifestation of East Asia's leadership in science, technology and innovation.

The intersection of government leadership and investment, nationwide collaboration within the business community and an enviable level of government, business and academic interaction has produced the kind of cooperation that allows the country to participate in high-intensity and expensive research and development. As a consequence, East Asia has made major contributions to such fields as aerospace, fusion energy, digital integration, renewable resources, pharmaceuticals, robotics and electrical machinery. In addition, most of the nations have faster and less complicated regulatory processes than those in the West. China's rapid technological advances are due, in part, to the country's authoritarian government and ability to marshal impressive human and financial resources for national innovation.

The development of new economy products and services has perhaps benefitted most from the expansion of East Asian consumer markets. For several generations, East Asian companies focused largely on serving foreign markets, with Japan being an outlier in this area. However, with well over half a billion members of the middle class and a growing number of wealthy people in China, Taiwan and South Korea, East Asia has become a distinctive and attractive market. Consumers in the region are demanding, pushing companies to produce good-quality products with attentive follow-up service. The East Asian countries, particularly China, are able to produce an interesting combination of both high-quality and high-cost products and lower quality, inexpensive manufacturing. Furthermore, East Asia has made a crucial transition from heavy and medium industry to the digital economy, setting the stage for continued 21st-century economic success.

Despite the region's global and regional economic success, the transitions in East Asia have not all been smooth. The rapid expansion of China's global engagement has created substantial uncertainty in the region. Tensions between China and Japan, China and South Korea, South Korea and Japan and the ongoing political struggles between China and Taiwan have created a near continuous swirl of political contestations, mounting rhetoric and strategic challenges. Taiwan continues to fight for diplomatic recognition, an effort that is being blocked by China at every turn; only 15 states officially recognize the country, most of them microstates and small nations. Additionally, the constant strain associated with the political and diplomatic chaos related to North Korea keeps the residents of the region on tenterhooks, worried about military aggression, especially nuclear weapons, political subterfuge, the perpetual poverty crises inside North Korea and the unpredictability of the world's most dangerous rogue state.

East Asia has a complex international presence. Japan remains one of the world's foremost donor nations, devoting billions of dollars a year to building positive and commercially beneficial relations with the developing world. Similarly, China, eager to gain access to urgently needed strategic resources, has made massive investments around the world, particularly through its Belt and Road Initiative, which has allocated hundreds of billions of dollars for infrastructure construction around the world. However, the Belt and Road strategy has struggled in recent years, a consequence of China's strained financial resources, overcommitments and rising costs around the world. While some Belt and Road projects have been very successful—approximately $575 billion of infrastructure, like roads, ports and railways, have been built or are underway (Bloomberg, 2019)—recently some countries have declined to participate in the Belt and Road projects, extricated themselves from local projects or are rethinking their collaborations with China.

The region has avoided international military entanglements but has greatly expanded its economic presence around the world, particularly through overseas direct foreign investments in natural resources, manufacturing and services. The inherent distrust of China's political and strategic ambitions has been shown in the global backlash about Huawei's 5G Internet technology and growing global concerns about the extent and reach of the Chinese surveillance state. But delving into the world of cyber security and technological warfare

226 *East Asia in the 21st century*

is not required to find evidence of profound and worrisome international conflicts. China's stance towards Taiwan is aggressive, and Taiwan stands firm in response. But, because it lacks the military wherewithal to stand up to China, Taiwan would rely heavily on American protection if tensions were to escalate. The prospect of a jump from angry rhetoric to military engagement is more likely than most appreciate. Another cause for concern is the erratic and unpredictable Kim Jong-un of North Korea, leaving East Asia perpetually on the edge. That North Korea is close to being nuclear armed raises both the stakes and concerns, particularly for the highly vulnerable South Korea. Another source of conflict is territorial disputes: a stand-off over the Senkaku Islands between China and Japan has the most potential to escalate into a major confrontation. These small, isolated and uninhabited islands seem inconsequential, but the combination of national strategic considerations and pure bravado has turned this small outpost into a potential flashpoint of East Asian affairs.

The South China Sea presents even greater danger. An enormous volume of traded goods passes through the Sea, which is also the focus of numerous and overlapping territorial and marine claims, vast fishing resources and oil and gas reserves. The large number of countries involved—China, Taiwan, Philippines, Vietnam, Malaysia and Brunei—and the complications of history, politics and economics make this area one of the most volatile in the world. The region is closely watched by the United States, which is well aware that armed conflict could sweep beyond the immediate region and draw in other nations. The South China Sea has been heavily militarized, raising the possibility that incidental contact could spark escalating conflict.

East Asia's international entanglements are complicated by internal political dynamics. Much of the world is highly concerned about the human rights abuses directed at the Uyghurs in China, but intervention is politically impossible. The even higher profile pro-democracy movement in Hong Kong has shaken the authority of the Chinese government over the city-state, empowered anti-Communist forces, and added a great sense of uncertainty about the internal governance of China. The world is also concerned about Taiwan, whose struggles with China's constant challenges to its existence create an international dynamic that influences domestic politics. South Korean politics remain tumultuous and passionate, with strong traditions of student and labour protests and intense criticism of government-corporate entanglements. Unlike other countries, Japan's vaunted political stability still holds, with the dominance of the Liberal Democratic Party firmly in place and a strong opposition largely lacking. As a region, the countries of East Asia reflect the domination of central governments. China's government is authoritarian in nature, while the rest balance a strong belief in the authority of the state and domestic democracy.

East Asia's engagement with the world has been accelerated by climate change and the intensive evidence of global interconnectedness. Carbon emissions, the poisoning of the planet's oceans and dangerously unpredictable weather have undermined the stability of nations, raised the bar on the regulation and control of pollutants and sparked a global debate about environmental responsibilities. China is the world's largest source of emissions and regularly endures climate calamities, like the dust storms that sweep in from Mongolia and blank out the sun in Beijing. Japan, in contrast, has some of the world's best environmental technologies and aggressive strategies such as smart electrical grids, but the country lacks its own sources of energy beyond contested nuclear power and a slowly growing renewables sector. To reinforce the contrast, Japan and China used to vary dramatically in their sense of urgency: China has until relatively recently avoided accepting responsibility for climate

East Asia in the 21st century 227

change amelioration, while Japan has been at the leading edge of environmental awareness, reflected in its leadership on the Kyoto Accord and the 2005 Aichi World's Fair (although Japan is building 22 new coal-fired power plants, which contradicts this environmental responsibility). With rising living standards across the region and considerable vulnerability to climate change effects, East Asia is intricately connected to the ecological transitions that are transforming the world.

The rapid and diverse transformation of East Asia and the relationships between the nations and the rest of the world has vaulted the region into global prominence. The increasingly close interconnections, particularly in business and consumer markets, have made the region far less reliant on the rest of the world. Importantly, the world's growing reliance on East Asia has not been matched by international understanding of the social, economic and political dynamics of China, Japan, North and South Korea, Taiwan, Hong Kong and Macau. The limited appreciation for the region has been masked by growing engagement with East Asian food and popular culture and distorted by systematic misunderstanding of the region's economic transitions and political aspirations.

It will take years, perhaps generations, for the world to reconcile itself to East Asian leadership, if not dominance. The barriers presented by multiple languages, cultural misunderstandings, diverse ideological and political systems, philosophical and religious traditions and complex economic and innovation systems make it difficult for people outside the region to make sense of the continuing transitions in the region. International student enrolments steadily enhance East Asian understanding of the rest of the world, particularly North America and Europe, but the presence of international students on Western campuses seems to have done little to improve Western appreciation of East Asian realities.

The rise of East Asia—both in the past and the present—can be interpreted in one of three ways: as a commercial opportunity (the opening of China to foreign trade in the 18th century and again in the 21st century); as a strategic advantage (the 19th-century establishment of Hong Kong as a British colony and the division of the Korean Peninsula during the Cold War); and as an economic threat (during the Japanese boom and following the rise of China). The imperatives of the coming decades, from heeding the urgent need for a global approach to climate change to developing the social and economic potential of digital technologies, require stronger engagement between East Asia and the rest of the world and a realization of the degree to which the political economy of East Asia will drive the destiny of the planet.

In 2020, the world changed in ways that few imagined and even fewer can understand. In December 2019, a new coronavirus—labelled COVID-19—was identified in Wuhan, China. While epidemiologists worried from the outset—the earlier SARS and H1N1 epidemics had begun in China—it took the world until March 2020 to see the disease for the serious threat that it would become. By March 2020, the severe outbreak in Wuhan had spread through much of China to South Korea and Japan and had erupted in Italy, from where it quickly reached across Europe and North America. The pandemic exploded globally in the ensuing months; by the end of May it had infected 5 million people and killed over 300,000, particularly among the elderly and the ill (European Centre for Disease Prevention and Control, 2020).

China (over 4,600 reported deaths as of October 2020, a number believed by many to be too low) attracted a great deal of public criticism for its actions, principally for not reporting the outbreak soon enough. But by May, Wuhan was out of lockdown, Shanghai Disneyland

228 *East Asia in the 21st century*

Park had reopened and China's economy was growing again. Taiwan, with the world's most effective response to the pandemic, recovered quickly and became the poster child for an effective response to a viral disease (seven deaths by mid-October). Japan (1,726 deaths) and South Korea (461 deaths), likewise, contained the pandemic more quickly than did the United Kingdom (45,500 deaths) and the United States (close to 228,000 fatalities).

The pandemic-inspired lockdowns almost froze the global economy in place, forcing governments into large-scale deficit spending, causing mass unemployment and forcing thousands of businesses into bankruptcy. Led by U.S. President Donald Trump, many commentators pointed an accusatory finger at China, threatening to disrupt trade and investment relations. Asia's century did not grind to a halt; East Asia produced some of the most effective government responses in the world and set out to lead the global economic recovery. In short order, however, the economic and political realities of the first two decades of the 21st century had been thrown out the window. With a weakened global economy, considerable political turmoil focused on the United States, the United Kingdom and Russia, significant distrust of China, strong evidence of East Asia's resilience, creative and government-business-citizen alliances and sufficient uncertainty to create opportunities for the bold, the 21st century faced a profound redefinition. While the nature of East Asia's role in the shape-changing world remains unknown, there is little doubt that the region will be more influential than in the past and at the centre of the economic and political configuration that seems destined to follow the 2020 pandemic (see Figure 11.1).

Figure 11.1 Army disinfecting city streets, Taiwan 2020.

East Asia in the 21st century 229

Bibliography

Bloomberg News. 2019 August 14. European Centre for Disease Prevention and Control. 2020. https://www.ecdc.europa.eu/en/geographical-distribution-2019-ncov-cases

World Bank GDP Tables. https://data.worldbank.org/indicator/NY.GDP.MKTP.CD?cid=GPD_29&locations=KR

Further Reading

Hayes, Peter and Chung-in Moon, eds. 2018. *The Future of East Asia*. London: Palgrave McMillan.

Shambaugh, David. 2016. *When China Rules the World*. Boston: Polity Books.

Index

Page numbers in "italic" indicate a figure and page numbers in "bold" indicate an illustration.

#MeToo movement in South Korea 120

Abe Shinzo 3, 81, 200, 201, 206, 209
Aichi World's Fair (2005) 227
Ainu 58
Air Defense Identification Zone (ADIZ) 204, 205
AKB48, Japanese pop group *194*
Akihito (Emperor) 78
Akishino (Crown Prince) 78
Alliance Against Moral and National
    Education 167
Allied Occupation of Japan 146
Alternate attendance system 61
Alvares, Jorge 179
amakudari 83
Amitabha Buddha 91
Amsden, Alice 214
Anime Japan 221
anti-China separatist movement in Hong Kong 168
Army disinfecting city streets, Taiwan *228*
Arrow, the (ship) 14; *Arrow* War, the 14
art, ink wash painting 189
artforms 189
Ashikaga period 60
Ashikaga Takauji 60
Asian brands 3
Asian financial crisis 122–123
Asian Institute for Policy Studies and Council on
    Foreign Relations survey on the U.S. military
    presence in South Korea 116
Asian Women's Fund 209
Asimo Robot *213*
Association of Korean Victims 208, 209
Astro Boy 193
Asuka period 57
atomic bombings of Hiroshima and Nagasaki 71,
    71, 96, 137, 199
Austronesian groups, stateless 142
Azuchi-Momoyama period 60

Babones, Salvatore, *Foreign Policy* 159
baby strike 123

Basic Law: Hong Kong 165–166, 167;
    Macau 183
Basic Research Promotion Law (1989) 217
Battle of Sekigahara 60
Beijing 10, 11
Beijing Convention 14
Belt and Road Initiative 29–31, *30*, 50, 225
birth rate: in Japan 123; in South Korea 123–124
Black Ships, Perry's 63
Blair, Tony 166
Bloomberg Innovation Index, South Korea 212
Blue House 111, *117*
Booksellers' disappearance in Hong Kong
    168–169
border and trade treaty, China and Russia 13
Boxers, the 15
bride trafficking 48, 124
Bridge on the River Kwai, The (film) 70
British Empire and trade with China 13
British Hong Kong 163–164
British opium smugglers, Chinese attack
    against 162
British Supplementary Treaty of the
    Bogue 162
Buddhism/Buddhists 1, 8, 38, 91, 153, 191;
    in East Asia 189, 191; in Hong Kong 176;
    in Japan 57, 60, 63, 77, 82, 89, 90, 91, 201;
    Jogyesa temple *122*; Nichiren 91; in Korea
    100, 101; in Macau 184; in South Korea 102,
    121, 136; in Taiwan 154; Tibetan 41, 42

Canadian Trade Office in Taipei *147*
capitalist economy, China as a 28
casino gambling and casino lights in Macau *185*;
    in Macau 184–186
Catholicism/Catholics 38, 104, 121; in
    China 39; in Macau 179, 180, 184; in South
    Korea 121
Causeway Bay Books 168–169
CCP National Party Congress Standing
    Committee 167
Central and Victoria Harbour (Hong Kong) *177*

232 *Index*

Central Committee, China's 22, 34, 35, 36; central government, in China 7, 17, 26, 37, 51, 67; in Hong Kong 166, 173
Chaebol and the South Korean economy 110, 112, 113–115, 117, 120, 121; and the Asian Financial Crisis 122–123
Chairman Kim 86, 138, 139
Charles, Prince 166
Chen Shui-bian 150, 153
Chiang Ching-kuo 156; and improvements in Taiwan 145;
Chiang Kai-shek 17, 20, 21, 145, 150; airport 153
Chief Executive and executive branch, Hong Kong's government 171
China 10; and abject poverty transformation 5; ageing population of 2, 3, 29, 48–49; Belt and Road Initiative of 29–31, *30*, 50, 225; birth rate in 48; border and trade treaty with Russia 13; branches of government in 34; and Britain tensions 14; British trade with 13; Buddhism and 153; as a capitalist economy 28; Central Committee 22, 34, 35, 36; collapse of the imperial system of 190; Communist Party institutions in 33–34; Constitution of 32; corruption and 26, 28, 32, 37, 43, 47, 51; COVID-19 pandemic and 227–228; Cultural Revolution of 19, 23–25, 51, 155, 163, 175, 182, 190; demographic challenges of 48–49; different periods in history of 7; and difficult concessions with foreign countries 14; early history of 6–11; economic growth of 5, 26–31, 50; economic liberalization of 26–31; effect of World War II on 1; election of premier of 33; environmental problems in 45, 195; foreign-led government in 10; and foreign trade 10; GDP of 1, 28, 216; geography and demography of 5; head of government of 33–34; Head of State 32–33; individual wealth of citizens 50; inequality in 8, 36, 45–46, 47, 51; as an innovative country 1; interwoven histories with Japan and South Korea 1; investment in higher education 46; isolationism and 11, 13, 14; Japan relations 203–204; and Japan war over the Korean peninsula 14; map of *6*; middle class in 5; migrant workers in 46–47; National Medium-to-Long-Term Plan for Science and Technology Development 216; National Party Congress 35–36; negotiations for handover of Macau 182; New-Generation Artificial Intelligence Development Plan 217; organizational parallelism of government in 33–34; and the outside world 26; paramount leaders of 19, 32; peasant rebellions in 10; People's Liberation Army 37; per capita incomes in 5; Politburo/Standing Committee 33–37, 47; political succession in 36–37;

political system of 31–32; population size and challenges posed 48–49; president and election of 32–33; provincial and local government in 37; quality of life in 5, 45, 46; religion in 38–39; resumption of civil war 20–21; reunification of 8; rise and fall of 16; rural unrests in 46–47; sex ratio in 48; society of 37–38; and the South China Sea 204–206; State Council of 33, 34, 35; state-managed capitalism in 5; states under the Jin dynasty 7; and supercomputing technology 212; and the Treaty of Shimonoseki 144; US relations 49–50; and Vatican agreement 39; *see also* People's Republic of China (PRC)
China Post 153
Chinese, resentment against foreigners 14
Chinese Academy of Social Sciences (2020) 48
Chinese Catholic Patriotic Association (CCPA) 39
Chinese Civil War 18, 19, 21, 33, 152, 181; in Hong Kong 175; in Taiwan 150, 154
Chinese Communist Party (CCP) 1, 3, 18, 145; and People's Republic of China 107; religion and 38; and sensitive issues 39–50
Chinese Constitution, freedom of religion in the 38
Chinese culture, golden age of 8
Chinese dictionary, standard 13
Chinese folk religions 38, 176, 184
Chinese inventions 1
Chinese society 37–38
Chinese-state-appointed bishops 39
Chinese superiority 11
Choi Soon-sil 125
Chondoist Chongu Party 129
chopsticks 188
Christianity: in Japan 91; in Taiwan 154
Christian organizations: numbers in China 38; and state repression in China 38
Chrysanthemum throne 78
Chun Doo-hwan 112
Chunghwa Post 153
Chun government, US support of 115
Civic Passion 174
civil service exams 101, 120, 190
civil war: China's in Taiwan 145–146; Korea 106–107; resumption of China's 20–21
Classical Japan 57
Clean Government Party (*Komeito*) 82
CoFesta 221
comfort women 207–210; lawsuits filed by and for the 209
Comintern (Communist International) 17
communism, spread in China of 17, 19, 75, 107
Communist Party of China (CPC) 17, 19, 24, 32, 35, 36 ; People's Liberation Army and 37; power of 33–34; suppression of by the KMT 145; weapons aimed at Taiwan and 151
Communist single party state 129

Index   233

Communist Youth League 36, 127
Comprehensive and Progressive Agreement for Trans-Pacific Partnership, Japan and 98
Confucianism 1, 3, 189–190; in Chinese society 37; and Confucius 1, 6–7; in East Asia 189–190; in Hong Kong 176; and Japan's political heritage 77; rejection of 17, 19; in South Korea 100, 101, 119, 121; in Taiwan 154
conscription, limited, ROC/Taiwanese Armed Forces and 156
Constitution: China's 32; Constitution of the Republic of China 149; of Hong Kong 171; Japan's 78, 84; of Macau 183; South Korea 129; South Korea's 117–118
Content Industry Promotion Law 220
Content Job Counselling Centre 221
Convention of Beijing (1860) 14
Cool Japan 193, *220*; Cool Japan Fund 221
coronavirus pandemic 227; and China's response to 29, 51; impact of on Macau's economy 185; Lunar New Year holidays 29; and Taiwan and WHO's meetings 147
corruption: in China 26, 28, 32, 37, 47, 51; within China's police and judiciary 43; in Japan 80; in Korea 101, 110, 113; under the Ming dynasty 11; in South Korea 114, 125
Council for Science and Technology Policy, Japan's 215
COVID-19 pandemic: China and 227–228; global impact of 227–228; South Korea's response to 126; *see also* coronavirus pandemic
creation story, Japan's 58
Crown Prince Akishino 78
Cultural Revolution 19, 23–25, 51, 155, 163, 175, 182, 190
Cyberport 220, 221

Dae Jang-geum 194
daimyo (feudal lords) 60
Daoism 1, 6, 8, 38, 100; in Taiwan 154
Declaration of Independence, Taiwanese intellectuals for Taiwan's 144
democracy, China and 42–43
Democratic Justice Party 112
Democratic Party, South Korea's 117
Democratic People's Republic of Korea (DPRK) 129; establishment of 126
Democratic Progressive Party (DPP) 149, 150
Democratic United Party 117
Deng Pufang 24
Deng Xiaoping 24–25, *25*, 27, 31, 32, 50, 163; "reform and opening" policies of 25–26
Denuclearization of the Korean Peninsula 132–135, 197
Diaoyu/Senkaku Islands dispute, between China and Japan 203–204

Diet 79; Houses of the 78
Dietrich, William 214
Digital Content Industries Promotion and Development Office 218
digital content sectors, support of 218–222
Digital Media City *219*
District Councils, Hong Kong's government 172
divine winds (*kamikaze*) 10, 59, 70
Dodge, Joseph 75
Dokdo/Takeshima conflict 210
Dokdo/Takeshima Islands *202*
Dutch East India Company, trading on Penghu Islands by 142

earthquakes 7, 12, 54, 81, 95, 96; Great Kanto Earthquake 67; Tohoku 96, 216
East Asian countries: and the 21st century 224–228; and 21st century economy 195–196; challenges faced by 196; innovation strategies in 222–223; low birth rates and 197; people-to-people connections 196; popular culture of the 193–195; shared culture of 188; shared values of 191–193; *see also* East Asian region
East Asian medicine, traditional (TEAM) 188
East Asian region: conflicts in 199; Confucianism and the 1; consumer markets in 225; economic growth of 224–225; historical memory in 206–207; and international military entanglements 225–226; and plans and policies for the future 215–218; political entanglements in 226; relationship between countries in 1; rise of 227; and technological advancement 212
economic boom, global and Chinese 5
economic bubble (Japan) and Plaza Accord 76–77
economic growth 213; and China 7, 29, 45, 49, 216; and Japan 66, 83, 84, 98; and North Korea 130; and South Korea 111, 113; and Taiwan 155
economic inequality, China's reduction of 8
Economic Planning Agency (EPA) 83
economy, COVID-19 pandemic and the global 227–228
Edo/Tokugawa era 60–64
education: in Japan 87–89; in South Korea 120–121
election campaigns: in Japan 79–80; in South Korea 118; in Taiwan 149–150
electoral system: of Hong Kong 172; of Macau 183; South Korea's 118
Emperor Akihito 78, 206
Emperor Go-Daigo 60
Emperor Hirohito 68, 71, 74, 206
Emperor Jimmu 78
Emperor Kotoku 57
Emperor Meiji 206
Emperor Naruhito 78

234 *Index*

Emperor Puyi 15, 16, 17
Emperor Wen 8
Emperor Wuzong 8
Empress Wu Zetian 8
European Union on an Economic Partnership
 Agreement, Japan and 98
Everybody Produces Steel campaign 22
Ewha Women's University (Seoul) 118, 125
Exclusive Economic Zone (EEZ) 205
extraterritoriality treaty between Britain and
 China 14

Fallows, James 214
Falun Gong or Falun Dafa 39, 44, 176
family reunions, North and South Korean 132
Far East 2; Russian 201
February 28 Incident/February 28 Massacre 145
feudal lords (*daimyo*) 60
Fifth National People's Congress 32
Fifth Republic, the 112
Fifth Science and Technology Basic Plan
 (2016–2020) 216
First Republic, the 109–110
First Science and Technology Basic Plan
 (1996–2001) 215
First Sino-Japanese War 144
First United Front 17
Five Classics (Confucian texts) 10, 190
Five Dynasties and Ten Kingdoms 10
folk religions, Chinese 38, 176, 184
Forbidden City 11
foreign brides 48, 124
foreign missionaries 14
Foreign Policy (Babones) 159
foreigners, samurai killing of *63*
Formosa 142
Fort Zeelandia 142
Four Books 190
Four Noble Truths of Buddhism 191
Fourth Republic, the 111–112
Fourth Science and Technology Basic Plan
 (2011–2015) 215
Freedom in the World Index 131
freedom of religion: in China 38; in Japan 78,
 90, 91
Freeman, Chris 214; *Technology Policy and
 Economic Performance* 214
French and the British war with China 14
Friedman, Milton 214
Frontier R&D National Project 217–218
Fujian province 17, 28, 33; Taiwan and 143, 151
Fukushima Daiichi nuclear plan 96
Fukuzawa Yukichi 65

G5 76
Gallup International and the WI Network of
 Market Research 176

Gangnam Style (Psy) 126, 195
Gang of Four 24, 25
General Agreement on Tariffs and Trade 84
Genghis Khan 10
Gerschenkron, Alexander 214
GINI coefficient, China's 46
global economic boom, China and 5
Go-Daigo (Emperor) 60
God Worshipping Society 14
Gorbachev, Mikhail 26
Goryeo period 101
Grand Canal, UNESCO world heritage site 8, *9*
Great Britain 13, 54, 63, 71, 161–166; Kowloon
 Peninsula and 14
Great Depression 68
Greater East Asia Co-Prosperity Sphere 1
Great Famine 19, 22
Great Kanto Earthquake 67
Great Leader, the 129
Great Leap Forward 19, 22–23, 38, 51, 175
Great Proletarian Cultural Revolution 23
Great Tohoku Earthquake 215–216
Great Wall of China 7, 8, *12*; and the Manchu
 clan 12; under the Ming dynasty 11
Great Wall of China 7
Guomindang (GMD)/Koumintang (KMT)
 (Nationalist Party) 17

Hallyu (the Korean wave) 126, 194
Han Chinese 12
Han dynasty 7
Heian period 58
Hein, Laura 207
Heritage Foundation's Economic Freedom
 Rankings 130
Hermit Kingdom 104
Hideki Tojo 206
Highly Advanced Nation (HAN) project 217
Hirohito (Emperor) 68, 71, 74, 206
Hiroshima, atomic bombing of *71*, 199
history textbooks, Japanese 207, 208
Ho Iat Seng 183
Honda's Humanoid Robot Asimo *213*
Hong Kong 2; British control of 163–164; ceding
 of to Britain 14, 162; China relation 165; and
 China transportation links 169; civil rights of
 citizens 168–169; Constitution of 171; defence
 forces 173; economy of 176–177; electoral
 system of 172; and the future 177; geography
 and demography of 171; government of
 171–174; history of 161–163; and income in
 equality 176; judiciary 172–173; Legislative
 Council (LegCo) 167; map of *162*; Moral and
 national education 167; National Security
 legislation changes 166–167; negotiations
 over 164–165; political parties in 173–174;
 population of 175–176; and relationships with

Index 235

mainland China 166–171; and religion 176; society 175–176; transfer of 166; Umbrella Movement 167–168; universal suffrage and citizens 167
Hong Kong Convention and Exhibition Centre 166
Hong Kong Special Administrative Region (SAR) 171
Hongwu Emperor 11
Hong Xiuquan 14
House of Councillors 79
human rights, in China 40, 42, 43–45, 82, 226; Association of Korean Victims and 208; Hong Kong and 174; North Korea and 86, 131

Identity and National Identification of Hong Kong People survey 175, *175*
Imperial Rescript on Education 66
India, Buddhism and 1
Industrial Revolution 13
ink wash painting, "Pine Trees" *189*
innovation systems, national 213–214; and science and technology 214–215
Institute for Information Industry (Triple I) 218
Instrument of Surrender, signing of *72*
Inter-Korean Liaison Office 135
International Atomic Energy 133
International Covenant on Economic, Social and Cultural Rights (ICESCR) 44
International Labour Organization 192
iron triangle 83
Islam 38, 40
Islamization, in Xinjiang 40
Itō Hirobumi 65

Japan: 21st century 1; administration of Taiwan 144–145; ageing population 2, 3, 216; birth rate in 54, 92; centralized political system of 57; challenges faced by 92–97; Comprehensive and Progressive Agreement for Trans-Pacific Partnership 98; Constitution 78, 84; and control of Taiwan 144–145; Council for Science and Technology Policy 215; creation story 58; discrimination and racism against in 56; economic bubble of 76–77; economy of 97–98; education in 87–89; effect of World War II on 1; election campaigns in 79–80; electoral system in 79; European Union on an Economic Partnership Agreement 98; and external influences 57; Fifth Science and Technology Basic Plan (2016–2020) 216; First Science and Technology Basic Plan (1996–2001) 215; Fourth Science and Technology Basic Plan (2011–2015) 215; GDP of 97; geography and demography of 54–56; government of 77; head of government of 78; head of state of 77–78; industrialization of 66; interwoven

histories with China and South Korea 1; invasions of 59–60; Kublai Khan invasion of 10; map of *55*; Northern Territories day 201;Occupation of 72–76; occupation of Korea 104–106; opposition parties in 81–82; and the outside world 61; periods in Japanese history 56; political culture of 77–80; political parties in 80–82; pollution challenges in 84; Portuguese traders in 60; post-war development of 76–77; post-war prime ministers of 82; quality of life in 63; religion in 89–92; and robotic implementations 212; and Russia relations 199–201; and the Russo-Japanese War 14; Science and Technology Basic Law/Plan and 215; Second Science and Technology Basic Plan in 2001, 215; Self-Defense Forces 84–86; Sino-China war and 67; society 87; Society 5.0 216; South Korea relations 201–203; and South Korea war time labour compensation 210; and territorial disputes/neighbours *200*; Third Science and Technology Basic Plan (2006–2010) 215; trade surplus with US 76
Japan Brand Strategy 220
Japan Business Federation (the *Keidanren*) 215
Japan Content Showcase 221
Japanese Alps 54
Japanese animation 193
Japanese: abductions of citizens 86; early years of 56–60; history, periods in 56; history textbooks 207, 208; imperialism 1; militarism 144–145; Nihonjinron 89; Parliament 78; pop group AKB48 *194*; war crime trials *74*
Jesuit Church of St. Paul 180
Jiang Qing 24
Jiang Zemin 31–32, 36, 37, 166
Jimmu (Emperor) 78
Jin dynasty 7, 10; and the reunification of China 8
Jogyesa Buddhist temple *122*
Johnson, Chalmers 82, 214
Joint Declaration of the Denuclearization of the Korean Peninsula 132
Jomon 57–58
Juche ideology 129
Jurchen 10

Kaesong Industrial Park 135–136
Kamakura period 59; military government of 60
Kamidana (God-shelf) 90
kamikaze (divine winds) 10, 59, 70
Kangxi dictionary 13
Kangxi Emperor 13
Keiretsu/Zaibatsu 73–74
Kim (Chairman) 139
Kim Dae-jung 111
Kim Il-sung 126, 127, *127*, 129
Kim Jong-il 128

236 *Index*

Kim Jong-un 128, 130
Kim-Trump summit *138*
Kim Young Sam 112
Kingdom of Middage 142
King Sejong *103*
Kishi Nobusuke 81
Kissinger, Henry 146
KMT-CCP Alliance 17
Kofun period 56, 57
Koga, Tatsuhiro 203
Koizumi, Junichiro 206
Komeito (Clean Government Party) 82
Kōno statement 208
Korea Creative Content Agency (KOCCA) 219, 221
Korea Institute for National Unification survey (2017) 135
Korean Armistice Agreement 115
Korean Central Intelligence Agency 111
Korean names 120
Korean Peninsula 1–2, 188; early history of 100–104; geography of 100; importance 139; and international conflict 100; isolationism and 104; and Japanese expansion into 14, 100; Japanese occupation of the 104–106, 126; political heritage of 107
Korean pop music (K-pop) 126
Korean popular culture 194
Korean Red Cross 132
Koreans, Japanese discrimination and racism against 56; killing of 67–68
Korean Social Democratic Party 129
Korean War 76, 113; North Korea after 129
Korean Wave (Hallyu) 126
Kotoku (Emperor) 57
Kowloon Peninsula ceded to Great Britain 14
Koxinga 143; siege to Fort Zeelandia 142
Kublai Khan 10, 59; and invasion of Japan 10
Kuomintang (KMT or Nationalist Party) 18, 20, 145, 150
Kuril archipelago/islands 199, 200
Kwangju massacre 115
Kyoto Accord 227

Lai, William Ching-te 149
Lam, Carrie 171
Laozi 1, 6
League of Social Democrats 174
Lee, Jasmine 124
Lee Myung-bak 125
Lee Teng-hui 145, 147, 151
Legislative Council (LegCo): Hong Kong 167, 171–172; Hong Kong's government 171–173
Legislative Yuan (Parliament) 149
legislature, South Korea's 118
Leung Chun-Ying 167
Liaodong Peninsula 14; ceded to Japan 144

Liberal Democratic Party, Japan 80–81, 209, 226
Li family 8
Li Hongzhi 39
Li Keqiang 33, 36
Lin Tse-hsu 161
literary developments 10
Liu Shaoqi 22, 23
localist parties 174
Long March 19–21, 25; map of *19*
Love Yourself 195
Lundval, Bengt-Åke 214
An Lushan 10; An Lushan Rebellion 10
lyric poetry 10

Ma Ying-jeou 152, *153*
Macau (Macao) 186; casino lights in *185*; Constitution of 183; coronavirus pandemic effect on economy of 185; defence forces 183–184; economy of 184–186; electoral system of 183; government of 183; head of government of 183; history of 179–183; inequality in 186; *map of 181*; negotiations for handover to China 182; political parties in 183; population of 184; under Portuguese rule 179–181; religion in 184; society 184
Mahayana 90
Malayo-Polynesian Aboriginal peoples 142
Manchu clan, Ming dynasty and the 12
Manchu culture, preservation of 13
Mandate of Heaven 7; Mongols and 10
Mandopop 195
Mao Zedong/Maoism 18, 27, 32, 33, 47, 145; actions of 19–20; Cultural Revolution of 19, 23–25, 51, 155, 163, 174, 182, 190; economic development model of 22–23, 26; and the founding of People's Republic of China 21; human rights and 43; nationalism during 51; population growth and 48
March of the Volunteers 166
Maritime powers, European 63
Maritime Silk Road 29, 31
Marxist ideas in China 17
mass political mobilization 17
Mass Transport Railway (the MRT) 164
May Fourth Movement 17
Medieval Japan 59
Meiji (Emperor) 77, 206; Meiji Japan 14; Meiji period 64–67
migrant workers, in China 46–47
Minamoto Yoritomo *59*
Ming China, foreign trade and 11
Ming dynasty 11; end of 142; and foreigners 11; reasons for fall of 12; remembered for 11
Ming government 142
Ming loyalist rebellion 13
Ming treasure voyages 11
Ministry of International Trade and Industry (MITI) 83–84

Miracle on the Han River 113, 125, 224
Miyazawa, Kiichi 208
mobilization, mass 118–119
Mongol conquest 10
Mongol empire, decline of 10–11
Mongols 12; and attempts to invade Japan 59
Moon Jae-in 117
Moscow 201; and the Chinese Communist Party 17
Mount Kumgang (Diamond Mountain) tourism project 136
Mudan Incident 144
Munk School of Global Affairs 43
Muramachi period 60
Murasaki Shikibu, *The Tale of Genji* 1, 58
Murayama, Tomoichi 209
Musha Incident 144; attack by Seediq Indigenous warriors 144
Muslim ethnic minority 39
Mutual Defense Treaty, between South Korea and the United States 115
MyCos 46

Nagasaki, atomic bombing of *71*
names, Korean 120
Nanjing Massacre 69, 207; *see also* Rape of Nanjing
Nara period 57
Naruhito (Emperor) 78
National Assembly (the *Gukhwe*) of, South Korea's 118
National Chengchi University Taiwan Independence versus Unification Survey 159
national innovation systems research 214
nationalism in China 17, 51; in Japan 68; in North Korea 131
Nationalist Party (Guomindang (GMD)/ Koumintang (KMT)) 17
Nationalist Party of China 150
National Medium-to-Long-Term Plan for Science and Technology Development, China's 216
National People's Congress (NPC) 32, 33, 34, 165, 172, 183; Standing Committee 35
National Revolutionary Army 17
National Security legislation, Macau's 186
naturalized South Koreans 124
neoliberal revolution 214
New Culture Movement 17
New-Generation Artificial Intelligence Development Plan 217
New Party 150
New Power Party 151; and Taiwanese independence 150
nine-mast treasure ships 11
Nixon, Richard 20, 49, 146
Nobel Prize winners, Japanese 215
Northern Expedition 17

Northern Song 10
Northern Territories/Kuril Islands dispute, between Japan and Russia 199–201; Day 201
North Korea: abductions of Japanese citizens 86; citizens defected to South Korea 131; denuclearization and 196; economy of 130–131; geography and demography of 126; human rights and 11; industrial centre of 126; and the outside world 131; and society 131–132; South Korea and US relations 136–139; and South Korean family reunions 132; South Korea relations 132; South Korea's concerns about 120
North Wei dynasty 8
NTT DoCoMo, Japan's 218
nuclear issue; North Korea and 132–135

oath-taking ceremony, Hong Kong's Council (LegCo) 174
Occupation of Japan 72–76
ocean expeditions by the Chinese 11
Oda Nobunaga 60
Oh, Jennifer 118
one-child policy 24, 27, 48; in Korea 124
"One Country, Two Systems" approach 159, 165
opium trade: addiction in China 13; Britain and China 13; British 172; Opium War 14; Second Opium War 14, 163, 181
organizational parallelism, China's government and 33–34
Organization for Economic Cooperation and Development (OECD) 214

pan-Blue coalition parties 150
pan-democratic parties 174
pan-Green parties 150
Parasite (film) 125
Park Chung-hee 110, 117; assassination of 111
Park Geun-hye 117, 125
Patten, Chris 164
Pearl Harbour 68
Pearl River Estuary *180*
peasant rebellions, in China 10
Penghu Islands, ceded to Japan 14
Peng Liyuan 33
People First Party 150
People's Liberation Army (PLA) 37, 183; in Hong Kong 173
People's Republic of China (PRC) 1, 3, 107, 146; early years of 21–22
Perry, Matthew 63
Pescadores Islands ceded to Japan 144
Philippines, Japanese occupation of 69–70
Plaza Accord 76–77
Politburo 36; Standing Committee of 33, 36
political economy, Japanese 82–84

238 *Index*

political succession, in China 36–37
popular culture: East Asian region's 193–195;
   export of 193
popular rights societies 65
Portuguese traders, arrival in Japan 60
postal system 10
post–World War II era 2
poverty, abject, in China's transformation 5
Prestowitz, Clyde 214
prime ministers, of post-war Japan 82
Prince Shotoku 57
pro-Beijing parties 173
pro-Communist organizations 173
Professional Commons 174
Programme for International Student Assessment
   (PISA) 2018 192, *193*
Protestantism 38
protests: in Hong Kong (2019) 169–171, *170*;
   and politics and South Korea 118–119;
   students 17
provincial and local government in China 37
Psy, *Gangnam Style* 126, 195
"puppet" government 129
Puyi (Emperor) 15, 16, 17

Qianlong Emperor 13
Qin dynasty 7
Qing (Manchu) government and Taiwan
   143–144
Qing dynasty 12–16
Qin Shi Huangdi 7
Quotations from Chairman Mao Zedong 23

Rape of Nanjing 207
Reagan, Ronald 214
Red Guards 23–24
Red Purge 75
Red Turban movement 11
religion: allowed in China 38; in Hong Kong
   176; in Japan 89–92; in Macau 184;
   prohibited in China 38; sinicization of 38; in
   South Korea 121
Republic of China (ROC)/Taiwan 15, 16,
   142–160; establishment of new government
   17; power vacuum in 17; *see also* Taiwan
Republic of Korea (ROK) *see* South Korea
Republican China, establishment of 16
Reunification: and Hong Kong 177; and Koreas
   129, 132, 135; and Taiwan 151, 158
Revolt of the Three Feudatories 13
Revolutionary Alliance 15, 17
Rhee Syngman 109
rice farming activities 188
Rich, John 49
ritualized suicide (*seppuku*) 70
robotic implementations and Japan 212
ROC Armed Forces 155

Royal Navy, and the Opium War 14; *see also*
   Second Opium War
rural unrests in China 46–47
Russian-Chinese border 14
Russo-Japanese War, Japan and 14

Sailor Moon 193
Saint Dominic's Church 180, *182*
samurai 59, 63, 65
San Francisco Peace Treaty 146, 200, 201
Satsuma Rebellion 65
science, technology and innovation (STI)
   leadership 212
Science and Technology Basic Law and Science
   and Technology Basic Plans (Japan) 215
Sea of Japan (East Sea) 54
Second Opium War 14, 163, 181
Second Republic, the 110
Second Science and Technology Basic Plan in
   2001, 215
Seediq Indigenous warriors 144
Sejong (king) *103*
Selden, Mark 207
Self-Defense Forces, Japan's 84–86
self-reliance, Juche ideology of 129
sensitive issues, and the CCP: democracy 42–43;
   the *Falun Gong or Falun Dafa* 39; human
   rights 42, 43–45; inequality of citizens 45–46;
   rural unrests and 46–47; Tibetan Autonomous
   Region (Tibet) 41–42; Xinjiang 39–40
Seoul Animation Centre 222, *222*
seppuku (ritualized suicide) 70
sex ratio in China 48
Shandong peninsula 17
Shang dynasty 6
Shanghai Communique 49, 146
Shanghai Industrial Technology Institute 216
Shimoda Treaty (1855) 199
Shinto Shrine 90, *91*
Shinzo Abe 81
ships, Chinese construction of 11
Shogun 58–62, *59*
Shotoku, Prince 57, 191
Showa period 56, 68–71
shui-mo-hua 189
Silk Road 7; Silk trade routes 8
sinicization of religion 38
Sino-American Mutual Defense Treaty 146
Sino-British Joint Declaration 165
Sino-Japanese relations 203–204
Sino-Japanese War 14
Six-Party Talk 134
Sixteen Kingdoms 8
Sixth Republic 112–113
Socialist Women's Union of Korea 129
social mobility, South Korea's lack of 125
Society 5.0 216

Society of Jesus (Jesuit) missionaries, arrival in Japan of 60
Society of the Righteous and Harmonious Fists 15
SOE Reform Program 28
Sokka Gakkai 82
Song Ci 10
Songdo's U-City 219
"Son of Heaven" 7
Soong James 150
South China Sea 204–206, 226
Southeast Asia, wars in 10
Southern and Northern Dynasties period 8
Southern Song 10
South Korea 107–109; #MeToo movement 120; ageing population of 123–124; Asian financial crisis' impact on 122–123; birth rate in 109, 119, 121, 123–124; chaebol and the economy 113–115; challenges faced by 123–125; child-rearing in 120; China relations 203; Christian population in 121; compensations from Japan for forced labour 210; and concerns about North Korea 120; and Confucian values in society 119; Constitution of 117–118; culture of 126; demography of 123–125; economic growth of 113; education and careers in 120–121; electoral of 118; environmental problems in 218; the Fifth Republic 112; the First Republic 109–110; the Fourth Republic 111–112; frustrations with the 'elites' of society 125; GDP of 125–126; gender roles in 119; government of 116–117; head of government of 117; head of state of 117; inequality of citizens 125; interwoven histories with Japan and China 1; Miracle on the Han River 125; National Assembly (the *Gukhwe*) of 118; naturalized South Koreans in 124; North Koreans defected to 131; political evolution after World War II 109–113; political parties in 118; political structure of 116–119; post-World War II 109–113; protests against U.S. military presence in 116; protests and politics in 118–119; religion in 121; the Second Republic 110; the Sixth Republic 112–113; the Third Republic 110–111; unemployment in 126; women in 119–120
South Korea Combined Forces Command 115
Soviet Republic of China 17
Soviet Union and North Korea 126
Special Administrative Region (SAR) 161, 165; *see also* Hong Kong
Special Administrative Region of Macau *see* Macau
Special Economic Zones (SEZs) 27–28
spy network 11
standard Chinese dictionary 13
Standing Committee of the Politburo 33–36
State Administration for Religious Affairs 38

State Council: China's 33, 34, 35; executive meetings of 35
state-managed capitalism in China 5
state-owned enterprises (SOEs): in China 27, 28, 216; in North Korea 130
student protests 17
Suga, Yoshihide 81
Sui dynasty 8; mega projects during the 8
sumi-e 189
sumukhwa 189
Sunflower Movement (2014) 150
Sunhyuk Kim 118
Sun Yat-sen 17; Guomindang (GMD)/ Koumintang (KMT) (Nationalist Party) and 18
supercomputing technology, and China 212
Supreme People's Assembly (SPA) 129
Swaine, Michael D. 51

Taiping Rebellion 14
Taisho period 67–68
Taiwan 1, 2; anti-government uprising in 145; ceded to Japan 14; China relations 156–159, 199; China unification discussions 159; Chinese Civil War 150; Chinese living in 142–143; Constitution of 149; COVID-19 response 147; current political structure 148–150; democratization of 145–146; de-sinicization of 153; economy of 154–155; election campaigns in 149–150; electoral system of 149–150; end of World War II transformation 159; geography of 142; government of 148–149; head of government and head of state 149; and international offices 147–148; Japan administration of 144–145; and Japanese rule 144; map of *143*; national uncertainty 159; political parties in 150–151; political situation from 1987 151–152; religion in 154; resistance against Japanese rule 144; society 153–154; US relations 156; *see also* Republic of China
Taiwan Democratic Republic 144
Taiwanese Aboriginal peoples 142
Taiwan People's Party 151, 152
Taiwan Post 153
Taiwan Relations Act (TRA) 156
Taiwan State Building Party 152
Takeshima/Dokdo Island dispute between Japan and South Korea 201–203
The Tale of Genji (Murasaki) 1, 58
Tanaka Kakuei 81
Tang dynasty 8–10, 189
Tapani Incident 144
Technology Policy and Economic Performance (Freeman) 214
Terminal High Altitude Area Defense (THAAD) anti-missile system 203
Thatcher, Margaret 214
Third Republic, the 110–111

240 *Index*

Third Science and Technology Basic Plan
(2006–2010) 215
Three Kingdoms of Korea 8
Tiananmen Square protests (1989) 25, 26,
47, 165
Tibetan Autonomous Region (Tibet) 41–42
Tibetan Buddhism 153
Tokugawa era 63, 190; abolishment of class
system 65; shogunate of 61
Tokugawa Ieyasu 60
Tokyo District Court, and the Association of
Korean Victims claim 209
Tokyo Game Show 221
Tokyo International Film Festival 221
Tokyo Olympics (1964) 76
Toyotomi Hideyoshi 60, 104
traditional East Asian medicine (TEAM) 188
Treaty of Nanjing (1842) 14, 162
Treaty of Nerchinsk 13
Treaty of Shimoda (1855) 199, 200
Treaty of Shimonoseki 66, 105, 144
Treaty of Versailles 17
Treaty on Basic Relations, between Japan and
the Republic of Korea 208
Truku indigenous people 144
Trump, Donald 76, 86, 228; and China's
response to tariffs 49; and Japan 93, 94; and
North Korea 137–138, *138*, 139; and South
Korea 115; and Taiwan 156
Trustpolitick 135
Tsai Ing-wen of 149
Tuoba 8
two-child policy 48

Umbrella Movement: in Hong Kong 167–167;
protests *168*
"underground" secret churches 39
unequal treaties between China and foreign
power 14
UNESCO world heritage site, in China 8
Union of Agricultural Workers of Korea 129
Union of Soviet Socialist Republics (USSR) 20,
75, 106
United Kingdom 2
United Nations Civil Aviation Organization 152
United Nations Economic Commission for Asia
203
Uprising of the Five Barbarians 8
US–China relations 49–50
U.S. Army military government,
South Korea and 109

Vatican diplomatic ties with China 39;
recognition of Taiwan 148
"Vatican of the Far East" 180
Victoria, Queen 13

Wade, Robert 214
war criminals 206
Warring States period 60
Wealth Partaking Scheme (WPS) 186
Welch, David 205
Wen (Emperor) 8
Western countries, and technological
advancement 14
West Germany 76
White Terror 145
Winter Olympics 139
Winter Sonata 194
Wong, Joseph 43
Workers' Party of Korea 128; of North Korea 129
working hours 192
World Health Organization (WHO); and
China's response to the coronavirus pandemic
51; exclusion of Taiwan from coronavirus
pandemic meetings 147; recognition of
Taiwan 147
World Intellectual Property Organization
(WIP0), patent applications statistics 212
world religions, history of 1
World War II 18, 19, 126, 144, 145, 159, 163,
199, 201, 203, 206; apology by Prime Minister
Murayama 209; and China's civil war 20–21;
comfort women during 69, 207–210; and East
Asia 2; forced labour 54; Japan after 1, 2,
66, 68, 224; Japanese history textbook 207;
prisoners of 70
Wushe Rebellion 144
Wu Zetian (Empress) 8
Wuzong (Emperor) 8

Xavier, Francis 60, 91
Xi Jinping 2, 3, 33, 36, 38, 152, *153*, 159, 168, 190
Xinhai Revolution 15, 19
Xinjiang 29, 38, 39–40, 44, 158
Yamato clan 57

Yasukuni Shrine 206–207; Japanese politicians'
visit to 206
Yayoi period 57
Yayoi settlements 57
Yellow Peril 67
Yongle Emperor 11
Yuan dynasty 10–11
Yusin Constitution 111

Zaibatsu/Keiretsu 73–74
Zainichi Koreans 54
Zheng Chenggong 142
Zheng He 11
Zhou dynasty 6; kings of 7
Zhou Enlai 49
Zhu Yuan Zhang 11; Ming dynasty and 11